You Can't Fight Crazy

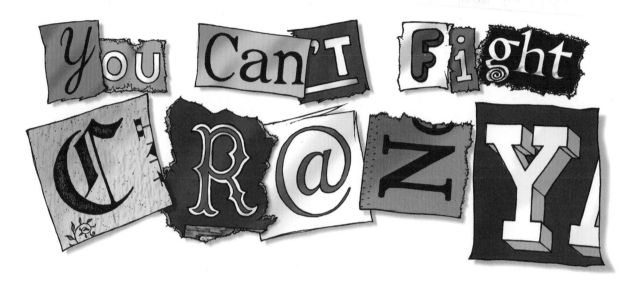

Other *Get Fuzzy* Books

The Dog Is Not a Toy (House Rule #4)

Fuzzy Logic: Get Fuzzy 2

The Get Fuzzy Experience: Are You Bucksperienced

I Would Have Bought You a Cat, But . . .

Blueprint for Disaster

Say Cheesy

Scrum Bums

I'm Ready for My Movie Contract

Take Our Cat, Please!

Ignorance, Thy Name Is Bucky

Dumbheart

Masters of the Nonsenseverse

Survival of the Filthiest

The Birth of Canis

The Fuzzy Bunch

Treasuries

Groovitude: A Get Fuzzy Treasury

Bucky Katt's Big Book of Fun

Loserpalooza

The Potpourrific Great Big Grab Bag of Get Fuzzy

Treasury of the Lost Litter Box

The Stinking

Jerktastic Park

You Can't Fight Crazy

a **GET FUZZY** collection

by darby conley

Andrews McMeel
Publishing

Kansas City • Sydney • London

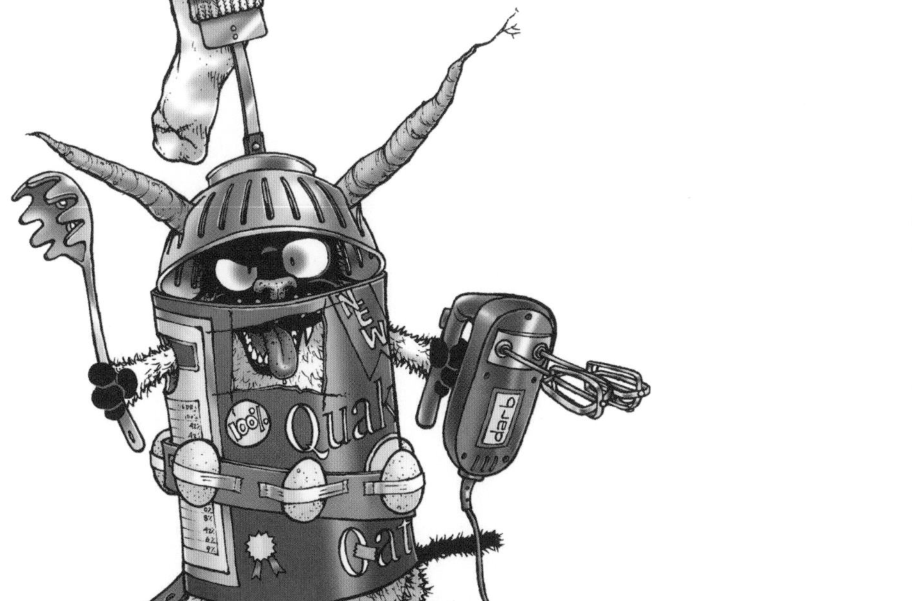
NEW
Quak
Gat
darb

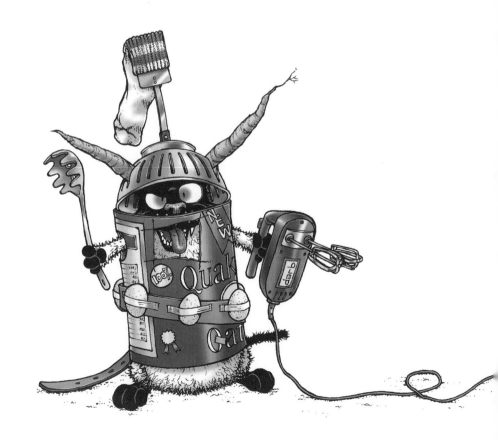

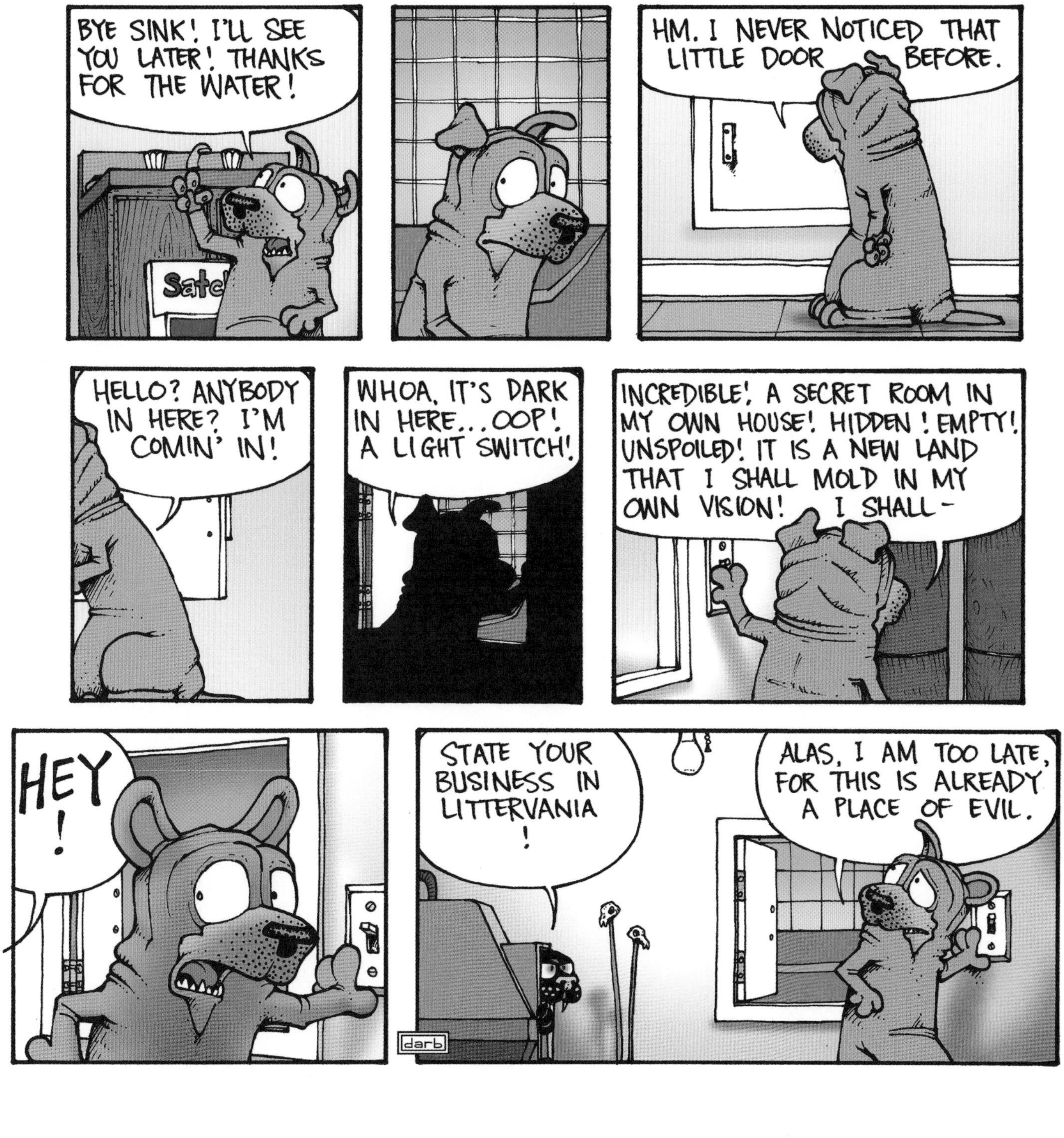
BYE SINK! I'LL SEE YOU LATER! THANKS FOR THE WATER!
HM. I NEVER NOTICED THAT LITTLE DOOR BEFORE.
HELLO? ANYBODY IN HERE? I'M COMIN' IN!
WHOA, IT'S DARK IN HERE...OOP! A LIGHT SWITCH!
INCREDIBLE! A SECRET ROOM IN MY OWN HOUSE! HIDDEN! EMPTY! UNSPOILED! IT IS A NEW LAND THAT I SHALL MOLD IN MY OWN VISION! I SHALL-
HEY!
STATE YOUR BUSINESS IN LITTERVANIA!
ALAS, I AM TOO LATE, FOR THIS IS ALREADY A PLACE OF EVIL.
darb

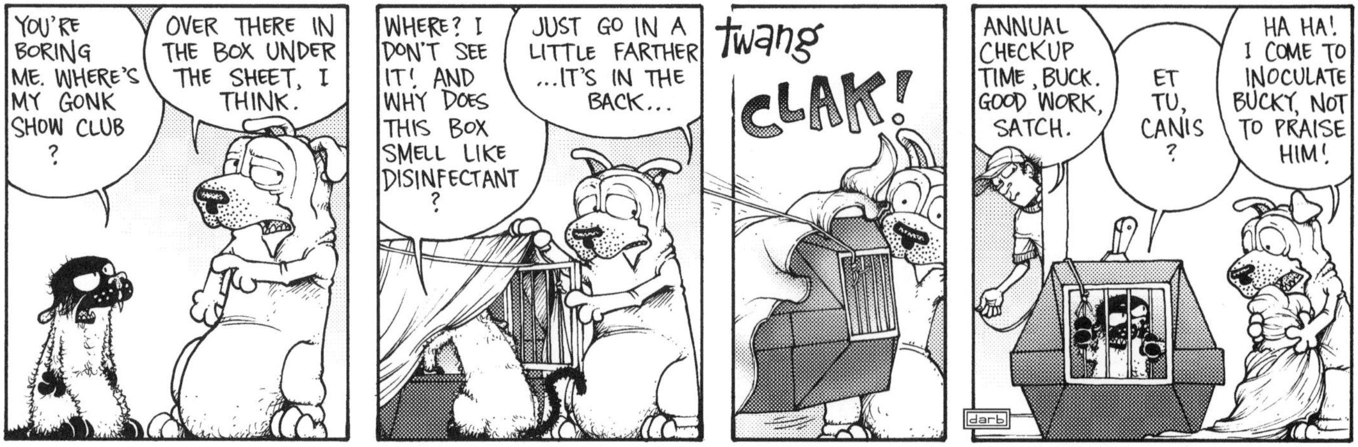
YOU'RE BORING ME. WHERE'S MY GONK SHOW CLUB ?
OVER THERE IN THE BOX UNDER THE SHEET, I THINK.
WHERE? I DON'T SEE IT! AND WHY DOES THIS BOX SMELL LIKE DISINFECTANT ?
JUST GO IN A LITTLE FARTHER ...IT'S IN THE BACK...
twang
CLAK!
ANNUAL CHECKUP TIME, BUCK. GOOD WORK, SATCH.
ET TU, CANIS ?
HA HA! I COME TO INOCULATE BUCKY, NOT TO PRAISE HIM!
darb

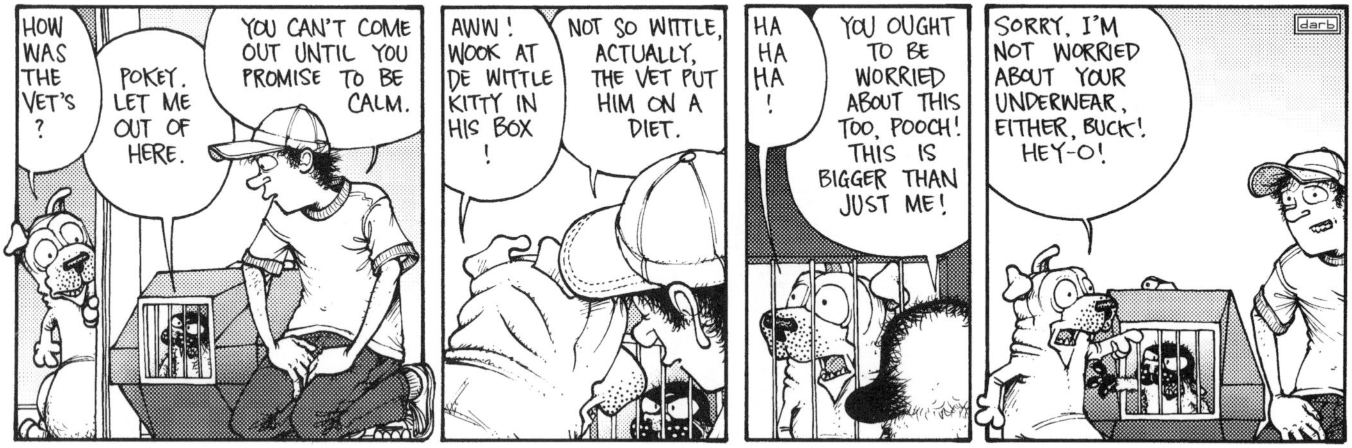
HOW WAS THE VET'S ?
POKEY. LET ME OUT OF HERE.
YOU CAN'T COME OUT UNTIL YOU PROMISE TO BE CALM.
AWW! WOOK AT DE WITTLE KITTY IN HIS BOX !
NOT SO WITTLE, ACTUALLY, THE VET PUT HIM ON A DIET.
HA HA HA !
YOU OUGHT TO BE WORRIED ABOUT THIS TOO, POOCH! THIS IS BIGGER THAN JUST ME!
darb
SORRY, I'M NOT WORRIED ABOUT YOUR UNDERWEAR, EITHER, BUCK! HEY-O!

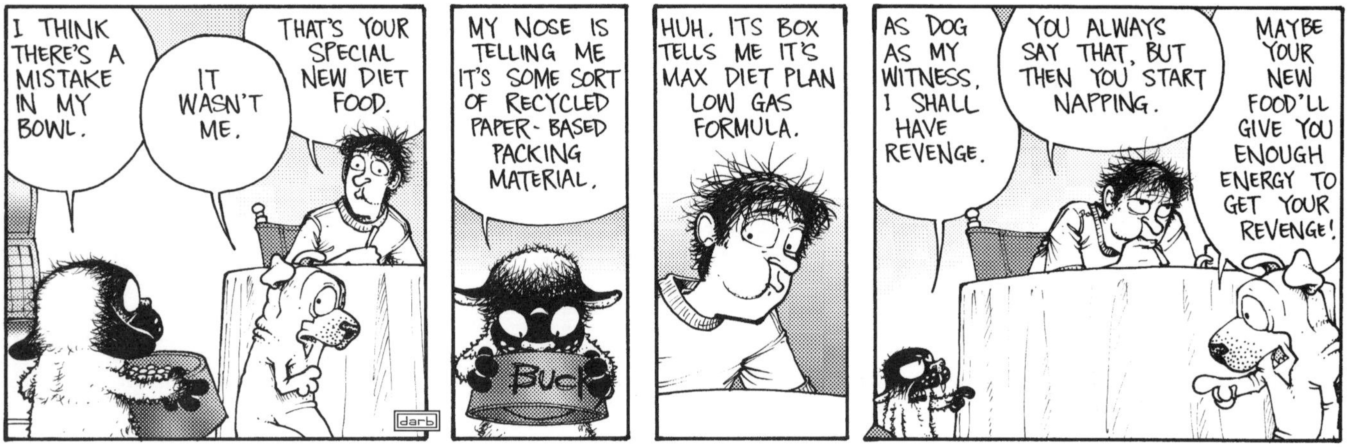
I THINK THERE'S A MISTAKE IN MY BOWL.
IT WASN'T ME.
THAT'S YOUR SPECIAL NEW DIET FOOD.
darb
MY NOSE IS TELLING ME IT'S SOME SORT OF RECYCLED PAPER-BASED PACKING MATERIAL.
BUCK
HUH. ITS BOX TELLS ME IT'S MAX DIET PLAN LOW GAS FORMULA.
AS DOG AS MY WITNESS, I SHALL HAVE REVENGE.
YOU ALWAYS SAY THAT, BUT THEN YOU START NAPPING.
MAYBE YOUR NEW FOOD'LL GIVE YOU ENOUGH ENERGY TO GET YOUR REVENGE!

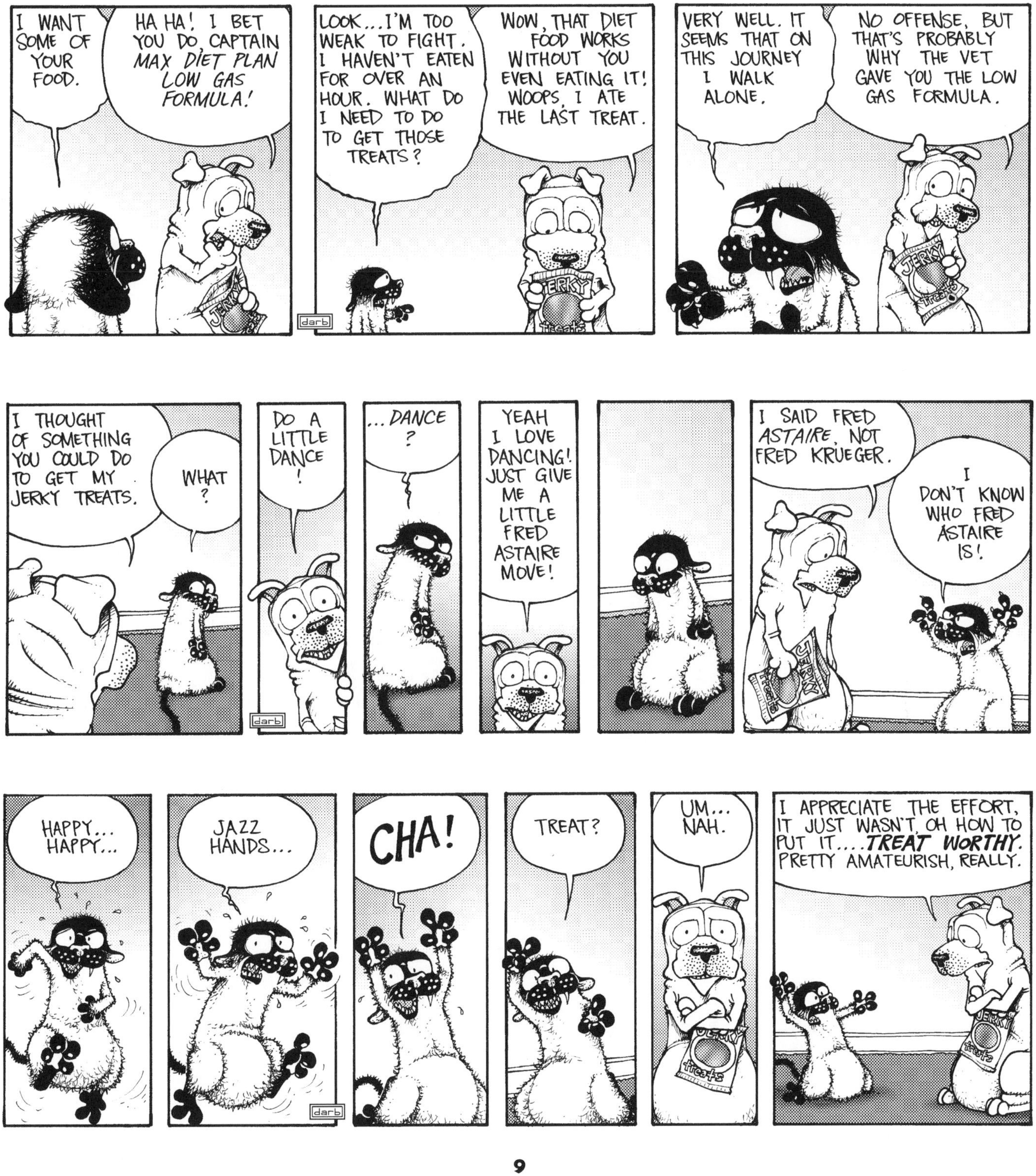
I WANT SOME OF YOUR FOOD.
HA HA! I BET YOU DO, CAPTAIN *MAX DIET PLAN LOW GAS FORMULA!*
JERKY
darb
LOOK...I'M TOO WEAK TO FIGHT. I HAVEN'T EATEN FOR OVER AN HOUR. WHAT DO I NEED TO DO TO GET THOSE TREATS?
WOW, THAT DIET FOOD WORKS WITHOUT YOU EVEN EATING IT! WOOPS, I ATE THE LAST TREAT.
JERKY treats
VERY WELL. IT SEEMS THAT ON THIS JOURNEY I WALK ALONE.
NO OFFENSE, BUT THAT'S PROBABLY WHY THE VET GAVE YOU THE LOW GAS FORMULA.
JERKY treats
I THOUGHT OF SOMETHING YOU COULD DO TO GET MY JERKY TREATS.
WHAT?
darb
DO A LITTLE DANCE!
...*DANCE*?
YEAH I LOVE DANCING! JUST GIVE ME A LITTLE FRED ASTAIRE MOVE!
I SAID FRED *ASTAIRE*, NOT FRED KRUEGER.
I DON'T KNOW WHO FRED ASTAIRE IS!
JERKY treats
HAPPY... HAPPY...
JAZZ HANDS...
darb
CHA!
TREAT?
UM... NAH.
JERKY treats
I APPRECIATE THE EFFORT, IT JUST WASN'T, OH HOW TO PUT IT....***TREAT WORTHY***. PRETTY AMATEURISH, REALLY.
JERKY treats

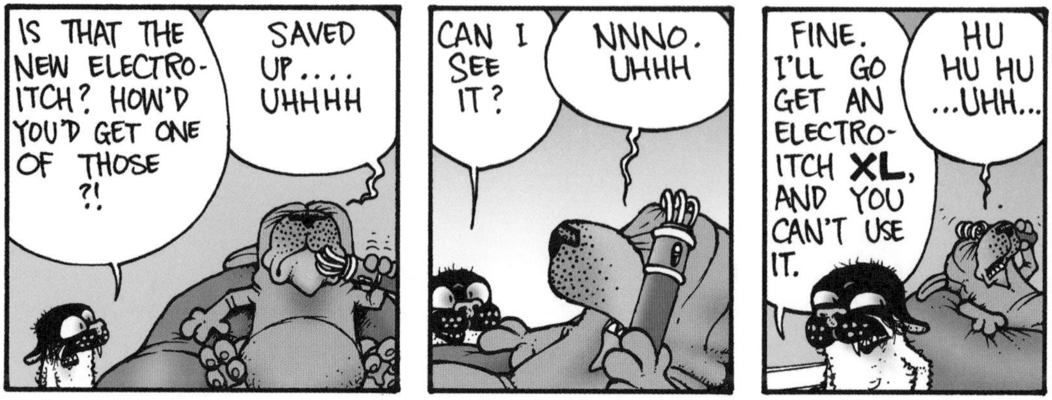
IS THAT THE NEW ELECTRO-ITCH? HOW'D YOU'D GET ONE OF THOSE ?!
SAVED UP.... UHHHH
CAN I SEE IT?
NNNO. UHHH
FINE. I'LL GO GET AN ELECTRO-ITCH **XL**, AND YOU CAN'T USE IT.
HU HU HU ...UHH...

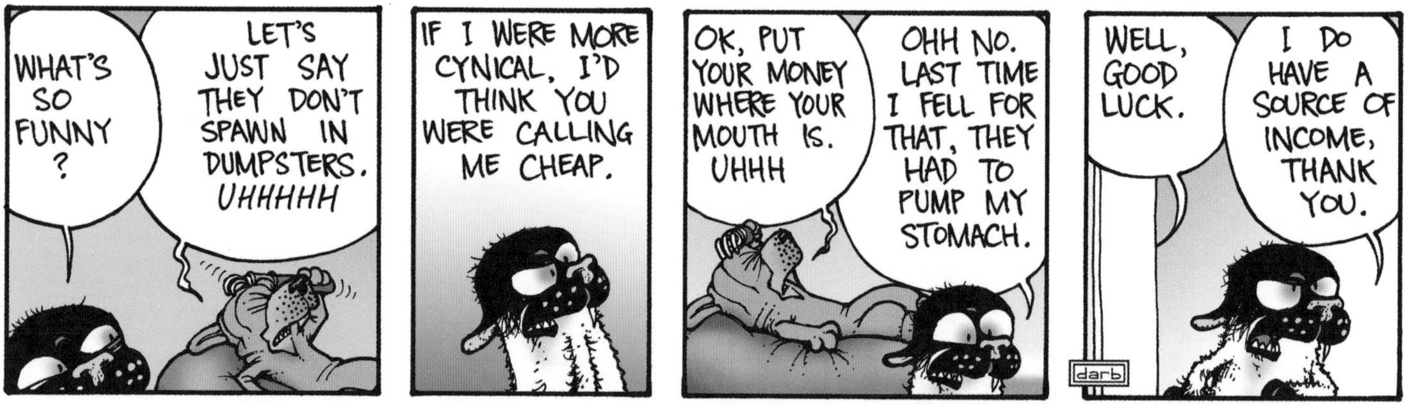
WHAT'S SO FUNNY?
LET'S JUST SAY THEY DON'T SPAWN IN DUMPSTERS. UHHHHH
IF I WERE MORE CYNICAL, I'D THINK YOU WERE CALLING ME CHEAP.
OK, PUT YOUR MONEY WHERE YOUR MOUTH IS. UHHH
OHH NO. LAST TIME I FELL FOR THAT, THEY HAD TO PUMP MY STOMACH.
darb
WELL, GOOD LUCK.
I DO HAVE A SOURCE OF INCOME, THANK YOU.

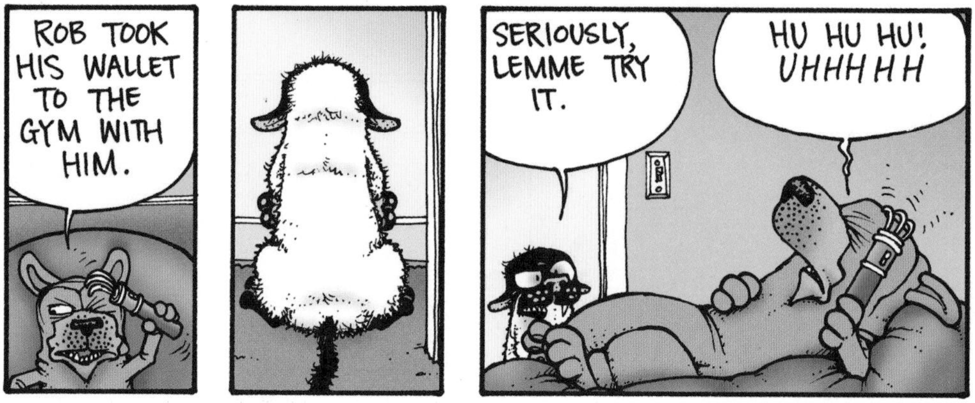
ROB TOOK HIS WALLET TO THE GYM WITH HIM.
SERIOUSLY, LEMME TRY IT.
HU HU HU! UHHHHH

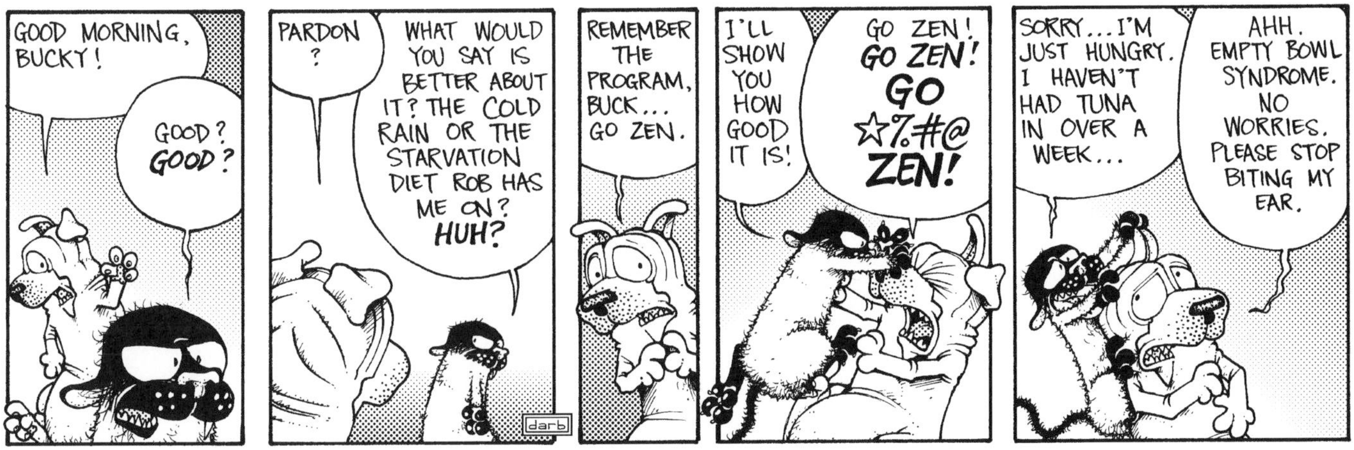
GOOD MORNING, BUCKY!
GOOD? **GOOD?**
PARDON?
WHAT WOULD YOU SAY IS BETTER ABOUT IT? THE COLD RAIN OR THE STARVATION DIET ROB HAS ME ON? **HUH?**
REMEMBER THE PROGRAM, BUCK... GO ZEN.
I'LL SHOW YOU HOW GOOD IT IS!
GO ZEN! **GO ZEN! GO ☆%#@ ZEN!**
SORRY... I'M JUST HUNGRY. I HAVEN'T HAD TUNA IN OVER A WEEK...
AHH. EMPTY BOWL SYNDROME. NO WORRIES. PLEASE STOP BITING MY EAR.
darb

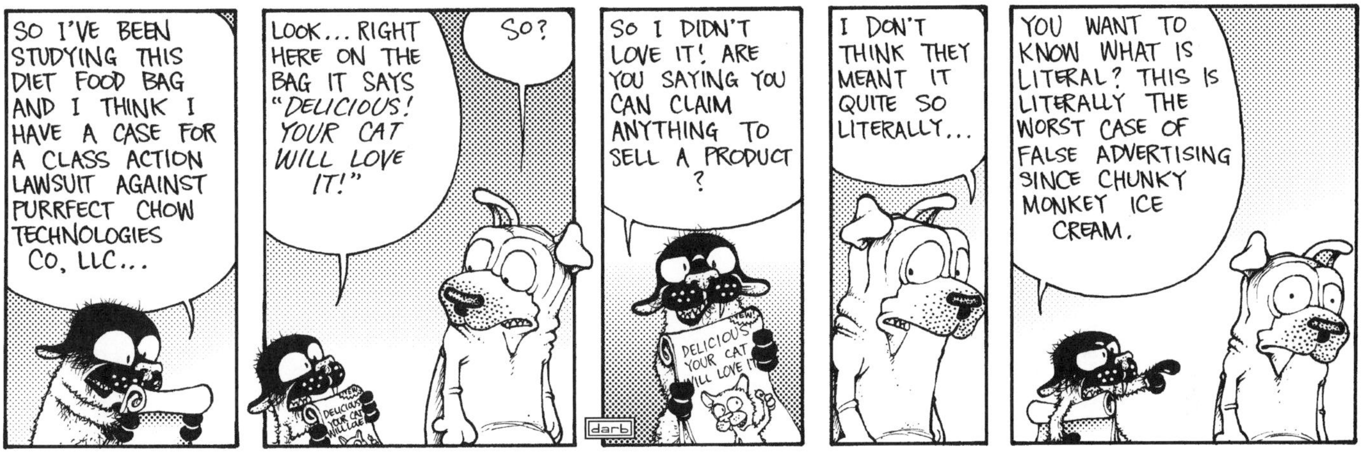
SO I'VE BEEN STUDYING THIS DIET FOOD BAG AND I THINK I HAVE A CASE FOR A CLASS ACTION LAWSUIT AGAINST PURRFECT CHOW TECHNOLOGIES CO, LLC...
LOOK... RIGHT HERE ON THE BAG IT SAYS "*DELICIOUS! YOUR CAT WILL LOVE IT!*"
SO?
SO I DIDN'T LOVE IT! ARE YOU SAYING YOU CAN CLAIM ANYTHING TO SELL A PRODUCT?
DELICIOUS! YOUR CAT WILL LOVE IT
I DON'T THINK THEY MEANT IT QUITE SO LITERALLY...
YOU WANT TO KNOW WHAT IS LITERAL? THIS IS LITERALLY THE WORST CASE OF FALSE ADVERTISING SINCE CHUNKY MONKEY ICE CREAM.
darb

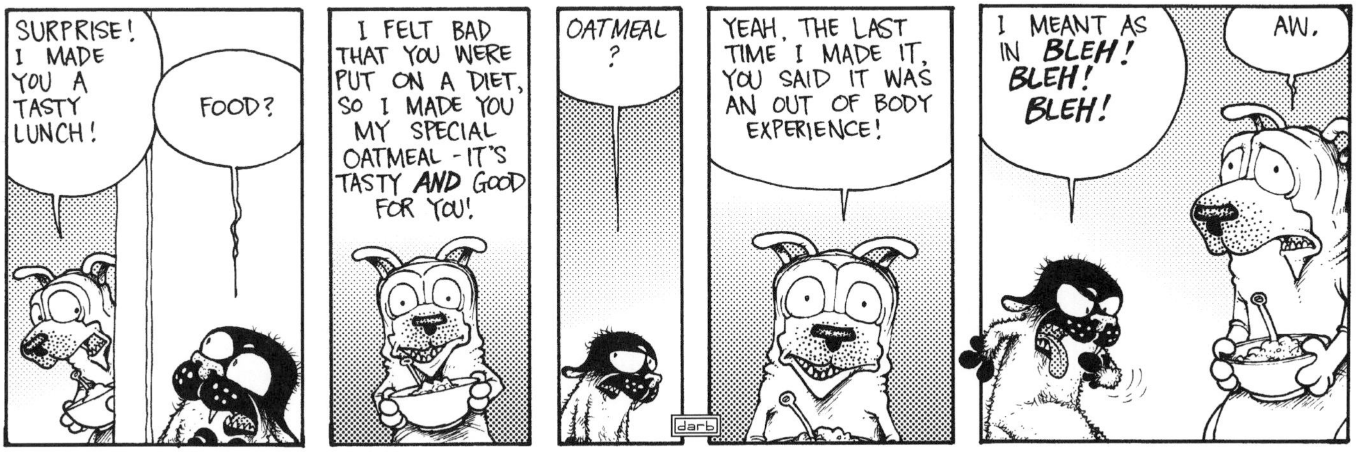
SURPRISE! I MADE YOU A TASTY LUNCH!
FOOD?
I FELT BAD THAT YOU WERE PUT ON A DIET, SO I MADE YOU MY SPECIAL OATMEAL - IT'S TASTY **AND** GOOD FOR YOU!
OATMEAL?
YEAH, THE LAST TIME I MADE IT, YOU SAID IT WAS AN OUT OF BODY EXPERIENCE!
I MEANT AS IN **BLEH! BLEH! BLEH!**
AW.
darb

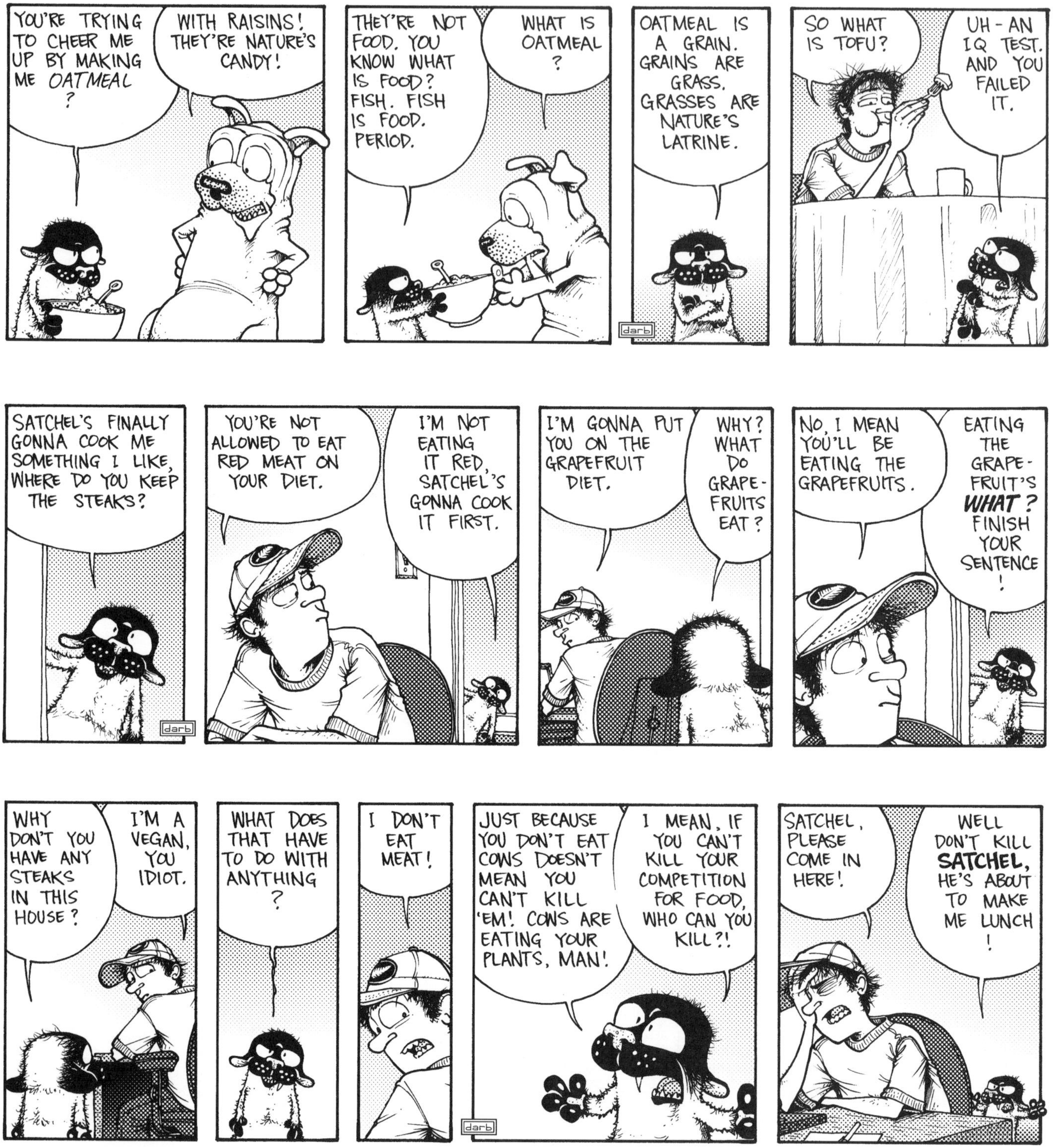

YOU'RE TRYING TO CHEER ME UP BY MAKING ME *OATMEAL* ?
WITH RAISINS! THEY'RE NATURE'S CANDY!
THEY'RE NOT FOOD. YOU KNOW WHAT IS FOOD? FISH. FISH IS FOOD. PERIOD.
WHAT IS OATMEAL ?
OATMEAL IS A GRAIN. GRAINS ARE GRASS. GRASSES ARE NATURE'S LATRINE.
SO WHAT IS TOFU?
UH-AN IQ TEST. AND YOU FAILED IT.
darb
SATCHEL'S FINALLY GONNA COOK ME SOMETHING I LIKE, WHERE DO YOU KEEP THE STEAKS?
YOU'RE NOT ALLOWED TO EAT RED MEAT ON YOUR DIET.
I'M NOT EATING IT RED, SATCHEL'S GONNA COOK IT FIRST.
I'M GONNA PUT YOU ON THE GRAPEFRUIT DIET.
WHY? WHAT DO GRAPE-FRUITS EAT?
NO, I MEAN YOU'LL BE EATING THE GRAPEFRUITS.
EATING THE GRAPE-FRUIT'S ***WHAT?*** FINISH YOUR SENTENCE !
darb
WHY DON'T YOU HAVE ANY STEAKS IN THIS HOUSE?
I'M A VEGAN, YOU IDIOT.
WHAT DOES THAT HAVE TO DO WITH ANYTHING ?
I DON'T EAT MEAT!
JUST BECAUSE YOU DON'T EAT COWS DOESN'T MEAN YOU CAN'T KILL 'EM! COWS ARE EATING YOUR PLANTS, MAN!
I MEAN, IF YOU CAN'T KILL YOUR COMPETITION FOR FOOD, WHO CAN YOU KILL?!
SATCHEL, PLEASE COME IN HERE!
WELL DON'T KILL **SATCHEL,** HE'S ABOUT TO MAKE ME LUNCH !
darb

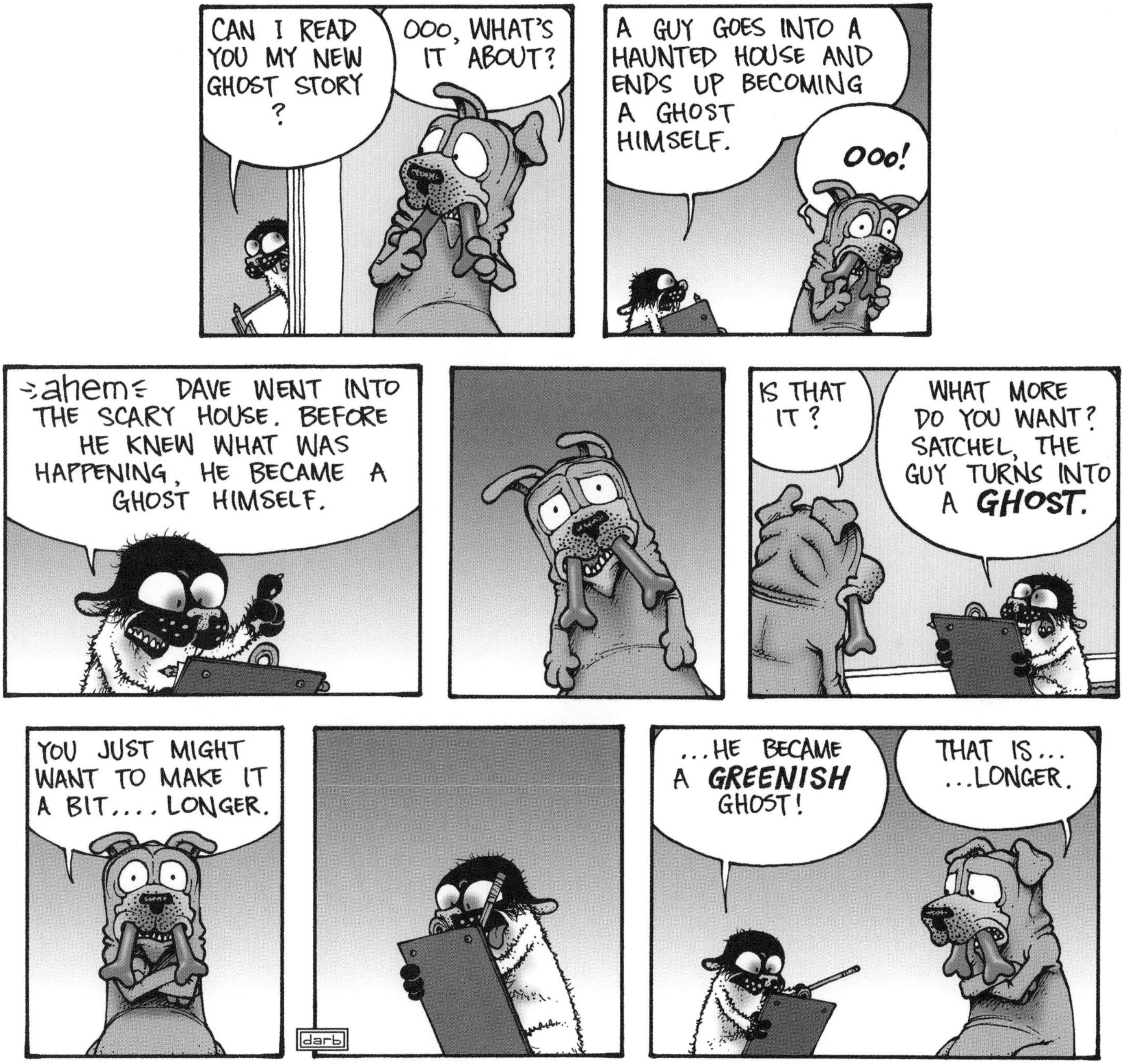
CAN I READ YOU MY NEW GHOST STORY?
OOO, WHAT'S IT ABOUT?
A GUY GOES INTO A HAUNTED HOUSE AND ENDS UP BECOMING A GHOST HIMSELF.
OOO!
ahem DAVE WENT INTO THE SCARY HOUSE. BEFORE HE KNEW WHAT WAS HAPPENING, HE BECAME A GHOST HIMSELF.
IS THAT IT?
WHAT MORE DO YOU WANT? SATCHEL, THE GUY TURNS INTO A **GHOST**.
YOU JUST MIGHT WANT TO MAKE IT A BIT.... LONGER.
darb
...HE BECAME A **GREENISH** GHOST!
THAT IS... ...LONGER.

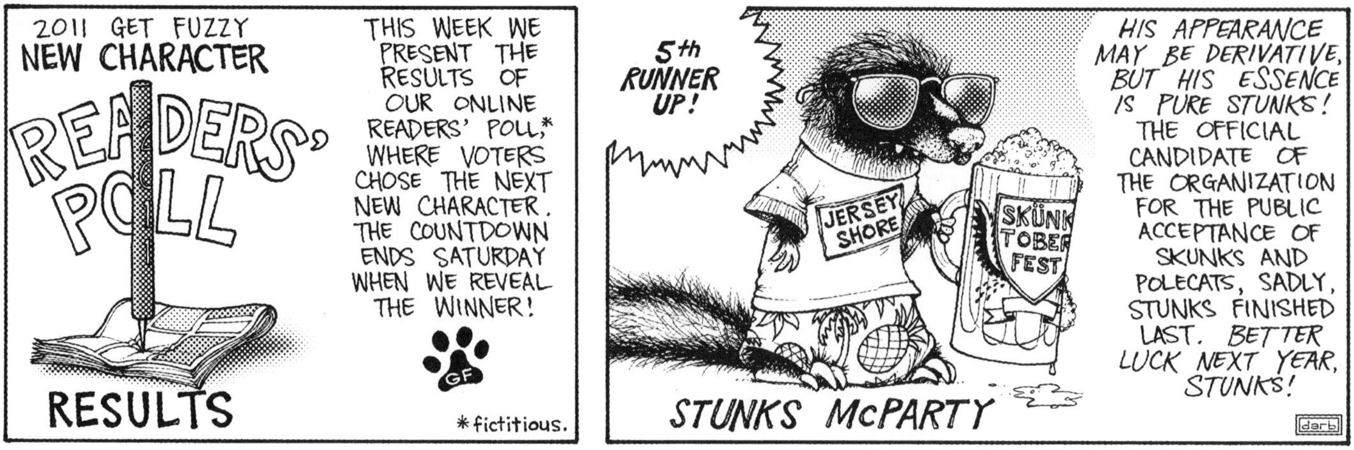
2011 GET FUZZY
NEW CHARACTER
READERS' POLL
RESULTS
THIS WEEK WE PRESENT THE RESULTS OF OUR ONLINE READERS' POLL,* WHERE VOTERS CHOSE THE NEXT NEW CHARACTER. THE COUNTDOWN ENDS SATURDAY WHEN WE REVEAL THE WINNER!
GF
*fictitious.
5th RUNNER UP!
JERSEY SHORE
SKÜNK TOBER FEST
HIS APPEARANCE MAY BE DERIVATIVE, BUT HIS ESSENCE IS PURE STUNKS! THE OFFICIAL CANDIDATE OF THE ORGANIZATION FOR THE PUBLIC ACCEPTANCE OF SKUNKS AND POLECATS, SADLY, STUNKS FINISHED LAST. BETTER LUCK NEXT YEAR, STUNKS!
STUNKS McPARTY
darb

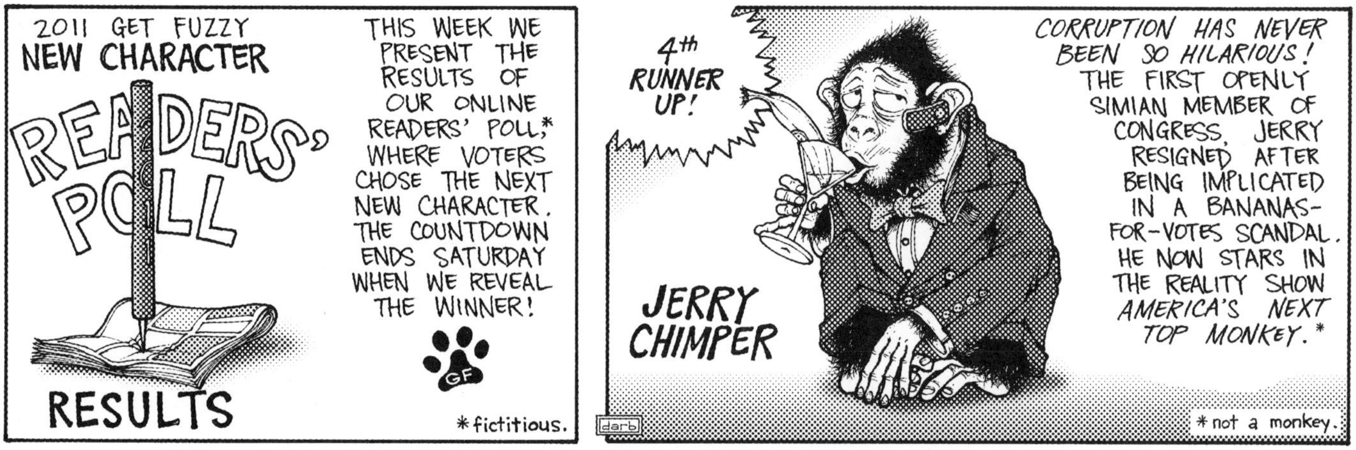
2011 GET FUZZY
NEW CHARACTER
READERS' POLL
RESULTS
THIS WEEK WE PRESENT THE RESULTS OF OUR ONLINE READERS' POLL,* WHERE VOTERS CHOSE THE NEXT NEW CHARACTER. THE COUNTDOWN ENDS SATURDAY WHEN WE REVEAL THE WINNER!
GF
*fictitious.
4th RUNNER UP!
CORRUPTION HAS NEVER BEEN SO HILARIOUS! THE FIRST OPENLY SIMIAN MEMBER OF CONGRESS, JERRY RESIGNED AFTER BEING IMPLICATED IN A BANANAS-FOR-VOTES SCANDAL. HE NOW STARS IN THE REALITY SHOW AMERICA'S NEXT TOP MONKEY.*
JERRY CHIMPER
darb
*not a monkey.

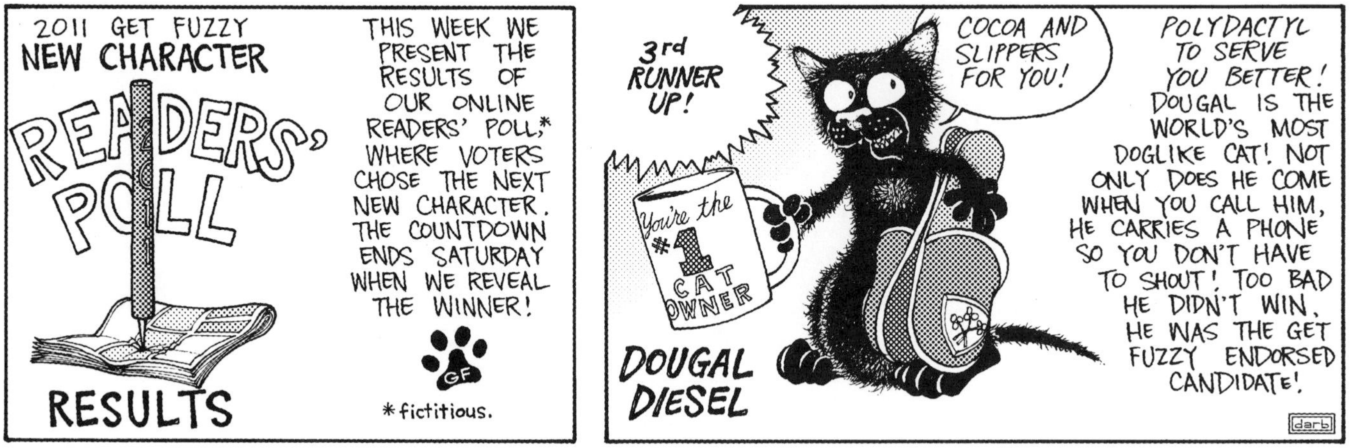
2011 GET FUZZY
NEW CHARACTER
READERS' POLL
RESULTS
THIS WEEK WE PRESENT THE RESULTS OF OUR ONLINE READERS' POLL,* WHERE VOTERS CHOSE THE NEXT NEW CHARACTER. THE COUNTDOWN ENDS SATURDAY WHEN WE REVEAL THE WINNER!
GF
*fictitious.
3rd RUNNER UP!
COCOA AND SLIPPERS FOR YOU!
You're the #1 CAT OWNER
POLYDACTYL TO SERVE YOU BETTER! DOUGAL IS THE WORLD'S MOST DOGLIKE CAT! NOT ONLY DOES HE COME WHEN YOU CALL HIM, HE CARRIES A PHONE SO YOU DON'T HAVE TO SHOUT! TOO BAD HE DIDN'T WIN. HE WAS THE GET FUZZY ENDORSED CANDIDATE!
DOUGAL DIESEL
darb

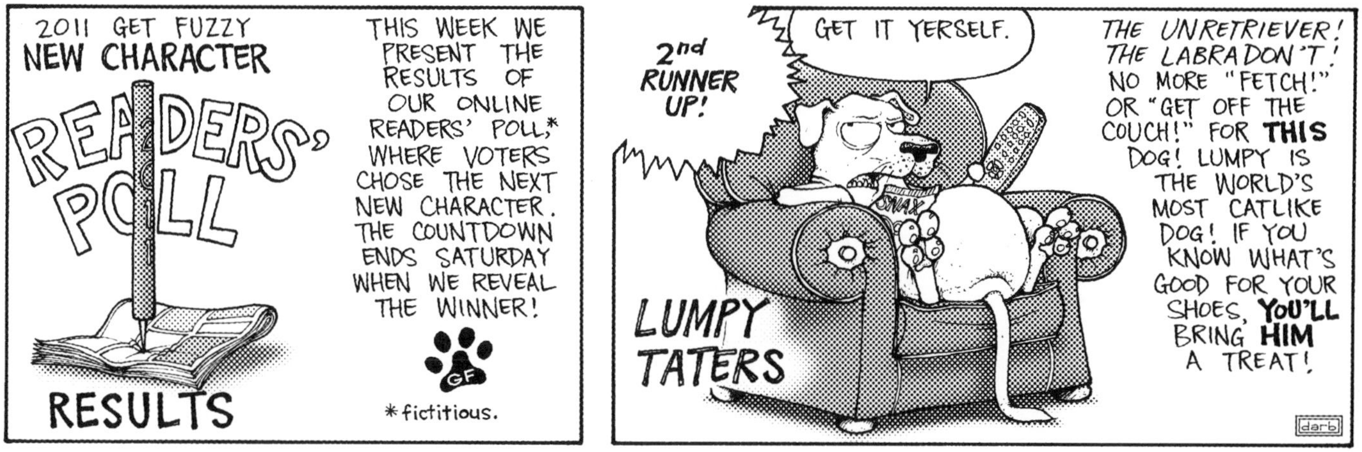
2011 GET FUZZY
NEW CHARACTER
READERS' POLL
RESULTS
THIS WEEK WE PRESENT THE RESULTS OF OUR ONLINE READERS' POLL,* WHERE VOTERS CHOSE THE NEXT NEW CHARACTER. THE COUNTDOWN ENDS SATURDAY WHEN WE REVEAL THE WINNER!
GF
* fictitious.
2nd RUNNER UP!
GET IT YERSELF.
SNAX
LUMPY TATERS
THE UNRETRIEVER! THE LABRADON'T! NO MORE "FETCH!" OR "GET OFF THE COUCH!" FOR THIS DOG! LUMPY IS THE WORLD'S MOST CATLIKE DOG! IF YOU KNOW WHAT'S GOOD FOR YOUR SHOES, YOU'LL BRING HIM A TREAT!
darb

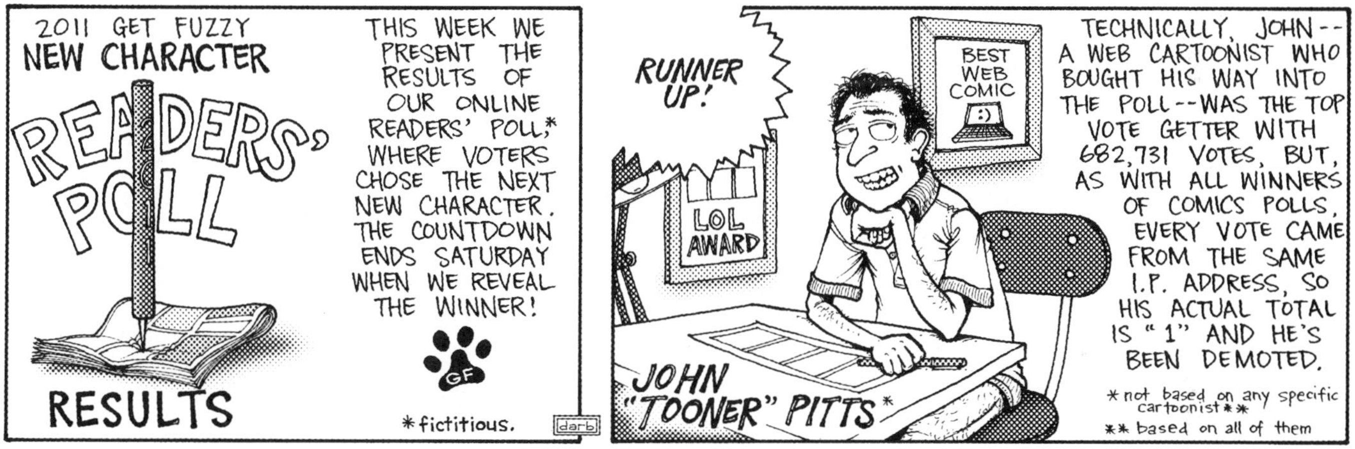
2011 GET FUZZY
NEW CHARACTER
READERS' POLL
RESULTS
THIS WEEK WE PRESENT THE RESULTS OF OUR ONLINE READERS' POLL,* WHERE VOTERS CHOSE THE NEXT NEW CHARACTER. THE COUNTDOWN ENDS SATURDAY WHEN WE REVEAL THE WINNER!
GF
* fictitious.
darb
RUNNER UP!
LOL AWARD
BEST WEB COMIC
:)
JOHN "TOONER" PITTS*
TECHNICALLY, JOHN -- A WEB CARTOONIST WHO BOUGHT HIS WAY INTO THE POLL -- WAS THE TOP VOTE GETTER WITH 682,731 VOTES, BUT, AS WITH ALL WINNERS OF COMICS POLLS, EVERY VOTE CAME FROM THE SAME I.P. ADDRESS, SO HIS ACTUAL TOTAL IS "1" AND HE'S BEEN DEMOTED.
* not based on any specific cartoonist**
** based on all of them

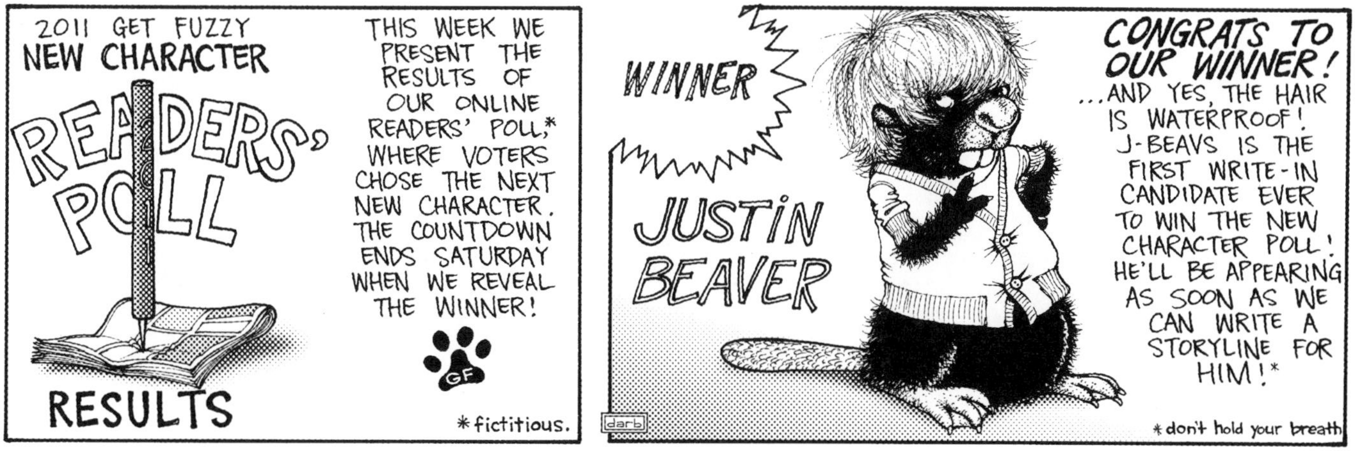
2011 GET FUZZY
NEW CHARACTER
READERS' POLL
RESULTS
THIS WEEK WE PRESENT THE RESULTS OF OUR ONLINE READERS' POLL,* WHERE VOTERS CHOSE THE NEXT NEW CHARACTER. THE COUNTDOWN ENDS SATURDAY WHEN WE REVEAL THE WINNER!
GF
* fictitious.
WINNER
JUSTIN BEAVER
CONGRATS TO OUR WINNER!
...AND YES, THE HAIR IS WATERPROOF! J-BEAVS IS THE FIRST WRITE-IN CANDIDATE EVER TO WIN THE NEW CHARACTER POLL! HE'LL BE APPEARING AS SOON AS WE CAN WRITE A STORYLINE FOR HIM!*
* don't hold your breath
darb

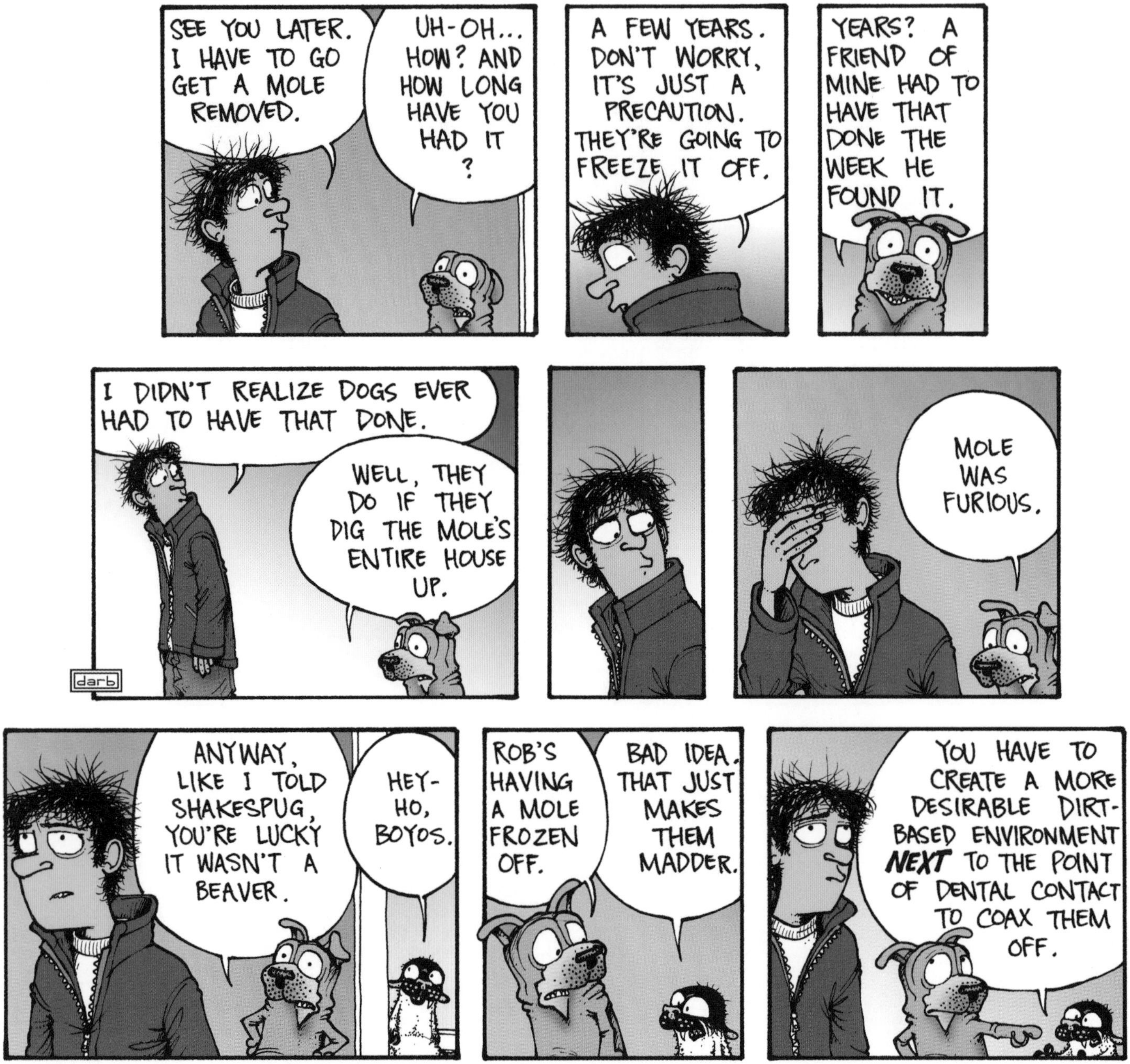
SEE YOU LATER. I HAVE TO GO GET A MOLE REMOVED.
UH-OH... HOW? AND HOW LONG HAVE YOU HAD IT ?
A FEW YEARS. DON'T WORRY, IT'S JUST A PRECAUTION. THEY'RE GOING TO FREEZE IT OFF.
YEARS? A FRIEND OF MINE HAD TO HAVE THAT DONE THE WEEK HE FOUND IT.
I DIDN'T REALIZE DOGS EVER HAD TO HAVE THAT DONE.
WELL, THEY DO IF THEY DIG THE MOLE'S ENTIRE HOUSE UP.
darb
MOLE WAS FURIOUS.
ANYWAY, LIKE I TOLD SHAKESPUG, YOU'RE LUCKY IT WASN'T A BEAVER.
HEY-HO, BOYOS.
ROB'S HAVING A MOLE FROZEN OFF.
BAD IDEA. THAT JUST MAKES THEM MADDER.
YOU HAVE TO CREATE A MORE DESIRABLE DIRT-BASED ENVIRONMENT NEXT TO THE POINT OF DENTAL CONTACT TO COAX THEM OFF.

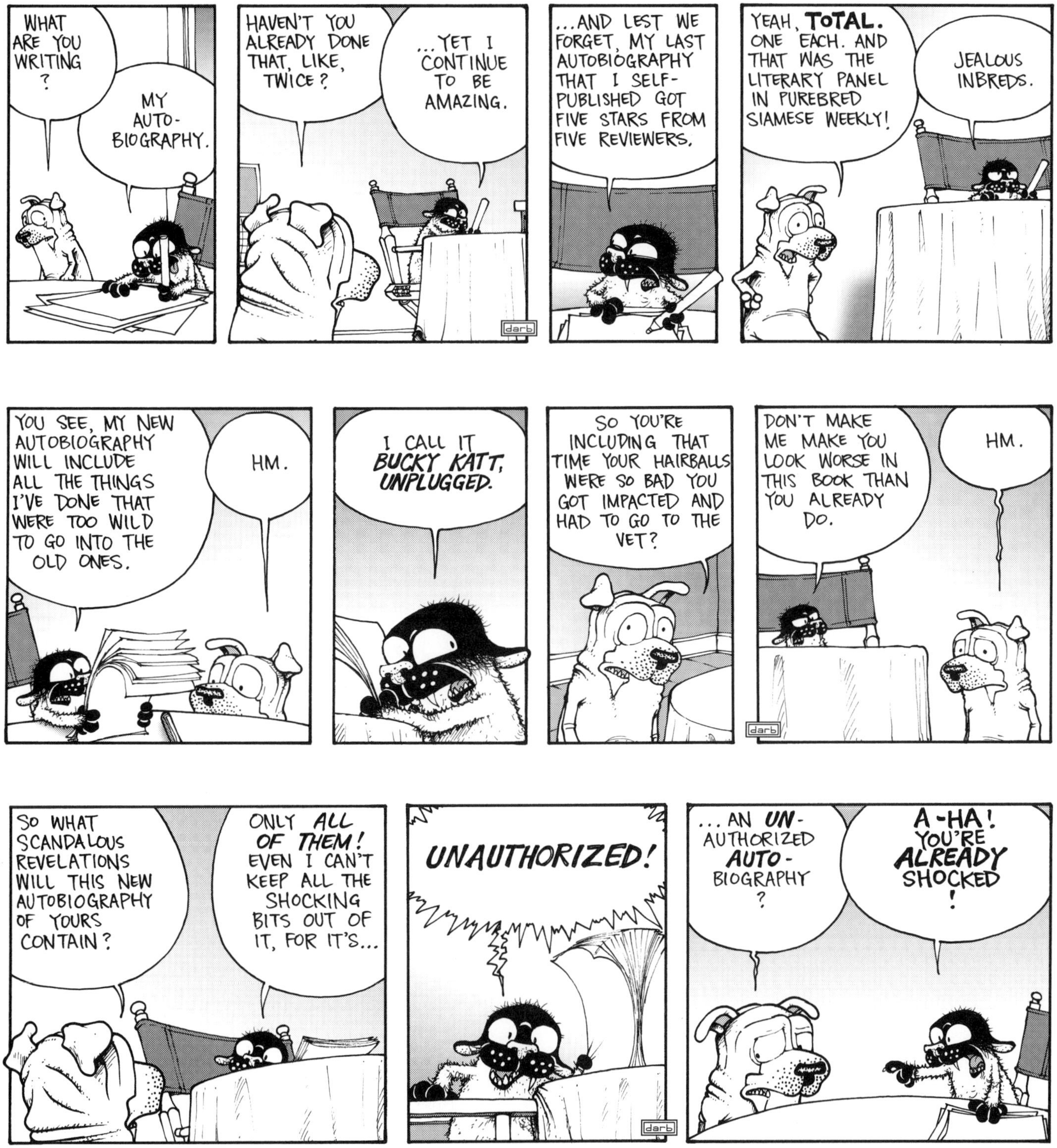
WHAT ARE YOU WRITING ?
MY AUTO-BIOGRAPHY.
HAVEN'T YOU ALREADY DONE THAT, LIKE, TWICE ?
...YET I CONTINUE TO BE AMAZING.
...AND LEST WE FORGET, MY LAST AUTOBIOGRAPHY THAT I SELF-PUBLISHED GOT FIVE STARS FROM FIVE REVIEWERS.
YEAH, TOTAL. ONE EACH. AND THAT WAS THE LITERARY PANEL IN PUREBRED SIAMESE WEEKLY!
JEALOUS INBREDS.
darb
YOU SEE, MY NEW AUTOBIOGRAPHY WILL INCLUDE ALL THE THINGS I'VE DONE THAT WERE TOO WILD TO GO INTO THE OLD ONES.
HM.
I CALL IT BUCKY KATT, UNPLUGGED.
SO YOU'RE INCLUDING THAT TIME YOUR HAIRBALLS WERE SO BAD YOU GOT IMPACTED AND HAD TO GO TO THE VET?
DON'T MAKE ME MAKE YOU LOOK WORSE IN THIS BOOK THAN YOU ALREADY DO.
HM.
darb
SO WHAT SCANDALOUS REVELATIONS WILL THIS NEW AUTOBIOGRAPHY OF YOURS CONTAIN ?
ONLY ALL OF THEM! EVEN I CAN'T KEEP ALL THE SHOCKING BITS OUT OF IT, FOR IT'S...
UNAUTHORIZED!
darb
...AN UN-AUTHORIZED AUTO-BIOGRAPHY ?
A-HA! YOU'RE ALREADY SHOCKED !

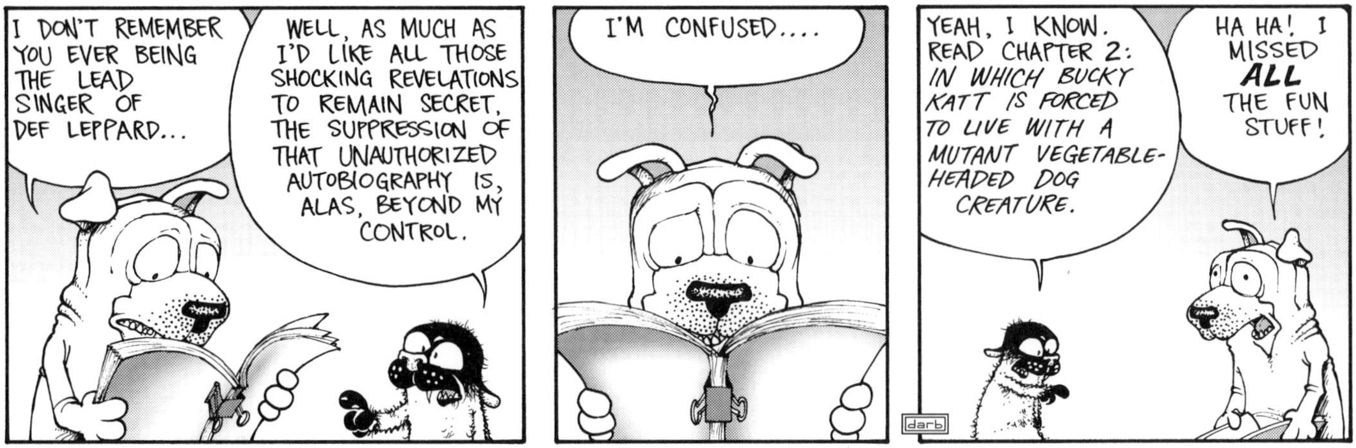
I DON'T REMEMBER YOU EVER BEING THE LEAD SINGER OF DEF LEPPARD...
WELL, AS MUCH AS I'D LIKE ALL THOSE SHOCKING REVELATIONS TO REMAIN SECRET, THE SUPPRESSION OF THAT UNAUTHORIZED AUTOBIOGRAPHY IS, ALAS, BEYOND MY CONTROL.
I'M CONFUSED....
YEAH, I KNOW. READ CHAPTER 2: *IN WHICH BUCKY KATT IS FORCED TO LIVE WITH A MUTANT VEGETABLE-HEADED DOG CREATURE.*
HA HA! I MISSED **ALL** THE FUN STUFF!
darb

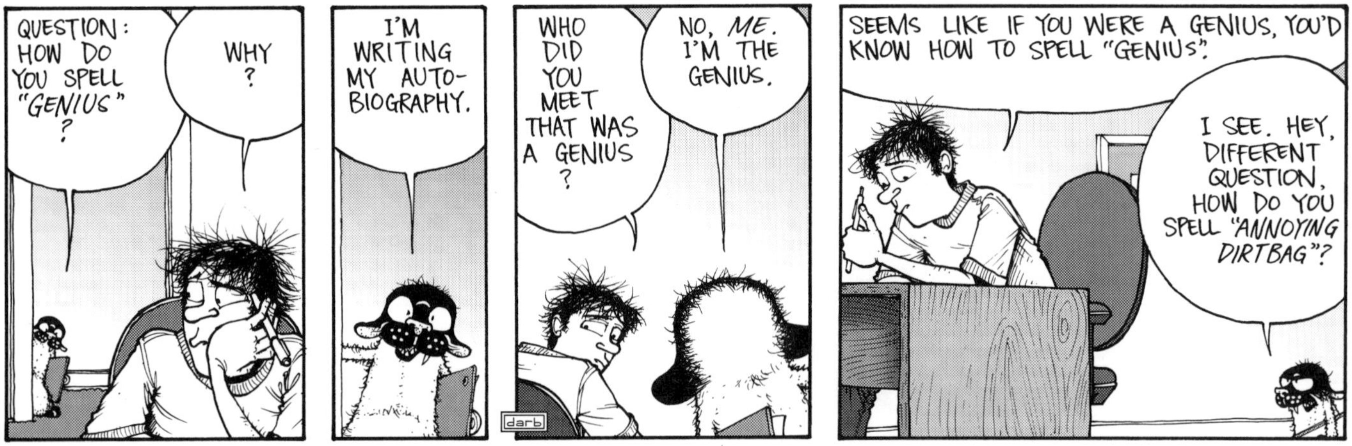
QUESTION: HOW DO YOU SPELL "*GENIUS*"?
WHY?
I'M WRITING MY AUTO-BIOGRAPHY.
WHO DID YOU MEET THAT WAS A GENIUS?
NO, *ME*. I'M THE GENIUS.
darb
SEEMS LIKE IF YOU WERE A GENIUS, YOU'D KNOW HOW TO SPELL "GENIUS".
I SEE. HEY, DIFFERENT QUESTION. HOW DO YOU SPELL "*ANNOYING DIRTBAG*"?

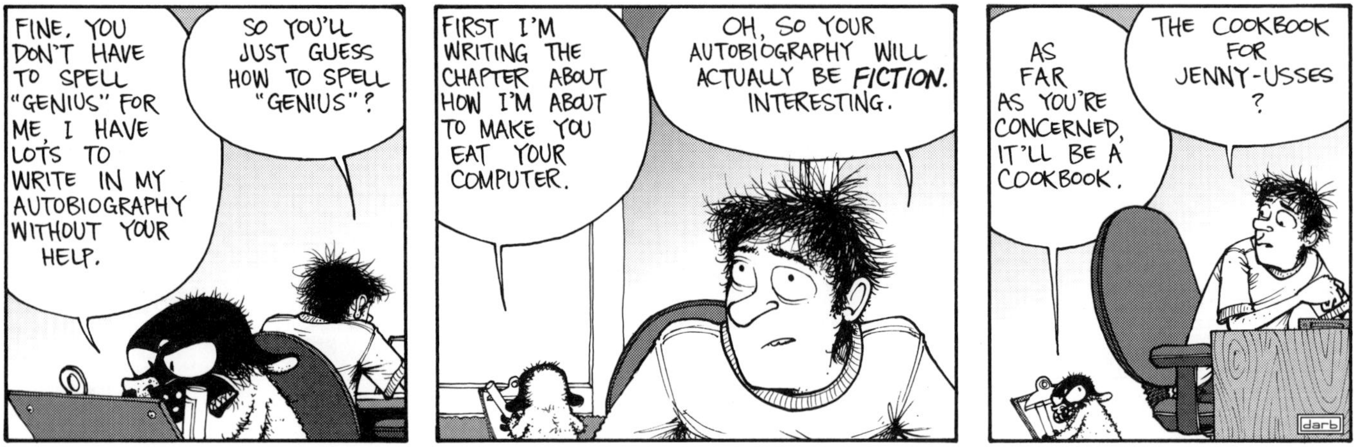
FINE. YOU DON'T HAVE TO SPELL "GENIUS" FOR ME. I HAVE LOTS TO WRITE IN MY AUTOBIOGRAPHY WITHOUT YOUR HELP.
SO YOU'LL JUST GUESS HOW TO SPELL "GENIUS"?
FIRST I'M WRITING THE CHAPTER ABOUT HOW I'M ABOUT TO MAKE YOU EAT YOUR COMPUTER.
OH, SO YOUR AUTOBIOGRAPHY WILL ACTUALLY BE ***FICTION***. INTERESTING.
AS FAR AS YOU'RE CONCERNED, IT'LL BE A COOKBOOK.
THE COOKBOOK FOR JENNY-USSES?
darb

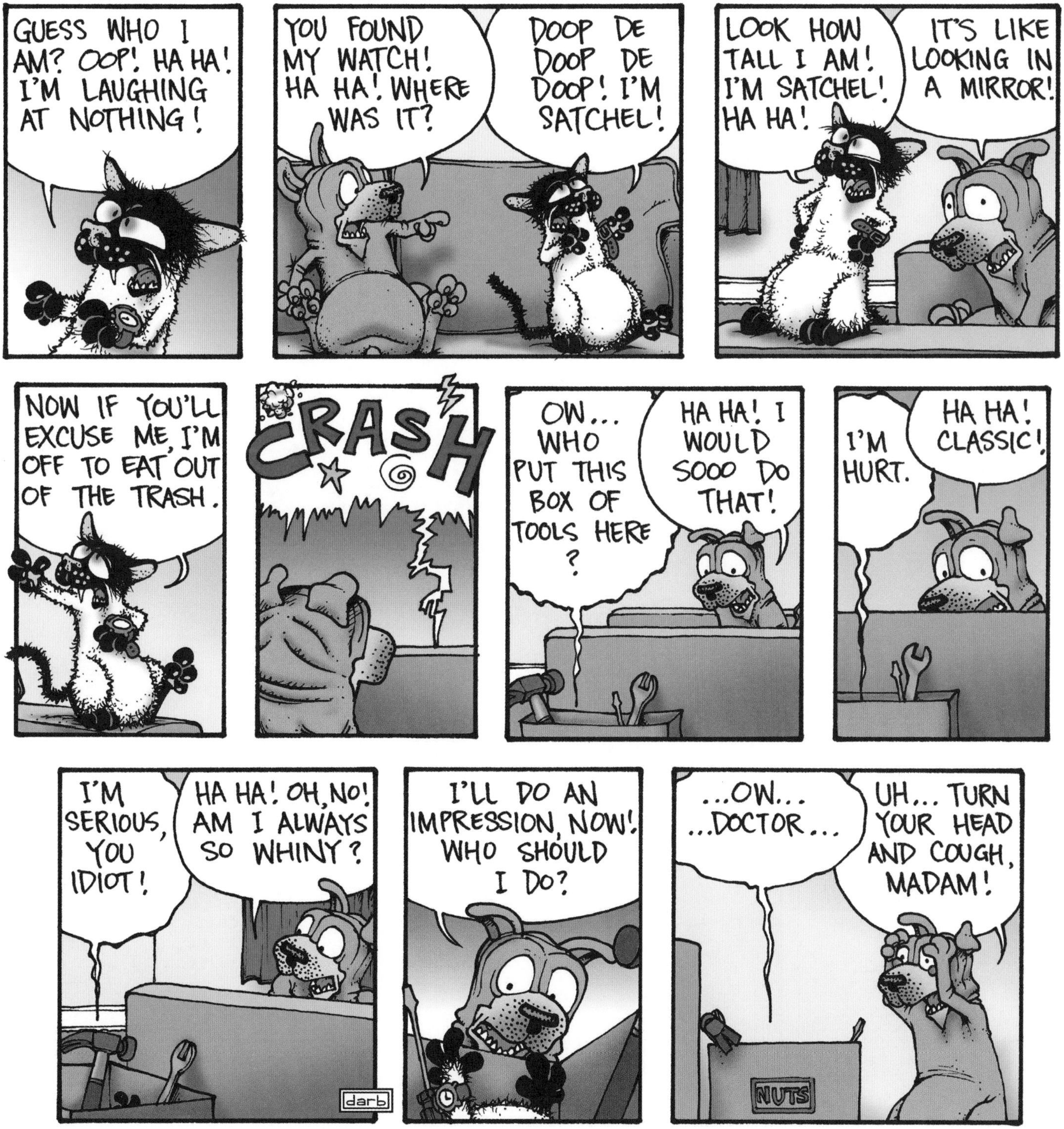
GUESS WHO I AM? OOP! HA HA! I'M LAUGHING AT NOTHING!
YOU FOUND MY WATCH! HA HA! WHERE WAS IT?
DOOP DE DOOP DE DOOP! I'M SATCHEL!
LOOK HOW TALL I AM! I'M SATCHEL! HA HA!
IT'S LIKE LOOKING IN A MIRROR!
NOW IF YOU'LL EXCUSE ME, I'M OFF TO EAT OUT OF THE TRASH.
CRASH
OW... WHO PUT THIS BOX OF TOOLS HERE?
HA HA! I WOULD SOOO DO THAT!
I'M HURT.
HA HA! CLASSIC!
I'M SERIOUS, YOU IDIOT!
HA HA! OH, NO! AM I ALWAYS SO WHINY?
darb
I'LL DO AN IMPRESSION, NOW! WHO SHOULD I DO?
...OW... ...DOCTOR...
UH... TURN YOUR HEAD AND COUGH, MADAM!
NUTS

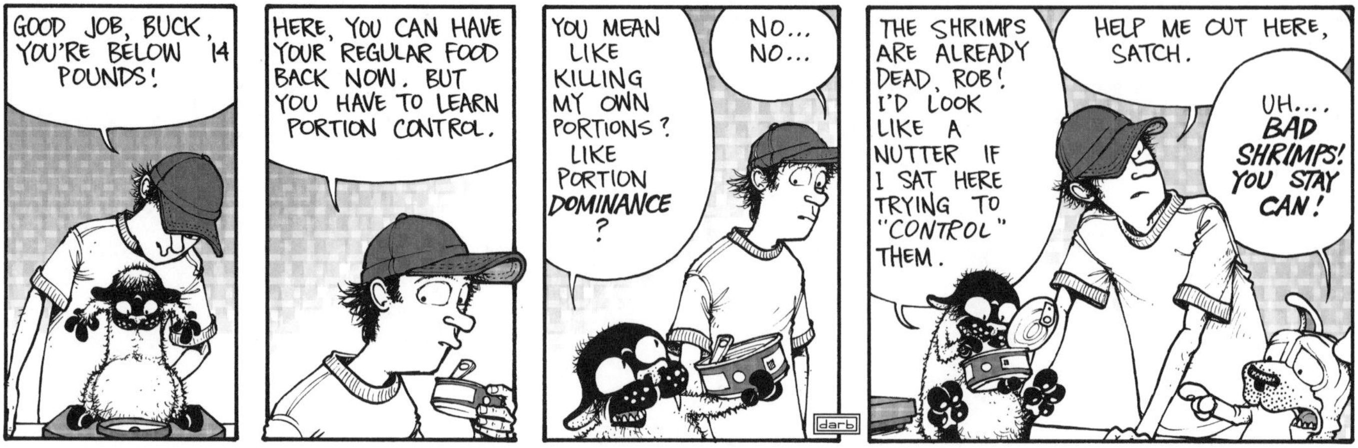
GOOD JOB, BUCK, YOU'RE BELOW 14 POUNDS!
HERE, YOU CAN HAVE YOUR REGULAR FOOD BACK NOW. BUT YOU HAVE TO LEARN PORTION CONTROL.
YOU MEAN LIKE KILLING MY OWN PORTIONS? LIKE PORTION **DOMINANCE**?
NO... NO...
THE SHRIMPS ARE ALREADY DEAD, ROB! I'D LOOK LIKE A NUTTER IF I SAT HERE TRYING TO "CONTROL" THEM.
HELP ME OUT HERE, SATCH.
UH.... **BAD SHRIMPS! YOU STAY CAN!**
darb

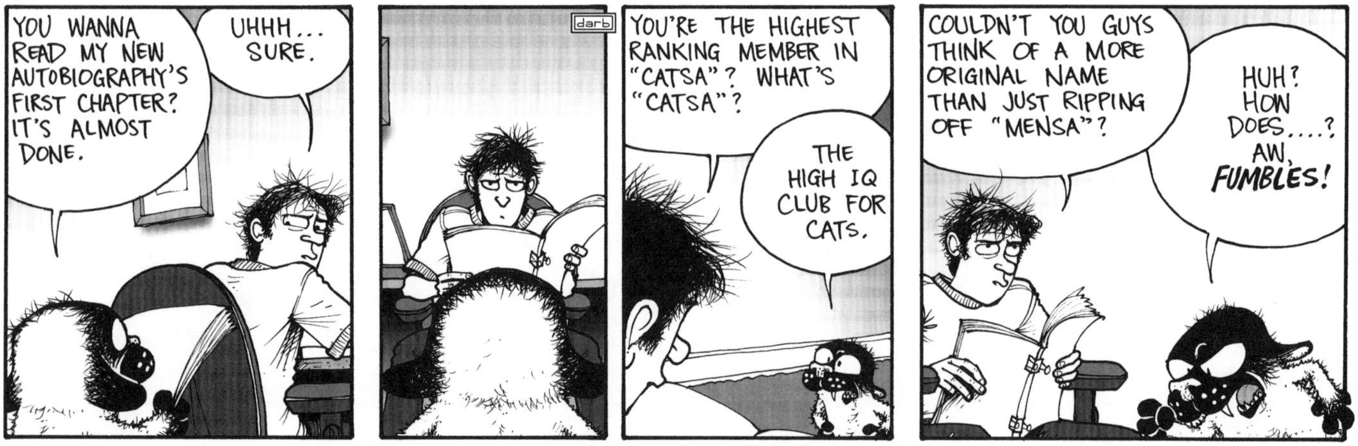
YOU WANNA READ MY NEW AUTOBIOGRAPHY'S FIRST CHAPTER? IT'S ALMOST DONE.
UHHH... SURE.
darb
YOU'RE THE HIGHEST RANKING MEMBER IN "CATSA"? WHAT'S "CATSA"?
THE HIGH IQ CLUB FOR CATS.
COULDN'T YOU GUYS THINK OF A MORE ORIGINAL NAME THAN JUST RIPPING OFF "MENSA"?
HUH? HOW DOES....? AW, **FUMBLES!**

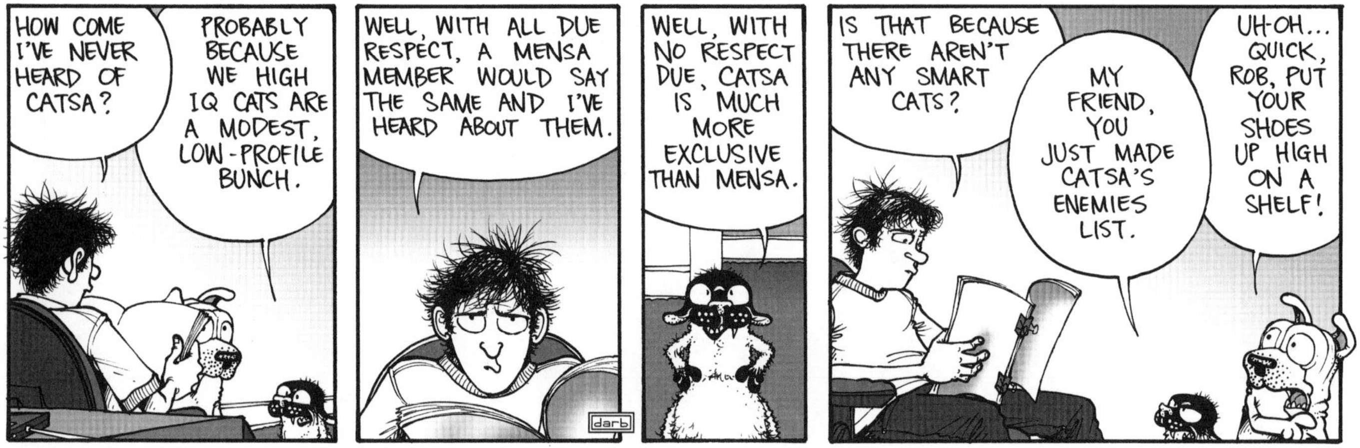
HOW COME I'VE NEVER HEARD OF CATSA?
PROBABLY BECAUSE WE HIGH IQ CATS ARE A MODEST, LOW-PROFILE BUNCH.
WELL, WITH ALL DUE RESPECT, A MENSA MEMBER WOULD SAY THE SAME AND I'VE HEARD ABOUT THEM.
darb
WELL, WITH NO RESPECT DUE, CATSA IS MUCH MORE EXCLUSIVE THAN MENSA.
IS THAT BECAUSE THERE AREN'T ANY SMART CATS?
MY FRIEND, YOU JUST MADE CATSA'S ENEMIES LIST.
UH-OH... QUICK, ROB, PUT YOUR SHOES UP HIGH ON A SHELF!

Panel 1: BUCKY, NOTHING IN YOUR AUTO-BIOGRAPHY IS TRUE. / JUST BECAUSE YOU DON'T KNOW IT DOESN'T MAKE IT UNTRUE.

Panel 2: HM. OK, I MUST HAVE BEEN OUT OF TOWN THE DAY YOU WON THE UFC BANTAMWEIGHT TITLE. / MUST HAVE BEEN.

Panel 3: I ALSO FORGOT THAT YOU INVENTED THE CURE FOR LYME DISEASE BUT WERE AMBUSHED BY DRUG COMPANY GOONS WHO STOLE YOUR NOTES AS YOU WERE ON YOUR WAY TO MAKE THE DRUG'S RECIPE PUBLIC. / I THINK YOU WERE ILL THAT DAY.

Panel 4: IT ALL SEEMS RATHER... SUPER-HUMAN. / NOT ALL OF IT IS ME BEING SUPER-HUMAN. SOME OF IT IS YOU BEING SUB-CAT.

Panel 5: I'M TAKING ADVANCE ORDERS FOR MY AUTO-BIOGRAPHY, DO YOU WANT 12 OR 13 COPIES? / ZERO, PLEASE.

Panel 6: COME ON, PINKISH, IT'S FOR CHARITY. / WHAT CHARITY?

Panel 7: HANDS ACROSS BUCKY. / THAT SOUNDS INAPPROPRIATE.

Panel 8: RELAX, H.A.B. IS JUST THE DOWN & DIRTY, GRASS LEVEL OF THE BUCKY MOVEMENT, OR B.M., AS I CALL IT.

Panel 9: SORRY, I WON'T BE PRE-ORDERING YOUR AUTO-BIOGRAPHY. / YOU'RE JUST JEALOUS OF MY AWESOME LIFE BECAUSE YOU'RE SO BORING.

Panel 10: I'M GOING TO PRETEND I DIDN'T HEAR THAT. / SEE? RIGHT THERE, THAT'S BORING.

Panel 11: FOR EXAMPLE, I WOULD LAY A BIGGY BUCKY BEATING ON YOU IF YOU CALLED ME BORING, BECAUSE *I'M* INTERESTING. / WELL, THAT JUST SOUNDS VIOLENT.

Panel 12: VIOLENCE IS INTERESTING! DON'T YOU WATCH TV, MAN?! / I FIND THE REMOTE MORE FUN THAN THE ACTUAL TV.

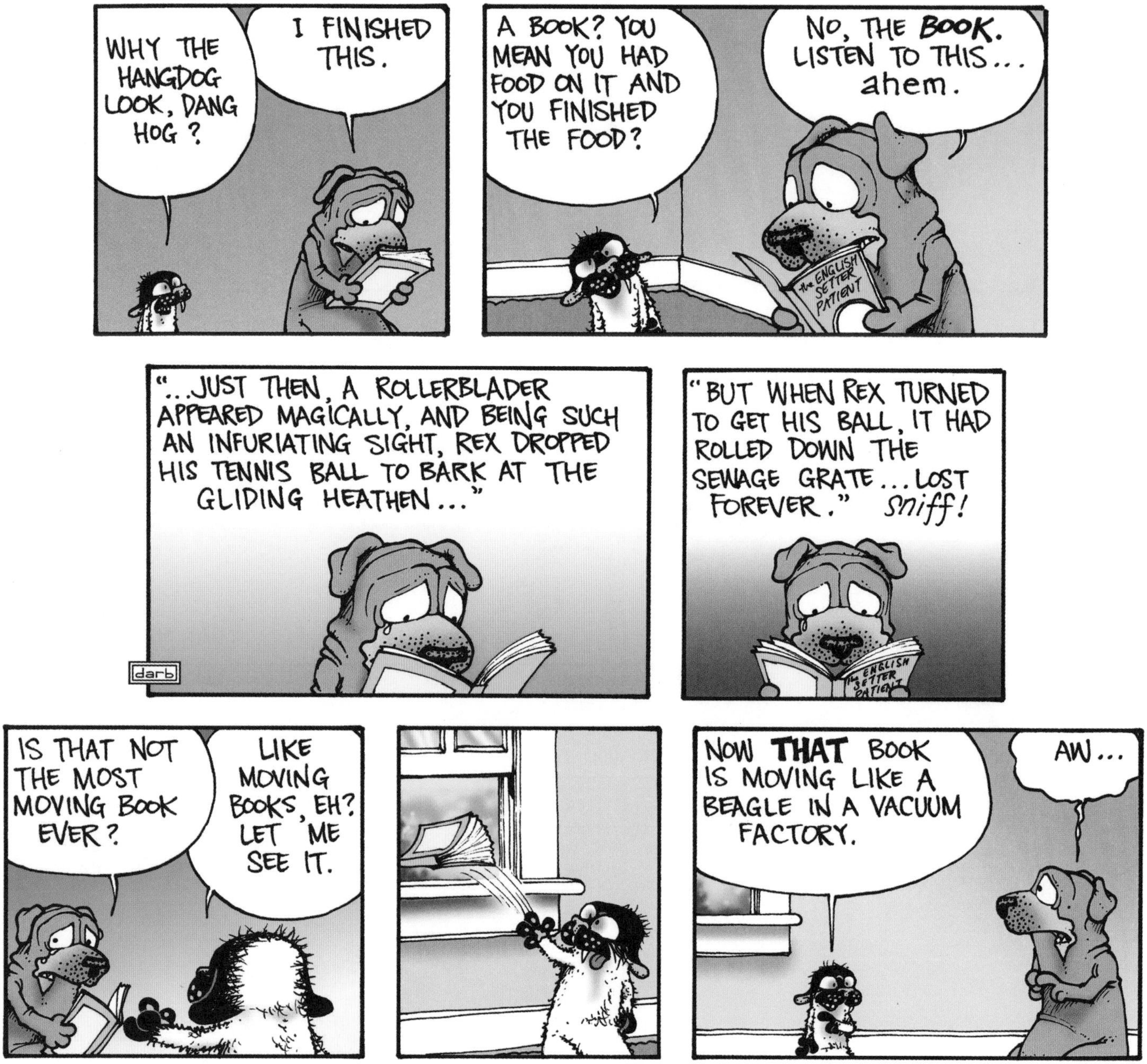
WHY THE HANGDOG LOOK, DANG HOG?
I FINISHED THIS.
A BOOK? YOU MEAN YOU HAD FOOD ON IT AND YOU FINISHED THE FOOD?
NO, THE BOOK. LISTEN TO THIS... ahem.
THE ENGLISH SETTER PATIENT
"...JUST THEN, A ROLLERBLADER APPEARED MAGICALLY, AND BEING SUCH AN INFURIATING SIGHT, REX DROPPED HIS TENNIS BALL TO BARK AT THE GLIDING HEATHEN..."
darb
"BUT WHEN REX TURNED TO GET HIS BALL, IT HAD ROLLED DOWN THE SEWAGE GRATE...LOST FOREVER." sniff!
IS THAT NOT THE MOST MOVING BOOK EVER?
LIKE MOVING BOOKS, EH? LET ME SEE IT.
NOW THAT BOOK IS MOVING LIKE A BEAGLE IN A VACUUM FACTORY.
AW...

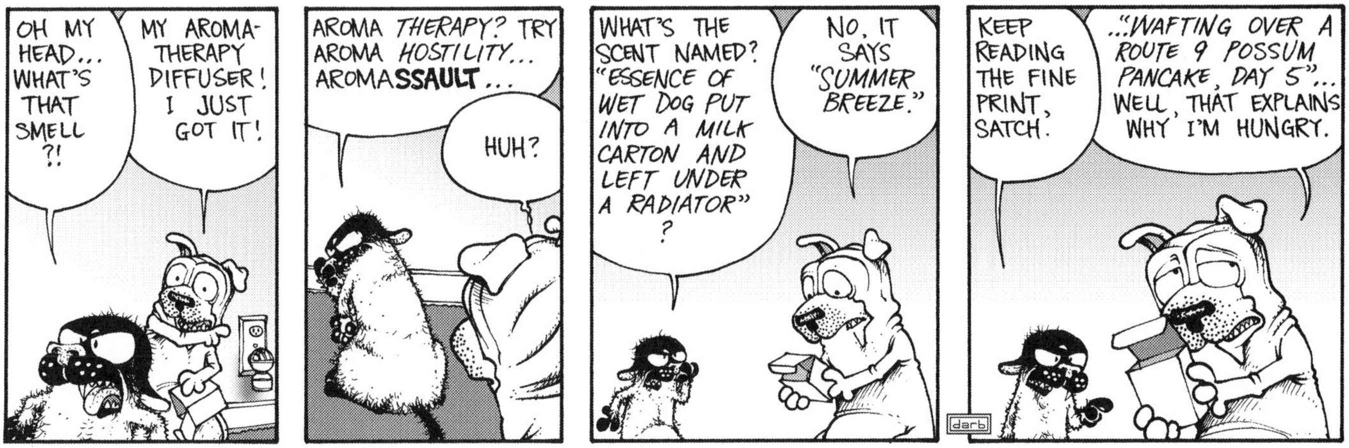
OH MY HEAD... WHAT'S THAT SMELL ?!
MY AROMA-THERAPY DIFFUSER! I JUST GOT IT!
AROMA THERAPY? TRY AROMA HOSTILITY... AROMASSAULT...
HUH?
WHAT'S THE SCENT NAMED? "ESSENCE OF WET DOG PUT INTO A MILK CARTON AND LEFT UNDER A RADIATOR" ?
NO, IT SAYS "SUMMER BREEZE."
KEEP READING THE FINE PRINT, SATCH.
..."WAFTING OVER A ROUTE 9 POSSUM PANCAKE, DAY 5"... WELL, THAT EXPLAINS WHY I'M HUNGRY.
darb

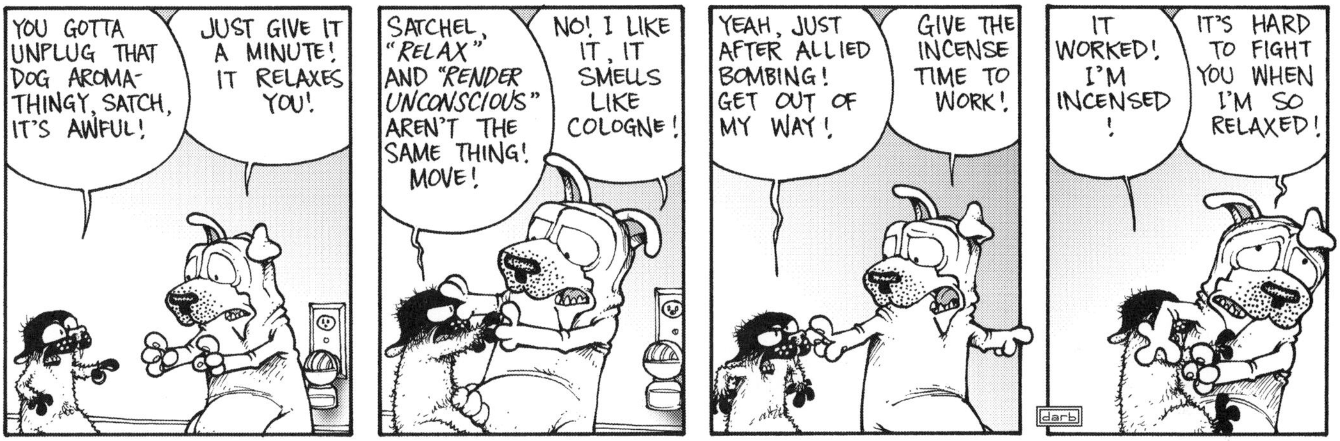
YOU GOTTA UNPLUG THAT DOG AROMA-THINGY, SATCH, IT'S AWFUL!
JUST GIVE IT A MINUTE! IT RELAXES YOU!
SATCHEL, "RELAX" AND "RENDER UNCONSCIOUS" AREN'T THE SAME THING! MOVE!
NO! I LIKE IT, IT SMELLS LIKE COLOGNE!
YEAH, JUST AFTER ALLIED BOMBING! GET OUT OF MY WAY!
GIVE THE INCENSE TIME TO WORK!
IT WORKED! I'M INCENSED!
IT'S HARD TO FIGHT YOU WHEN I'M SO RELAXED!
darb

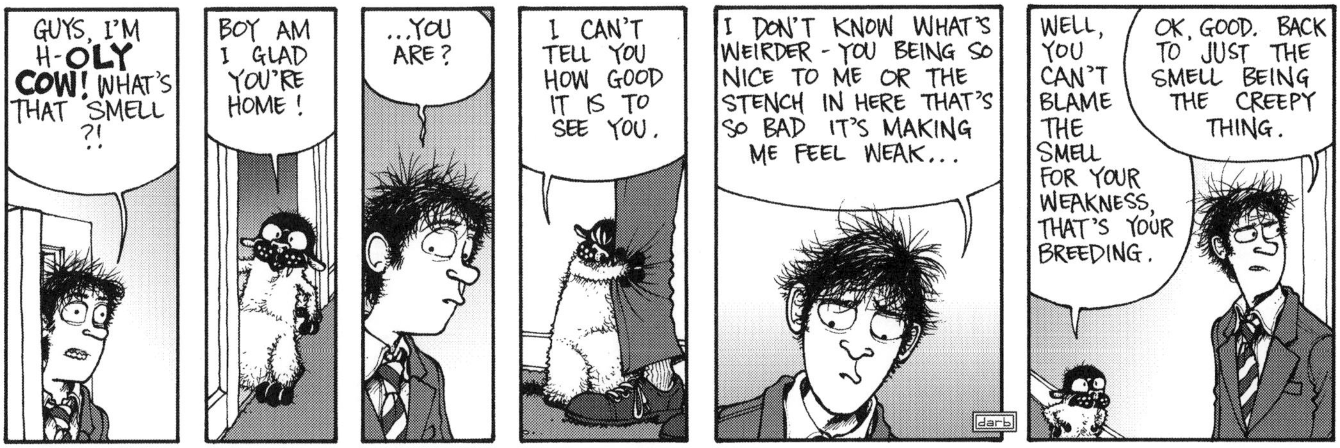
GUYS, I'M H-OLY COW! WHAT'S THAT SMELL ?!
BOY AM I GLAD YOU'RE HOME!
...YOU ARE?
I CAN'T TELL YOU HOW GOOD IT IS TO SEE YOU.
I DON'T KNOW WHAT'S WEIRDER - YOU BEING SO NICE TO ME OR THE STENCH IN HERE THAT'S SO BAD IT'S MAKING ME FEEL WEAK...
WELL, YOU CAN'T BLAME THE SMELL FOR YOUR WEAKNESS, THAT'S YOUR BREEDING.
OK, GOOD. BACK TO JUST THE SMELL BEING THE CREEPY THING.
darb

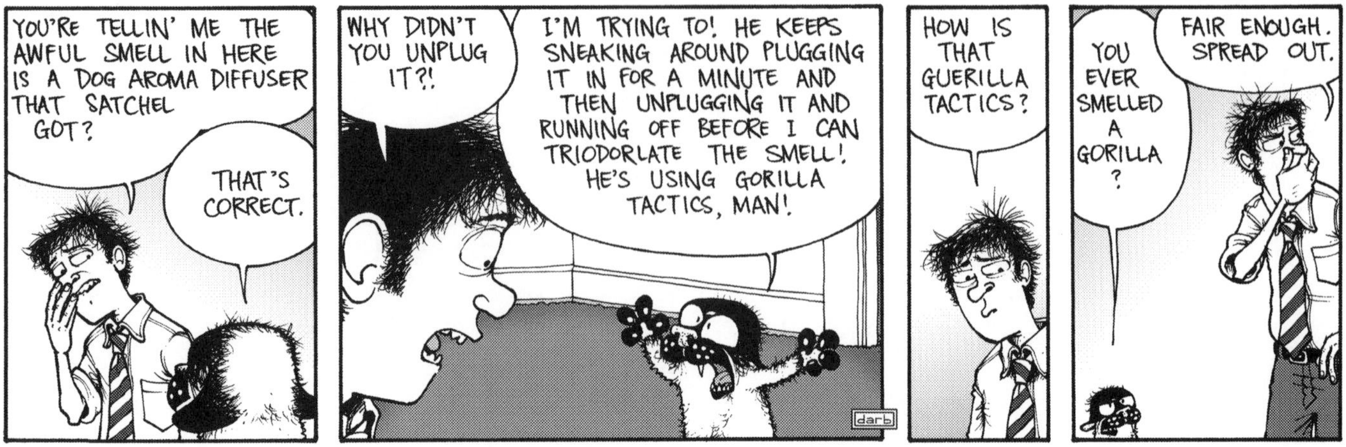
YOU'RE TELLIN' ME THE AWFUL SMELL IN HERE IS A DOG AROMA DIFFUSER THAT SATCHEL GOT?
THAT'S CORRECT.
WHY DIDN'T YOU UNPLUG IT?!
I'M TRYING TO! HE KEEPS SNEAKING AROUND PLUGGING IT IN FOR A MINUTE AND THEN UNPLUGGING IT AND RUNNING OFF BEFORE I CAN TRIODORLATE THE SMELL! HE'S USING GORILLA TACTICS, MAN!
HOW IS THAT GUERILLA TACTICS?
YOU EVER SMELLED A GORILLA?
FAIR ENOUGH. SPREAD OUT.

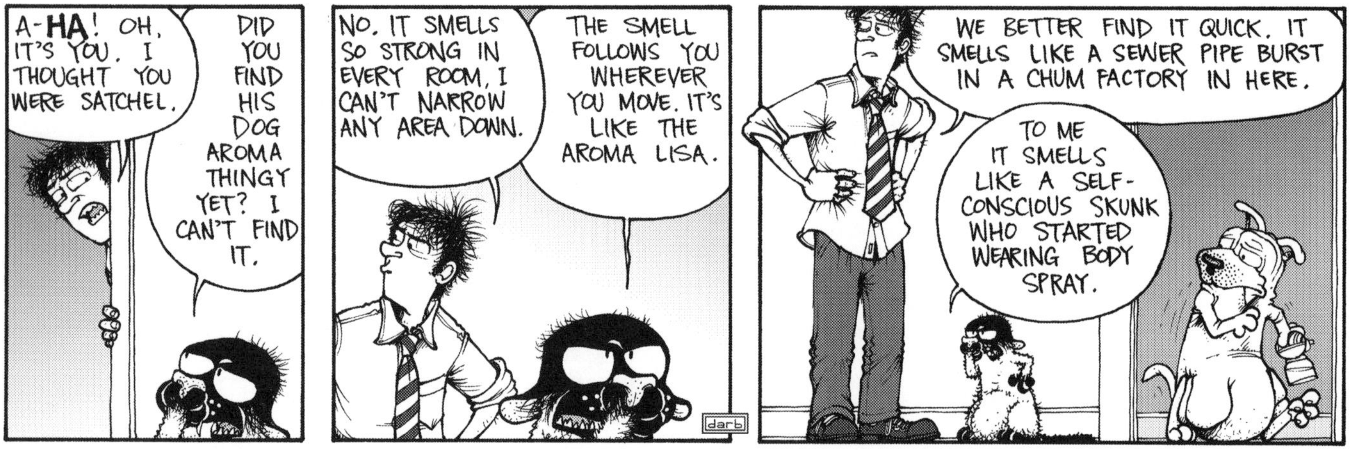
A-HA! OH, IT'S YOU. I THOUGHT YOU WERE SATCHEL.
DID YOU FIND HIS DOG AROMA THINGY YET? I CAN'T FIND IT.
NO. IT SMELLS SO STRONG IN EVERY ROOM, I CAN'T NARROW ANY AREA DOWN.
THE SMELL FOLLOWS YOU WHEREVER YOU MOVE. IT'S LIKE THE AROMA LISA.
WE BETTER FIND IT QUICK. IT SMELLS LIKE A SEWER PIPE BURST IN A CHUM FACTORY IN HERE.
TO ME IT SMELLS LIKE A SELF-CONSCIOUS SKUNK WHO STARTED WEARING BODY SPRAY.

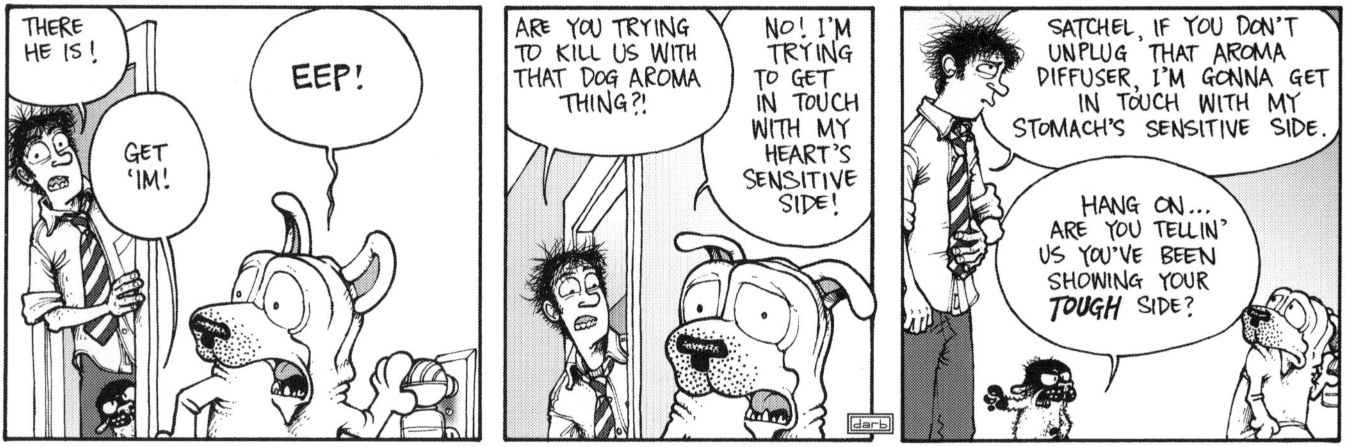
THERE HE IS!
GET 'IM!
EEP!
ARE YOU TRYING TO KILL US WITH THAT DOG AROMA THING?!
NO! I'M TRYING TO GET IN TOUCH WITH MY HEART'S SENSITIVE SIDE!
SATCHEL, IF YOU DON'T UNPLUG THAT AROMA DIFFUSER, I'M GONNA GET IN TOUCH WITH MY STOMACH'S SENSITIVE SIDE.
HANG ON... ARE YOU TELLIN' US YOU'VE BEEN SHOWING YOUR TOUGH SIDE?

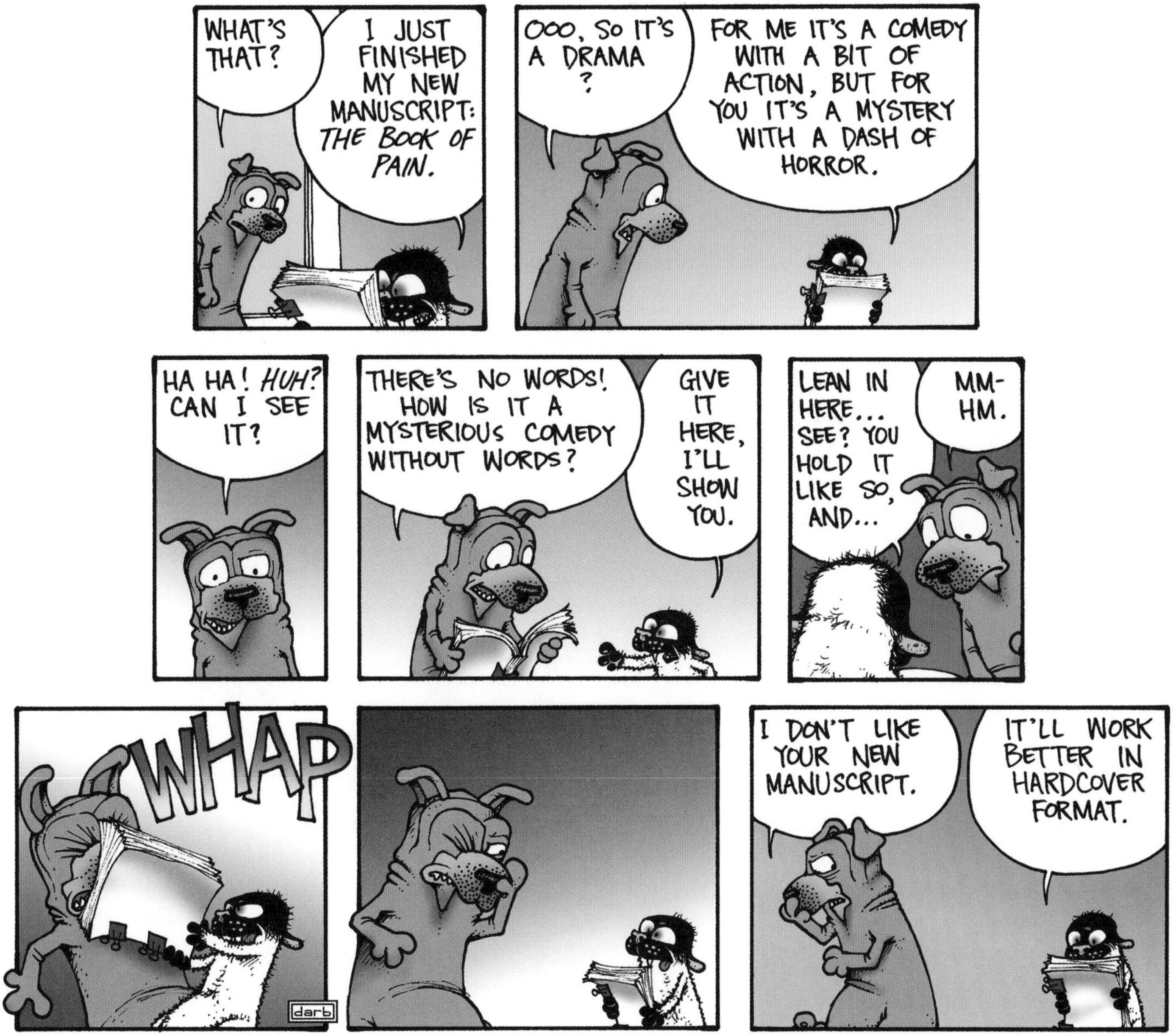
WHAT'S THAT?
I JUST FINISHED MY NEW MANUSCRIPT: *THE BOOK OF PAIN*.
OOO, SO IT'S A DRAMA?
FOR ME IT'S A COMEDY WITH A BIT OF ACTION, BUT FOR YOU IT'S A MYSTERY WITH A DASH OF HORROR.
HA HA! *HUH?* CAN I SEE IT?
THERE'S NO WORDS! HOW IS IT A MYSTERIOUS COMEDY WITHOUT WORDS?
GIVE IT HERE, I'LL SHOW YOU.
LEAN IN HERE... SEE? YOU HOLD IT LIKE SO, AND...
MM-HM.
WHAP
darb
I DON'T LIKE YOUR NEW MANUSCRIPT.
IT'LL WORK BETTER IN HARDCOVER FORMAT.

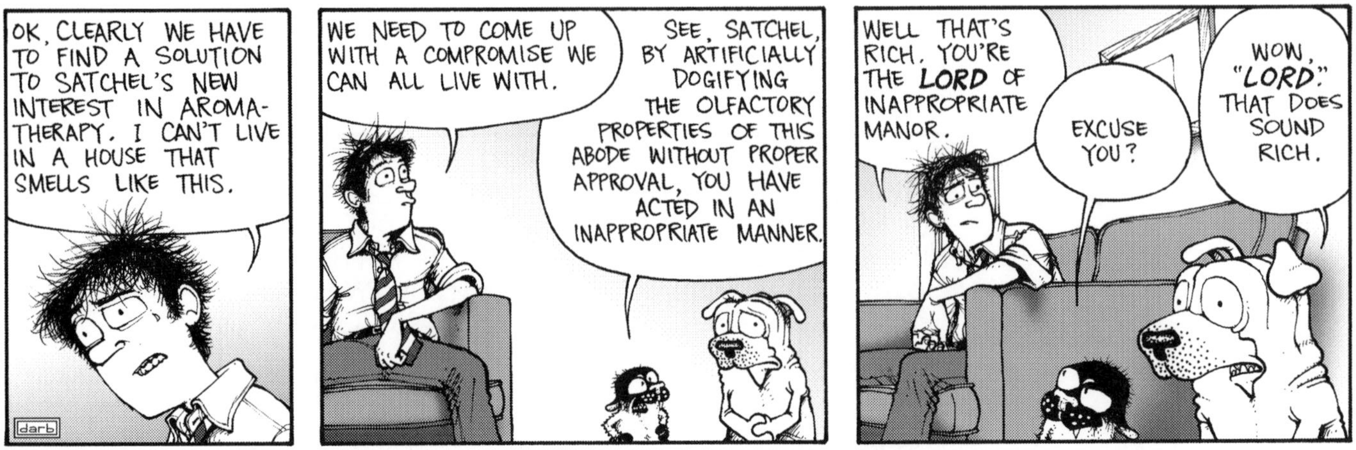
OK, CLEARLY WE HAVE TO FIND A SOLUTION TO SATCHEL'S NEW INTEREST IN AROMA-THERAPY. I CAN'T LIVE IN A HOUSE THAT SMELLS LIKE THIS.
darb
WE NEED TO COME UP WITH A COMPROMISE WE CAN ALL LIVE WITH.
SEE, SATCHEL, BY ARTIFICIALLY DOGIFYING THE OLFACTORY PROPERTIES OF THIS ABODE WITHOUT PROPER APPROVAL, YOU HAVE ACTED IN AN INAPPROPRIATE MANNER.
WELL THAT'S RICH. YOU'RE THE **LORD** OF INAPPROPRIATE MANOR.
EXCUSE YOU?
WOW, "**LORD**." THAT DOES SOUND RICH.

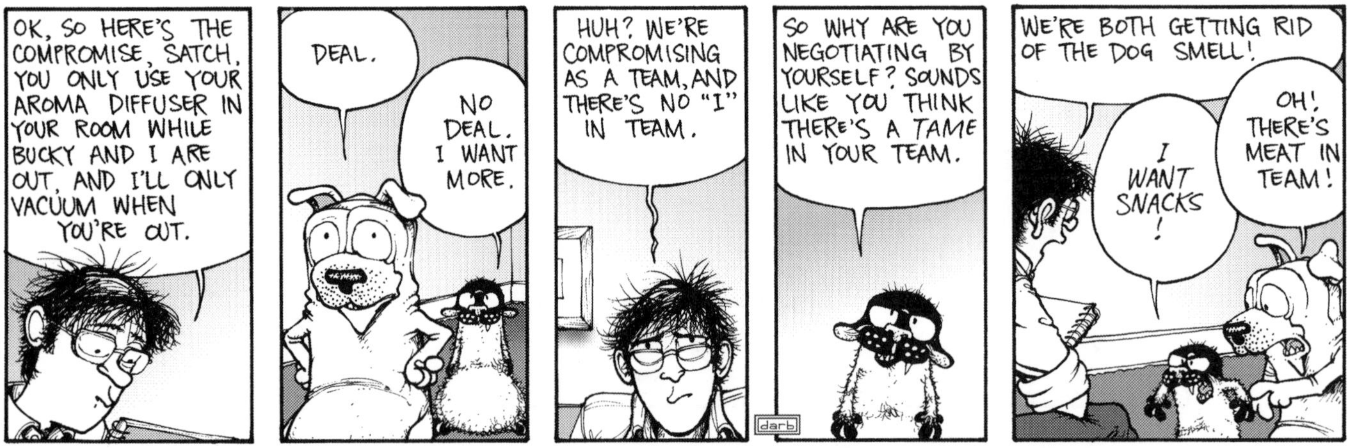
OK, SO HERE'S THE COMPROMISE, SATCH. YOU ONLY USE YOUR AROMA DIFFUSER IN YOUR ROOM WHILE BUCKY AND I ARE OUT, AND I'LL ONLY VACUUM WHEN YOU'RE OUT.
DEAL.
NO DEAL. I WANT MORE.
HUH? WE'RE COMPROMISING AS A TEAM, AND THERE'S NO "I" IN TEAM.
darb
SO WHY ARE YOU NEGOTIATING BY YOURSELF? SOUNDS LIKE YOU THINK THERE'S A *TAME* IN YOUR TEAM.
WE'RE BOTH GETTING RID OF THE DOG SMELL!
I WANT SNACKS!
OH! THERE'S MEAT IN TEAM!

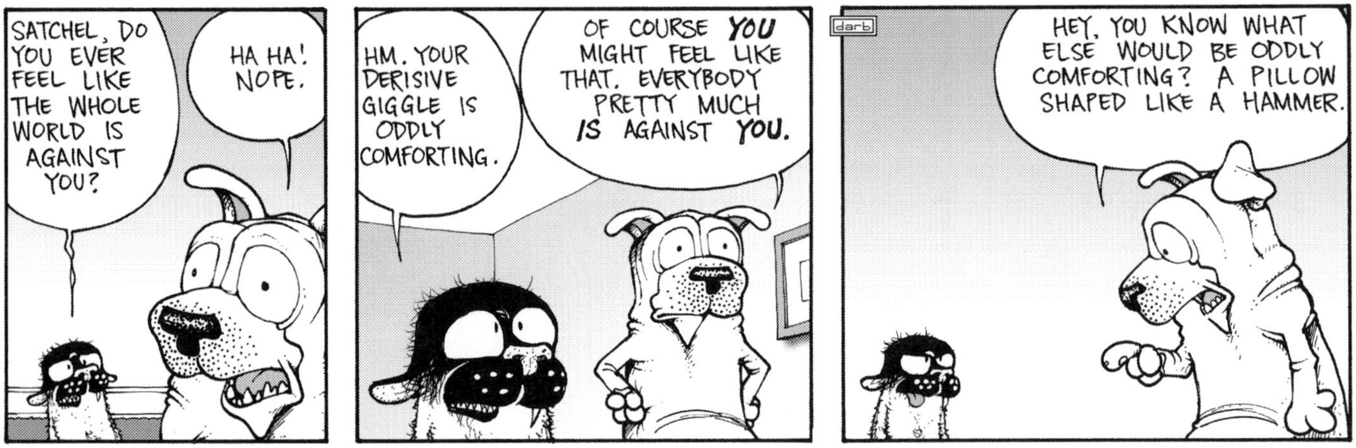
SATCHEL, DO YOU EVER FEEL LIKE THE WHOLE WORLD IS AGAINST YOU?
HA HA! NOPE.
HM. YOUR DERISIVE GIGGLE IS ODDLY COMFORTING.
OF COURSE **YOU** MIGHT FEEL LIKE THAT. EVERYBODY PRETTY MUCH **IS** AGAINST **YOU**.
darb
HEY, YOU KNOW WHAT ELSE WOULD BE ODDLY COMFORTING? A PILLOW SHAPED LIKE A HAMMER.

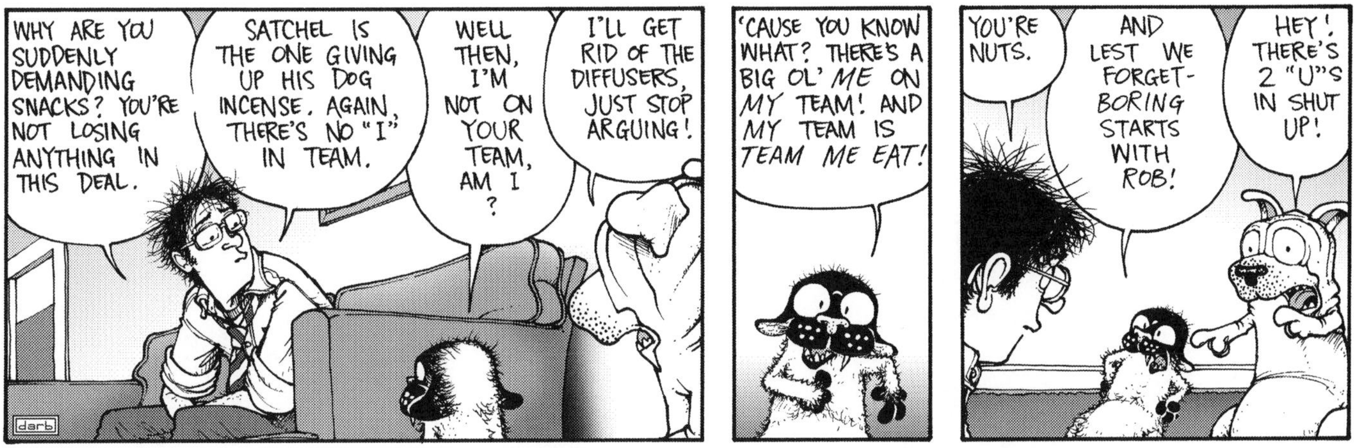
WHY ARE YOU SUDDENLY DEMANDING SNACKS? YOU'RE NOT LOSING ANYTHING IN THIS DEAL.
SATCHEL IS THE ONE GIVING UP HIS DOG INCENSE. AGAIN, THERE'S NO "I" IN TEAM.
WELL THEN, I'M NOT ON YOUR TEAM, AM I?
I'LL GET RID OF THE DIFFUSERS, JUST STOP ARGUING!
'CAUSE YOU KNOW WHAT? THERE'S A BIG OL' *ME* ON *MY* TEAM! AND *MY* TEAM IS *TEAM ME EAT!*
YOU'RE NUTS.
AND LEST WE FORGET- *BORING* STARTS WITH *ROB!*
HEY! THERE'S 2 "U"S IN SHUT UP!

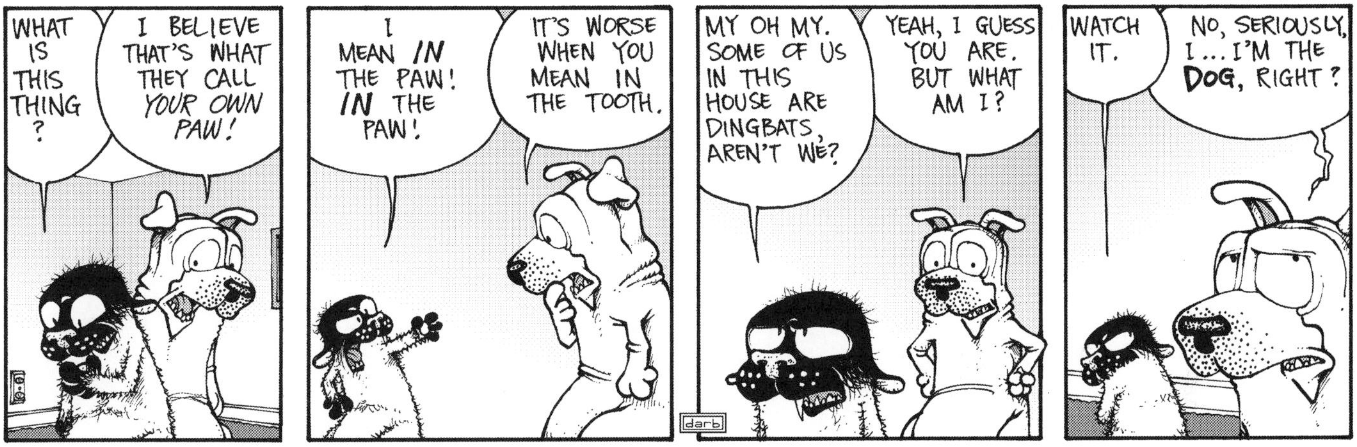
WHAT IS THIS THING?
I BELIEVE THAT'S WHAT THEY CALL *YOUR OWN PAW!*
I MEAN ***IN*** THE PAW! ***IN*** THE PAW!
IT'S WORSE WHEN YOU MEAN IN THE TOOTH.
MY OH MY. SOME OF US IN THIS HOUSE ARE DINGBATS, AREN'T WE?
YEAH, I GUESS YOU ARE. BUT WHAT AM I?
WATCH IT.
NO, SERIOUSLY, I... I'M THE **DOG**, RIGHT?

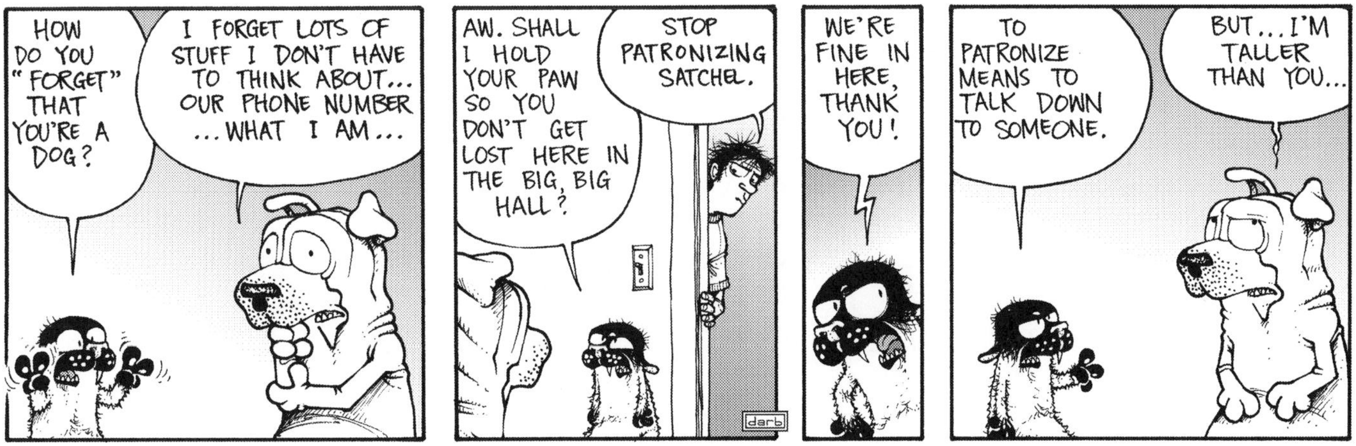
HOW DO YOU "FORGET" THAT YOU'RE A DOG?
I FORGET LOTS OF STUFF I DON'T HAVE TO THINK ABOUT... OUR PHONE NUMBER ...WHAT I AM...
AW. SHALL I HOLD YOUR PAW SO YOU DON'T GET LOST HERE IN THE BIG, BIG HALL?
STOP PATRONIZING SATCHEL.
WE'RE FINE IN HERE, THANK YOU!
TO PATRONIZE MEANS TO TALK DOWN TO SOMEONE.
BUT... I'M TALLER THAN YOU...

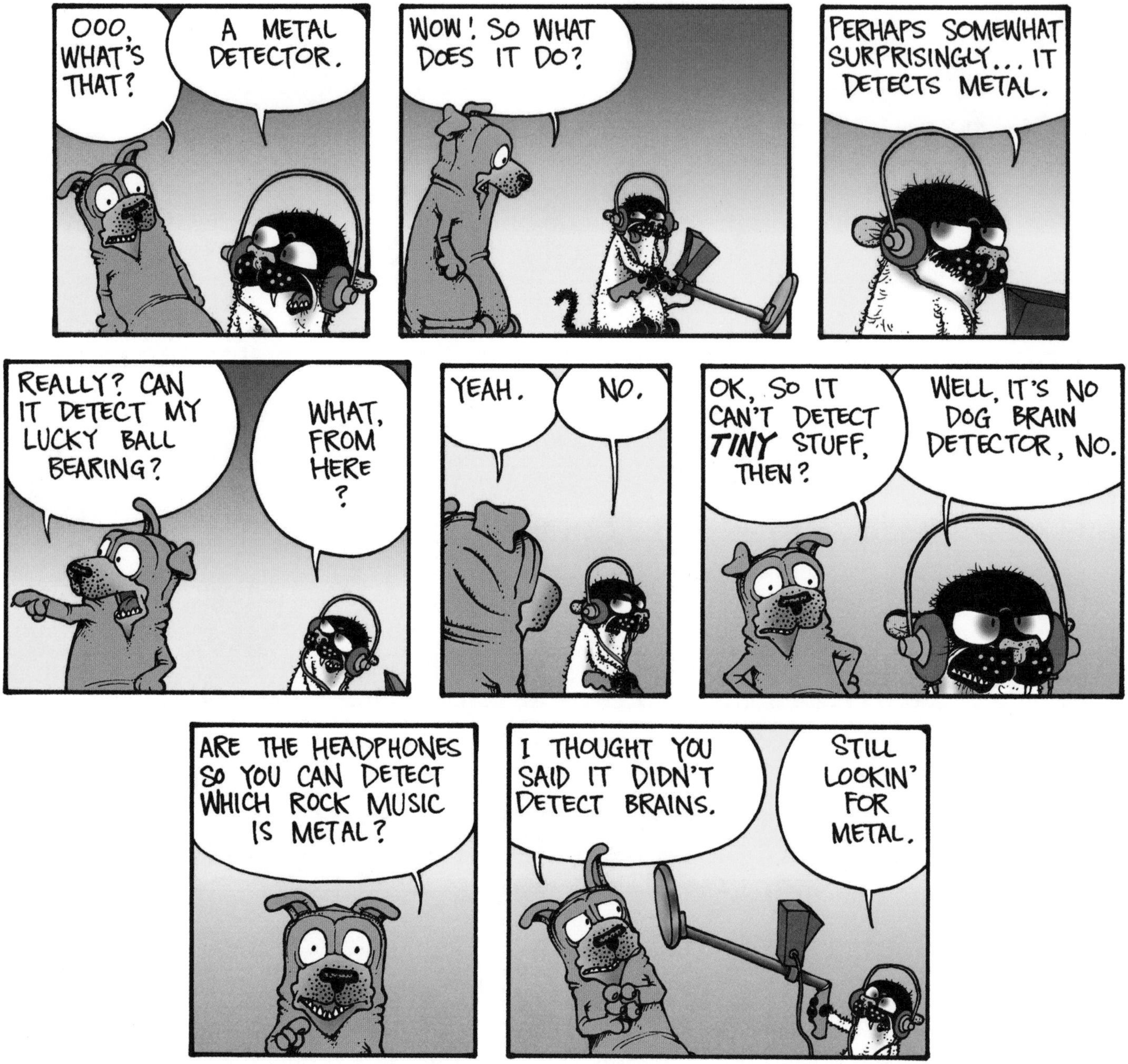
OOO, WHAT'S THAT?
A METAL DETECTOR.
WOW! SO WHAT DOES IT DO?
PERHAPS SOMEWHAT SURPRISINGLY... IT DETECTS METAL.
REALLY? CAN IT DETECT MY LUCKY BALL BEARING?
WHAT, FROM HERE?
YEAH.
NO.
OK, SO IT CAN'T DETECT *TINY* STUFF, THEN?
WELL, IT'S NO DOG BRAIN DETECTOR, NO.
ARE THE HEADPHONES SO YOU CAN DETECT WHICH ROCK MUSIC IS METAL?
I THOUGHT YOU SAID IT DIDN'T DETECT BRAINS.
STILL LOOKIN' FOR METAL.

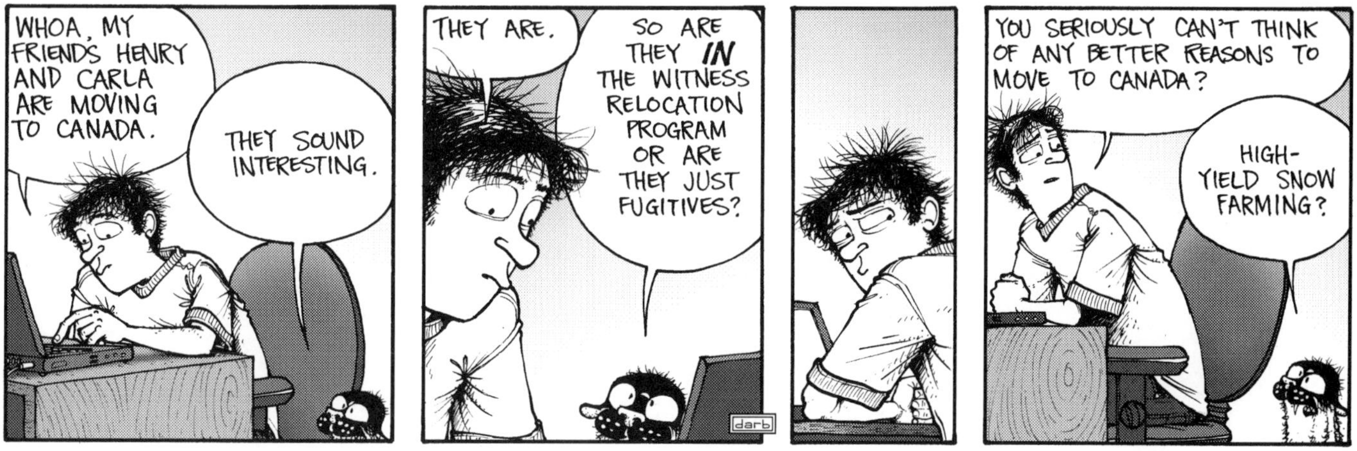
WHOA, MY FRIENDS HENRY AND CARLA ARE MOVING TO CANADA.
THEY SOUND INTERESTING.
THEY ARE.
SO ARE THEY *IN* THE WITNESS RELOCATION PROGRAM OR ARE THEY JUST FUGITIVES?
YOU SERIOUSLY CAN'T THINK OF ANY BETTER REASONS TO MOVE TO CANADA?
HIGH-YIELD SNOW FARMING?

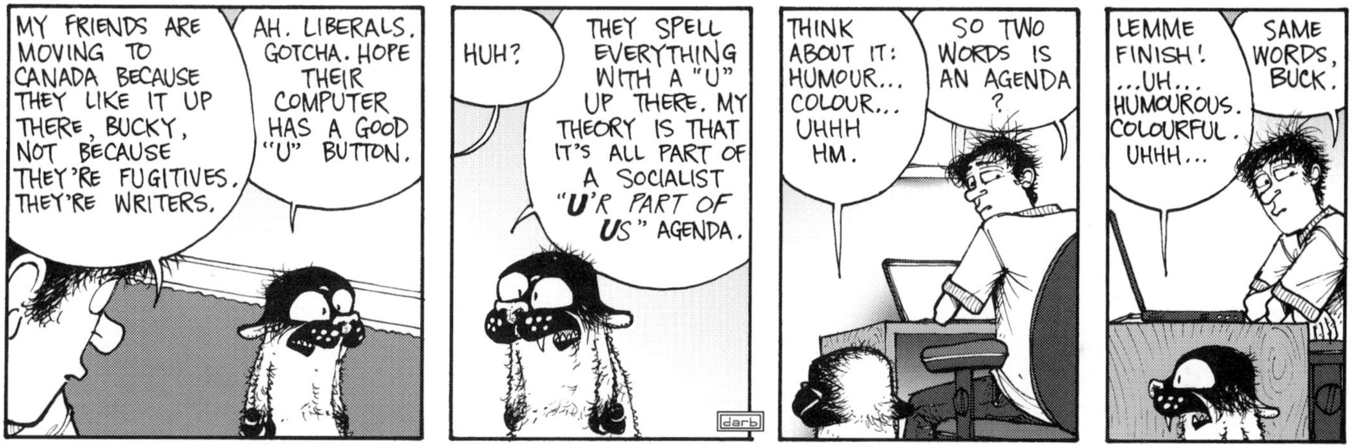
MY FRIENDS ARE MOVING TO CANADA BECAUSE THEY LIKE IT UP THERE, BUCKY, NOT BECAUSE THEY'RE FUGITIVES. THEY'RE WRITERS.
AH. LIBERALS. GOTCHA. HOPE THEIR COMPUTER HAS A GOOD "U" BUTTON.
HUH?
THEY SPELL EVERYTHING WITH A "U" UP THERE. MY THEORY IS THAT IT'S ALL PART OF A SOCIALIST "*U'R PART OF US*" AGENDA.
THINK ABOUT IT: HUMOUR... COLOUR... UHHH HM.
SO TWO WORDS IS AN AGENDA?
LEMME FINISH! ...UH... HUMOUROUS. COLOURFUL. UHHH...
SAME WORDS, BUCK.

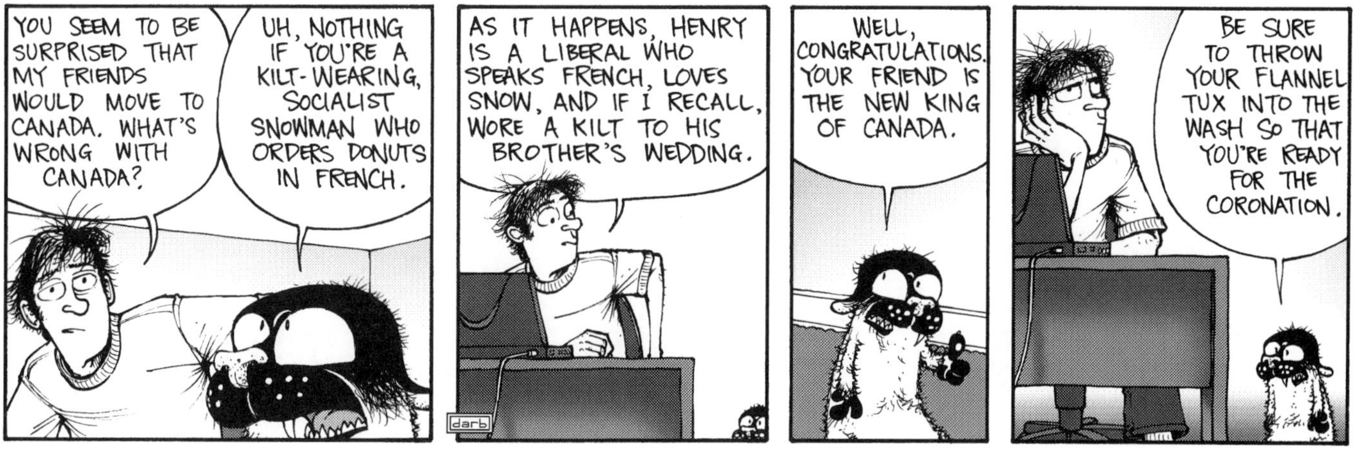
YOU SEEM TO BE SURPRISED THAT MY FRIENDS WOULD MOVE TO CANADA. WHAT'S WRONG WITH CANADA?
UH, NOTHING IF YOU'RE A KILT-WEARING, SOCIALIST SNOWMAN WHO ORDERS DONUTS IN FRENCH.
AS IT HAPPENS, HENRY IS A LIBERAL WHO SPEAKS FRENCH, LOVES SNOW, AND IF I RECALL, WORE A KILT TO HIS BROTHER'S WEDDING.
WELL, CONGRATULATIONS. YOUR FRIEND IS THE NEW KING OF CANADA.
BE SURE TO THROW YOUR FLANNEL TUX INTO THE WASH SO THAT YOU'RE READY FOR THE CORONATION.

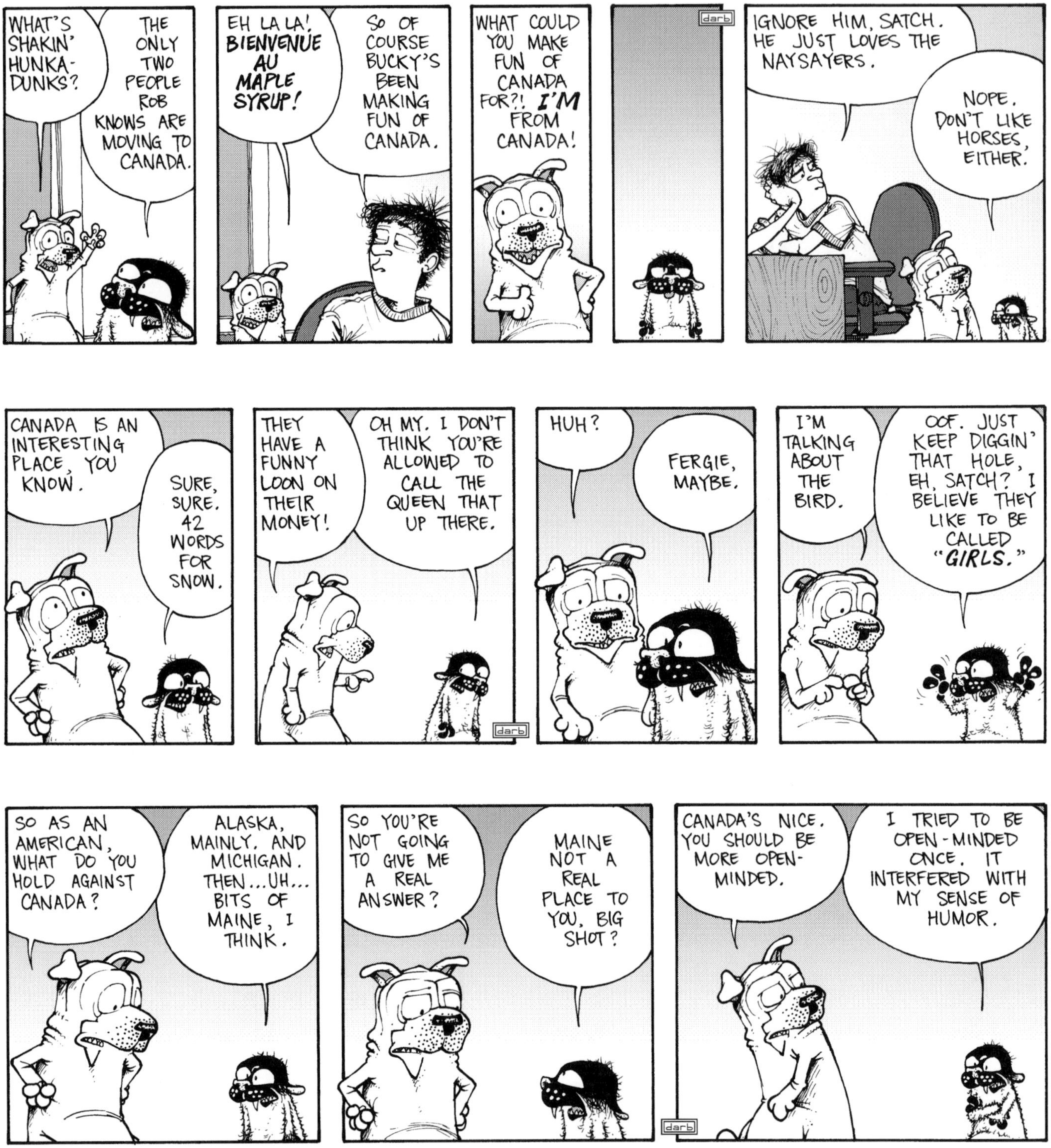
WHAT'S SHAKIN' HUNKA-DUNKS?
THE ONLY TWO PEOPLE ROB KNOWS ARE MOVING TO CANADA.
EH LA LA! BIENVENUE AU MAPLE SYRUP!
SO OF COURSE BUCKY'S BEEN MAKING FUN OF CANADA.
WHAT COULD YOU MAKE FUN OF CANADA FOR?! I'M FROM CANADA!
IGNORE HIM, SATCH. HE JUST LOVES THE NAYSAYERS.
NOPE. DON'T LIKE HORSES, EITHER.
CANADA IS AN INTERESTING PLACE, YOU KNOW.
SURE, SURE. 42 WORDS FOR SNOW.
THEY HAVE A FUNNY LOON ON THEIR MONEY!
OH MY. I DON'T THINK YOU'RE ALLOWED TO CALL THE QUEEN THAT UP THERE.
HUH?
FERGIE, MAYBE.
I'M TALKING ABOUT THE BIRD.
OOF. JUST KEEP DIGGIN' THAT HOLE, EH, SATCH? I BELIEVE THEY LIKE TO BE CALLED "GIRLS."
SO AS AN AMERICAN, WHAT DO YOU HOLD AGAINST CANADA?
ALASKA, MAINLY. AND MICHIGAN. THEN...UH... BITS OF MAINE, I THINK.
SO YOU'RE NOT GOING TO GIVE ME A REAL ANSWER?
MAINE NOT A REAL PLACE TO YOU, BIG SHOT?
CANADA'S NICE. YOU SHOULD BE MORE OPEN-MINDED.
I TRIED TO BE OPEN-MINDED ONCE. IT INTERFERED WITH MY SENSE OF HUMOR.

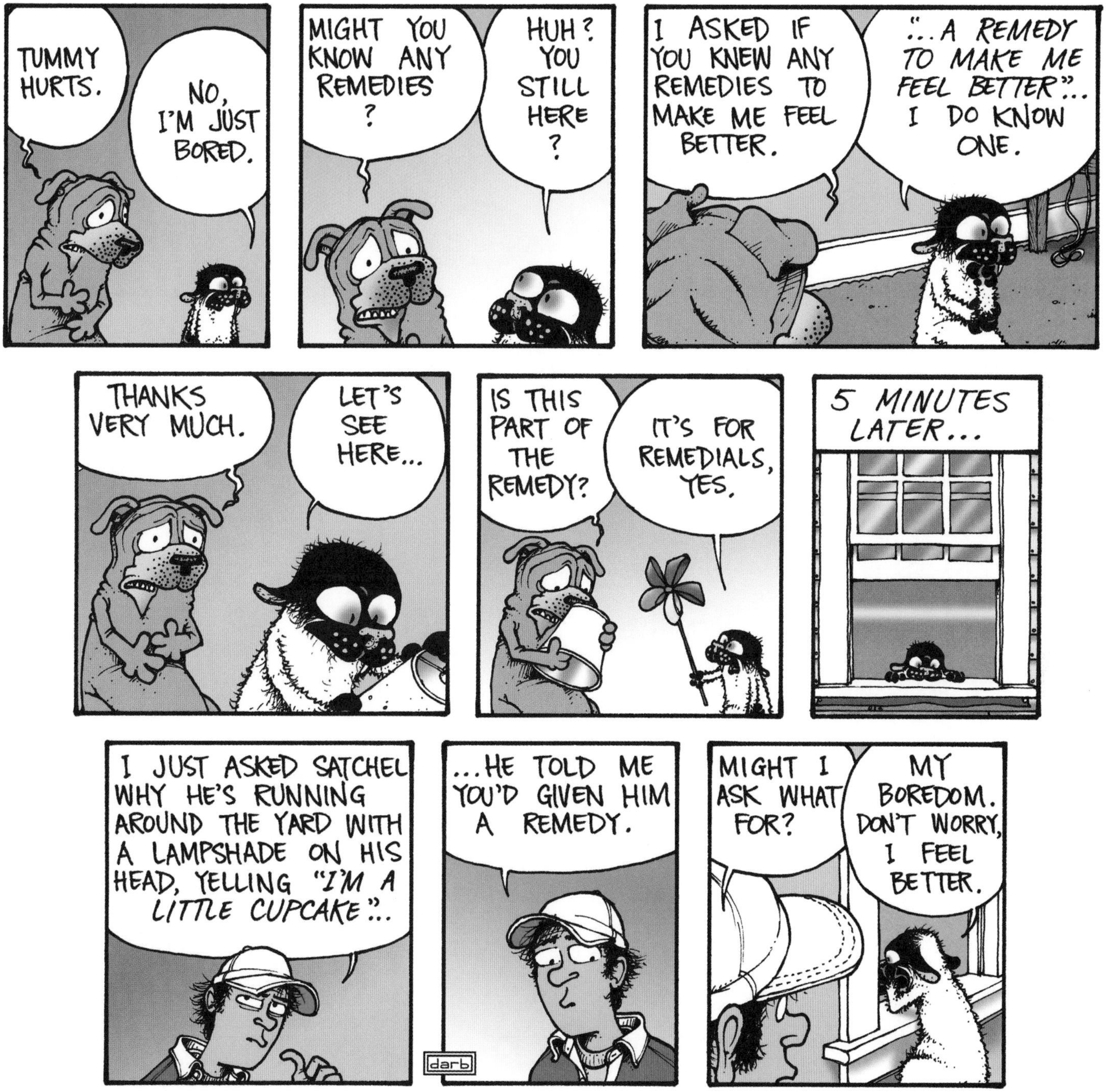
TUMMY HURTS.
NO, I'M JUST BORED.
MIGHT YOU KNOW ANY REMEDIES ?
HUH? YOU STILL HERE ?
I ASKED IF YOU KNEW ANY REMEDIES TO MAKE ME FEEL BETTER.
"...A *REMEDY TO MAKE ME FEEL BETTER*"... I DO KNOW ONE.
THANKS VERY MUCH.
LET'S SEE HERE...
IS THIS PART OF THE REMEDY?
IT'S FOR REMEDIALS, YES.
5 MINUTES LATER...
I JUST ASKED SATCHEL WHY HE'S RUNNING AROUND THE YARD WITH A LAMPSHADE ON HIS HEAD, YELLING "*I'M A LITTLE CUPCAKE*"...
darb
...HE TOLD ME YOU'D GIVEN HIM A REMEDY.
MIGHT I ASK WHAT FOR?
MY BOREDOM. DON'T WORRY, I FEEL BETTER.

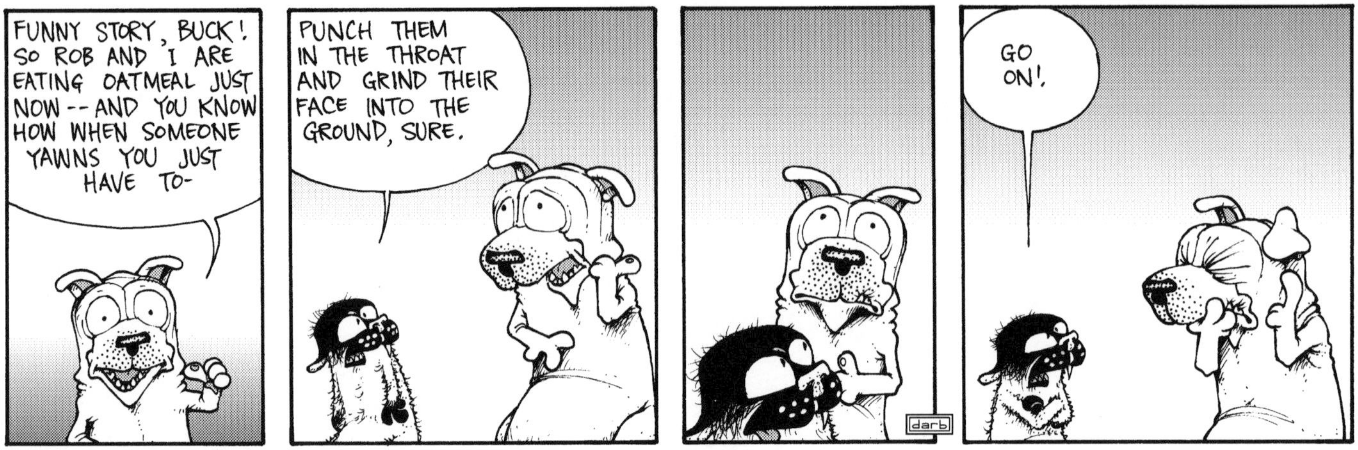
FUNNY STORY, BUCK! SO ROB AND I ARE EATING OATMEAL JUST NOW -- AND YOU KNOW HOW WHEN SOMEONE YAWNS YOU JUST HAVE TO-
PUNCH THEM IN THE THROAT AND GRIND THEIR FACE INTO THE GROUND, SURE.
GO ON!

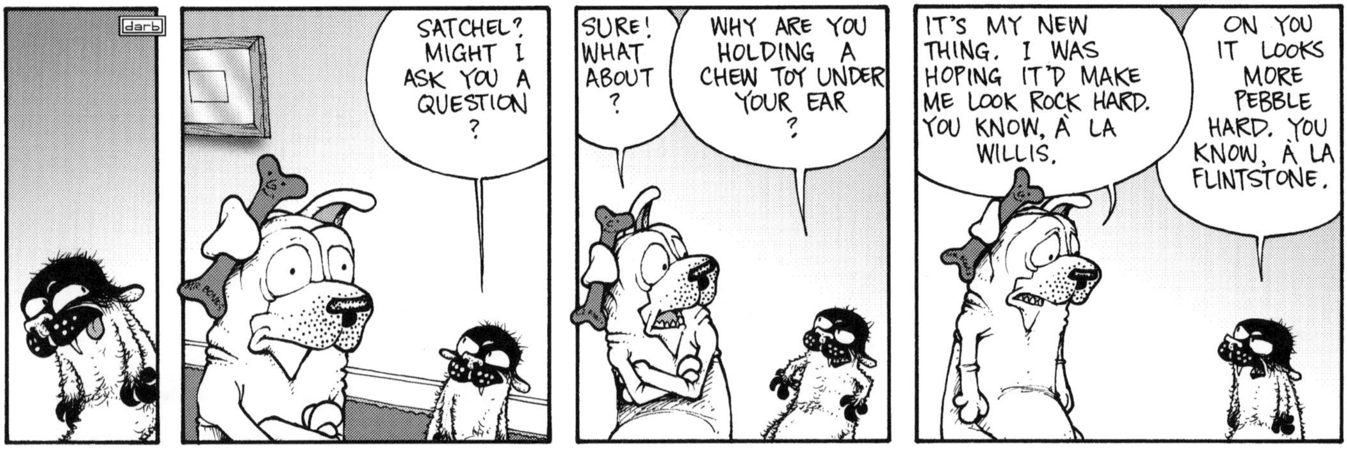
SATCHEL? MIGHT I ASK YOU A QUESTION?
SURE! WHAT ABOUT?
WHY ARE YOU HOLDING A CHEW TOY UNDER YOUR EAR?
IT'S MY NEW THING. I WAS HOPING IT'D MAKE ME LOOK ROCK HARD. YOU KNOW, À LA WILLIS.
ON YOU IT LOOKS MORE PEBBLE HARD. YOU KNOW, À LA FLINTSTONE.

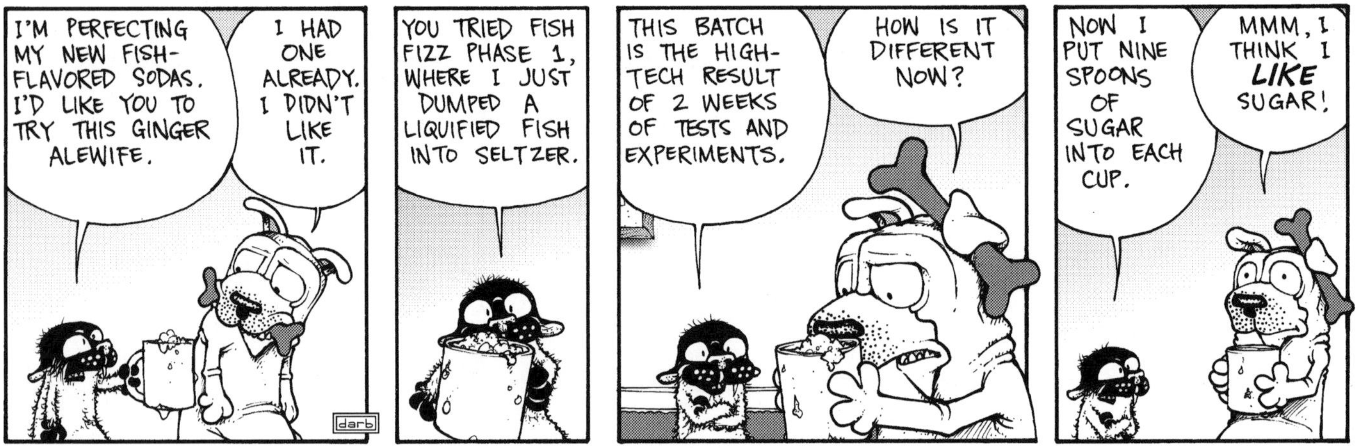
I'M PERFECTING MY NEW FISH-FLAVORED SODAS. I'D LIKE YOU TO TRY THIS GINGER ALEWIFE.
I HAD ONE ALREADY. I DIDN'T LIKE IT.
YOU TRIED FISH FIZZ PHASE 1, WHERE I JUST DUMPED A LIQUIFIED FISH INTO SELTZER.
THIS BATCH IS THE HIGH-TECH RESULT OF 2 WEEKS OF TESTS AND EXPERIMENTS.
HOW IS IT DIFFERENT NOW?
NOW I PUT NINE SPOONS OF SUGAR INTO EACH CUP.
MMM, I THINK I ***LIKE*** SUGAR!

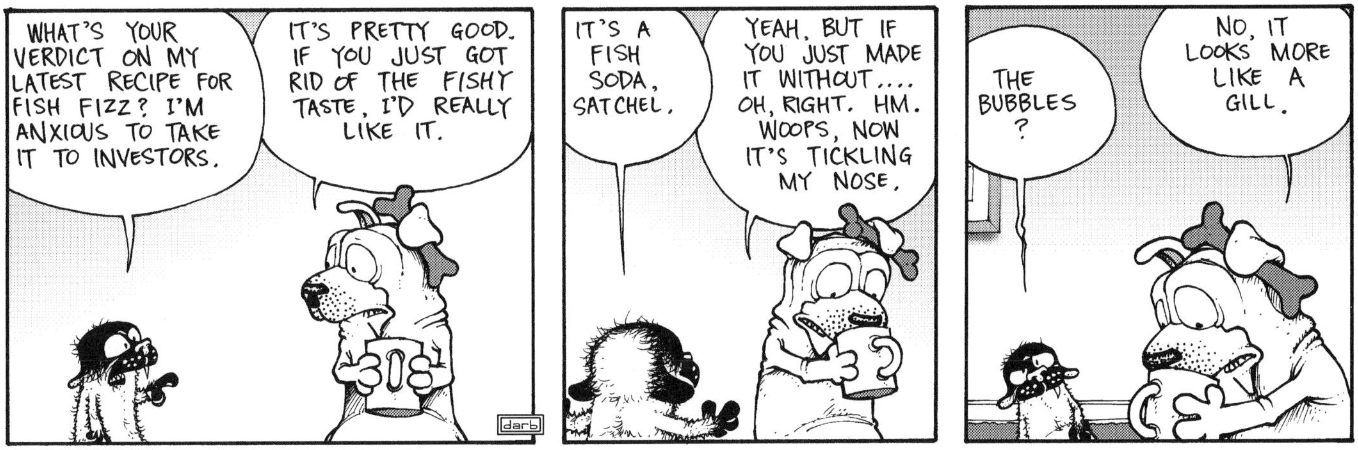
WHAT'S YOUR VERDICT ON MY LATEST RECIPE FOR FISH FIZZ? I'M ANXIOUS TO TAKE IT TO INVESTORS.
IT'S PRETTY GOOD. IF YOU JUST GOT RID OF THE FISHY TASTE, I'D REALLY LIKE IT.
darb
IT'S A FISH SODA, SATCHEL.
YEAH, BUT IF YOU JUST MADE IT WITHOUT.... OH, RIGHT. HM. WOOPS, NOW IT'S TICKLING MY NOSE.
THE BUBBLES?
NO, IT LOOKS MORE LIKE A GILL.

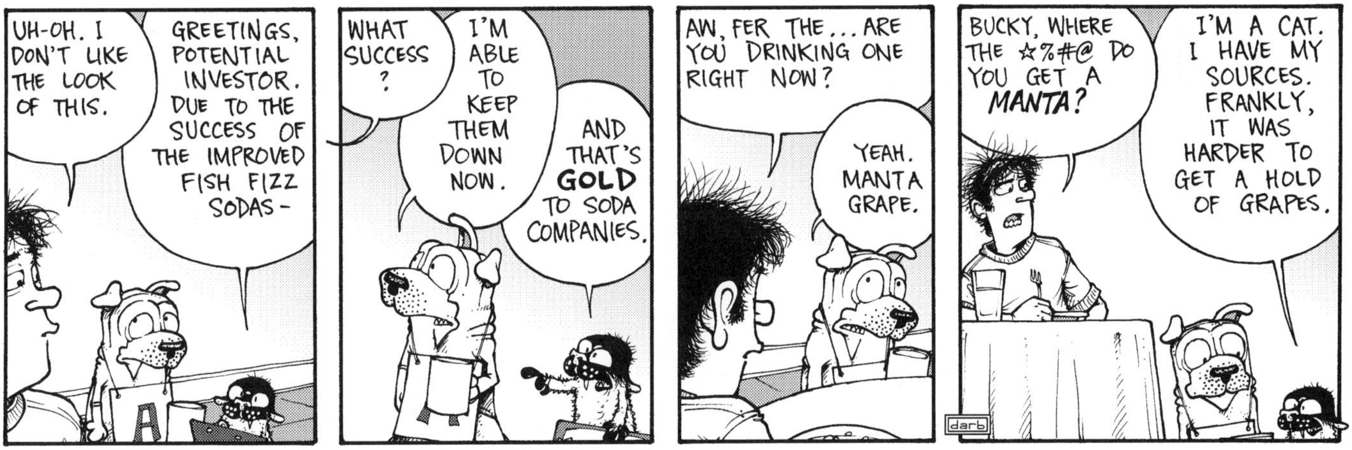
UH-OH. I DON'T LIKE THE LOOK OF THIS.
GREETINGS, POTENTIAL INVESTOR. DUE TO THE SUCCESS OF THE IMPROVED FISH FIZZ SODAS-
WHAT SUCCESS?
I'M ABLE TO KEEP THEM DOWN NOW.
AND THAT'S GOLD TO SODA COMPANIES.
AW, FER THE... ARE YOU DRINKING ONE RIGHT NOW?
YEAH. MANTA GRAPE.
darb
BUCKY, WHERE THE ☆%#@ DO YOU GET A MANTA?
I'M A CAT. I HAVE MY SOURCES. FRANKLY, IT WAS HARDER TO GET A HOLD OF GRAPES.

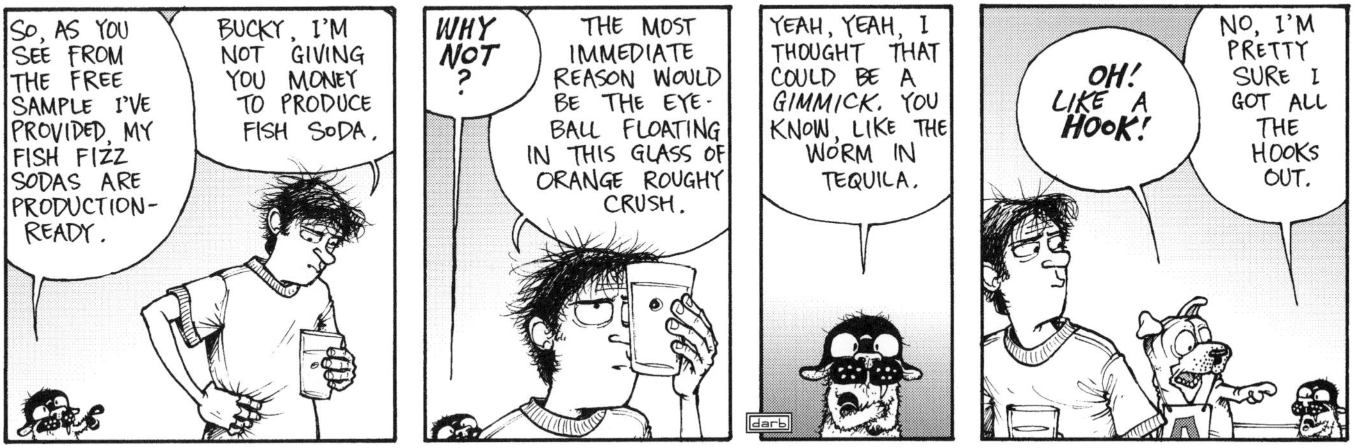
SO, AS YOU SEE FROM THE FREE SAMPLE I'VE PROVIDED, MY FISH FIZZ SODAS ARE PRODUCTION-READY.
BUCKY, I'M NOT GIVING YOU MONEY TO PRODUCE FISH SODA.
WHY NOT?
THE MOST IMMEDIATE REASON WOULD BE THE EYE-BALL FLOATING IN THIS GLASS OF ORANGE ROUGHY CRUSH.
YEAH, YEAH, I THOUGHT THAT COULD BE A GIMMICK. YOU KNOW, LIKE THE WORM IN TEQUILA.
darb
OH! LIKE A HOOK!
NO, I'M PRETTY SURE I GOT ALL THE HOOKS OUT.

ROB WANTS TO KNOW IF YOU'RE EATING WITH US TONIGHT.

WHAT ARE YOU HAVING?

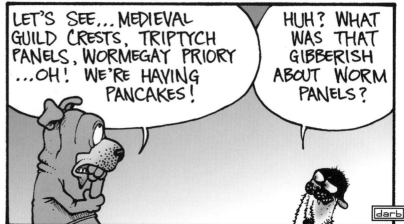

LET'S SEE,... MEDIEVAL GUILD CRESTS, TRIPTYCH PANELS, WORMEGAY PRIORY ...OH! WE'RE HAVING PANCAKES!

HUH? WHAT WAS THAT GIBBERISH ABOUT WORM PANELS?

MY MNEMONIC DEVICE? THAT'S HOW I REMEMBER THE DINNER SCHEDULE. MEDIEVAL GUILD CREST MEANS MONDAY GRILLED CHEESE, TRIPTYCH PANELS MEANS TUESDAY PASTA, WORMEGAY—

THAT TAKES MORE WORK THAN JUST REMEMBERING THE MEAL.

NO, NO, IT'S A MNEMONIC DEVICE.

BUT IT'S HARDER TO REMEMBER THAN THE ACTUAL SCHEDULE! IT'S A MORONIC DEVICE!

YOU KNOW THOSE PEOPLE WHO FIND HIDDEN MEANINGS IN BACKWARDS MUSIC? I CHALLENGE THEM TO FIND ANY MEANING IN WHAT YOU SAY FORWARDS.

BY THE WAY, HERETIC DONGLES TOMORROW. WITH FRIES.

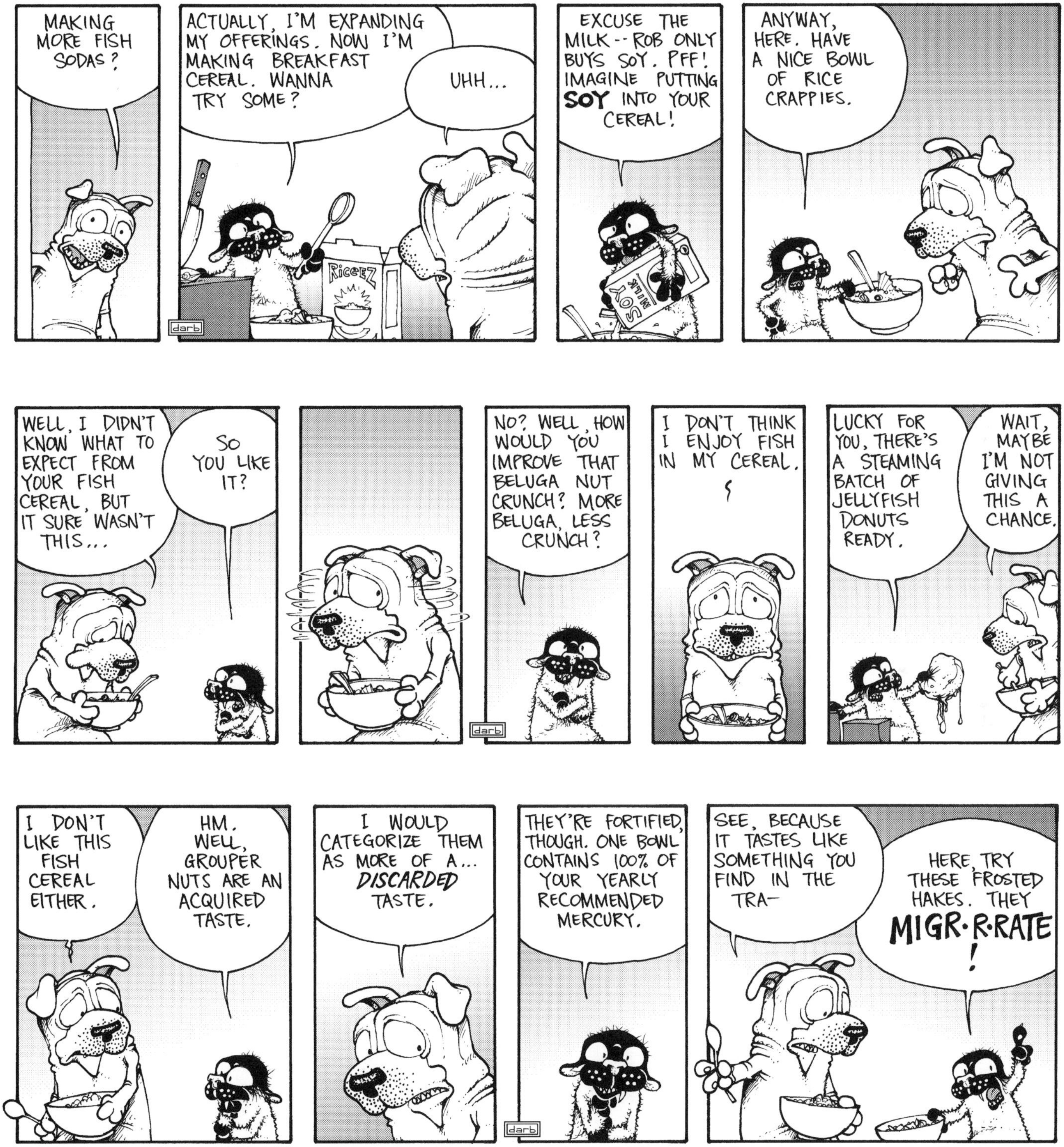
MAKING MORE FISH SODAS?
ACTUALLY, I'M EXPANDING MY OFFERINGS. NOW I'M MAKING BREAKFAST CEREAL. WANNA TRY SOME?
UHH...
RiceeZ
darb
EXCUSE THE MILK--ROB ONLY BUYS SOY. PFF! IMAGINE PUTTING **SOY** INTO YOUR CEREAL!
SOY MILK
ANYWAY, HERE. HAVE A NICE BOWL OF RICE CRAPPIES.
WELL, I DIDN'T KNOW WHAT TO EXPECT FROM YOUR FISH CEREAL, BUT IT SURE WASN'T THIS...
SO YOU LIKE IT?
darb
NO? WELL, HOW WOULD YOU IMPROVE THAT BELUGA NUT CRUNCH? MORE BELUGA, LESS CRUNCH?
I DON'T THINK I ENJOY FISH IN MY CEREAL.
LUCKY FOR YOU, THERE'S A STEAMING BATCH OF JELLYFISH DONUTS READY.
WAIT, MAYBE I'M NOT GIVING THIS A CHANCE.
I DON'T LIKE THIS FISH CEREAL EITHER.
HM. WELL, GROUPER NUTS ARE AN ACQUIRED TASTE.
I WOULD CATEGORIZE THEM AS MORE OF A... *DISCARDED* TASTE.
darb
THEY'RE FORTIFIED, THOUGH. ONE BOWL CONTAINS 100% OF YOUR YEARLY RECOMMENDED MERCURY.
SEE, BECAUSE IT TASTES LIKE SOMETHING YOU FIND IN THE TRA—
HERE, TRY THESE FROSTED HAKES. THEY **MIGR-R-RATE**!

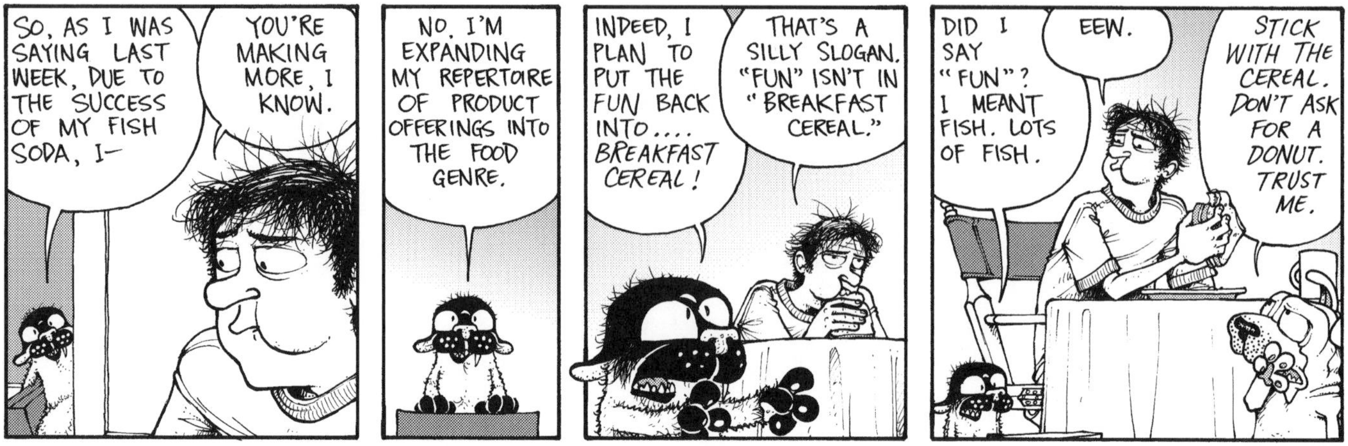
SO, AS I WAS SAYING LAST WEEK, DUE TO THE SUCCESS OF MY FISH SODA, I—
YOU'RE MAKING MORE, I KNOW.
NO. I'M EXPANDING MY REPERTOIRE OF PRODUCT OFFERINGS INTO THE FOOD GENRE.
INDEED, I PLAN TO PUT THE FUN BACK INTO.... BREAKFAST CEREAL!
THAT'S A SILLY SLOGAN. "FUN" ISN'T IN "BREAKFAST CEREAL."
DID I SAY "FUN"? I MEANT FISH. LOTS OF FISH.
EEW.
STICK WITH THE CEREAL. DON'T ASK FOR A DONUT. TRUST ME.

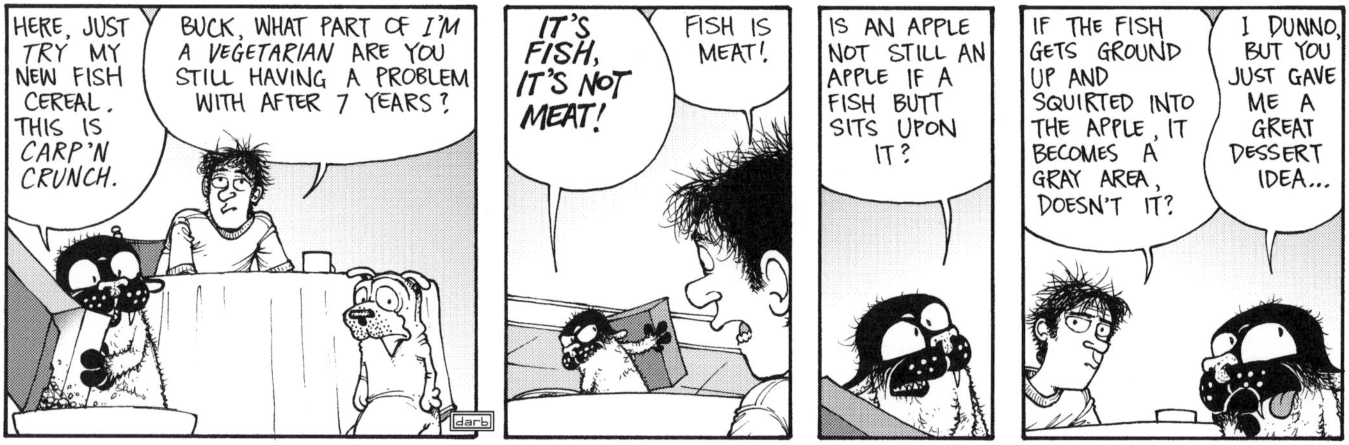
HERE, JUST TRY MY NEW FISH CEREAL. THIS IS CARP'N CRUNCH.
BUCK, WHAT PART OF I'M A VEGETARIAN ARE YOU STILL HAVING A PROBLEM WITH AFTER 7 YEARS?
darb
IT'S FISH, IT'S NOT MEAT!
FISH IS MEAT!
IS AN APPLE NOT STILL AN APPLE IF A FISH BUTT SITS UPON IT?
IF THE FISH GETS GROUND UP AND SQUIRTED INTO THE APPLE, IT BECOMES A GRAY AREA, DOESN'T IT?
I DUNNO, BUT YOU JUST GAVE ME A GREAT DESSERT IDEA...

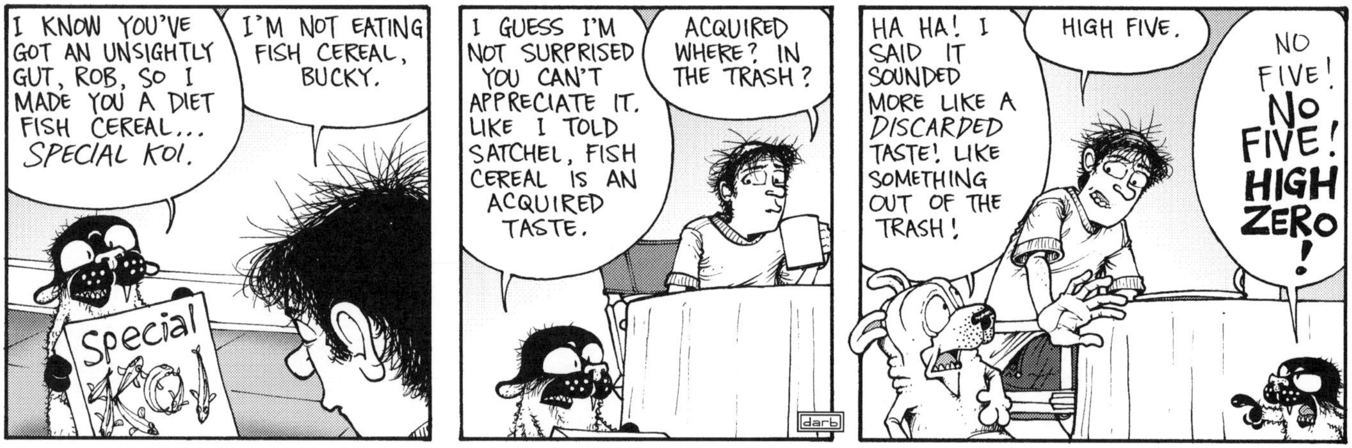
I KNOW YOU'VE GOT AN UNSIGHTLY GUT, ROB, SO I MADE YOU A DIET FISH CEREAL... SPECIAL KOI.
I'M NOT EATING FISH CEREAL, BUCKY.
Special KOI
I GUESS I'M NOT SURPRISED YOU CAN'T APPRECIATE IT. LIKE I TOLD SATCHEL, FISH CEREAL IS AN ACQUIRED TASTE.
ACQUIRED WHERE? IN THE TRASH?
darb
HA HA! I SAID IT SOUNDED MORE LIKE A DISCARDED TASTE! LIKE SOMETHING OUT OF THE TRASH!
HIGH FIVE.
NO FIVE! NO FIVE! HIGH ZERO!

WE NEED MORE SELTZER, PINKISH.

FOR WHAT? YOU DON'T DRINK SELTZER.

I'VE IDENTIFIED A GAP IN THE SOFT DRINK MARKET. I'M EXPERIMENTING WITH FLAVORS.

OH, NO.

I'M CREATING THE WORLD'S FIRST LINE OF FISH-FLAVORED SODA. WOULD YOU LIKE TO TRY...

...A COOL, REFRESHING *CARPA-COLA*?

EEW! NO!

WATCHIN' THE OL' GUT, EH? I HEAR YA. TRY A DIET SPRAT.

UH... NO.

MELLO YELLOFIN? MUSKELLUNGE DEW?

NO.

JOLT?

THERE'S ALREADY A SODA NAMED JOLT.

BUT DOES EACH CAN CONTAIN A LIVE EEL CAPABLE OF DELIVERING 500 VOLTS VIA LIP?

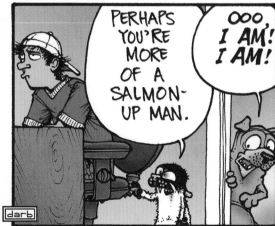

PERHAPS YOU'RE MORE OF A SALMON-UP MAN.

OOO, *I AM! I AM!*

darb

37

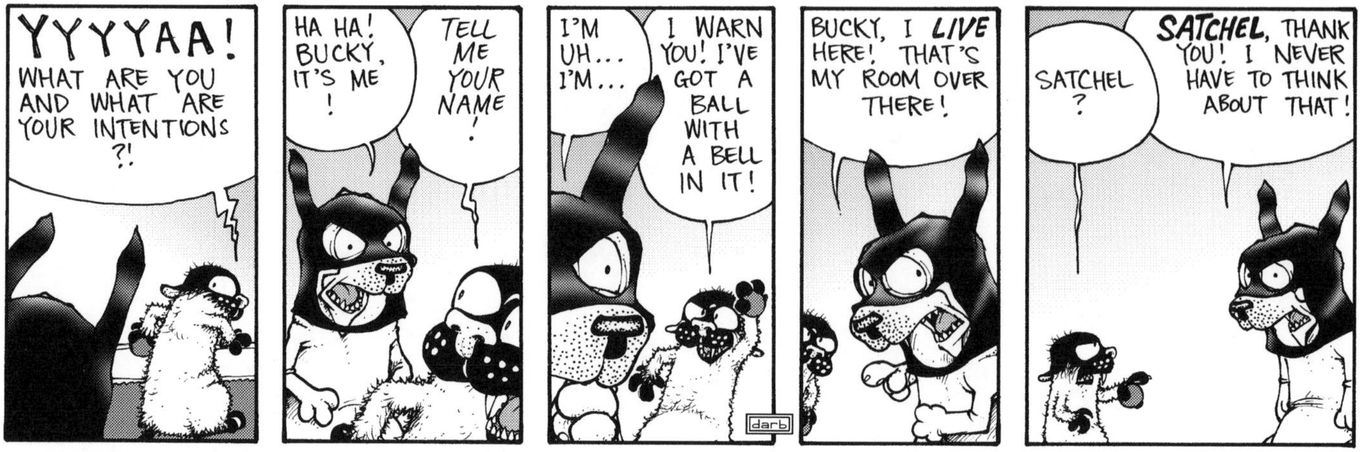
YYYYAA!
WHAT ARE YOU AND WHAT ARE YOUR INTENTIONS ?!
HA HA! BUCKY, IT'S ME !
TELL ME YOUR NAME !
I'M UH... I'M...
I WARN YOU! I'VE GOT A BALL WITH A BELL IN IT!
darb
BUCKY, I **LIVE** HERE! THAT'S MY ROOM OVER THERE!
SATCHEL ?
SATCHEL, THANK YOU! I NEVER HAVE TO THINK ABOUT THAT!

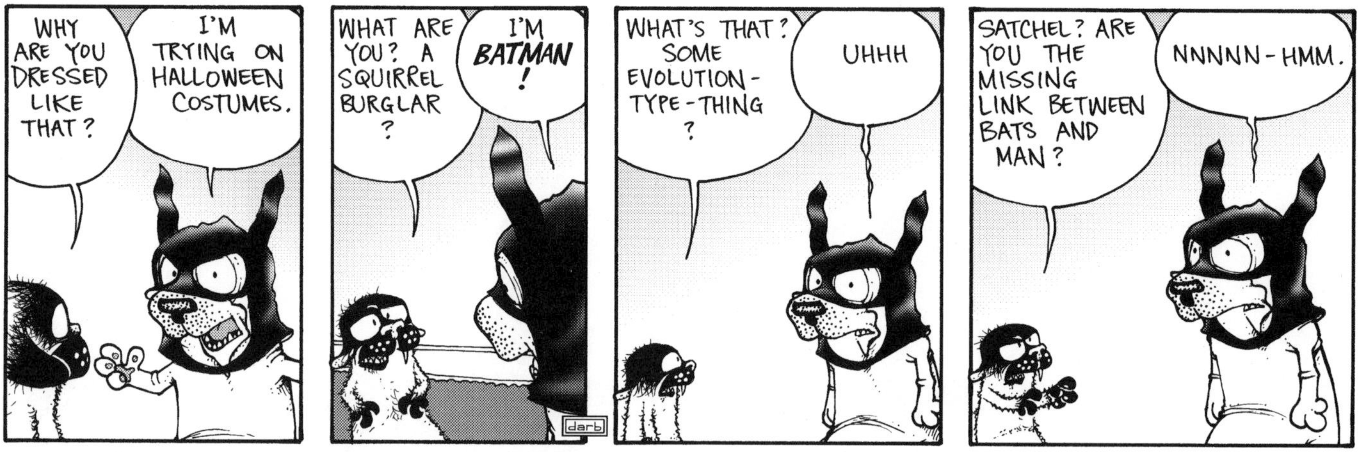
WHY ARE YOU DRESSED LIKE THAT?
I'M TRYING ON HALLOWEEN COSTUMES.
WHAT ARE YOU? A SQUIRREL BURGLAR ?
I'M **BATMAN** !
darb
WHAT'S THAT? SOME EVOLUTION-TYPE-THING ?
UHHH
SATCHEL? ARE YOU THE MISSING LINK BETWEEN BATS AND MAN?
NNNNN-HMM.

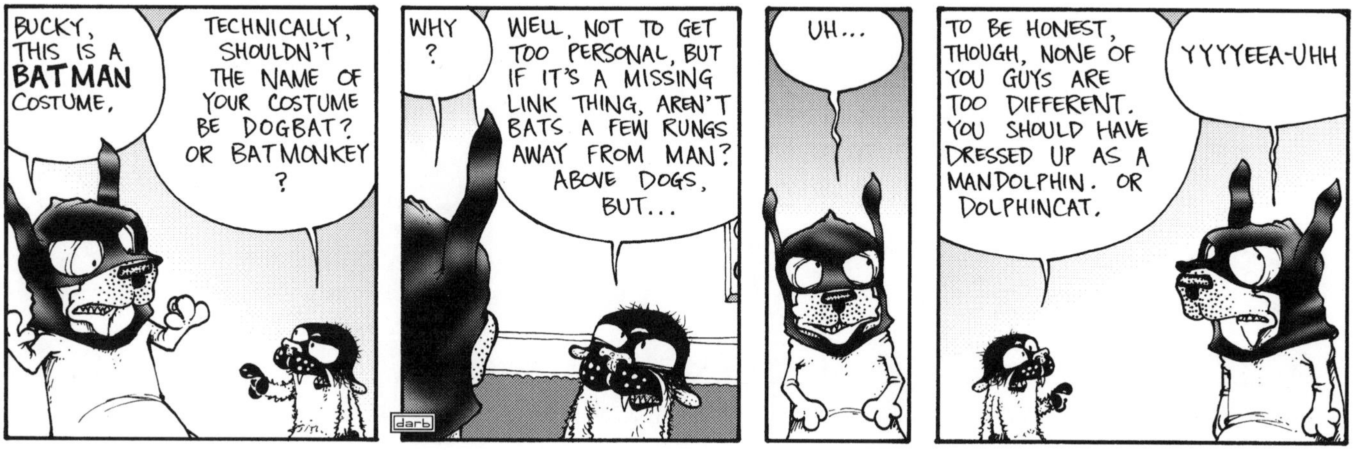
BUCKY, THIS IS A **BATMAN** COSTUME.
TECHNICALLY, SHOULDN'T THE NAME OF YOUR COSTUME BE DOGBAT? OR BATMONKEY ?
WHY ?
WELL, NOT TO GET TOO PERSONAL, BUT IF IT'S A MISSING LINK THING, AREN'T BATS A FEW RUNGS AWAY FROM MAN? ABOVE DOGS, BUT...
darb
UH...
TO BE HONEST, THOUGH, NONE OF YOU GUYS ARE TOO DIFFERENT. YOU SHOULD HAVE DRESSED UP AS A MANDOLPHIN. OR DOLPHINCAT.
YYYYEEA-UHH

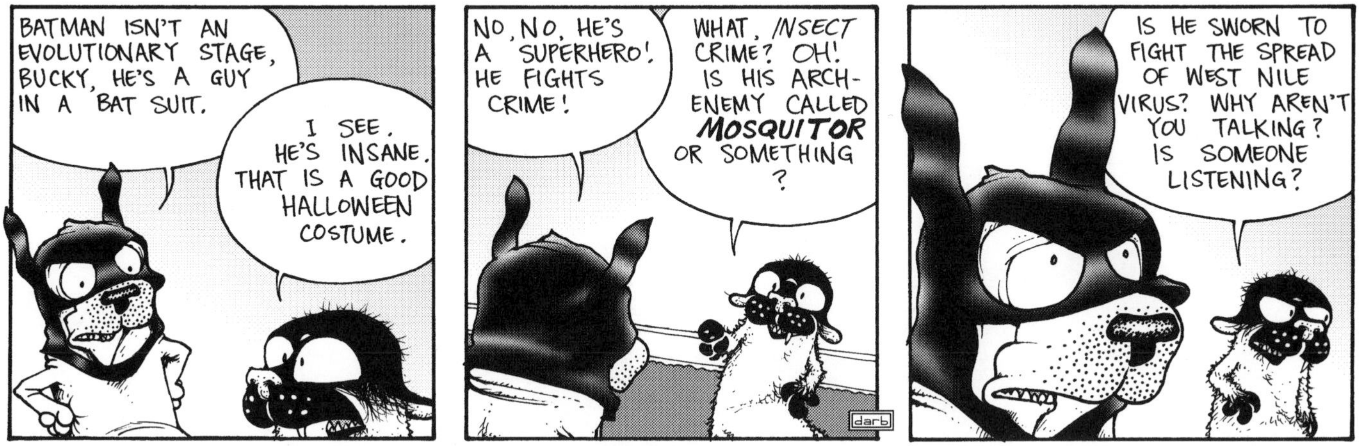
BATMAN ISN'T AN EVOLUTIONARY STAGE, BUCKY, HE'S A GUY IN A BAT SUIT.
I SEE. HE'S INSANE. THAT IS A GOOD HALLOWEEN COSTUME.
NO, NO. HE'S A SUPERHERO! HE FIGHTS CRIME!
WHAT, *INSECT* CRIME? OH! IS HIS ARCH-ENEMY CALLED **MOSQUITOR** OR SOMETHING ?
IS HE SWORN TO FIGHT THE SPREAD OF WEST NILE VIRUS? WHY AREN'T YOU TALKING? IS SOMEONE LISTENING?
darb

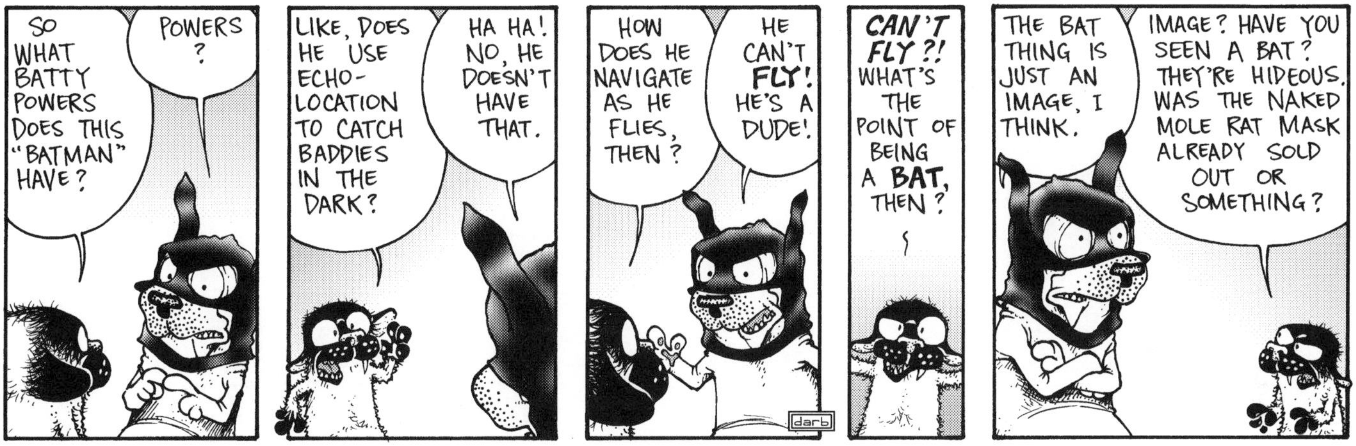
SO WHAT BATTY POWERS DOES THIS "BATMAN" HAVE?
POWERS ?
LIKE, DOES HE USE ECHO-LOCATION TO CATCH BADDIES IN THE DARK?
HA HA! NO, HE DOESN'T HAVE THAT.
HOW DOES HE NAVIGATE AS HE FLIES, THEN ?
HE CAN'T **FLY**! HE'S A DUDE!
darb
CAN'T FLY?! WHAT'S THE POINT OF BEING A **BAT**, THEN ?
THE BAT THING IS JUST AN IMAGE, I THINK.
IMAGE? HAVE YOU SEEN A BAT? THEY'RE HIDEOUS. WAS THE NAKED MOLE RAT MASK ALREADY SOLD OUT OR SOMETHING?

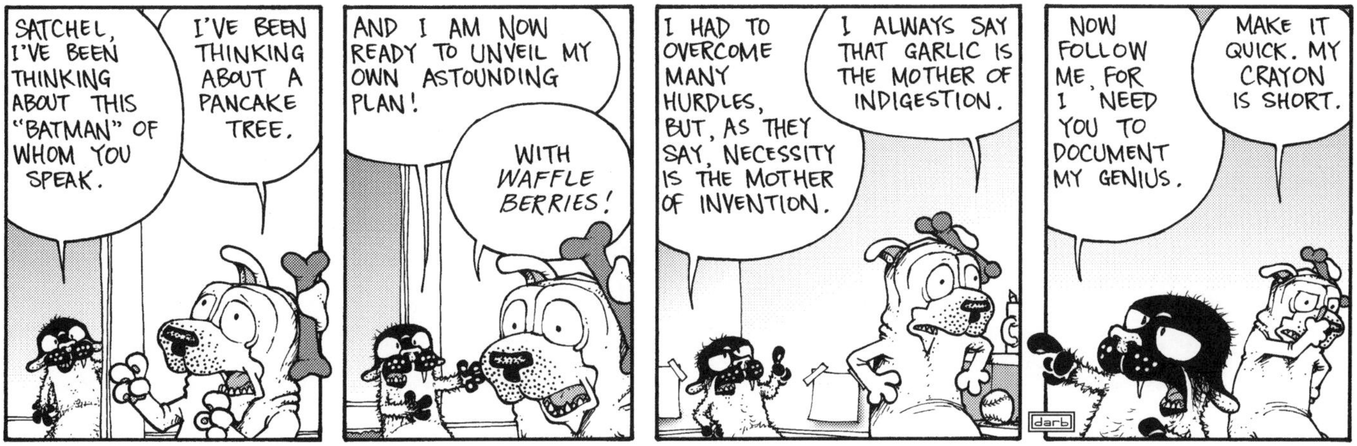
SATCHEL, I'VE BEEN THINKING ABOUT THIS "BATMAN" OF WHOM YOU SPEAK.
I'VE BEEN THINKING ABOUT A PANCAKE TREE.
AND I AM NOW READY TO UNVEIL MY OWN ASTOUNDING PLAN!
WITH *WAFFLE BERRIES!*
I HAD TO OVERCOME MANY HURDLES, BUT, AS THEY SAY, NECESSITY IS THE MOTHER OF INVENTION.
I ALWAYS SAY THAT GARLIC IS THE MOTHER OF INDIGESTION.
darb
NOW FOLLOW ME, FOR I NEED YOU TO DOCUMENT MY GENIUS.
MAKE IT QUICK. MY CRAYON IS SHORT.

WHOA, WHOA, WHOA, WHAT ARE YOU DOING?!

I'M PAINTING. MY BRUSH FELL UNDER THE LADDER.

WELL DON'T GO CRAWLING UNDER IT! GOING UNDER A LADDER IS BAD LUCK!

BAD LUCK?

LIKE BREAKING A MIRROR OR OPENING AN UMBRELLA INDOORS! I LIVE WITH YOU! DON'T TURN ME INTO SOME KIND OF COSMIC COLLATERAL DAMAGE!

OH, MY. SO WE'RE DOOMING MRS. CHU AS SHE WALKS AROUND DOWNSTAIRS!

HUH?

WHAT HAPPENS WHEN THERE'S A LADDER ON TOP OF A SKYSCRAPER? IS *EVERYBODY* BELOW IT UNLUCKY? THAT SEEMS A TAD UNFAIR.

OH! WHAT ABOUT THAT TIME ROB CRACKED HIS SUNGLASSES?! THEY'RE NOT MIRRORS, BUT THEY'RE MIRROR *COATED!*

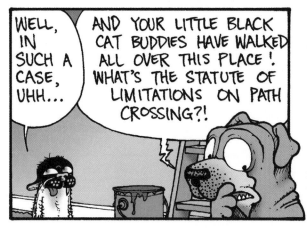

WELL, IN SUCH A CASE, UHH...

AND YOUR LITTLE BLACK CAT BUDDIES HAVE WALKED ALL OVER THIS PLACE! WHAT'S THE STATUTE OF LIMITATIONS ON PATH CROSSING?!

OK, NOW, I WOULD CLASSIFY THIS AS A BIT OF BAD KARMA FOR YOU.

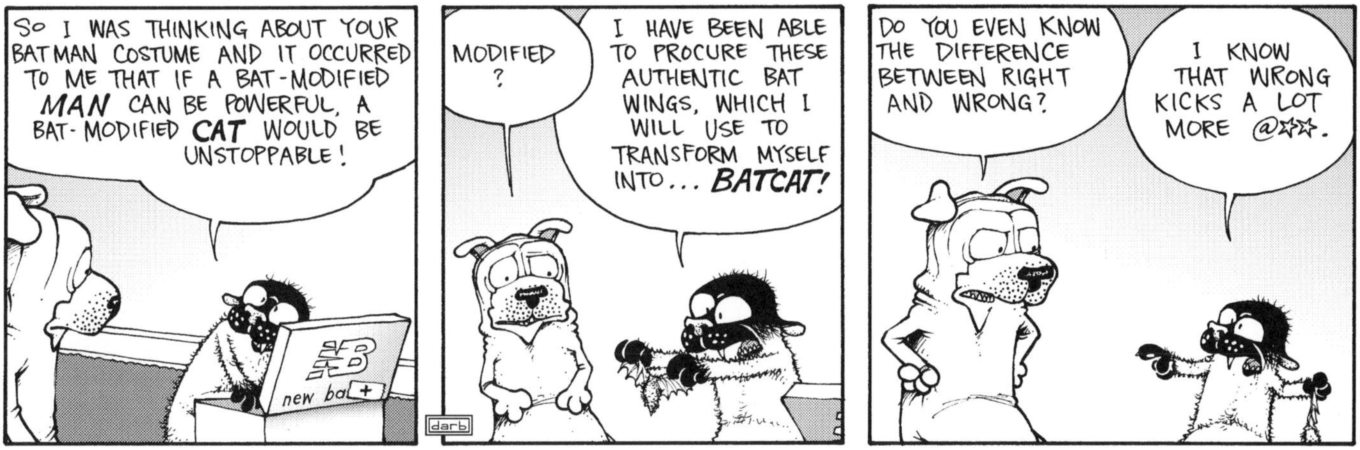
SO I WAS THINKING ABOUT YOUR BATMAN COSTUME AND IT OCCURRED TO ME THAT IF A BAT-MODIFIED MAN CAN BE POWERFUL, A BAT-MODIFIED CAT WOULD BE UNSTOPPABLE!
new ba
darb
MODIFIED?
I HAVE BEEN ABLE TO PROCURE THESE AUTHENTIC BAT WINGS, WHICH I WILL USE TO TRANSFORM MYSELF INTO... BATCAT!
DO YOU EVEN KNOW THE DIFFERENCE BETWEEN RIGHT AND WRONG?
I KNOW THAT WRONG KICKS A LOT MORE @☆☆.

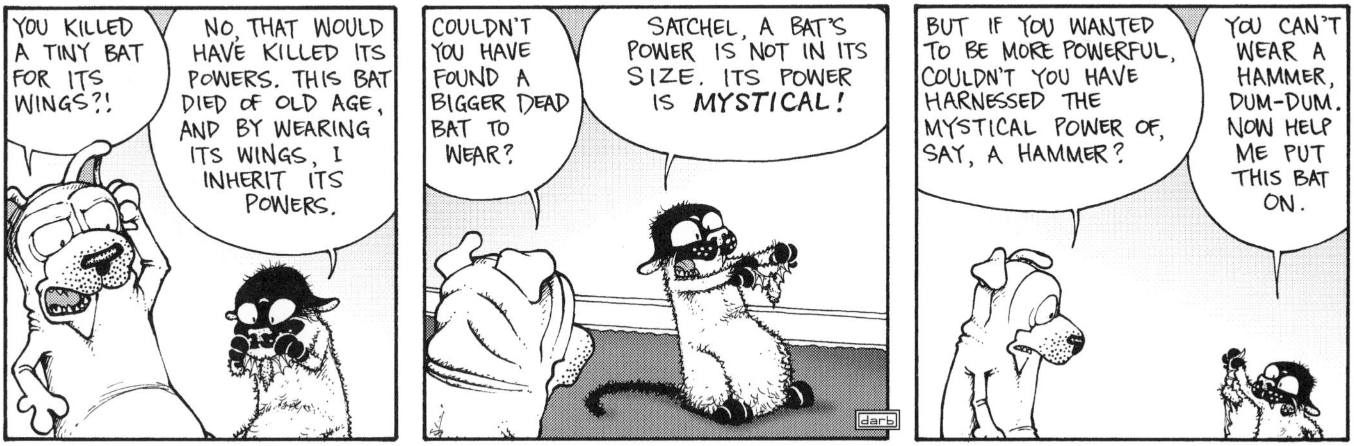
YOU KILLED A TINY BAT FOR ITS WINGS?!
NO, THAT WOULD HAVE KILLED ITS POWERS. THIS BAT DIED OF OLD AGE, AND BY WEARING ITS WINGS, I INHERIT ITS POWERS.
COULDN'T YOU HAVE FOUND A BIGGER DEAD BAT TO WEAR?
SATCHEL, A BAT'S POWER IS NOT IN ITS SIZE. ITS POWER IS MYSTICAL!
darb
BUT IF YOU WANTED TO BE MORE POWERFUL, COULDN'T YOU HAVE HARNESSED THE MYSTICAL POWER OF, SAY, A HAMMER?
YOU CAN'T WEAR A HAMMER, DUM-DUM. NOW HELP ME PUT THIS BAT ON.

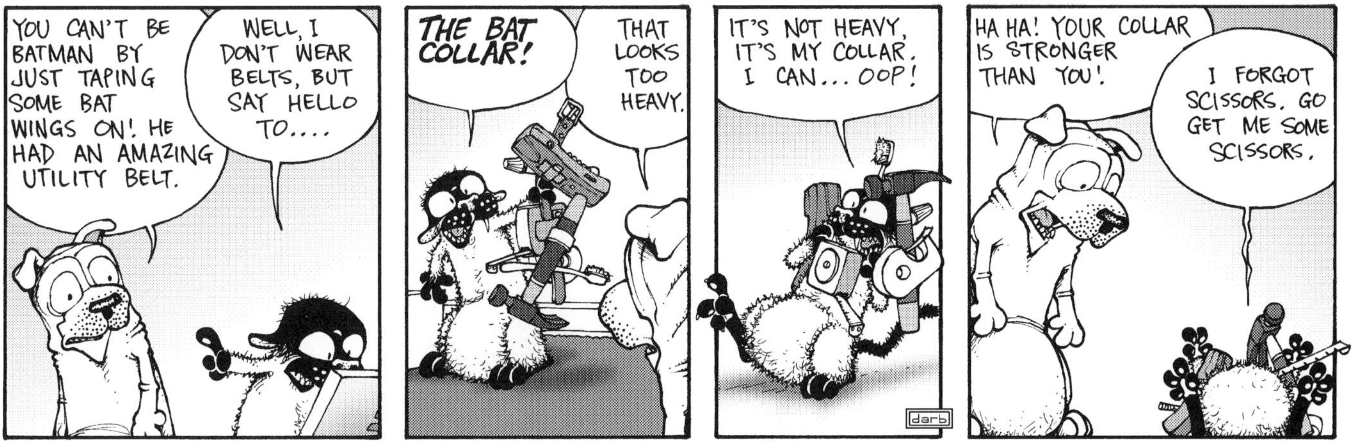
YOU CAN'T BE BATMAN BY JUST TAPING SOME BAT WINGS ON! HE HAD AN AMAZING UTILITY BELT.
WELL, I DON'T WEAR BELTS, BUT SAY HELLO TO....
THE BAT COLLAR!
THAT LOOKS TOO HEAVY.
IT'S NOT HEAVY, IT'S MY COLLAR. I CAN... OOP!
darb
HA HA! YOUR COLLAR IS STRONGER THAN YOU!
I FORGOT SCISSORS. GO GET ME SOME SCISSORS.

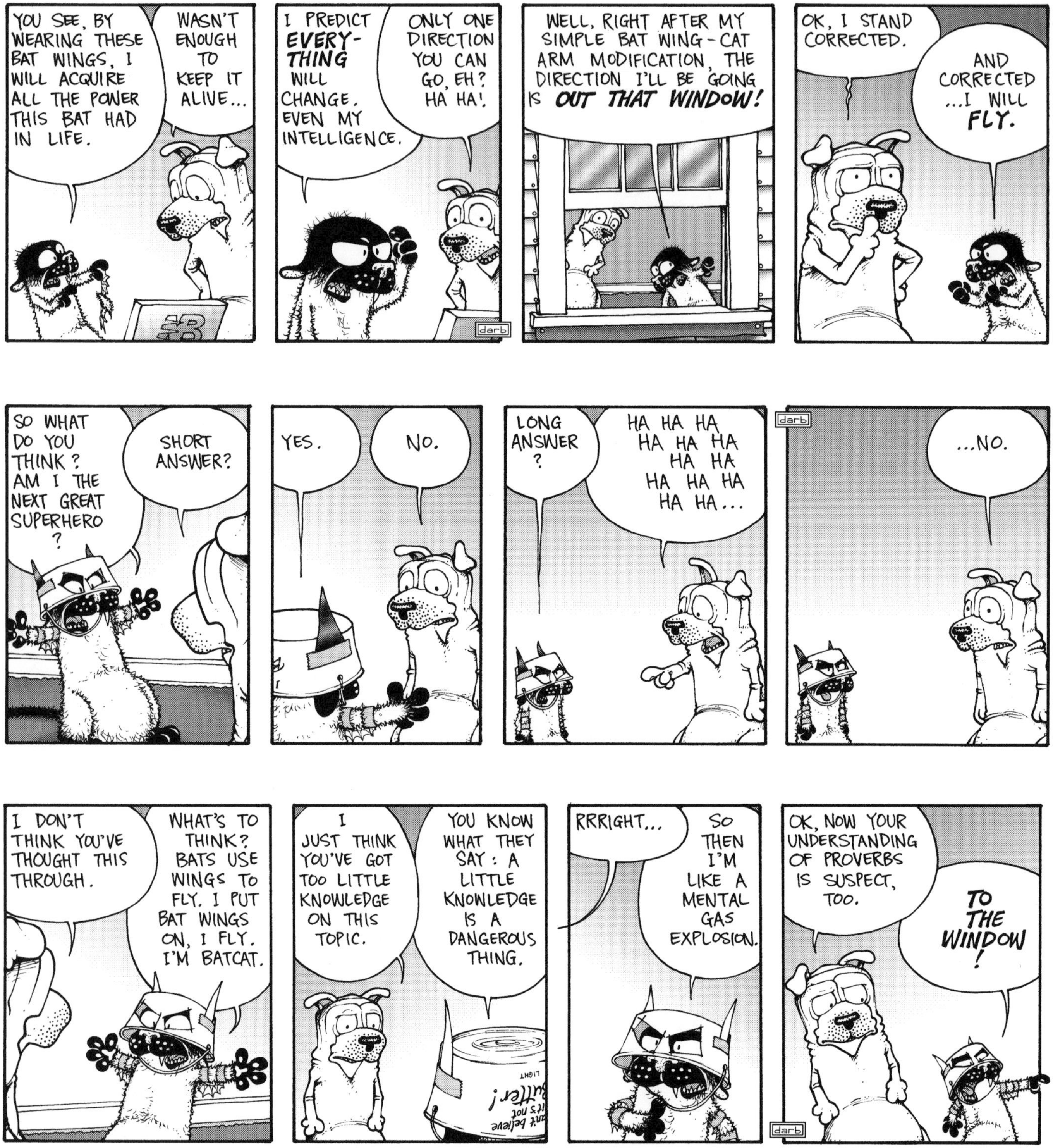
YOU SEE, BY WEARING THESE BAT WINGS, I WILL ACQUIRE ALL THE POWER THIS BAT HAD IN LIFE.
WASN'T ENOUGH TO KEEP IT ALIVE...
I PREDICT EVERY-THING WILL CHANGE. EVEN MY INTELLIGENCE.
ONLY ONE DIRECTION YOU CAN GO, EH? HA HA!
WELL, RIGHT AFTER MY SIMPLE BAT WING-CAT ARM MODIFICATION, THE DIRECTION I'LL BE GOING IS OUT THAT WINDOW!
OK, I STAND CORRECTED.
AND CORRECTED ...I WILL FLY.
SO WHAT DO YOU THINK? AM I THE NEXT GREAT SUPERHERO?
SHORT ANSWER?
YES.
NO.
LONG ANSWER?
HA HA HA HA HA HA HA HA HA HA HA HA HA...
...NO.
I DON'T THINK YOU'VE THOUGHT THIS THROUGH.
WHAT'S TO THINK? BATS USE WINGS TO FLY. I PUT BAT WINGS ON, I FLY. I'M BATCAT.
I JUST THINK YOU'VE GOT TOO LITTLE KNOWLEDGE ON THIS TOPIC.
YOU KNOW WHAT THEY SAY: A LITTLE KNOWLEDGE IS A DANGEROUS THING.
RRRIGHT...
SO THEN I'M LIKE A MENTAL GAS EXPLOSION.
OK, NOW YOUR UNDERSTANDING OF PROVERBS IS SUSPECT, TOO.
TO THE WINDOW!

WATCHING SINGING ON TV? GIVEN UP ON EVER BEING COOL, EH? BRAVE.

WHAT'S WRONG WITH SINGING?

IT'S USELESS IN TODAY'S iPAD AND ATARI CULTURE. IT'S PRIMITIVE.

...SAID THE GUY WHO CLEANS HIS BUTT WITH HIS MOUTH.

SEE, OTHER FORMS OF ENTERTAINISM HAVE PASSED SINGING BY.

MM-HM.

IN FACT, WEBSTER DEFINES SINGING AS CAVEMAN WAILING.

WELL THAT'S WRONG.

I'LL SHOW YOU. *WEBSTER! GET IN HERE!*

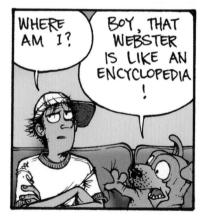

A-O.

WHAT'S THE DEFINITION OF SINGING?

CAVEMAN WAILING.

WHERE AM I?

BOY, THAT WEBSTER IS LIKE AN ENCYCLOPEDIA!

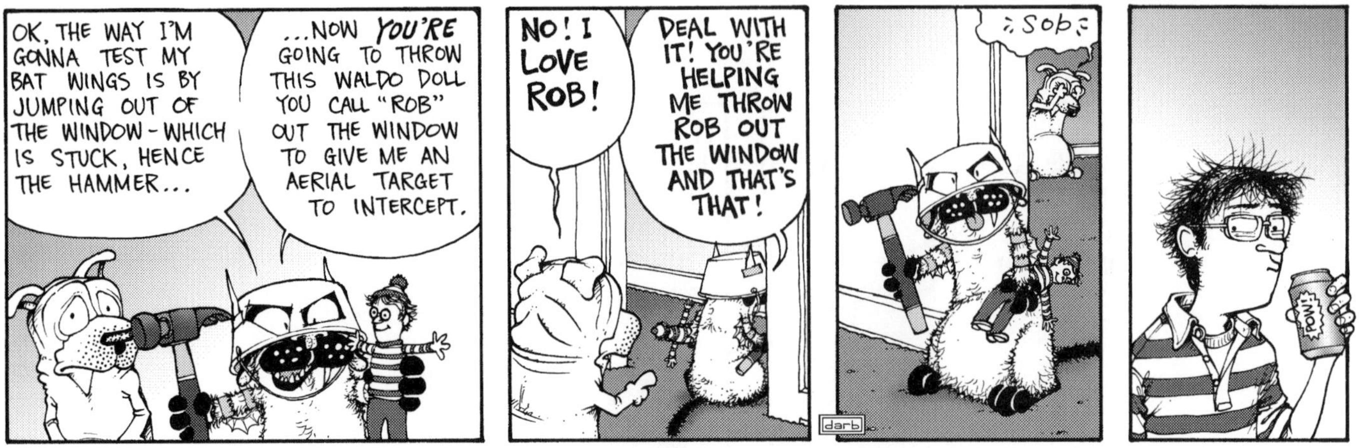
OK, THE WAY I'M GONNA TEST MY BAT WINGS IS BY JUMPING OUT OF THE WINDOW - WHICH IS STUCK, HENCE THE HAMMER...
...NOW YOU'RE GOING TO THROW THIS WALDO DOLL YOU CALL "ROB" OUT THE WINDOW TO GIVE ME AN AERIAL TARGET TO INTERCEPT.
NO! I LOVE ROB!
DEAL WITH IT! YOU'RE HELPING ME THROW ROB OUT THE WINDOW AND THAT'S THAT!
SOB
darb

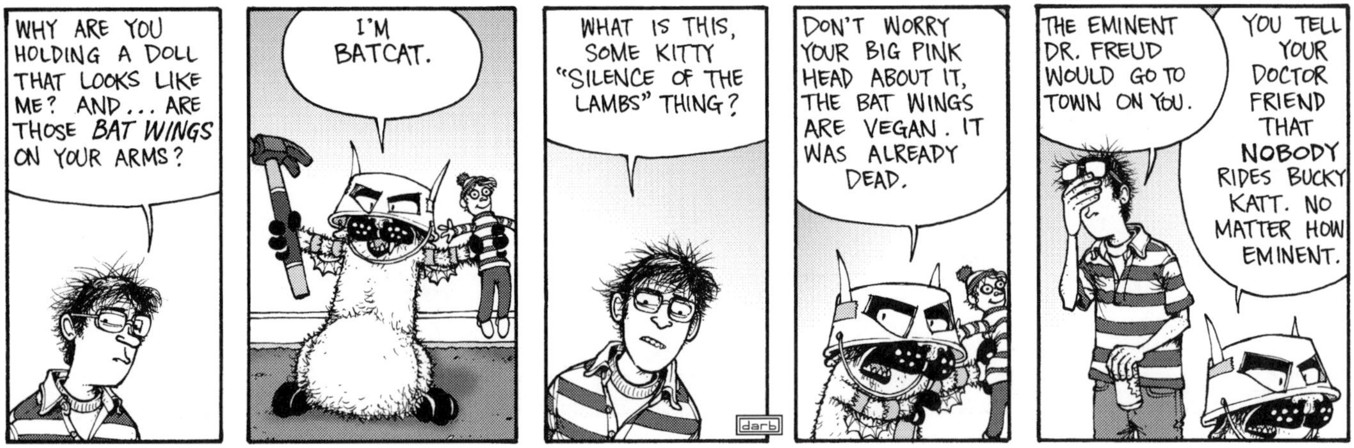
WHY ARE YOU HOLDING A DOLL THAT LOOKS LIKE ME? AND... ARE THOSE BAT WINGS ON YOUR ARMS?
I'M BATCAT.
WHAT IS THIS, SOME KITTY "SILENCE OF THE LAMBS" THING?
darb
DON'T WORRY YOUR BIG PINK HEAD ABOUT IT, THE BAT WINGS ARE VEGAN. IT WAS ALREADY DEAD.
THE EMINENT DR. FREUD WOULD GO TO TOWN ON YOU.
YOU TELL YOUR DOCTOR FRIEND THAT NOBODY RIDES BUCKY KATT. NO MATTER HOW EMINENT.

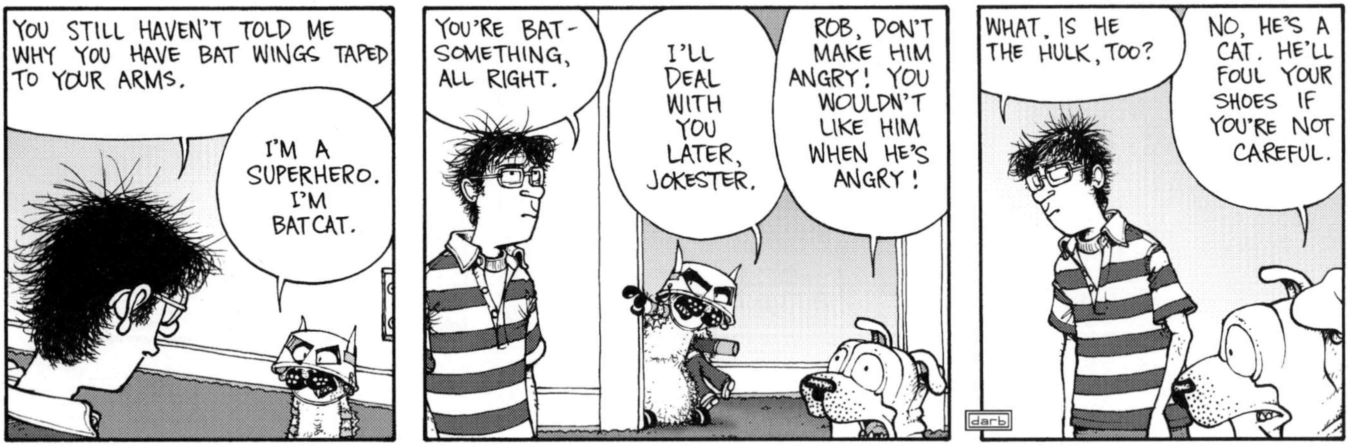
YOU STILL HAVEN'T TOLD ME WHY YOU HAVE BAT WINGS TAPED TO YOUR ARMS.
I'M A SUPERHERO. I'M BATCAT.
YOU'RE BAT-SOMETHING, ALL RIGHT.
I'LL DEAL WITH YOU LATER, JOKESTER.
ROB, DON'T MAKE HIM ANGRY! YOU WOULDN'T LIKE HIM WHEN HE'S ANGRY!
darb
WHAT, IS HE THE HULK, TOO?
NO, HE'S A CAT. HE'LL FOUL YOUR SHOES IF YOU'RE NOT CAREFUL.

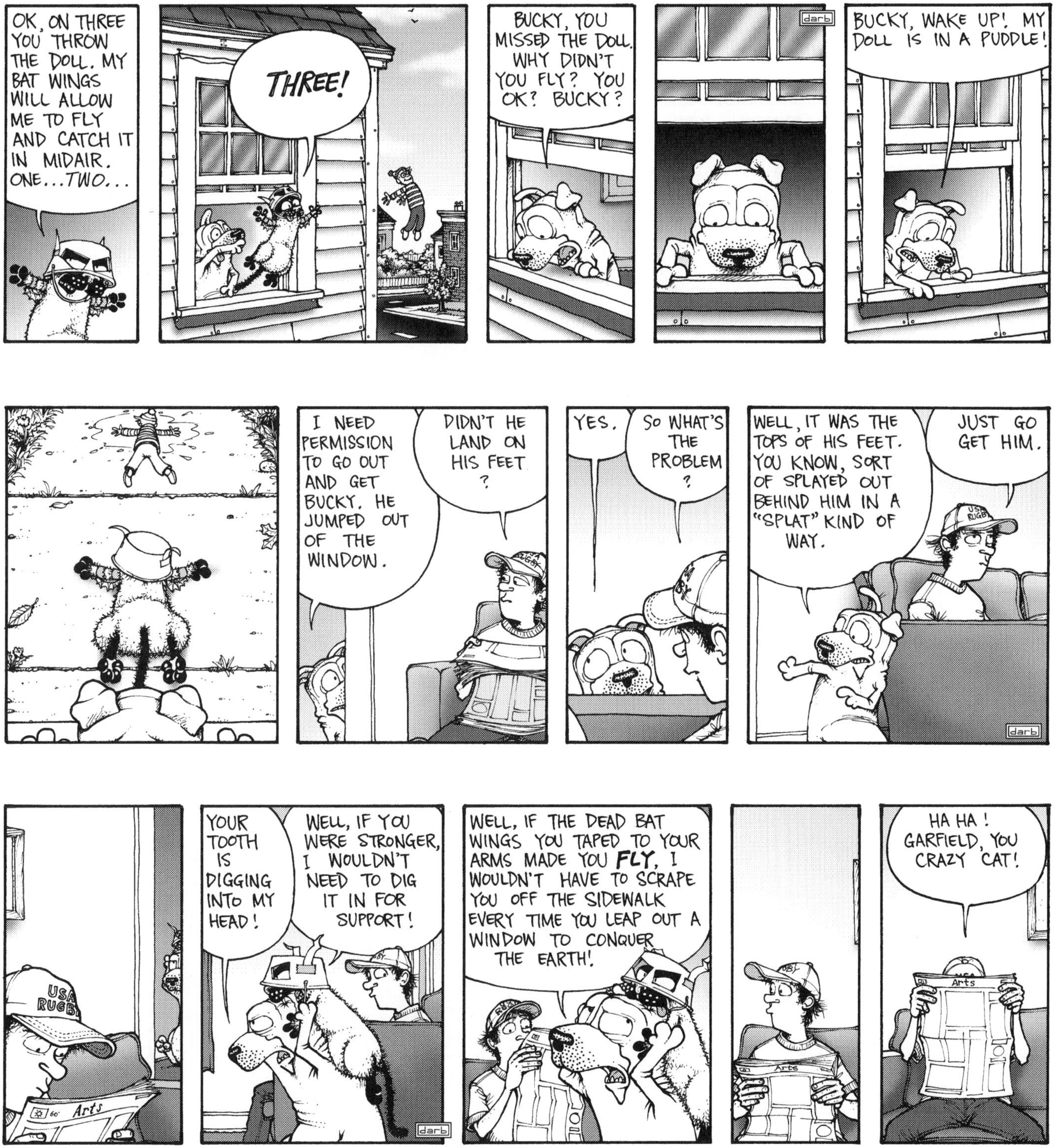
OK, ON THREE YOU THROW THE DOLL. MY BAT WINGS WILL ALLOW ME TO FLY AND CATCH IT IN MIDAIR. ONE...TWO...
THREE!
BUCKY, YOU MISSED THE DOLL. WHY DIDN'T YOU FLY? YOU OK? BUCKY?
darb
BUCKY, WAKE UP! MY DOLL IS IN A PUDDLE!
I NEED PERMISSION TO GO OUT AND GET BUCKY. HE JUMPED OUT OF THE WINDOW.
DIDN'T HE LAND ON HIS FEET?
YES.
SO WHAT'S THE PROBLEM?
WELL, IT WAS THE TOPS OF HIS FEET. YOU KNOW, SORT OF SPLAYED OUT BEHIND HIM IN A "SPLAT" KIND OF WAY.
JUST GO GET HIM.
darb
USA RUGBY
Arts
YOUR TOOTH IS DIGGING INTO MY HEAD!
WELL, IF YOU WERE STRONGER, I WOULDN'T NEED TO DIG IT IN FOR SUPPORT!
darb
WELL, IF THE DEAD BAT WINGS YOU TAPED TO YOUR ARMS MADE YOU FLY, I WOULDN'T HAVE TO SCRAPE YOU OFF THE SIDEWALK EVERY TIME YOU LEAP OUT A WINDOW TO CONQUER THE EARTH!
Arts
HA HA! GARFIELD, YOU CRAZY CAT!
Arts

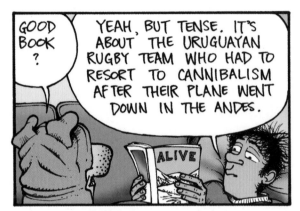

GOOD BOOK?

YEAH, BUT TENSE. IT'S ABOUT THE URUGUAYAN RUGBY TEAM WHO HAD TO RESORT TO CANNIBALISM AFTER THEIR PLANE WENT DOWN IN THE ANDES.

OH MY! HOW AWFUL!

JUDGE NOT. FOR YOU KNOW NOT THE MADNESS OF PANIC.

PARDON?

FOR EVEN I, BUCKY KATT, HAVE KNOWN THE DARK MANIA OF DESPERATION.

ONCE, IN MY DARK PAST, MY PREDICAMENT WAS SO DIRE THAT I, TOO, WAS TESTED: *COULD I EAT A FELLOW CAT?*

WHAT HAPPENED?!

HE WOKE UP AND BEAT THE ✰%#@ OUT OF ME. HE WAS A MAINE COON.

IN THE END, I HAD TO GO **ALL THE WAY TO THE STORE** FOR FOOD.

HA HA! YOU'RE A CAN'TIBAL!

darb

THE MORAL? NEVER TRY TO EAT SOMEONE BIGGER THAN YOU.

BRILLIANT.

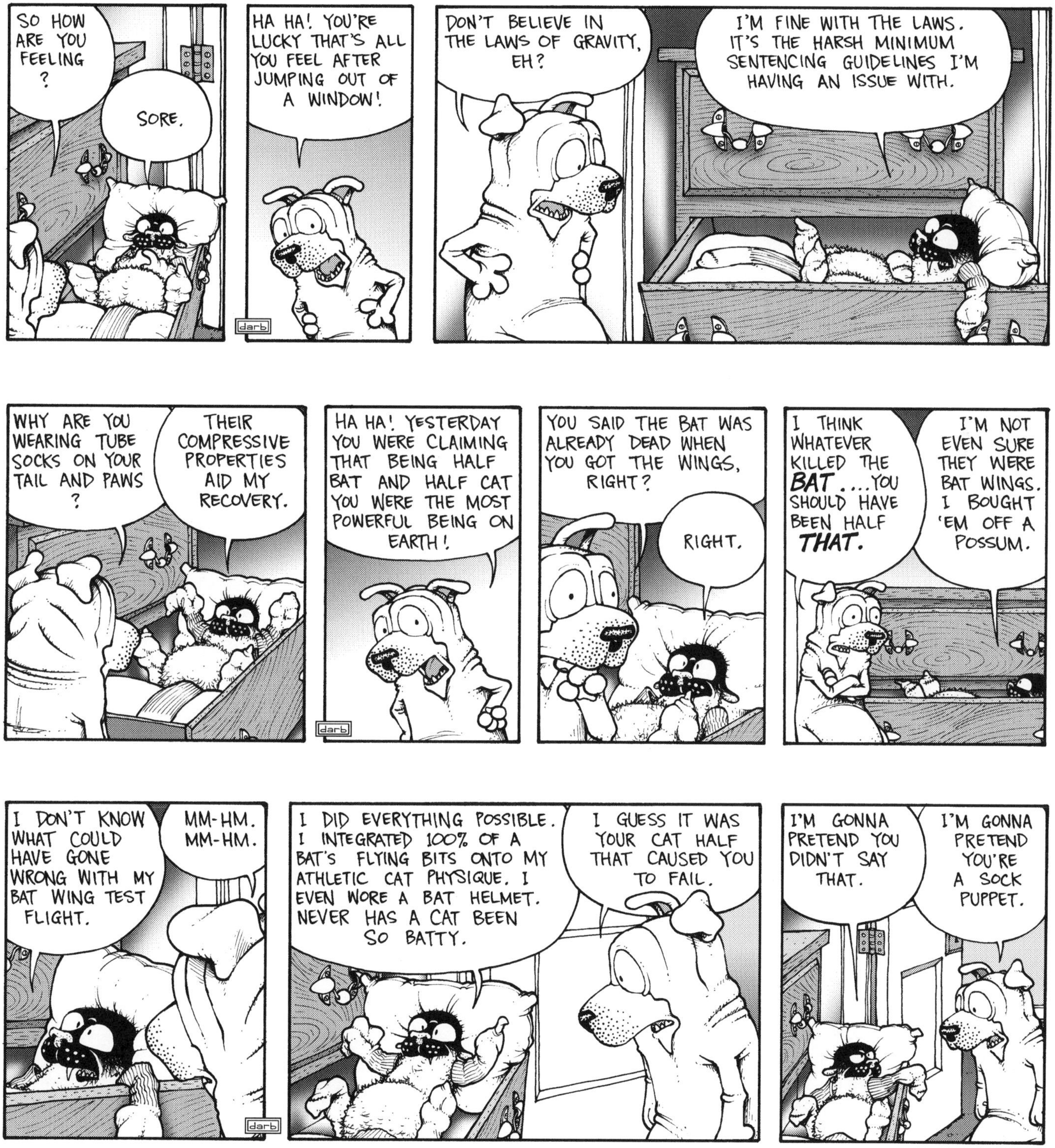
SO HOW ARE YOU FEELING ?
SORE.
darb
HA HA! YOU'RE LUCKY THAT'S ALL YOU FEEL AFTER JUMPING OUT OF A WINDOW!
DON'T BELIEVE IN THE LAWS OF GRAVITY, EH?
I'M FINE WITH THE LAWS. IT'S THE HARSH MINIMUM SENTENCING GUIDELINES I'M HAVING AN ISSUE WITH.
WHY ARE YOU WEARING TUBE SOCKS ON YOUR TAIL AND PAWS ?
THEIR COMPRESSIVE PROPERTIES AID MY RECOVERY.
darb
HA HA! YESTERDAY YOU WERE CLAIMING THAT BEING HALF BAT AND HALF CAT YOU WERE THE MOST POWERFUL BEING ON EARTH!
YOU SAID THE BAT WAS ALREADY DEAD WHEN YOU GOT THE WINGS, RIGHT?
RIGHT.
I THINK WHATEVER KILLED THE BAT....YOU SHOULD HAVE BEEN HALF THAT.
I'M NOT EVEN SURE THEY WERE BAT WINGS. I BOUGHT 'EM OFF A POSSUM.
I DON'T KNOW WHAT COULD HAVE GONE WRONG WITH MY BAT WING TEST FLIGHT.
MM-HM. MM-HM.
darb
I DID EVERYTHING POSSIBLE. I INTEGRATED 100% OF A BAT'S FLYING BITS ONTO MY ATHLETIC CAT PHYSIQUE. I EVEN WORE A BAT HELMET. NEVER HAS A CAT BEEN SO BATTY.
I GUESS IT WAS YOUR CAT HALF THAT CAUSED YOU TO FAIL.
I'M GONNA PRETEND YOU DIDN'T SAY THAT.
I'M GONNA PRETEND YOU'RE A SOCK PUPPET.

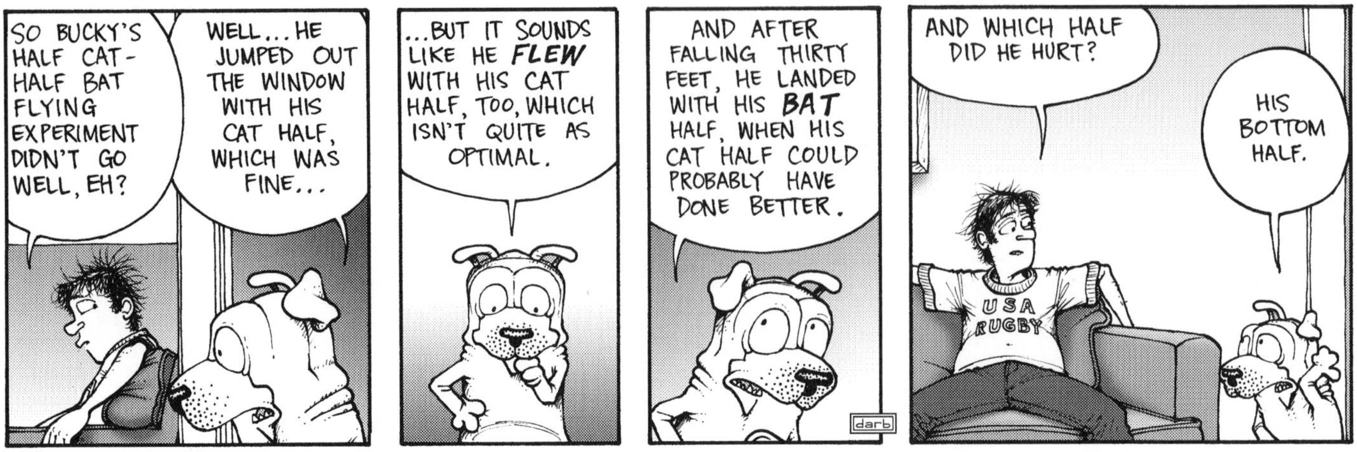
SO BUCKY'S HALF CAT-HALF BAT FLYING EXPERIMENT DIDN'T GO WELL, EH?
WELL... HE JUMPED OUT THE WINDOW WITH HIS CAT HALF, WHICH WAS FINE...
...BUT IT SOUNDS LIKE HE FLEW WITH HIS CAT HALF, TOO, WHICH ISN'T QUITE AS OPTIMAL.
AND AFTER FALLING THIRTY FEET, HE LANDED WITH HIS BAT HALF, WHEN HIS CAT HALF COULD PROBABLY HAVE DONE BETTER.
darb
AND WHICH HALF DID HE HURT?
HIS BOTTOM HALF.
USA RUGBY

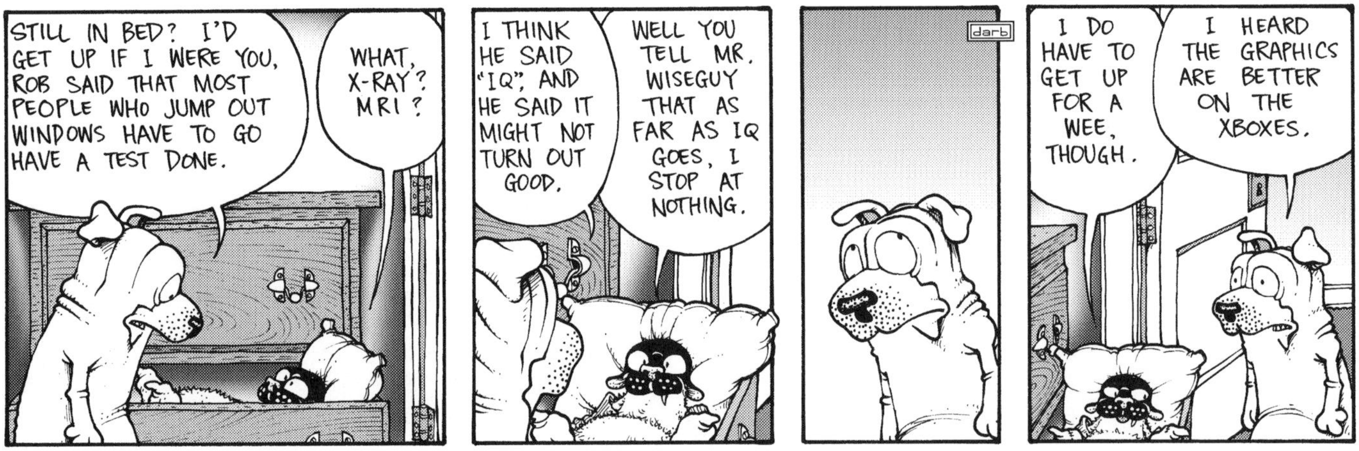
STILL IN BED? I'D GET UP IF I WERE YOU, ROB SAID THAT MOST PEOPLE WHO JUMP OUT WINDOWS HAVE TO GO HAVE A TEST DONE.
WHAT, X-RAY? MRI?
I THINK HE SAID "IQ," AND HE SAID IT MIGHT NOT TURN OUT GOOD.
WELL YOU TELL MR. WISEGUY THAT AS FAR AS IQ GOES, I STOP AT NOTHING.
darb
I DO HAVE TO GET UP FOR A WEE, THOUGH.
I HEARD THE GRAPHICS ARE BETTER ON THE XBOXES.

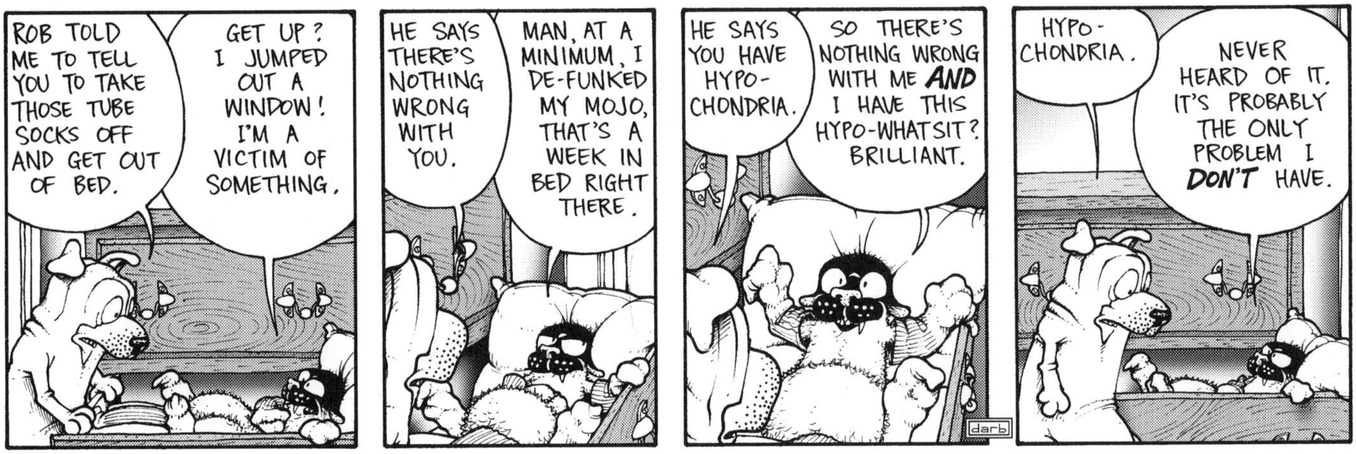
ROB TOLD ME TO TELL YOU TO TAKE THOSE TUBE SOCKS OFF AND GET OUT OF BED.
GET UP? I JUMPED OUT A WINDOW! I'M A VICTIM OF SOMETHING.
HE SAYS THERE'S NOTHING WRONG WITH YOU.
MAN, AT A MINIMUM, I DE-FUNKED MY MOJO, THAT'S A WEEK IN BED RIGHT THERE.
HE SAYS YOU HAVE HYPO-CHONDRIA.
SO THERE'S NOTHING WRONG WITH ME AND I HAVE THIS HYPO-WHATSIT? BRILLIANT.
darb
HYPO-CHONDRIA.
NEVER HEARD OF IT. IT'S PROBABLY THE ONLY PROBLEM I DON'T HAVE.

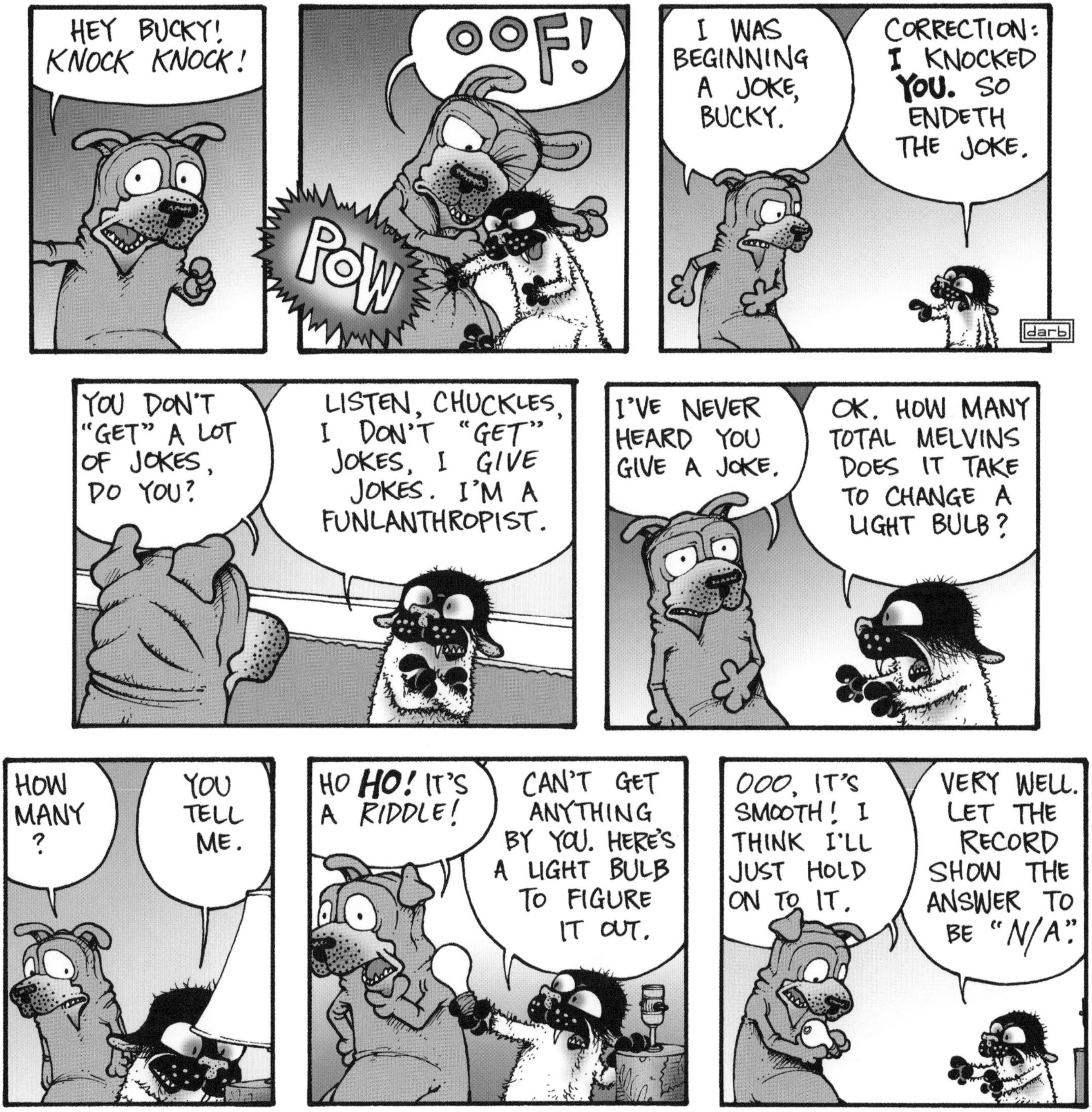
HEY BUCKY! KNOCK KNOCK!
OOF!
POW
I WAS BEGINNING A JOKE, BUCKY.
CORRECTION: I KNOCKED YOU. SO ENDETH THE JOKE.
darb
YOU DON'T "GET" A LOT OF JOKES, DO YOU?
LISTEN, CHUCKLES, I DON'T "GET" JOKES, I GIVE JOKES. I'M A FUNLANTHROPIST.
I'VE NEVER HEARD YOU GIVE A JOKE.
OK. HOW MANY TOTAL MELVINS DOES IT TAKE TO CHANGE A LIGHT BULB?
HOW MANY ?
YOU TELL ME.
HO HO! IT'S A RIDDLE!
CAN'T GET ANYTHING BY YOU. HERE'S A LIGHT BULB TO FIGURE IT OUT.
OOO, IT'S SMOOTH! I THINK I'LL JUST HOLD ON TO IT.
VERY WELL. LET THE RECORD SHOW THE ANSWER TO BE "N/A".

Panel 1:
PSST! BUCKY? CAN I SLEEP OUTSIDE OF YOUR DOOR TONIGHT?

WHY?

Panel 2:
THE NOVEL I'M READING GOT ME SCARED.

FOR THE LAST TIME, THAT'S NOT A NOVEL, IT'S A VACUUM CLEANER USER'S MANUAL.

Panel 3:
NO, NO, DIFFERENT NOVEL... BUT THANKS, NOW I'M TOO SCARED TO SLEEP ON THE FLOOR, TOO.

Panel 4:
WHAT BOOK GOT YOU SO SCARED THAT YOU CAN'T SLEEP ALONE?

IT'S ABOUT ..... A MOTHMAN.

Panel 5:
OH... KAYYY. AND WHAT HAPPENS TO HIM THAT'S SO SCARY?

Panel 6:
NO, HE IS THE SCARY BIT!

THE... THE MOTHMAN?

Panel 7:
YES! I CAN'T EVEN TURN MY LIGHT OFF!

THERE'S YOUR PROBLEM, TURN YOUR LIGHT OFF AND THE KITCHEN LIGHT ON AND HE WON'T BOTHER YOU!

Panel 8:
WHO IS THIS "MOTHMAN" YOU'RE SO AFRAID OF?

WELL, HE HAS RED, GLOWING EYES, TEN-FOOT WINGS, AND WHEREVER HE GOES, CHAOS FOLLOWS.

Panel 9:
SO HE DOES EXIST?

SOME PEOPLE SAY HE'S JUST AN URBAN LEGEND, BUT HE'S BEEN SEEN IN WEST VIRGINIA.

Panel 10:
CLEARLY HE'S NO URBAN LEGEND, THEN.

HE ISN'T?

Panel 11:
NO. HE SOUNDS LIKE MORE OF A SUB-URBAN LEGEND. DARE I SAY, MAYBE EVEN A RURAL LEGEND.

OHHHH, THAT SOUNDS SCARIER.

Panel 1

SATCHEL, THERE'S NO REASON TO FEAR MOTHMEN, EVEN IF THEY DO EXIST.

NO?

Panel 2

IN FACT, BEING PART MOTH NERFS AN OTHERWISE POTENTIALLY SCARY MUTANT. EVEN SOMETHING LIKE A MOTHIGATOR.

Panel 3

IT'S NOT THAT *NO* INSECT COULD EVER BE SCARY, BUT IT'D TAKE MORE THAN A "MOTHMAN." LIKE, SAY, A BUMBLE BEAR.... OR A TARANTULION.

Panel 4

A SPIDER ISN'T AN INSECT.

TECHNICALLY, NEITHER IS A TARANTULION, BUT I STILL WOULDN'T MESS WITH ONE.

Panel 5

I DECLARE YOUR ROOM TO BE FREE OF MOTHS-- MAN-LIKE OR OTHERWISE.

I'M STILL SCARED.

Panel 6

SATCHEL... THE TOUGHEST MOTHMAN CAN BE DEFEATED WITH A CAN OF BEER AND A PIECE OF DOUBLE-SIDED TAPE.

Panel 7

AND LO BEHOLD! FOR THE MAGIC BLOCKAGE OF CEDAR SHALL PROTECTORATE US FROM THE EVIL MOTHMAN: FLITTY, THE BULB BONKER!

Panel 8

SOMEHOW I DON'T THINK YOU'RE TAKING MY FEELINGS SERIOUSLY.

OF COURSE, IF WE SQUISH FLITTY, WE STILL HAVE TO DEAL WITH HIS EVIL HENCH-BUGS: BUTTERFLY BOY AND THE CATERPILLAR KID!

Panel 9

WHAT ARE YOU GUYS YELLING ABOUT? IT'S 3 IN THE MORNING!

Panel 10

SATCHEL'S AFRAID OF MOTHMEN.

HE HAS BIG, RED, GLOW-IN-THE-DARK EYES AND HE SURPRISES YOU IN YOUR BED.

Panel 11

THAT'S JUST A SUPERSTITION.

PFF. IT'S AN OK-STITION, AT BEST.

Panel 12

CAN I SLEEP ON YOUR BED?

SURE.

ROBERT, BEWARE THE MOTHDOG! HE LEAVES SURPRISES IN YOUR BED!

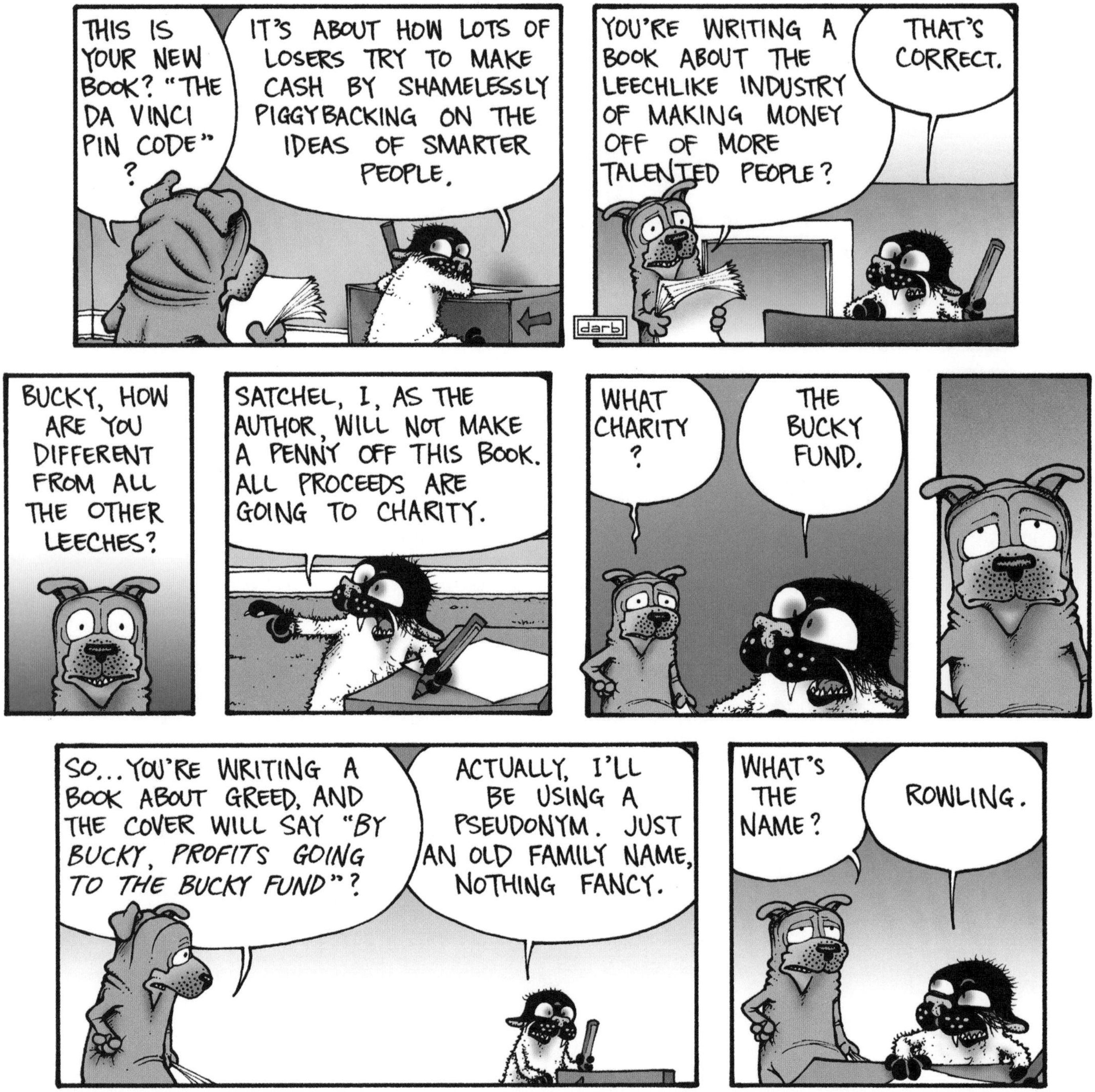
THIS IS YOUR NEW BOOK? "THE DA VINCI PIN CODE"?
IT'S ABOUT HOW LOTS OF LOSERS TRY TO MAKE CASH BY SHAMELESSLY PIGGYBACKING ON THE IDEAS OF SMARTER PEOPLE.
YOU'RE WRITING A BOOK ABOUT THE LEECHLIKE INDUSTRY OF MAKING MONEY OFF OF MORE TALENTED PEOPLE?
THAT'S CORRECT.
darb
BUCKY, HOW ARE YOU DIFFERENT FROM ALL THE OTHER LEECHES?
SATCHEL, I, AS THE AUTHOR, WILL NOT MAKE A PENNY OFF THIS BOOK. ALL PROCEEDS ARE GOING TO CHARITY.
WHAT CHARITY?
THE BUCKY FUND.
SO... YOU'RE WRITING A BOOK ABOUT GREED, AND THE COVER WILL SAY "BY BUCKY, PROFITS GOING TO THE BUCKY FUND"?
ACTUALLY, I'LL BE USING A PSEUDONYM. JUST AN OLD FAMILY NAME, NOTHING FANCY.
WHAT'S THE NAME?
ROWLING.

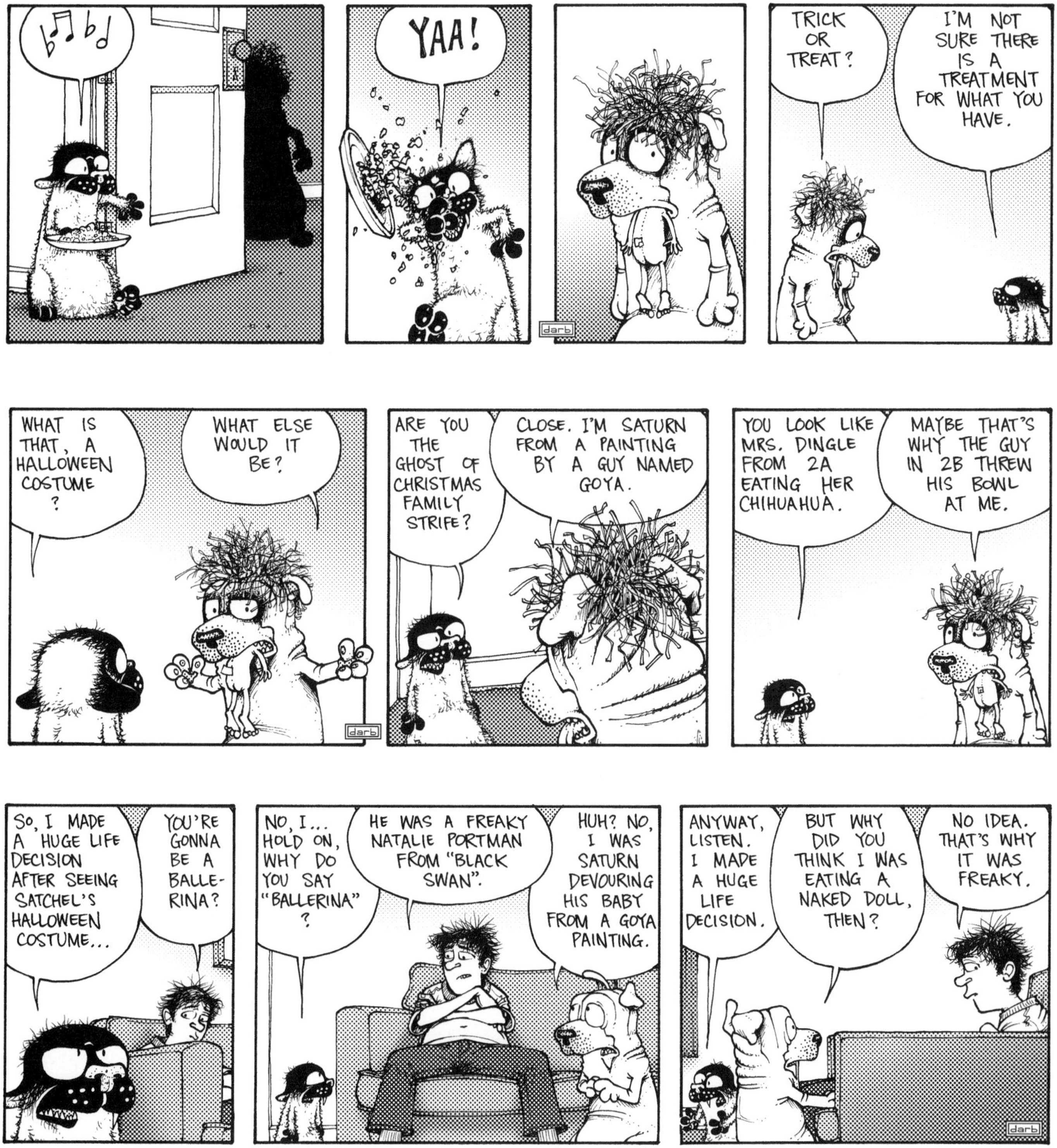
YAA!
TRICK OR TREAT?
I'M NOT SURE THERE IS A TREATMENT FOR WHAT YOU HAVE.
WHAT IS THAT, A HALLOWEEN COSTUME?
WHAT ELSE WOULD IT BE?
ARE YOU THE GHOST OF CHRISTMAS FAMILY STRIFE?
CLOSE. I'M SATURN FROM A PAINTING BY A GUY NAMED GOYA.
YOU LOOK LIKE MRS. DINGLE FROM 2A EATING HER CHIHUAHUA.
MAYBE THAT'S WHY THE GUY IN 2B THREW HIS BOWL AT ME.
SO, I MADE A HUGE LIFE DECISION AFTER SEEING SATCHEL'S HALLOWEEN COSTUME...
YOU'RE GONNA BE A BALLERINA?
NO, I... HOLD ON, WHY DO YOU SAY "BALLERINA"?
HE WAS A FREAKY NATALIE PORTMAN FROM "BLACK SWAN".
HUH? NO, I WAS SATURN DEVOURING HIS BABY FROM A GOYA PAINTING.
ANYWAY, LISTEN. I MADE A HUGE LIFE DECISION.
BUT WHY DID YOU THINK I WAS EATING A NAKED DOLL, THEN?
NO IDEA. THAT'S WHY IT WAS FREAKY.

Panel 1:
SO WHAT'S THIS BIG LIFE CHANGE YOU'RE TALKING ABOUT?

WELL, I'M SURE YOU AND ROBERT HAVE NOTICED MY HEIGHTENED SENSE OF BEING TODAY...

Panel 3:
ANYWAY.... I HAVE BECOME A TEACHER OF ENLIGHTENED INDIANA SPIRITUALITY.

Panel 4:
HA HA! WHAT'S THAT, HOOSIERISM? DO YOU LECTURE AT THE HINDI 500?

I DON'T FOLLOW YOU.

HA HA! NOR I YOU.

Panel 5:
YOU'RE A SPIRITUAL ADVISOR ALL OF A SUDDEN?

I'VE DECIDED I HAVE E.S.P. AND I'M PSYCHIC. I'M BASICALLY A JACK OF ALL BRAINS.

Panel 6:
I'LL REFRAIN FROM ADDING TO THAT TITLE.

MY PSYCHIC POWERS SENSE A "BUT"...

HA HA! EWW! THAT SURE PUTS THE *ICK* IN *PSYCHIC*!

Panel 7:
EXCUSE YOU?

WHAT IS THAT POWER CALLED? **A.**S.P.?

Panel 8:
HOW DID SEEING SATCHEL IN HIS HALLOWEEN COSTUME INSPIRE YOU TO BE A SPIRITUAL ADVISOR?

ROB, WHEN SATCHEL ACTUALLY MANAGED TO SCARE ME, I REALIZED I HAD TO GET A HANDLE ON MY BRAIN.

Panel 9:
LIKE HIPPIE SELF-AWARENESS?

IT'S NOT JUST ABOUT SELF-A-*WHERE*-NESS, IT'S ALSO ABOUT SELF-A-*WHO*-NESS, SELF-A-*WHAT*-NESS AND THE BIG ONE: SELF-A-*WHY*-NESS.

Panel 10:
YOU'RE A FOOL.

NOPE. NOT AWARE OF THAT.

54

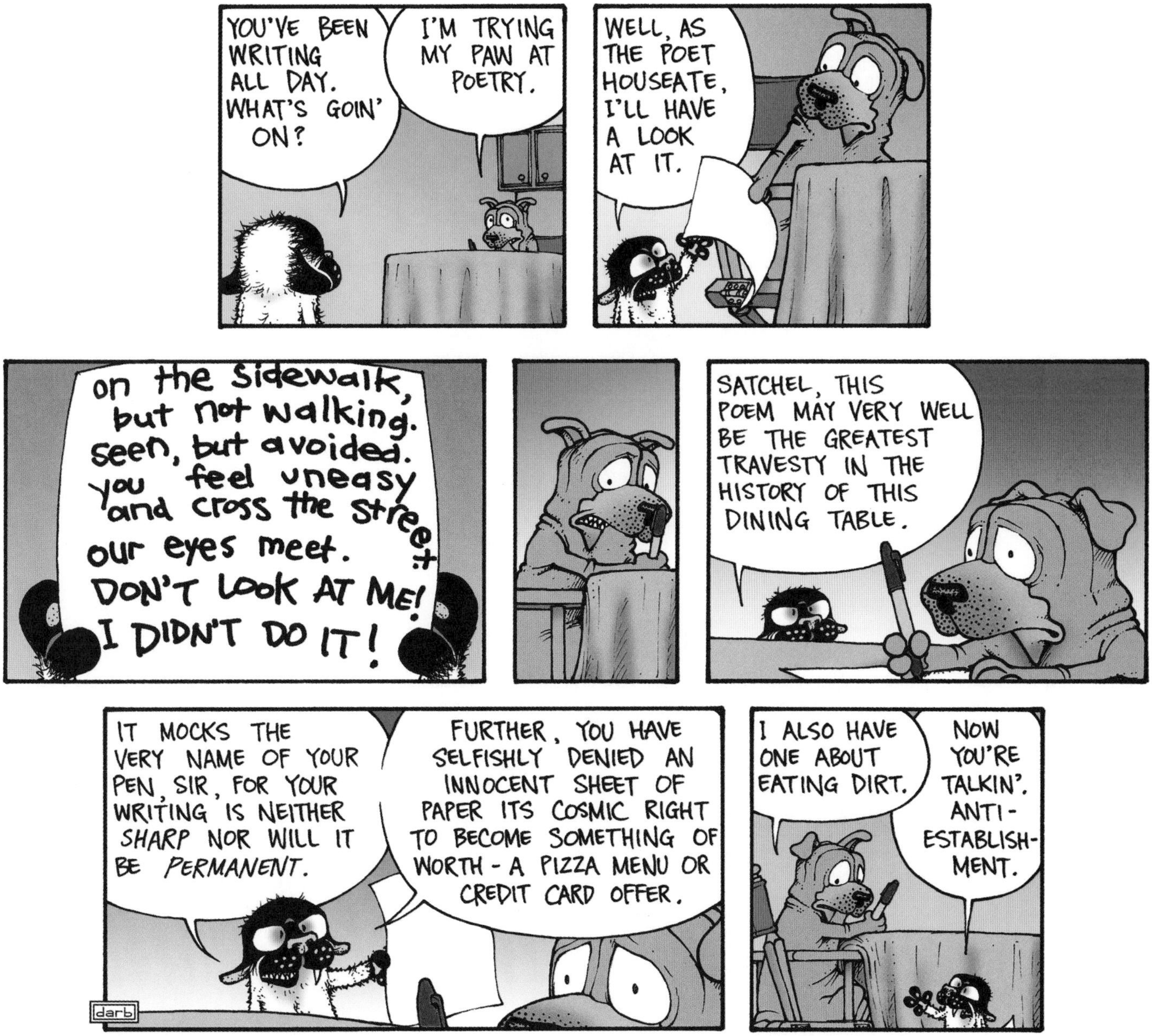
YOU'VE BEEN WRITING ALL DAY. WHAT'S GOIN' ON?
I'M TRYING MY PAW AT POETRY.
WELL, AS THE POET HOUSEATE, I'LL HAVE A LOOK AT IT.
on the sidewalk, but not walking. seen, but avoided. you feel uneasy and cross the street our eyes meet. DON'T LOOK AT ME! I DIDN'T DO IT!
SATCHEL, THIS POEM MAY VERY WELL BE THE GREATEST TRAVESTY IN THE HISTORY OF THIS DINING TABLE.
IT MOCKS THE VERY NAME OF YOUR PEN, SIR, FOR YOUR WRITING IS NEITHER *SHARP* NOR WILL IT BE *PERMANENT*.
FURTHER, YOU HAVE SELFISHLY DENIED AN INNOCENT SHEET OF PAPER ITS COSMIC RIGHT TO BECOME SOMETHING OF WORTH - A PIZZA MENU OR CREDIT CARD OFFER.
darb
I ALSO HAVE ONE ABOUT EATING DIRT.
NOW YOU'RE TALKIN'. ANTI-ESTABLISHMENT.

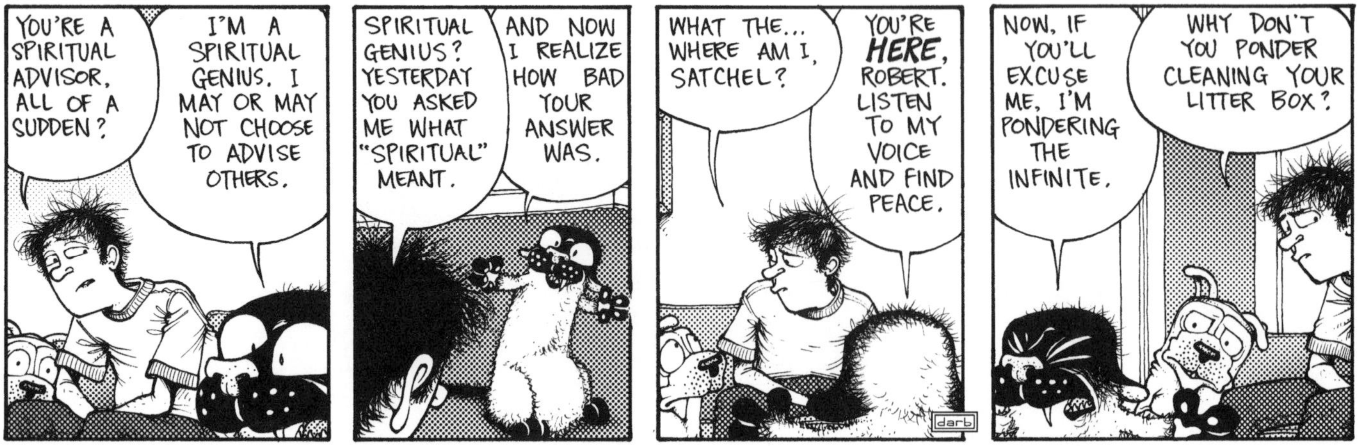
YOU'RE A SPIRITUAL ADVISOR, ALL OF A SUDDEN?
I'M A SPIRITUAL GENIUS. I MAY OR MAY NOT CHOOSE TO ADVISE OTHERS.
SPIRITUAL GENIUS? YESTERDAY YOU ASKED ME WHAT "SPIRITUAL" MEANT.
AND NOW I REALIZE HOW BAD YOUR ANSWER WAS.
WHAT THE... WHERE AM I, SATCHEL?
YOU'RE **HERE**, ROBERT. LISTEN TO MY VOICE AND FIND PEACE.
darb
NOW, IF YOU'LL EXCUSE ME, I'M PONDERING THE INFINITE.
WHY DON'T YOU PONDER CLEANING YOUR LITTER BOX?

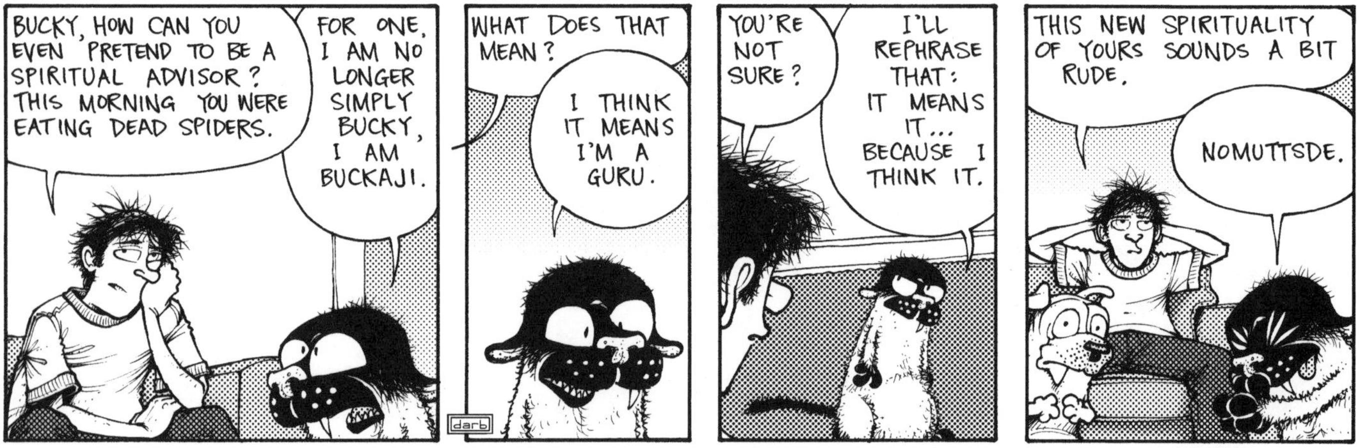
BUCKY, HOW CAN YOU EVEN PRETEND TO BE A SPIRITUAL ADVISOR? THIS MORNING YOU WERE EATING DEAD SPIDERS.
FOR ONE, I AM NO LONGER SIMPLY BUCKY, I AM BUCKAJI.
darb
WHAT DOES THAT MEAN?
I THINK IT MEANS I'M A GURU.
YOU'RE NOT SURE?
I'LL REPHRASE THAT: IT MEANS IT... BECAUSE I THINK IT.
THIS NEW SPIRITUALITY OF YOURS SOUNDS A BIT RUDE.
NOMUTTSDE.

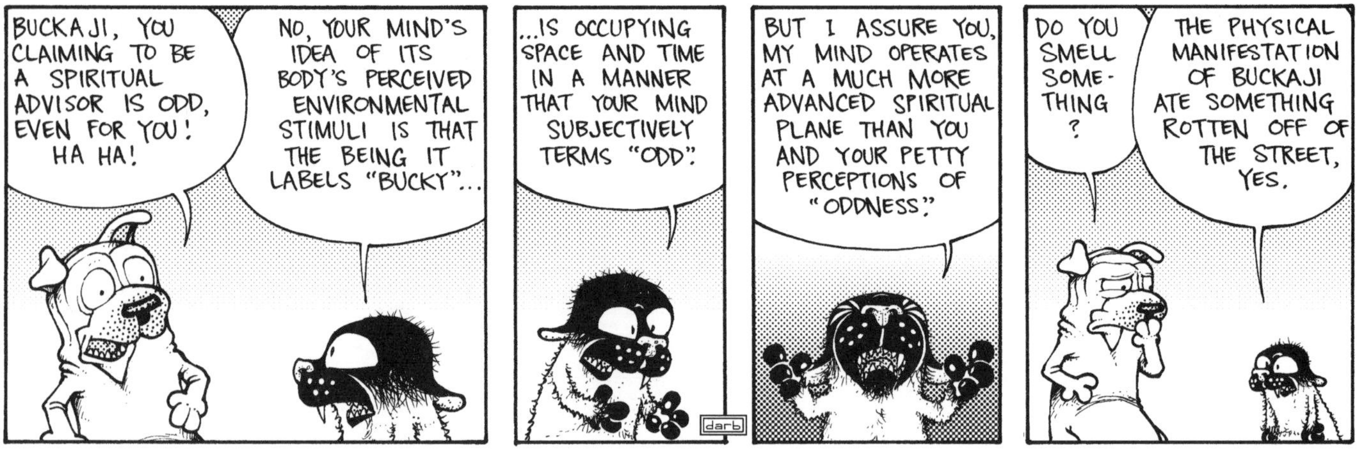
BUCKAJI, YOU CLAIMING TO BE A SPIRITUAL ADVISOR IS ODD, EVEN FOR YOU! HA HA!
NO, YOUR MIND'S IDEA OF ITS BODY'S PERCEIVED ENVIRONMENTAL STIMULI IS THAT THE BEING IT LABELS "BUCKY"...
...IS OCCUPYING SPACE AND TIME IN A MANNER THAT YOUR MIND SUBJECTIVELY TERMS "ODD".
darb
BUT I ASSURE YOU, MY MIND OPERATES AT A MUCH MORE ADVANCED SPIRITUAL PLANE THAN YOU AND YOUR PETTY PERCEPTIONS OF "ODDNESS."
DO YOU SMELL SOME-THING?
THE PHYSICAL MANIFESTATION OF BUCKAJI ATE SOMETHING ROTTEN OFF OF THE STREET, YES.

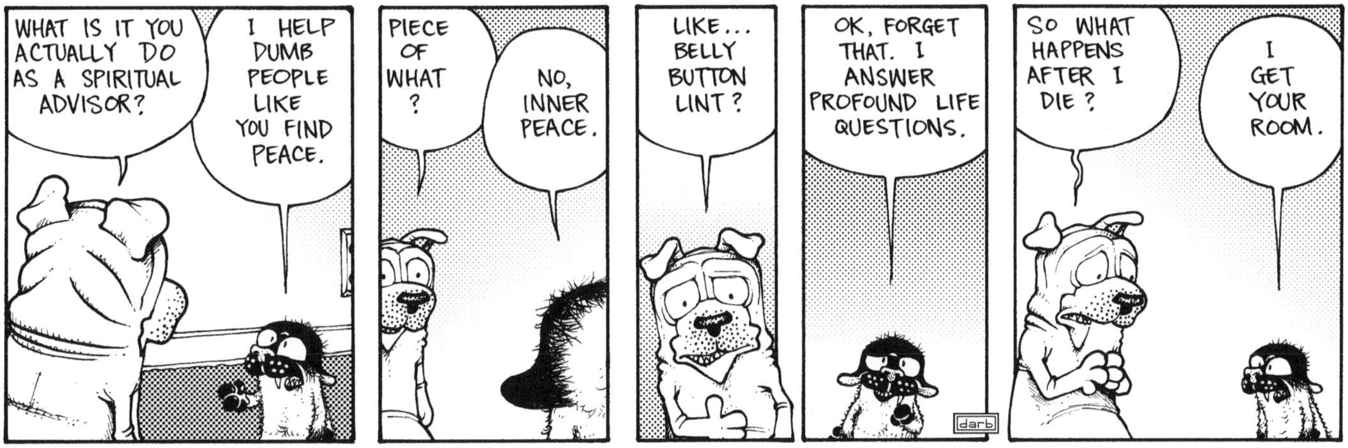
WHAT IS IT YOU ACTUALLY DO AS A SPIRITUAL ADVISOR?
I HELP DUMB PEOPLE LIKE YOU FIND PEACE.
PIECE OF WHAT?
NO, INNER PEACE.
LIKE... BELLY BUTTON LINT?
OK, FORGET THAT. I ANSWER PROFOUND LIFE QUESTIONS.
darb
SO WHAT HAPPENS AFTER I DIE?
I GET YOUR ROOM.

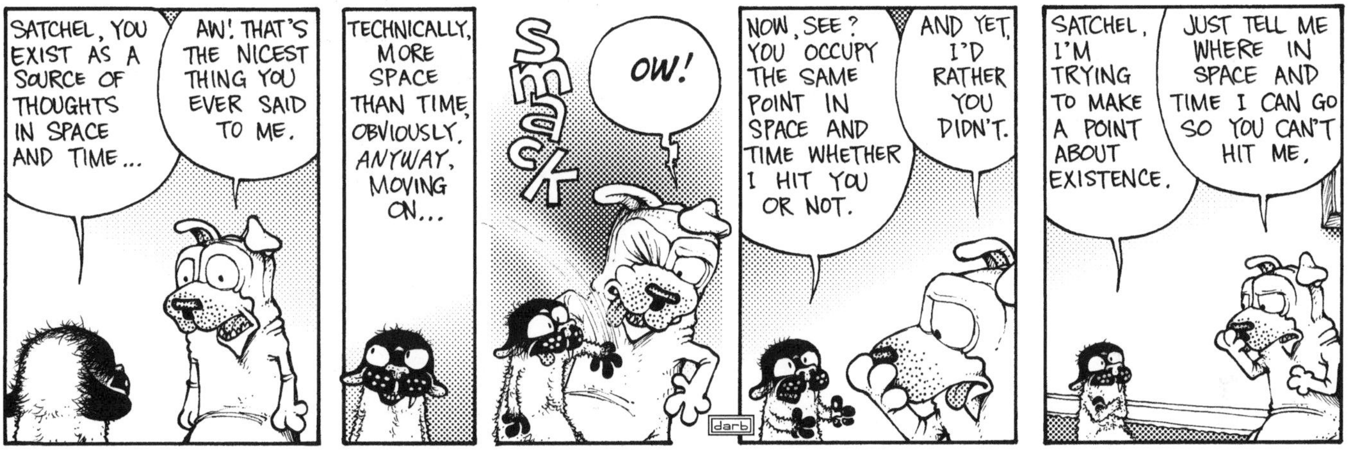
SATCHEL, YOU EXIST AS A SOURCE OF THOUGHTS IN SPACE AND TIME...
AW! THAT'S THE NICEST THING YOU EVER SAID TO ME.
TECHNICALLY, MORE SPACE THAN TIME, OBVIOUSLY. ANYWAY, MOVING ON...
SMACK
OW!
darb
NOW, SEE? YOU OCCUPY THE SAME POINT IN SPACE AND TIME WHETHER I HIT YOU OR NOT.
AND YET, I'D RATHER YOU DIDN'T.
SATCHEL, I'M TRYING TO MAKE A POINT ABOUT EXISTENCE.
JUST TELL ME WHERE IN SPACE AND TIME I CAN GO SO YOU CAN'T HIT ME.

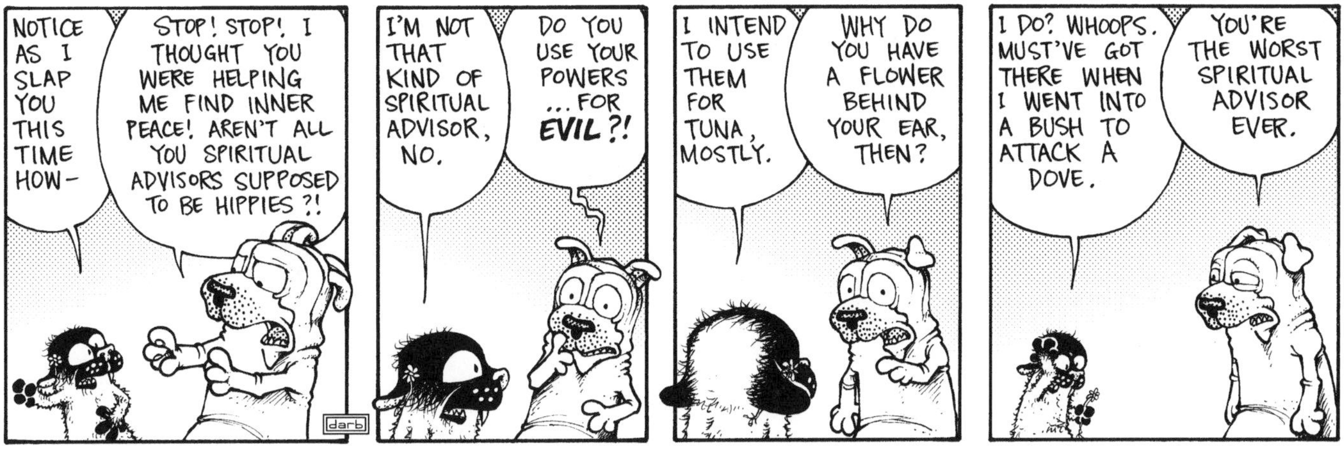
NOTICE AS I SLAP YOU THIS TIME HOW-
STOP! STOP! I THOUGHT YOU WERE HELPING ME FIND INNER PEACE! AREN'T ALL YOU SPIRITUAL ADVISORS SUPPOSED TO BE HIPPIES?!
darb
I'M NOT THAT KIND OF SPIRITUAL ADVISOR, NO.
DO YOU USE YOUR POWERS ...FOR EVIL?!
I INTEND TO USE THEM FOR TUNA, MOSTLY.
WHY DO YOU HAVE A FLOWER BEHIND YOUR EAR, THEN?
I DO? WHOOPS. MUST'VE GOT THERE WHEN I WENT INTO A BUSH TO ATTACK A DOVE.
YOU'RE THE WORST SPIRITUAL ADVISOR EVER.

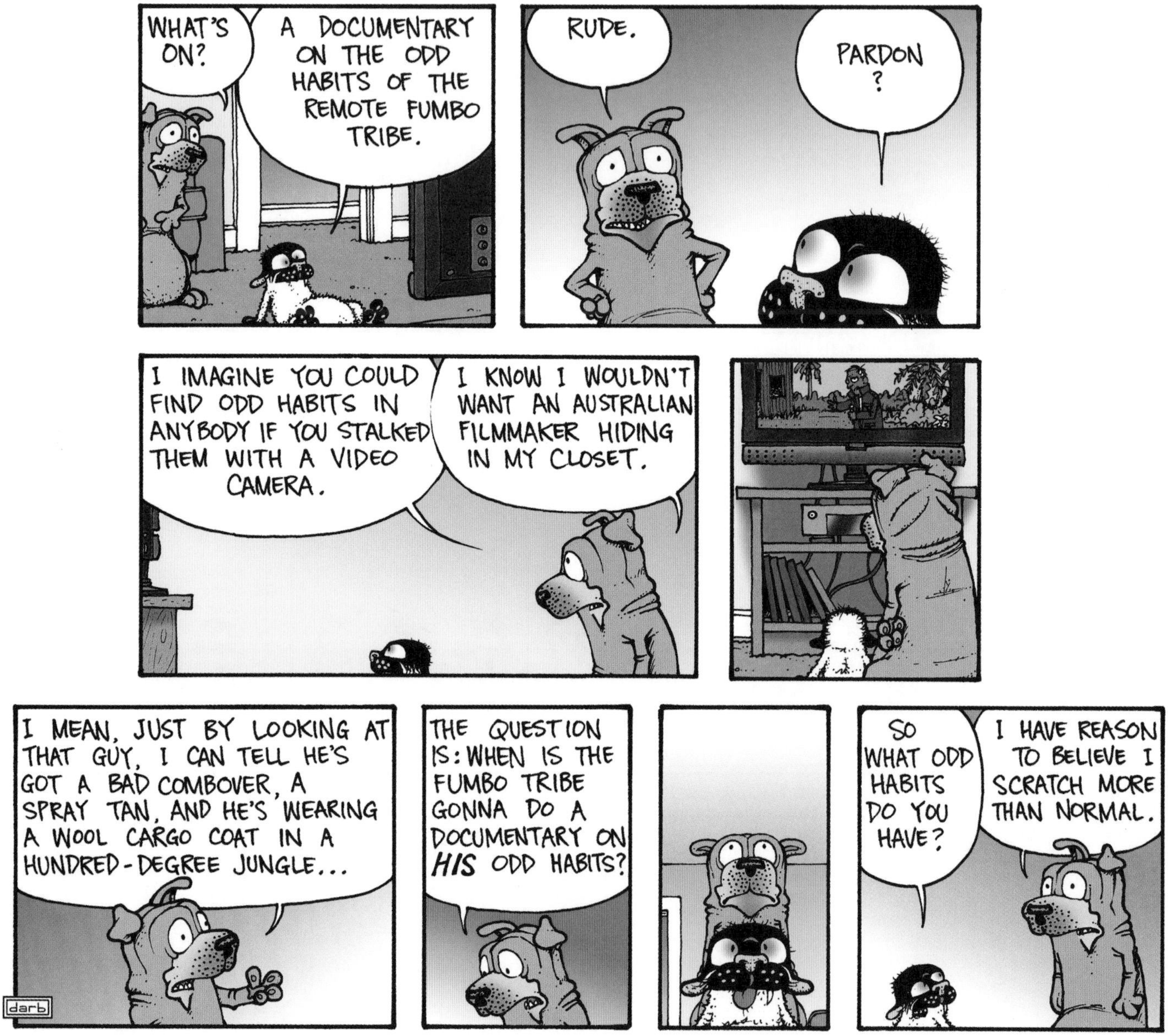
WHAT'S ON?
A DOCUMENTARY ON THE ODD HABITS OF THE REMOTE FUMBO TRIBE.
RUDE.
PARDON?
I IMAGINE YOU COULD FIND ODD HABITS IN ANYBODY IF YOU STALKED THEM WITH A VIDEO CAMERA.
I KNOW I WOULDN'T WANT AN AUSTRALIAN FILMMAKER HIDING IN MY CLOSET.
I MEAN, JUST BY LOOKING AT THAT GUY, I CAN TELL HE'S GOT A BAD COMBOVER, A SPRAY TAN, AND HE'S WEARING A WOOL CARGO COAT IN A HUNDRED-DEGREE JUNGLE...
darb
THE QUESTION IS: WHEN IS THE FUMBO TRIBE GONNA DO A DOCUMENTARY ON *HIS* ODD HABITS?
SO WHAT ODD HABITS DO YOU HAVE?
I HAVE REASON TO BELIEVE I SCRATCH MORE THAN NORMAL.

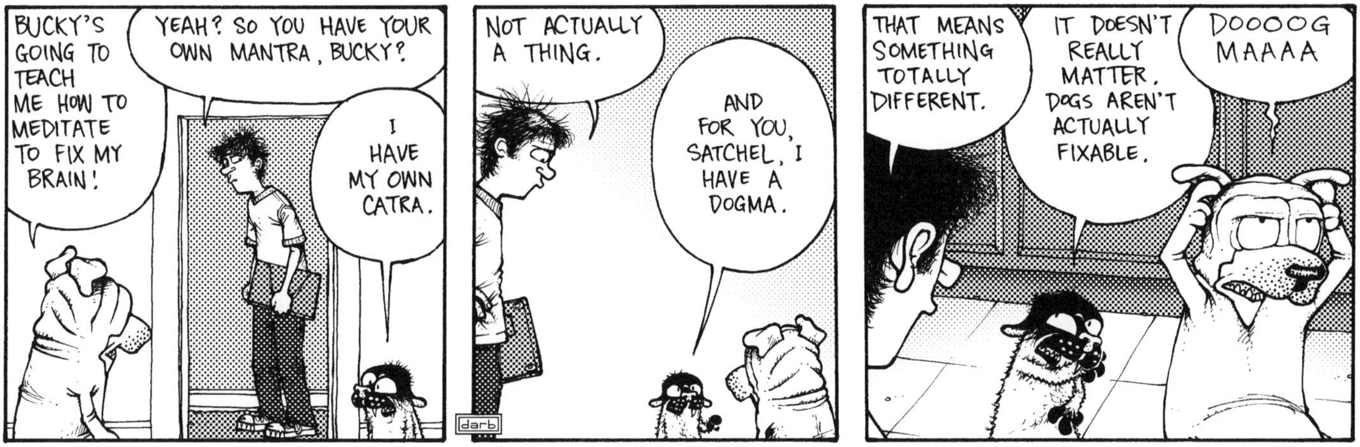
BUCKY'S GOING TO TEACH ME HOW TO MEDITATE TO FIX MY BRAIN!
YEAH? SO YOU HAVE YOUR OWN MANTRA, BUCKY?
I HAVE MY OWN CATRA.
NOT ACTUALLY A THING.
AND FOR YOU, SATCHEL, I HAVE A DOGMA.
THAT MEANS SOMETHING TOTALLY DIFFERENT.
IT DOESN'T REALLY MATTER. DOGS AREN'T ACTUALLY FIXABLE.
DOOOOG MAAAAA

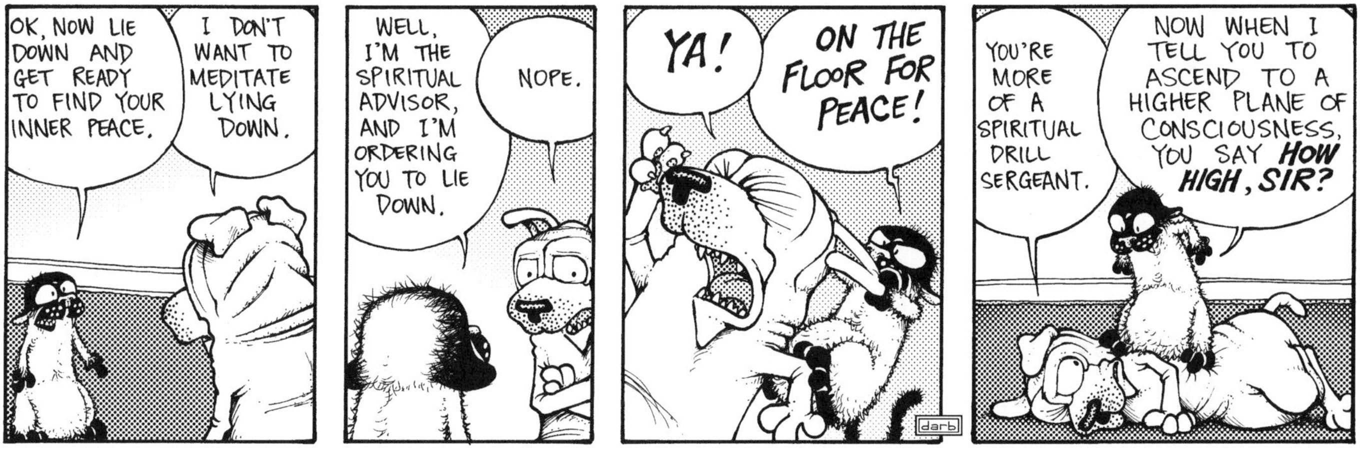
OK, NOW LIE DOWN AND GET READY TO FIND YOUR INNER PEACE.
I DON'T WANT TO MEDITATE LYING DOWN.
WELL, I'M THE SPIRITUAL ADVISOR, AND I'M ORDERING YOU TO LIE DOWN.
NOPE.
YA!
ON THE FLOOR FOR PEACE!
YOU'RE MORE OF A SPIRITUAL DRILL SERGEANT.
NOW WHEN I TELL YOU TO ASCEND TO A HIGHER PLANE OF CONSCIOUSNESS, YOU SAY HOW HIGH, SIR?

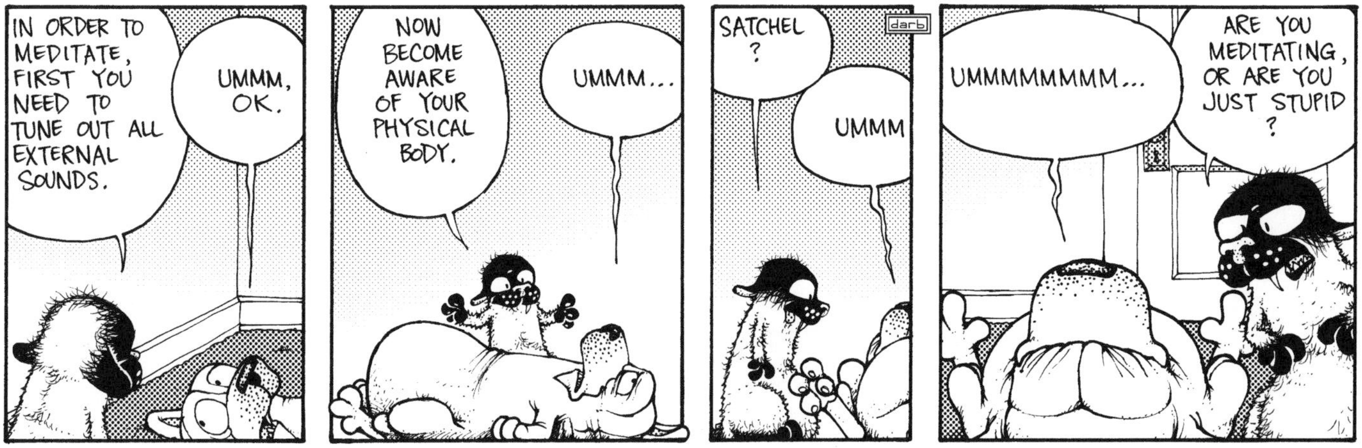
IN ORDER TO MEDITATE, FIRST YOU NEED TO TUNE OUT ALL EXTERNAL SOUNDS.
UMMM, OK.
NOW BECOME AWARE OF YOUR PHYSICAL BODY.
UMMM...
SATCHEL?
UMMM
UMMMMMMMM...
ARE YOU MEDITATING, OR ARE YOU JUST STUPID?

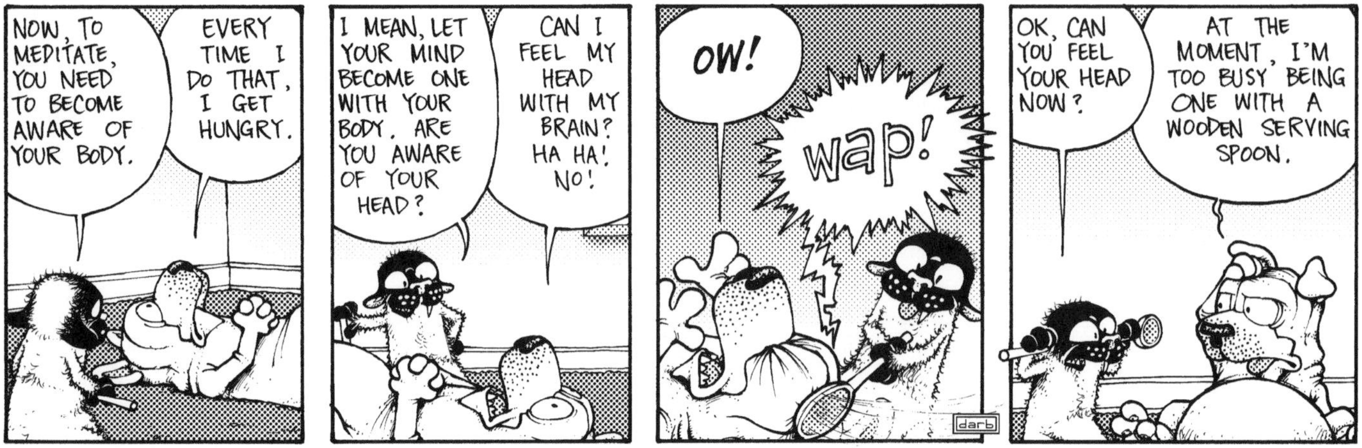
NOW, TO MEDITATE, YOU NEED TO BECOME AWARE OF YOUR BODY.
EVERY TIME I DO THAT, I GET HUNGRY.
I MEAN, LET YOUR MIND BECOME ONE WITH YOUR BODY. ARE YOU AWARE OF YOUR HEAD?
CAN I FEEL MY HEAD WITH MY BRAIN? HA HA! NO!
OW!
wap!
OK, CAN YOU FEEL YOUR HEAD NOW?
AT THE MOMENT, I'M TOO BUSY BEING ONE WITH A WOODEN SERVING SPOON.
darb

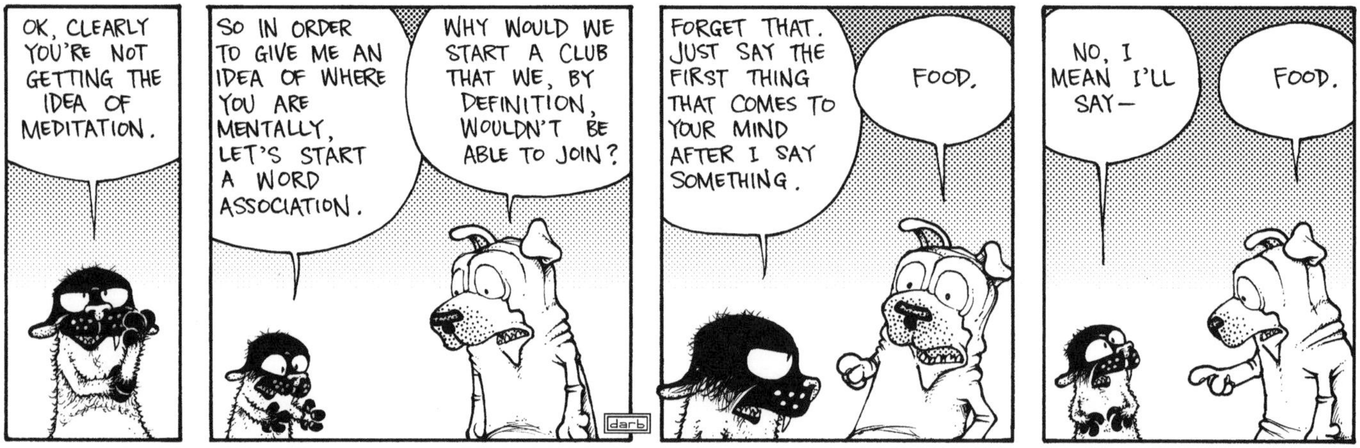
OK, CLEARLY YOU'RE NOT GETTING THE IDEA OF MEDITATION.
SO IN ORDER TO GIVE ME AN IDEA OF WHERE YOU ARE MENTALLY, LET'S START A WORD ASSOCIATION.
WHY WOULD WE START A CLUB THAT WE, BY DEFINITION, WOULDN'T BE ABLE TO JOIN?
darb
FORGET THAT. JUST SAY THE FIRST THING THAT COMES TO YOUR MIND AFTER I SAY SOMETHING.
FOOD.
NO, I MEAN I'LL SAY—
FOOD.

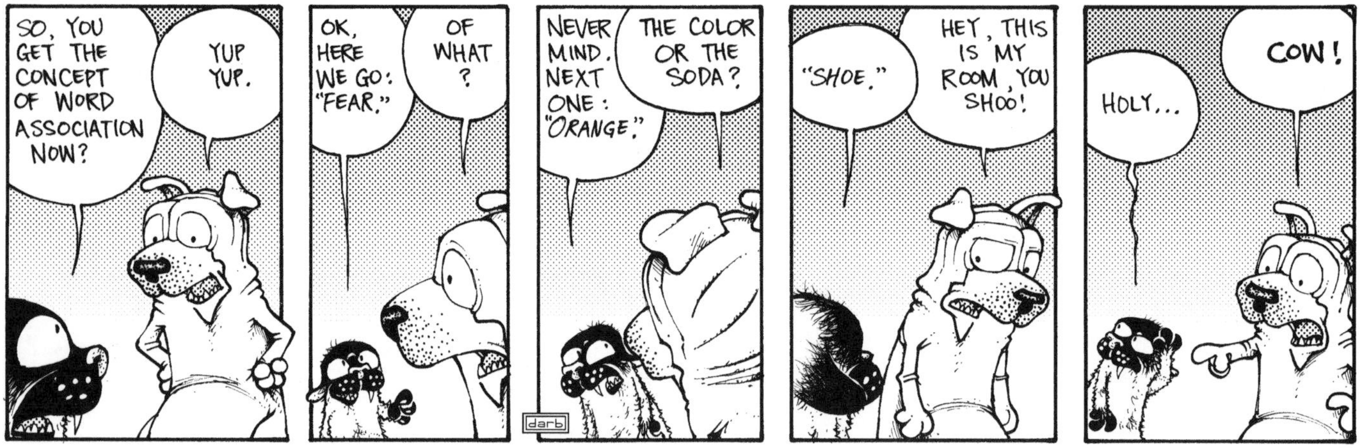
SO, YOU GET THE CONCEPT OF WORD ASSOCIATION NOW?
YUP YUP.
OK, HERE WE GO: "FEAR."
OF WHAT?
darb
NEVER MIND. NEXT ONE: "ORANGE."
THE COLOR OR THE SODA?
"SHOE."
HEY, THIS IS MY ROOM, YOU SHOO!
HOLY...
COW!

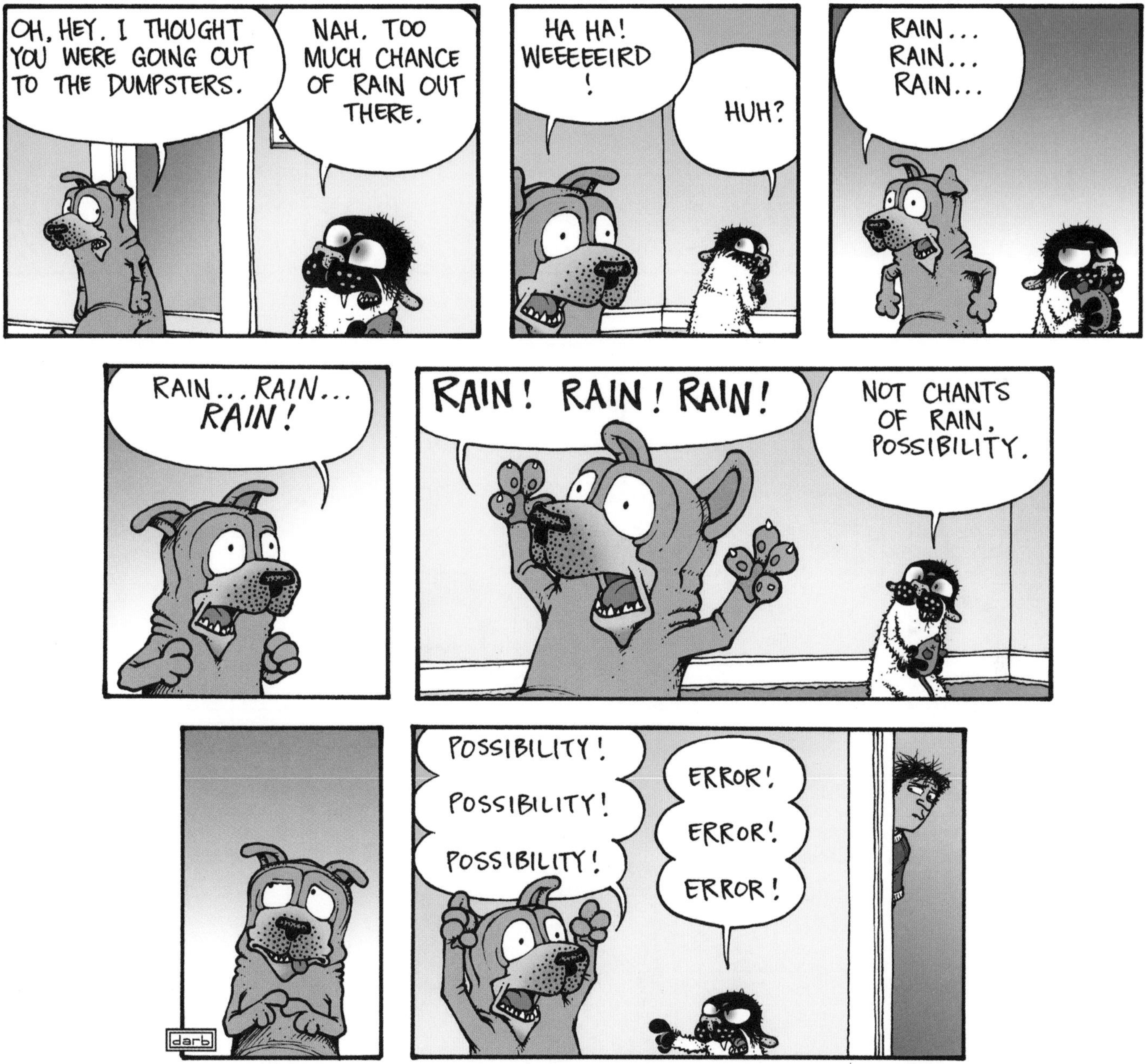
OH, HEY. I THOUGHT YOU WERE GOING OUT TO THE DUMPSTERS.
NAH. TOO MUCH CHANCE OF RAIN OUT THERE.
HA HA! WEEEEEIRD !
HUH?
RAIN... RAIN... RAIN...
RAIN... RAIN... RAIN!
RAIN! RAIN! RAIN!
NOT CHANTS OF RAIN, POSSIBILITY.
darb
POSSIBILITY!
POSSIBILITY!
POSSIBILITY!
ERROR!
ERROR!
ERROR!

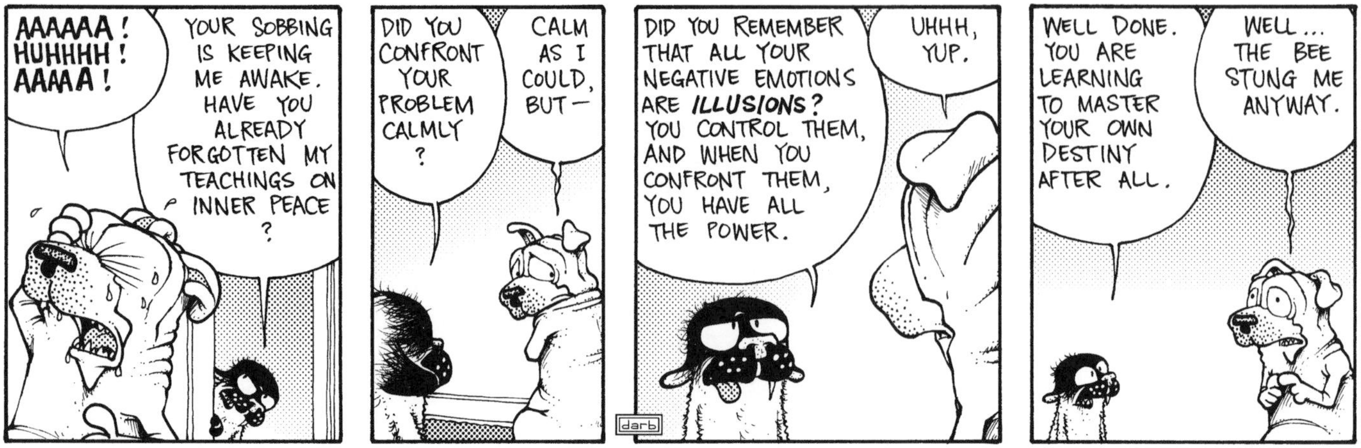
AAAAAA! HUHHHH! AAAAA!
YOUR SOBBING IS KEEPING ME AWAKE. HAVE YOU ALREADY FORGOTTEN MY TEACHINGS ON INNER PEACE?
DID YOU CONFRONT YOUR PROBLEM CALMLY?
CALM AS I COULD, BUT—
darb
DID YOU REMEMBER THAT ALL YOUR NEGATIVE EMOTIONS ARE ILLUSIONS? YOU CONTROL THEM, AND WHEN YOU CONFRONT THEM, YOU HAVE ALL THE POWER.
UHHH, YUP.
WELL DONE. YOU ARE LEARNING TO MASTER YOUR OWN DESTINY AFTER ALL.
WELL... THE BEE STUNG ME ANYWAY.

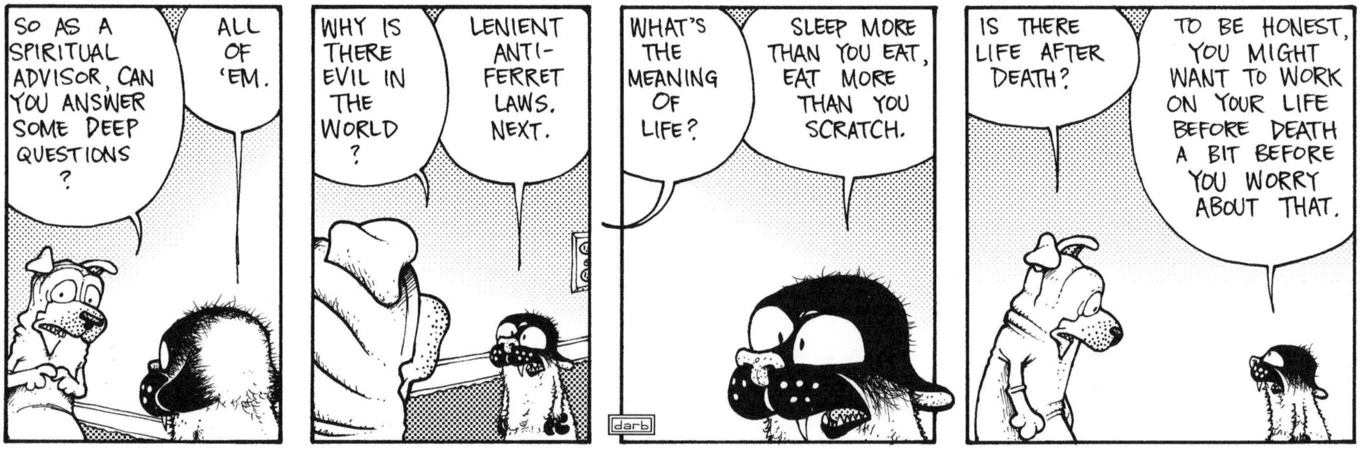
SO AS A SPIRITUAL ADVISOR, CAN YOU ANSWER SOME DEEP QUESTIONS?
ALL OF 'EM.
WHY IS THERE EVIL IN THE WORLD?
LENIENT ANTI-FERRET LAWS. NEXT.
darb
WHAT'S THE MEANING OF LIFE?
SLEEP MORE THAN YOU EAT, EAT MORE THAN YOU SCRATCH.
IS THERE LIFE AFTER DEATH?
TO BE HONEST, YOU MIGHT WANT TO WORK ON YOUR LIFE BEFORE DEATH A BIT BEFORE YOU WORRY ABOUT THAT.

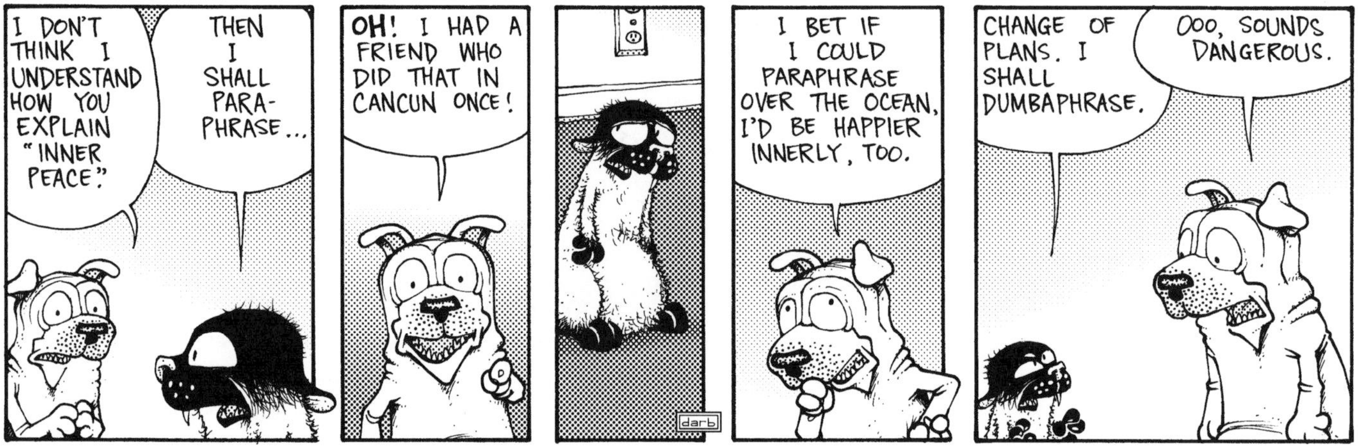
I DON'T THINK I UNDERSTAND HOW YOU EXPLAIN "INNER PEACE."
THEN I SHALL PARA-PHRASE...
OH! I HAD A FRIEND WHO DID THAT IN CANCUN ONCE!
darb
I BET IF I COULD PARAPHRASE OVER THE OCEAN, I'D BE HAPPIER INNERLY, TOO.
CHANGE OF PLANS. I SHALL DUMBAPHRASE.
OOO, SOUNDS DANGEROUS.

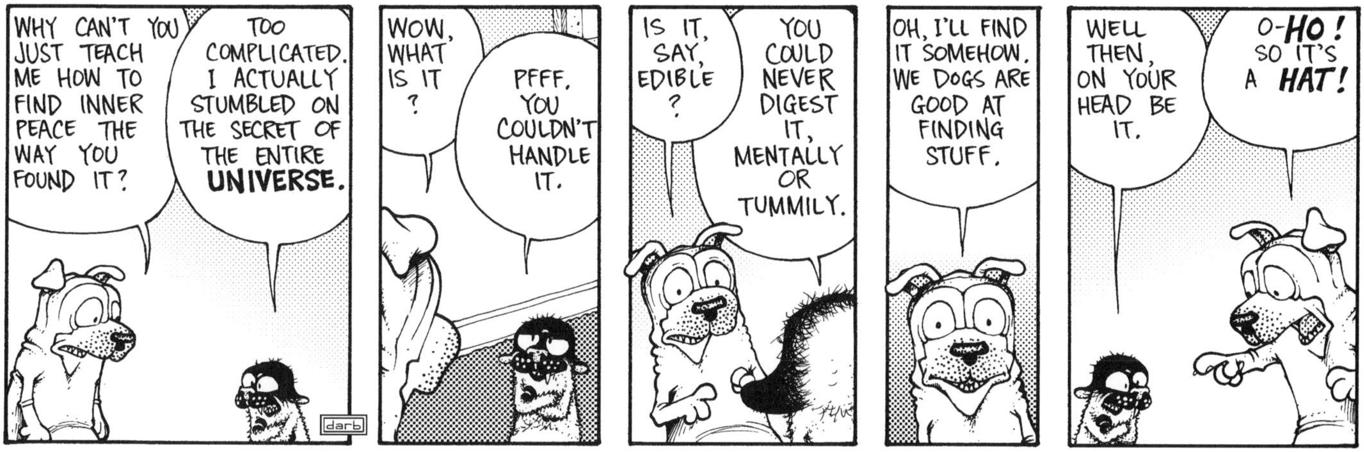
WHY CAN'T YOU JUST TEACH ME HOW TO FIND INNER PEACE THE WAY YOU FOUND IT?
TOO COMPLICATED. I ACTUALLY STUMBLED ON THE SECRET OF THE ENTIRE UNIVERSE.
WOW, WHAT IS IT?
PFFF. YOU COULDN'T HANDLE IT.
IS IT, SAY, EDIBLE?
YOU COULD NEVER DIGEST IT, MENTALLY OR TUMMILY.
OH, I'LL FIND IT SOMEHOW. WE DOGS ARE GOOD AT FINDING STUFF.
WELL THEN, ON YOUR HEAD BE IT.
O-HO! SO IT'S A HAT!
darb

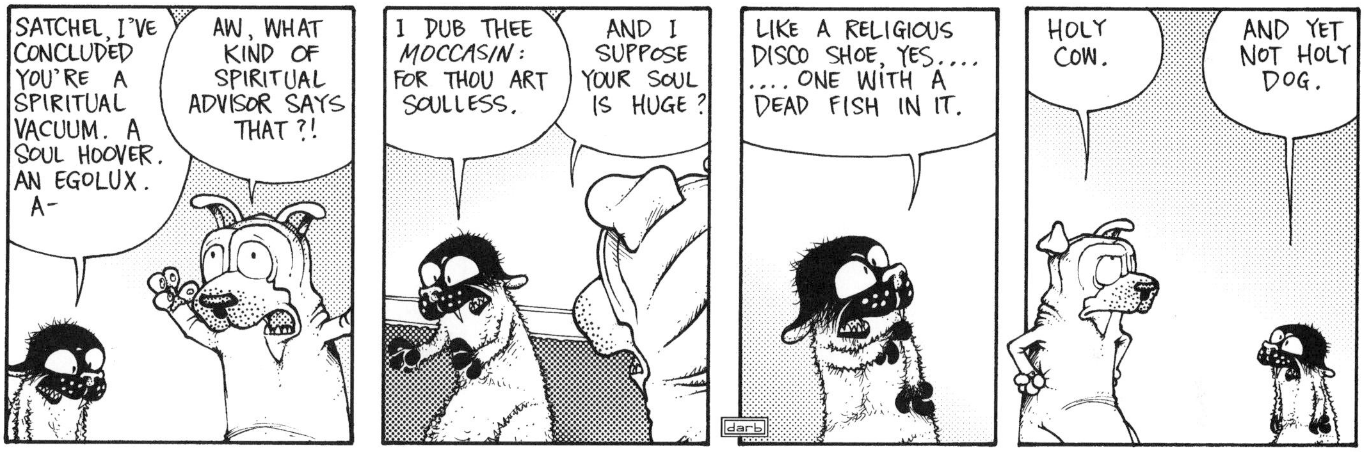
SATCHEL, I'VE CONCLUDED YOU'RE A SPIRITUAL VACUUM. A SOUL HOOVER. AN EGOLUX. A-
AW, WHAT KIND OF SPIRITUAL ADVISOR SAYS THAT?!
I DUB THEE MOCCASIN: FOR THOU ART SOULLESS.
AND I SUPPOSE YOUR SOUL IS HUGE?
darb
LIKE A RELIGIOUS DISCO SHOE, YES.... ....ONE WITH A DEAD FISH IN IT.
HOLY COW.
AND YET NOT HOLY DOG.

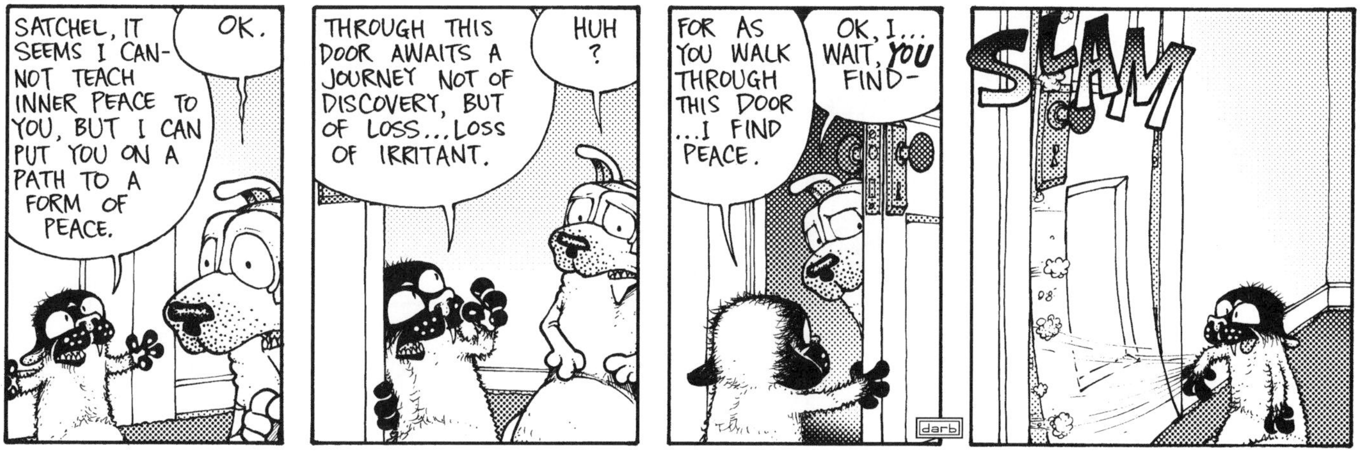
SATCHEL, IT SEEMS I CANNOT TEACH INNER PEACE TO YOU, BUT I CAN PUT YOU ON A PATH TO A FORM OF PEACE.
OK.
THROUGH THIS DOOR AWAITS A JOURNEY NOT OF DISCOVERY, BUT OF LOSS...LOSS OF IRRITANT.
HUH?
FOR AS YOU WALK THROUGH THIS DOOR ...I FIND PEACE.
OK, I... WAIT, YOU FIND-
darb
SLAM

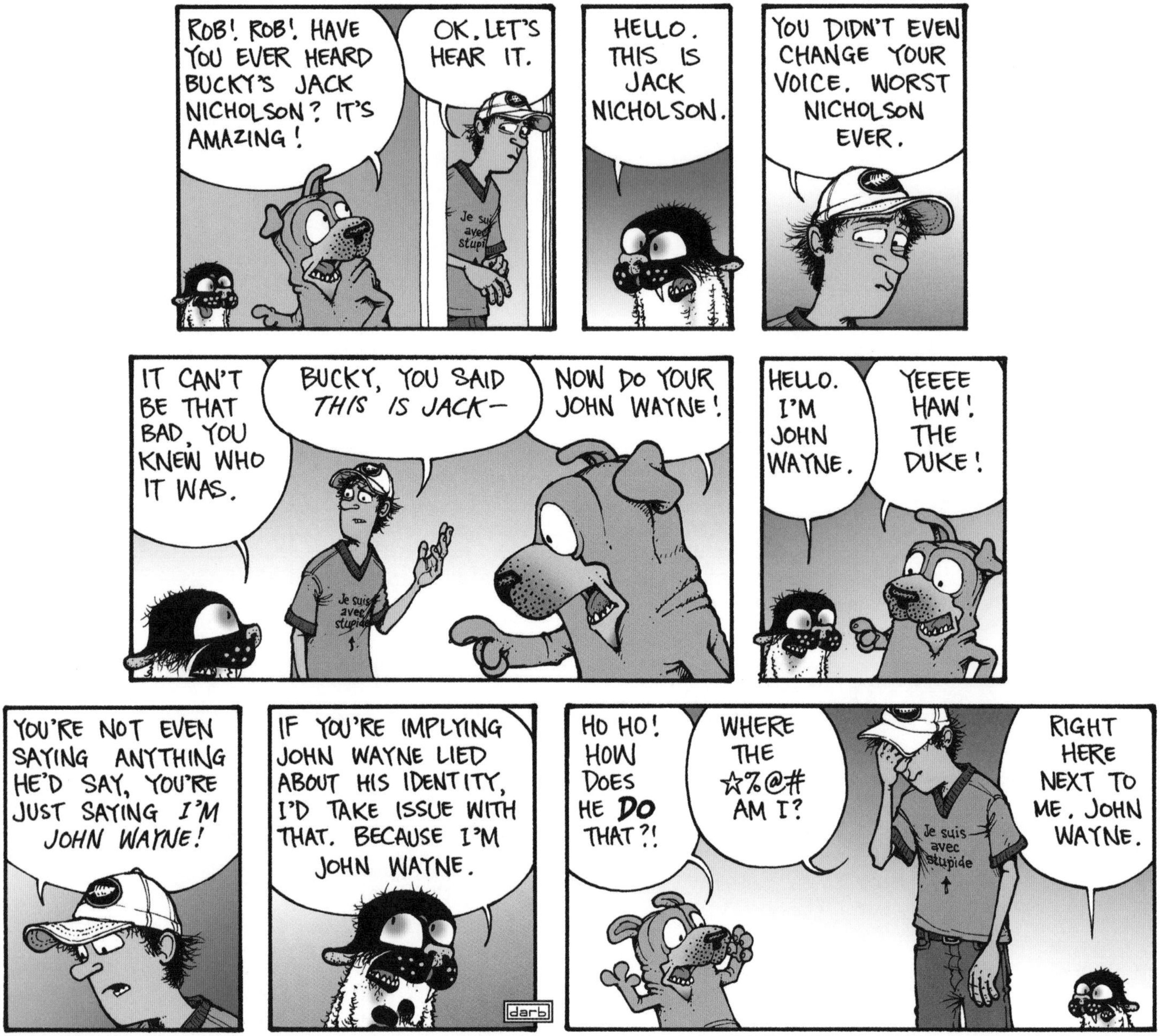
ROB! ROB! HAVE YOU EVER HEARD BUCKY'S JACK NICHOLSON? IT'S AMAZING!
OK. LET'S HEAR IT.
Je suis avec stupide
HELLO. THIS IS JACK NICHOLSON.
YOU DIDN'T EVEN CHANGE YOUR VOICE. WORST NICHOLSON EVER.
IT CAN'T BE THAT BAD. YOU KNEW WHO IT WAS.
BUCKY, YOU SAID *THIS IS JACK*—
NOW DO YOUR JOHN WAYNE!
Je suis avec stupide
HELLO. I'M JOHN WAYNE.
YEEEE HAW! THE DUKE!
YOU'RE NOT EVEN SAYING ANYTHING HE'D SAY. YOU'RE JUST SAYING *I'M JOHN WAYNE!*
IF YOU'RE IMPLYING JOHN WAYNE LIED ABOUT HIS IDENTITY, I'D TAKE ISSUE WITH THAT. BECAUSE I'M JOHN WAYNE.
darb
HO HO! HOW DOES HE **DO** THAT?!
WHERE THE ☆%@# AM I?
RIGHT HERE NEXT TO ME. JOHN WAYNE.
Je suis avec stupide

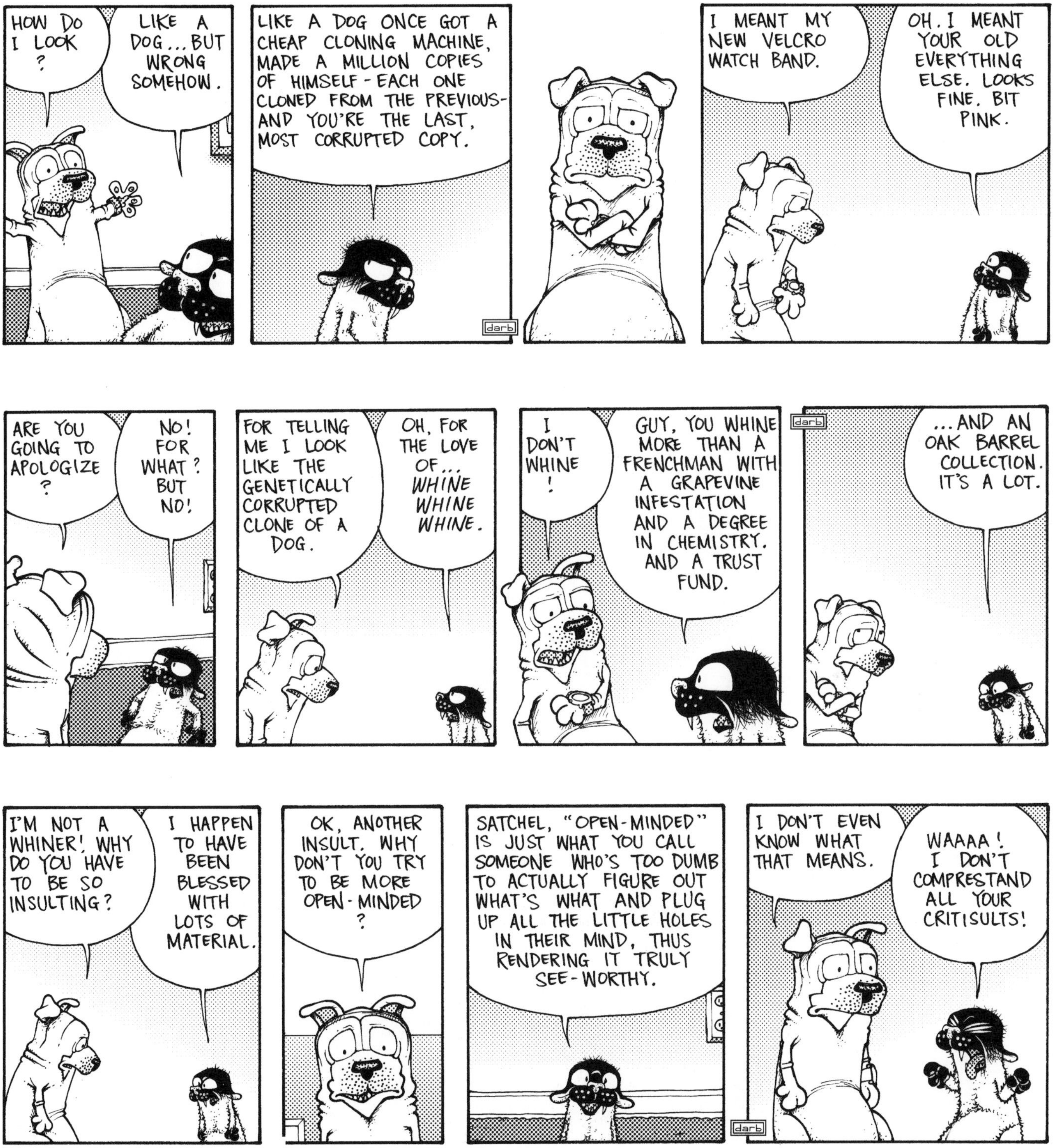
HOW DO I LOOK?
LIKE A DOG... BUT WRONG SOMEHOW.
LIKE A DOG ONCE GOT A CHEAP CLONING MACHINE, MADE A MILLION COPIES OF HIMSELF - EACH ONE CLONED FROM THE PREVIOUS - AND YOU'RE THE LAST, MOST CORRUPTED COPY.
darb
I MEANT MY NEW VELCRO WATCH BAND.
OH. I MEANT YOUR OLD EVERYTHING ELSE. LOOKS FINE. BIT PINK.
ARE YOU GOING TO APOLOGIZE?
NO! FOR WHAT? BUT NO!
FOR TELLING ME I LOOK LIKE THE GENETICALLY CORRUPTED CLONE OF A DOG.
OH, FOR THE LOVE OF... *WHINE WHINE WHINE.*
I DON'T WHINE!
GUY, YOU WHINE MORE THAN A FRENCHMAN WITH A GRAPEVINE INFESTATION AND A DEGREE IN CHEMISTRY. AND A TRUST FUND.
darb
...AND AN OAK BARREL COLLECTION. IT'S A LOT.
I'M NOT A WHINER! WHY DO YOU HAVE TO BE SO INSULTING?
I HAPPEN TO HAVE BEEN BLESSED WITH LOTS OF MATERIAL.
OK, ANOTHER INSULT. WHY DON'T YOU TRY TO BE MORE OPEN-MINDED?
SATCHEL, "OPEN-MINDED" IS JUST WHAT YOU CALL SOMEONE WHO'S TOO DUMB TO ACTUALLY FIGURE OUT WHAT'S WHAT AND PLUG UP ALL THE LITTLE HOLES IN THEIR MIND, THUS RENDERING IT TRULY SEE-WORTHY.
darb
I DON'T EVEN KNOW WHAT THAT MEANS.
WAAAA! I DON'T COMPRESTAND ALL YOUR CRITISULTS!

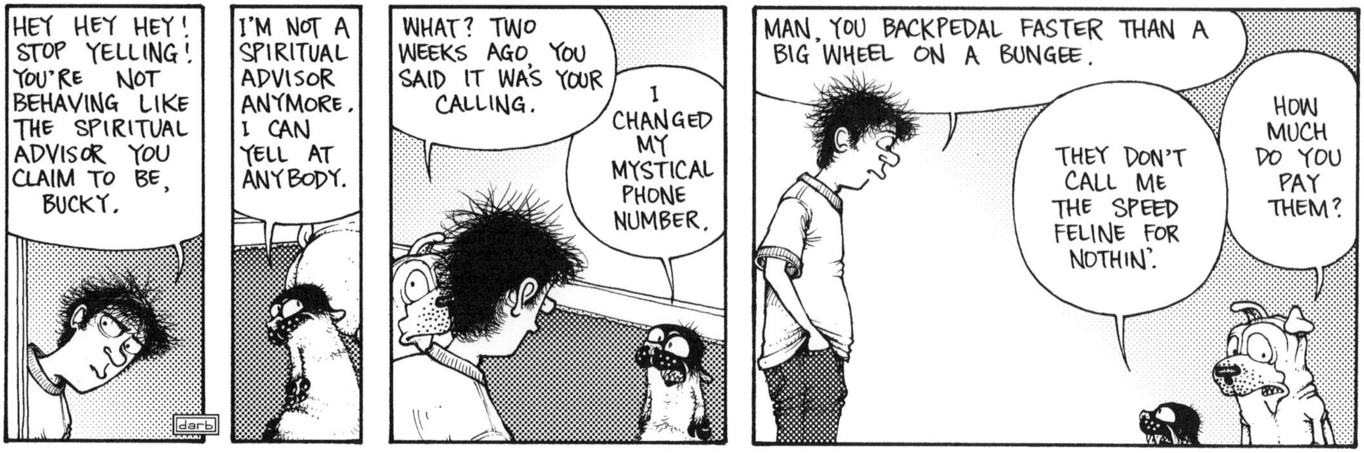
HEY HEY HEY! STOP YELLING! YOU'RE NOT BEHAVING LIKE THE SPIRITUAL ADVISOR YOU CLAIM TO BE, BUCKY.
darb
I'M NOT A SPIRITUAL ADVISOR ANYMORE. I CAN YELL AT ANYBODY.
WHAT? TWO WEEKS AGO, YOU SAID IT WAS YOUR CALLING.
I CHANGED MY MYSTICAL PHONE NUMBER.
MAN, YOU BACKPEDAL FASTER THAN A BIG WHEEL ON A BUNGEE.
THEY DON'T CALL ME THE SPEED FELINE FOR NOTHIN'.
HOW MUCH DO YOU PAY THEM?

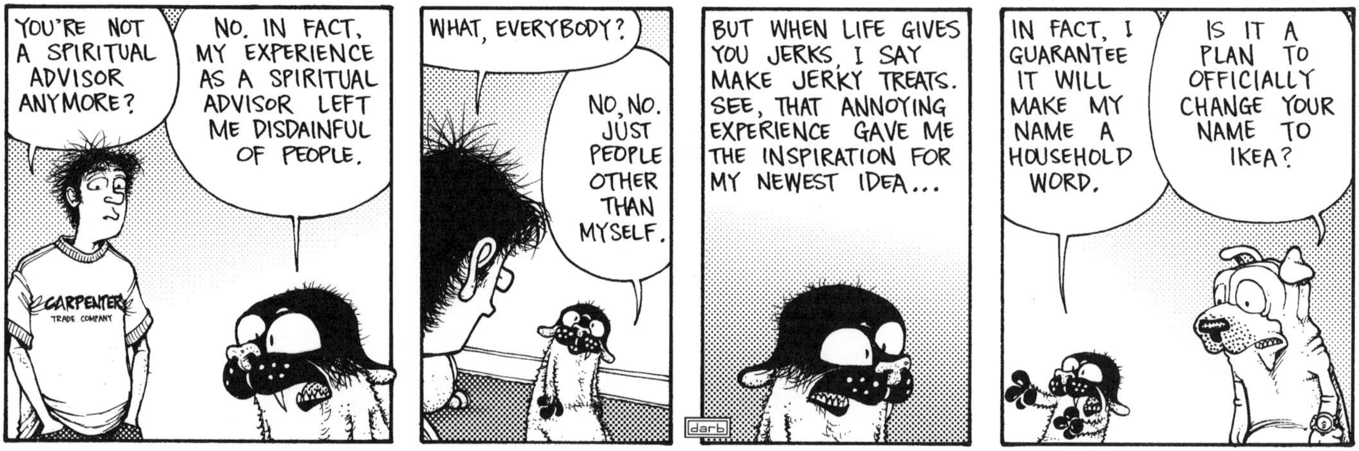
YOU'RE NOT A SPIRITUAL ADVISOR ANYMORE?
NO. IN FACT, MY EXPERIENCE AS A SPIRITUAL ADVISOR LEFT ME DISDAINFUL OF PEOPLE.
CARPENTER TRADE COMPANY
WHAT, EVERYBODY?
NO, NO. JUST PEOPLE OTHER THAN MYSELF.
BUT WHEN LIFE GIVES YOU JERKS, I SAY MAKE JERKY TREATS. SEE, THAT ANNOYING EXPERIENCE GAVE ME THE INSPIRATION FOR MY NEWEST IDEA...
darb
IN FACT, I GUARANTEE IT WILL MAKE MY NAME A HOUSEHOLD WORD.
IS IT A PLAN TO OFFICIALLY CHANGE YOUR NAME TO IKEA?

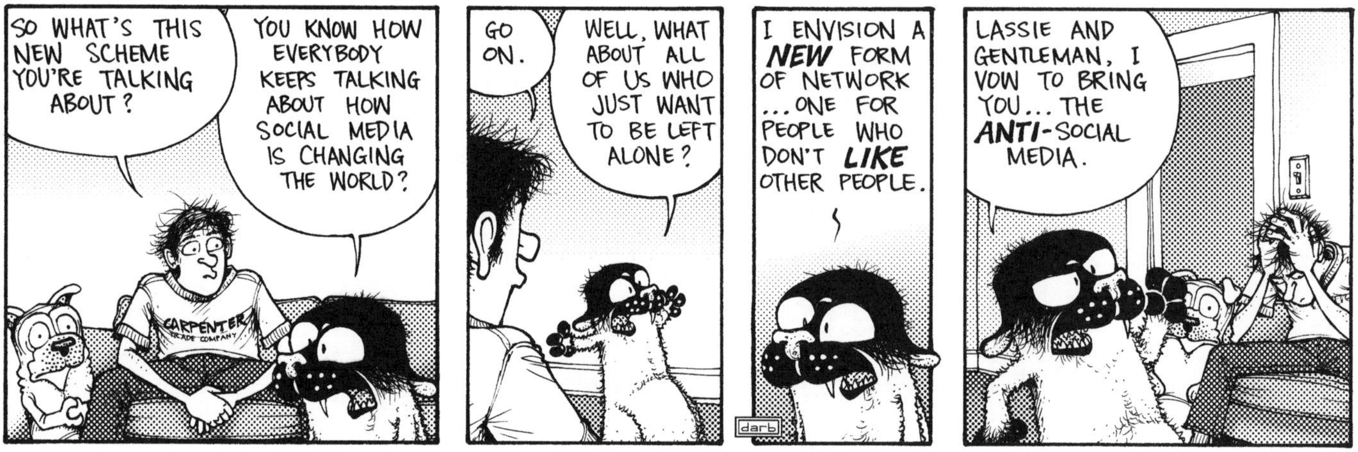
SO WHAT'S THIS NEW SCHEME YOU'RE TALKING ABOUT?
YOU KNOW HOW EVERYBODY KEEPS TALKING ABOUT HOW SOCIAL MEDIA IS CHANGING THE WORLD?
CARPENTER TRADE COMPANY
GO ON.
WELL, WHAT ABOUT ALL OF US WHO JUST WANT TO BE LEFT ALONE?
darb
I ENVISION A **NEW** FORM OF NETWORK ...ONE FOR PEOPLE WHO DON'T **LIKE** OTHER PEOPLE.
LASSIE AND GENTLEMAN, I VOW TO BRING YOU... THE **ANTI**-SOCIAL MEDIA.

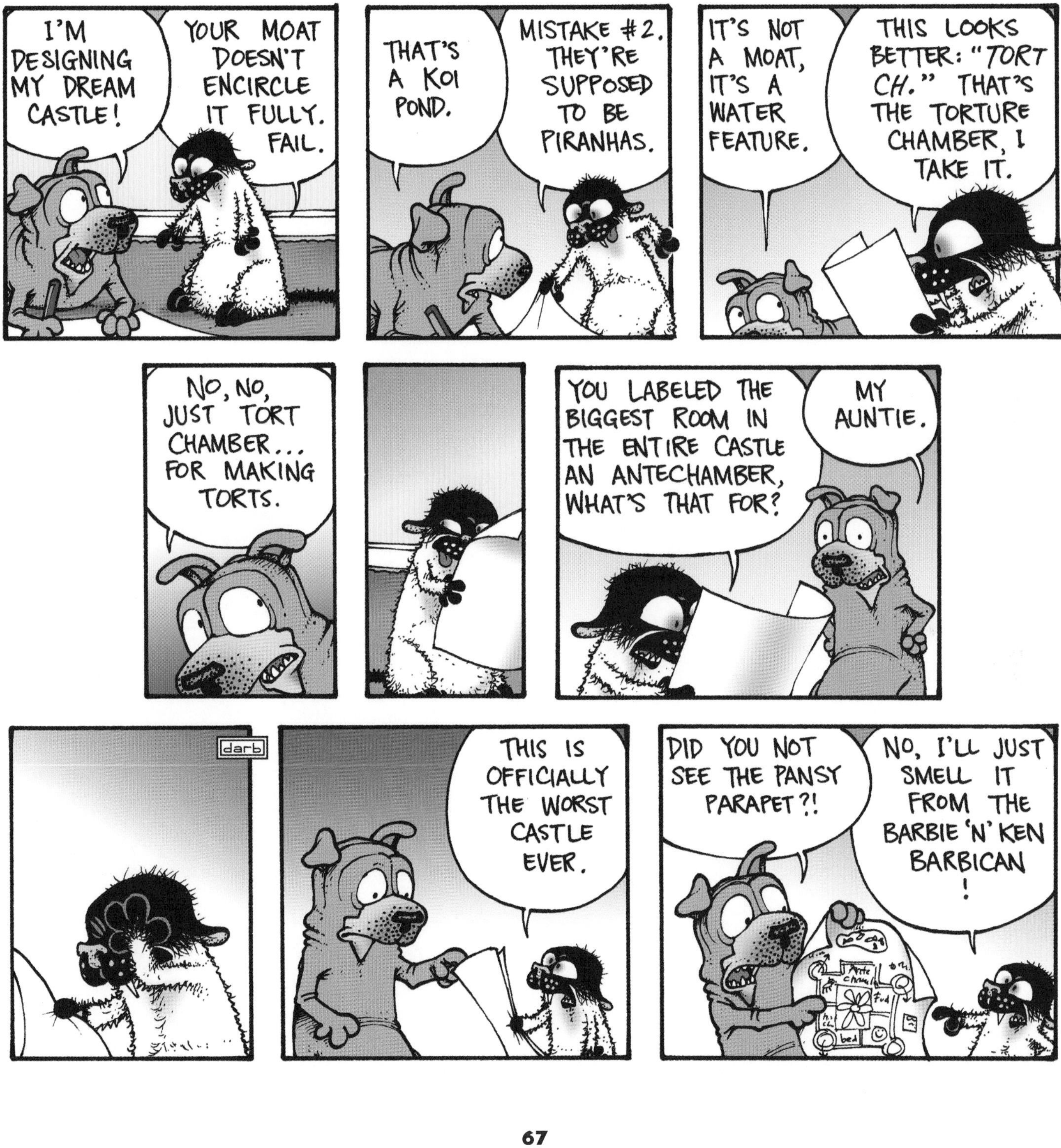
I'M DESIGNING MY DREAM CASTLE!
YOUR MOAT DOESN'T ENCIRCLE IT FULLY. FAIL.
THAT'S A KOI POND.
MISTAKE #2. THEY'RE SUPPOSED TO BE PIRANHAS.
IT'S NOT A MOAT, IT'S A WATER FEATURE.
THIS LOOKS BETTER: "TORT CH." THAT'S THE TORTURE CHAMBER, I TAKE IT.
NO, NO, JUST TORT CHAMBER... FOR MAKING TORTS.
YOU LABELED THE BIGGEST ROOM IN THE ENTIRE CASTLE AN ANTECHAMBER, WHAT'S THAT FOR?
MY AUNTIE.
darb
THIS IS OFFICIALLY THE WORST CASTLE EVER.
DID YOU NOT SEE THE PANSY PARAPET?!
NO, I'LL JUST SMELL IT FROM THE BARBIE 'N' KEN BARBICAN!

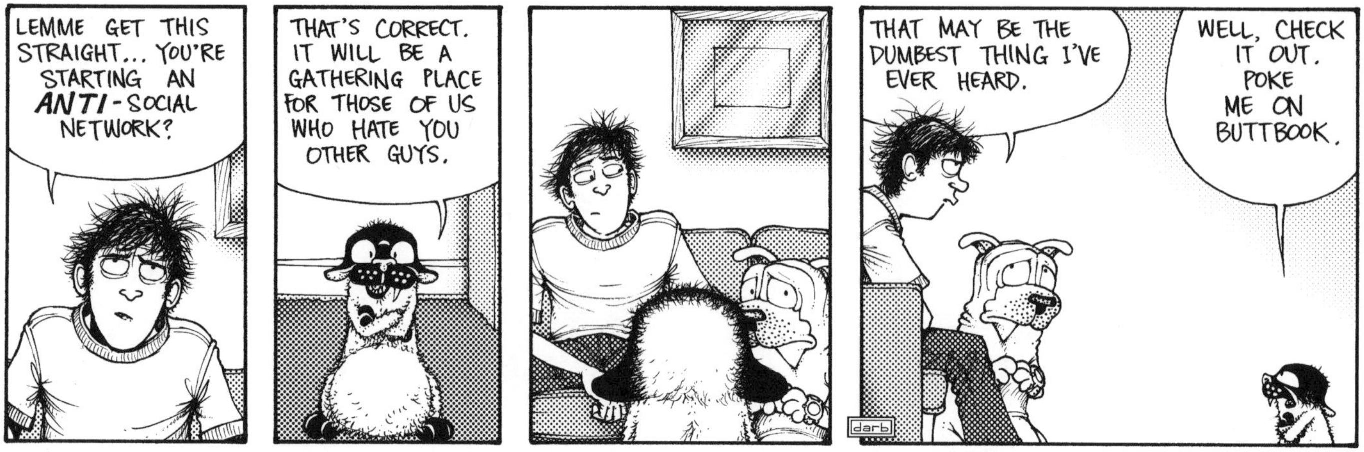
LEMME GET THIS STRAIGHT... YOU'RE STARTING AN ANTI-SOCIAL NETWORK?
THAT'S CORRECT. IT WILL BE A GATHERING PLACE FOR THOSE OF US WHO HATE YOU OTHER GUYS.
THAT MAY BE THE DUMBEST THING I'VE EVER HEARD.
WELL, CHECK IT OUT. POKE ME ON BUTTBOOK.
darb

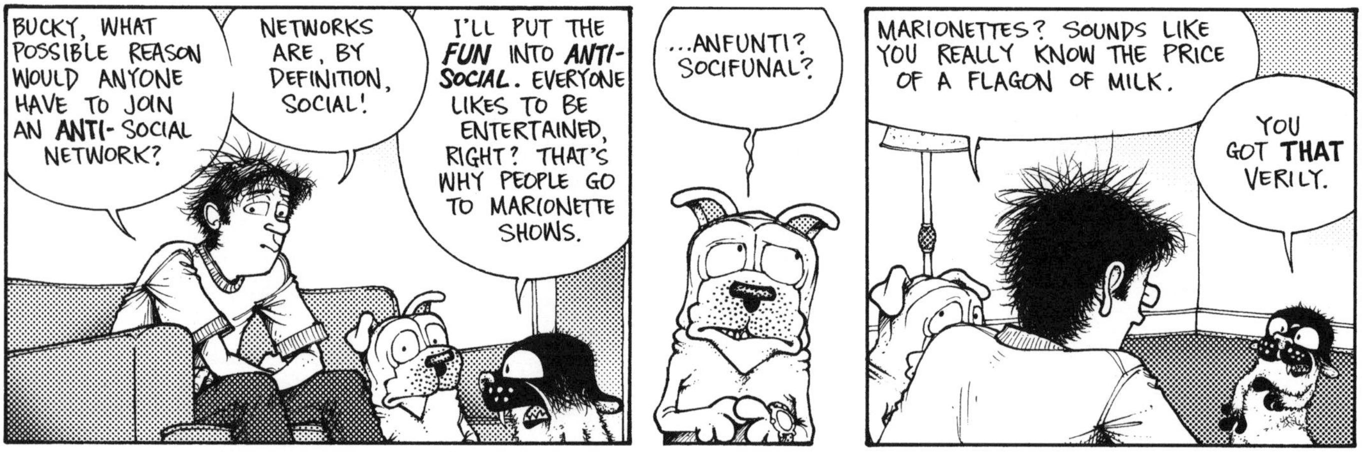
BUCKY, WHAT POSSIBLE REASON WOULD ANYONE HAVE TO JOIN AN ANTI-SOCIAL NETWORK?
NETWORKS ARE, BY DEFINITION, SOCIAL!
I'LL PUT THE FUN INTO ANTI-SOCIAL. EVERYONE LIKES TO BE ENTERTAINED, RIGHT? THAT'S WHY PEOPLE GO TO MARIONETTE SHOWS.
...ANFUNTI? SOCIFUNAL?
MARIONETTES? SOUNDS LIKE YOU REALLY KNOW THE PRICE OF A FLAGON OF MILK.
YOU GOT THAT VERILY.

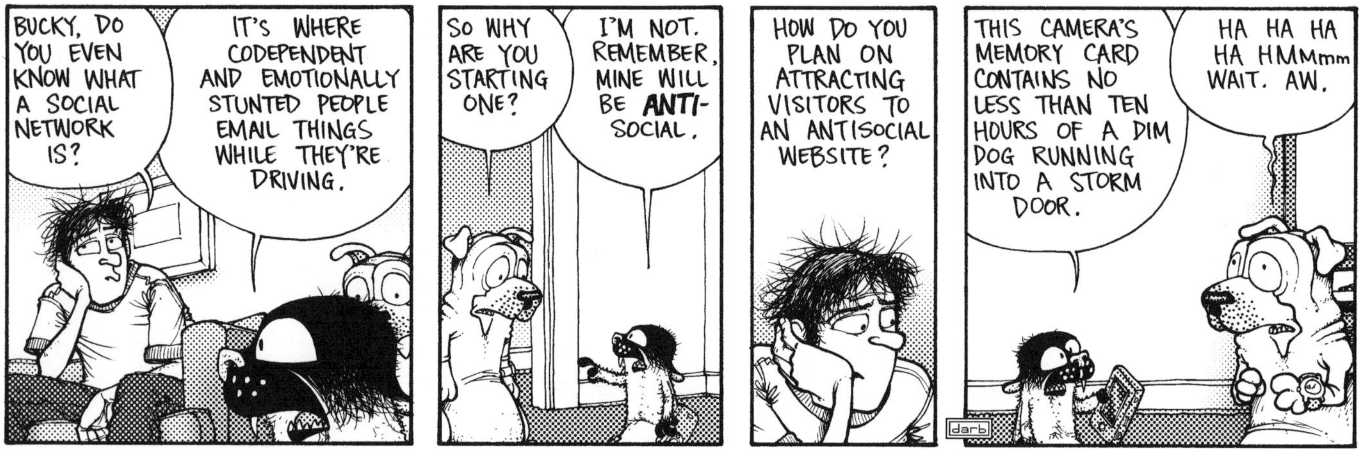
BUCKY, DO YOU EVEN KNOW WHAT A SOCIAL NETWORK IS?
IT'S WHERE CODEPENDENT AND EMOTIONALLY STUNTED PEOPLE EMAIL THINGS WHILE THEY'RE DRIVING.
SO WHY ARE YOU STARTING ONE?
I'M NOT. REMEMBER, MINE WILL BE ANTI-SOCIAL.
HOW DO YOU PLAN ON ATTRACTING VISITORS TO AN ANTISOCIAL WEBSITE?
darb
THIS CAMERA'S MEMORY CARD CONTAINS NO LESS THAN TEN HOURS OF A DIM DOG RUNNING INTO A STORM DOOR.
HA HA HA HA HMMmm WAIT. AW.

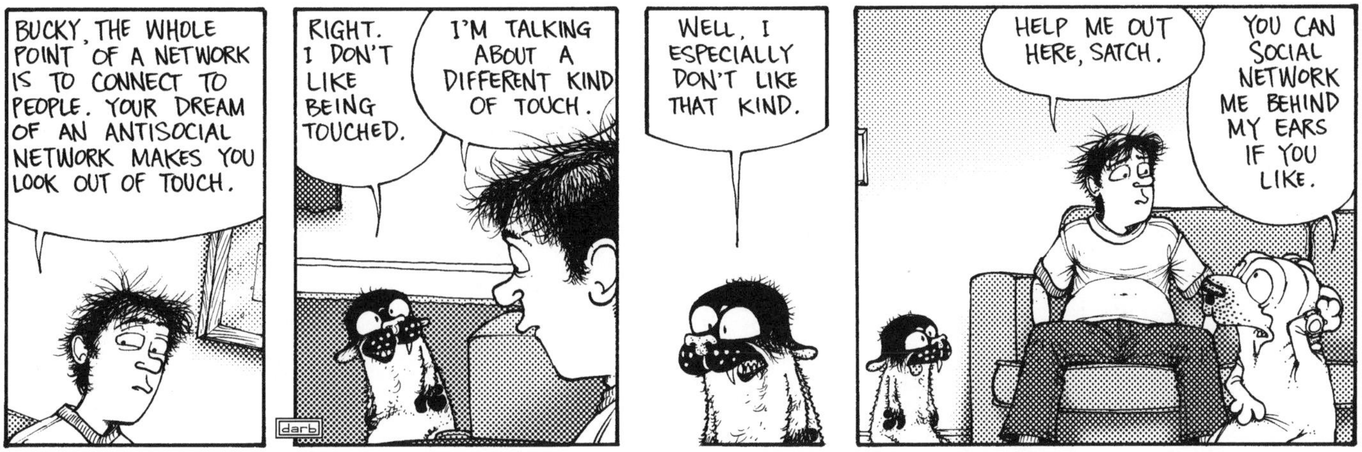
BUCKY, THE WHOLE POINT OF A NETWORK IS TO CONNECT TO PEOPLE. YOUR DREAM OF AN ANTISOCIAL NETWORK MAKES YOU LOOK OUT OF TOUCH.
RIGHT. I DON'T LIKE BEING TOUCHED.
I'M TALKING ABOUT A DIFFERENT KIND OF TOUCH.
WELL, I ESPECIALLY DON'T LIKE THAT KIND.
HELP ME OUT HERE, SATCH.
YOU CAN SOCIAL NETWORK ME BEHIND MY EARS IF YOU LIKE.

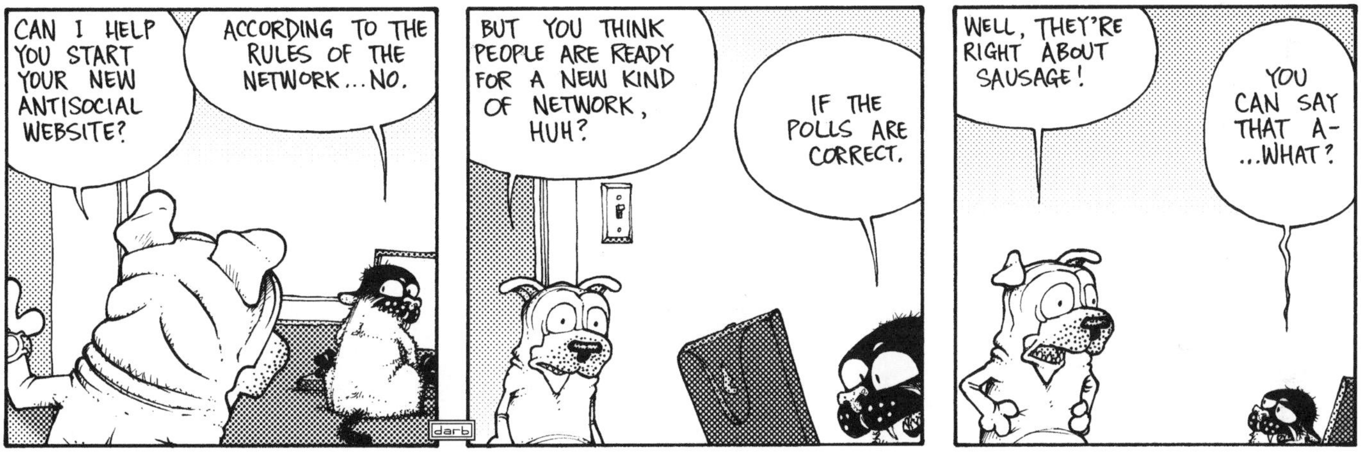
CAN I HELP YOU START YOUR NEW ANTISOCIAL WEBSITE?
ACCORDING TO THE RULES OF THE NETWORK... NO.
BUT YOU THINK PEOPLE ARE READY FOR A NEW KIND OF NETWORK, HUH?
IF THE POLLS ARE CORRECT.
WELL, THEY'RE RIGHT ABOUT SAUSAGE!
YOU CAN SAY THAT A- ...WHAT?

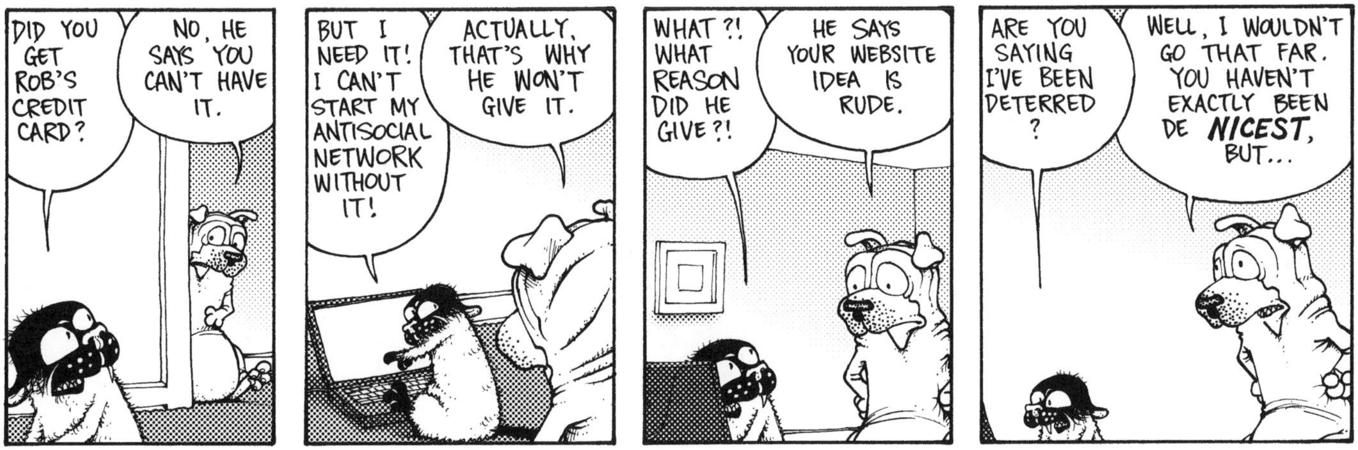
DID YOU GET ROB'S CREDIT CARD?
NO, HE SAYS YOU CAN'T HAVE IT.
BUT I NEED IT! I CAN'T START MY ANTISOCIAL NETWORK WITHOUT IT!
ACTUALLY, THAT'S WHY HE WON'T GIVE IT.
WHAT?! WHAT REASON DID HE GIVE?!
HE SAYS YOUR WEBSITE IDEA IS RUDE.
ARE YOU SAYING I'VE BEEN DETERRED?
WELL, I WOULDN'T GO THAT FAR. YOU HAVEN'T EXACTLY BEEN DE NICEST, BUT...

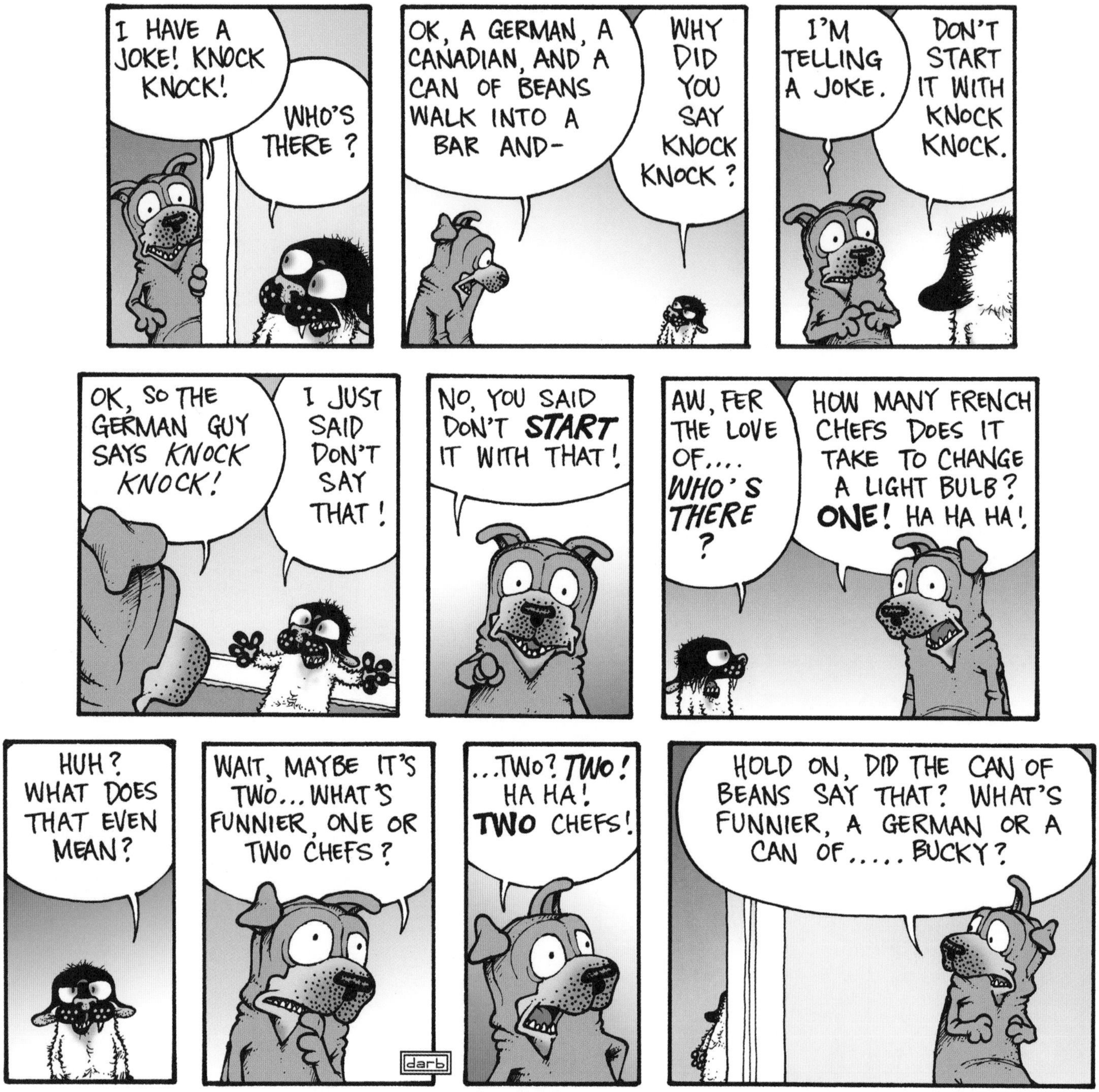
I HAVE A JOKE! KNOCK KNOCK!
WHO'S THERE?
OK, A GERMAN, A CANADIAN, AND A CAN OF BEANS WALK INTO A BAR AND-
WHY DID YOU SAY KNOCK KNOCK?
I'M TELLING A JOKE.
DON'T START IT WITH KNOCK KNOCK.
OK, SO THE GERMAN GUY SAYS KNOCK KNOCK!
I JUST SAID DON'T SAY THAT!
NO, YOU SAID DON'T START IT WITH THAT!
AW, FER THE LOVE OF.... WHO'S THERE?
HOW MANY FRENCH CHEFS DOES IT TAKE TO CHANGE A LIGHT BULB? ONE! HA HA HA!
HUH? WHAT DOES THAT EVEN MEAN?
WAIT, MAYBE IT'S TWO... WHAT'S FUNNIER, ONE OR TWO CHEFS?
darb
...TWO? TWO! HA HA! TWO CHEFS!
HOLD ON, DID THE CAN OF BEANS SAY THAT? WHAT'S FUNNIER, A GERMAN OR A CAN OF..... BUCKY?

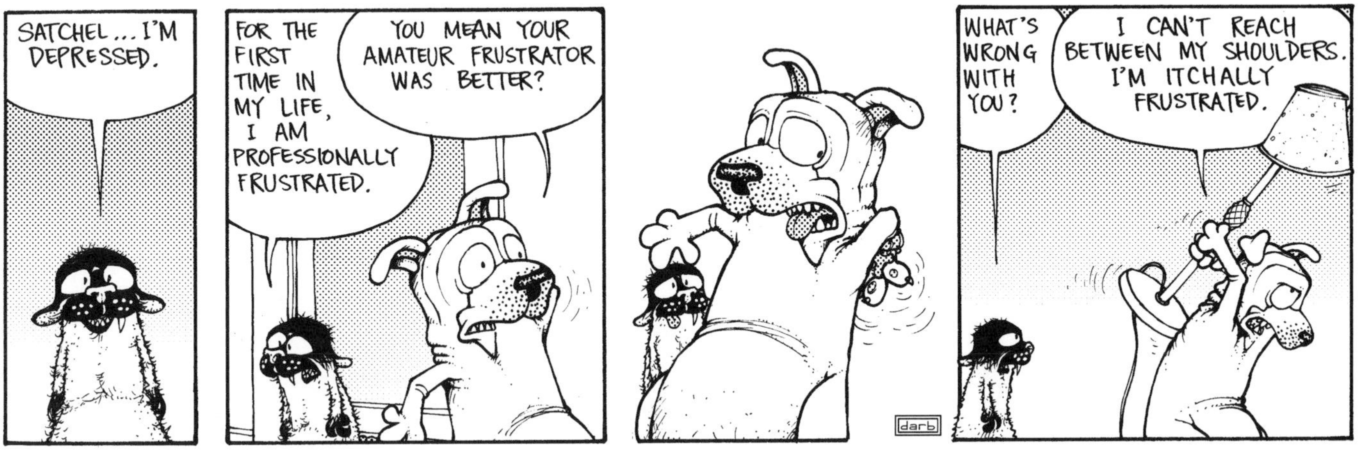
SATCHEL... I'M DEPRESSED.
FOR THE FIRST TIME IN MY LIFE, I AM PROFESSIONALLY FRUSTRATED.
YOU MEAN YOUR AMATEUR FRUSTRATOR WAS BETTER?
WHAT'S WRONG WITH YOU?
I CAN'T REACH BETWEEN MY SHOULDERS. I'M ITCHALLY FRUSTRATED.
darb

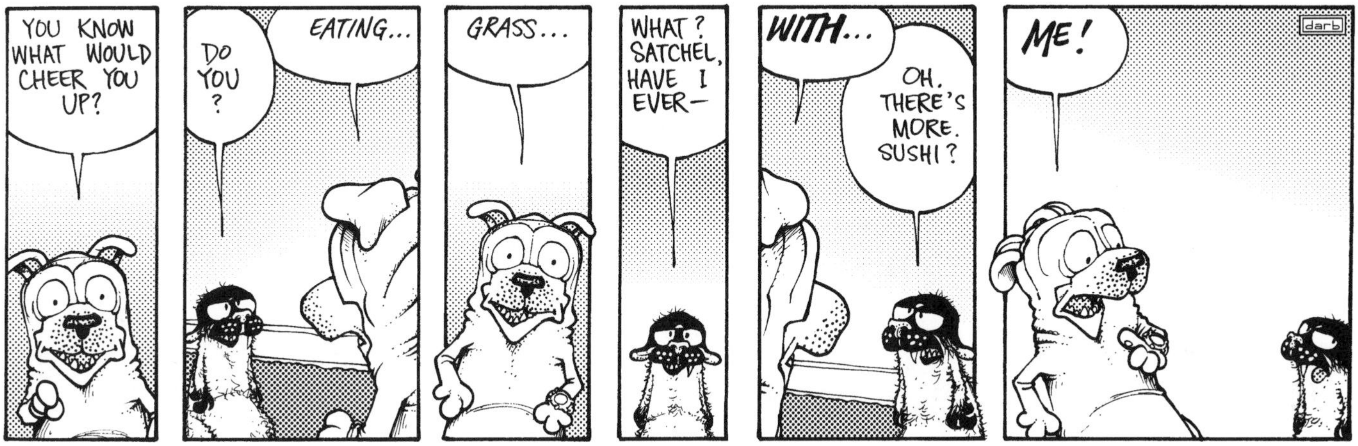
YOU KNOW WHAT WOULD CHEER YOU UP?
DO YOU ?
EATING...
GRASS...
WHAT? SATCHEL, HAVE I EVER—
WITH...
OH. THERE'S MORE. SUSHI?
ME!
darb

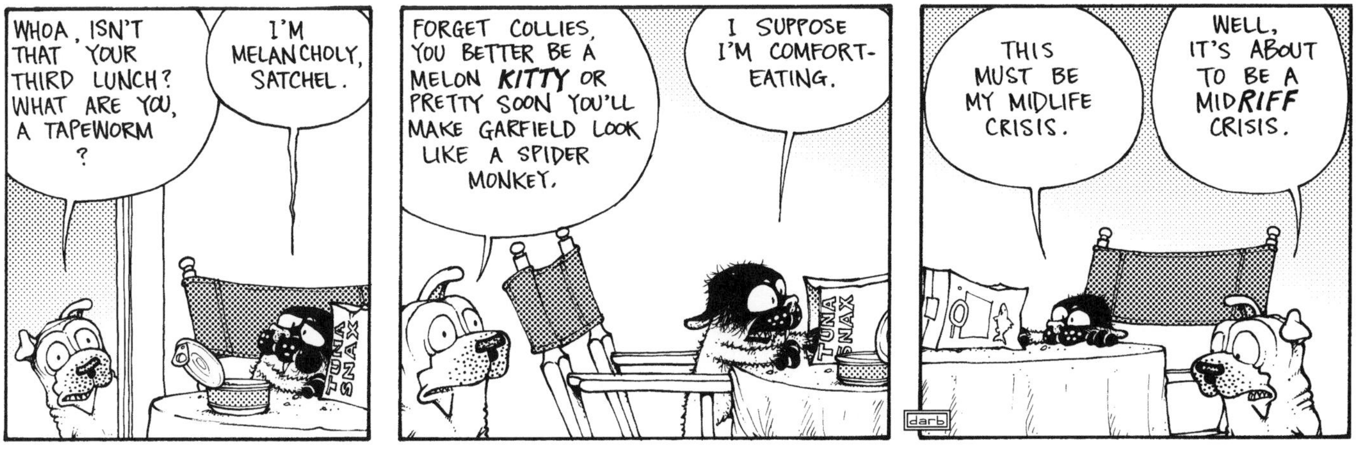
WHOA, ISN'T THAT YOUR THIRD LUNCH? WHAT ARE YOU, A TAPEWORM ?
I'M MELANCHOLY, SATCHEL.
FORGET COLLIES, YOU BETTER BE A MELON KITTY OR PRETTY SOON YOU'LL MAKE GARFIELD LOOK LIKE A SPIDER MONKEY.
I SUPPOSE I'M COMFORT-EATING.
TUNA SNAX
darb
THIS MUST BE MY MIDLIFE CRISIS.
WELL, IT'S ABOUT TO BE A MIDRIFF CRISIS.

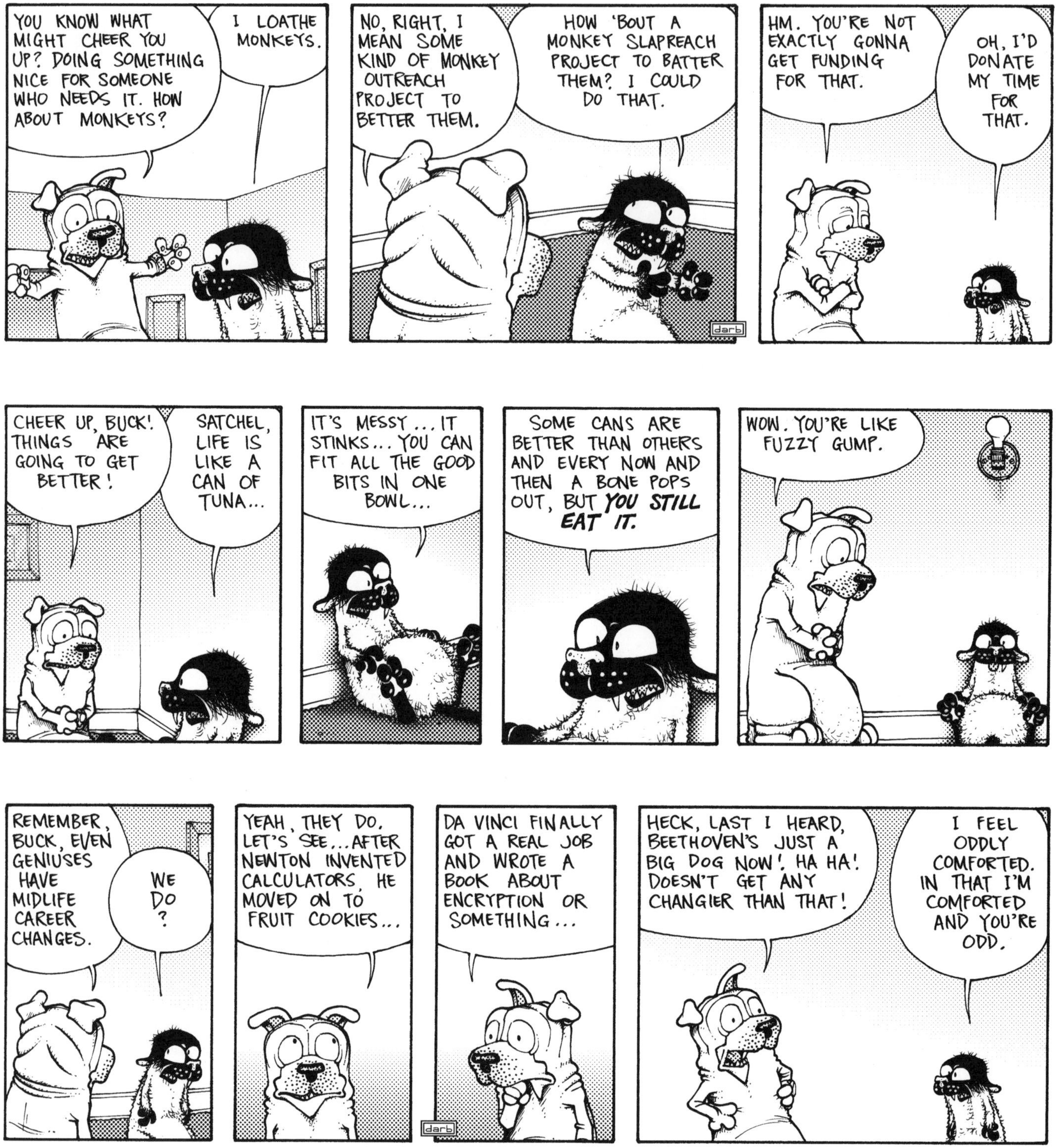
YOU KNOW WHAT MIGHT CHEER YOU UP? DOING SOMETHING NICE FOR SOMEONE WHO NEEDS IT. HOW ABOUT MONKEYS?
I LOATHE MONKEYS.
NO, RIGHT, I MEAN SOME KIND OF MONKEY OUTREACH PROJECT TO BETTER THEM.
HOW 'BOUT A MONKEY SLAPREACH PROJECT TO BATTER THEM? I COULD DO THAT.
HM. YOU'RE NOT EXACTLY GONNA GET FUNDING FOR THAT.
OH, I'D DONATE MY TIME FOR THAT.
CHEER UP, BUCK! THINGS ARE GOING TO GET BETTER!
SATCHEL, LIFE IS LIKE A CAN OF TUNA...
IT'S MESSY ... IT STINKS... YOU CAN FIT ALL THE GOOD BITS IN ONE BOWL...
SOME CANS ARE BETTER THAN OTHERS AND EVERY NOW AND THEN A BONE POPS OUT, BUT YOU STILL EAT IT.
WOW. YOU'RE LIKE FUZZY GUMP.
REMEMBER, BUCK, EVEN GENIUSES HAVE MIDLIFE CAREER CHANGES.
WE DO?
YEAH, THEY DO. LET'S SEE... AFTER NEWTON INVENTED CALCULATORS, HE MOVED ON TO FRUIT COOKIES...
DA VINCI FINALLY GOT A REAL JOB AND WROTE A BOOK ABOUT ENCRYPTION OR SOMETHING...
HECK, LAST I HEARD, BEETHOVEN'S JUST A BIG DOG NOW! HA HA! DOESN'T GET ANY CHANGIER THAN THAT!
I FEEL ODDLY COMFORTED. IN THAT I'M COMFORTED AND YOU'RE ODD.

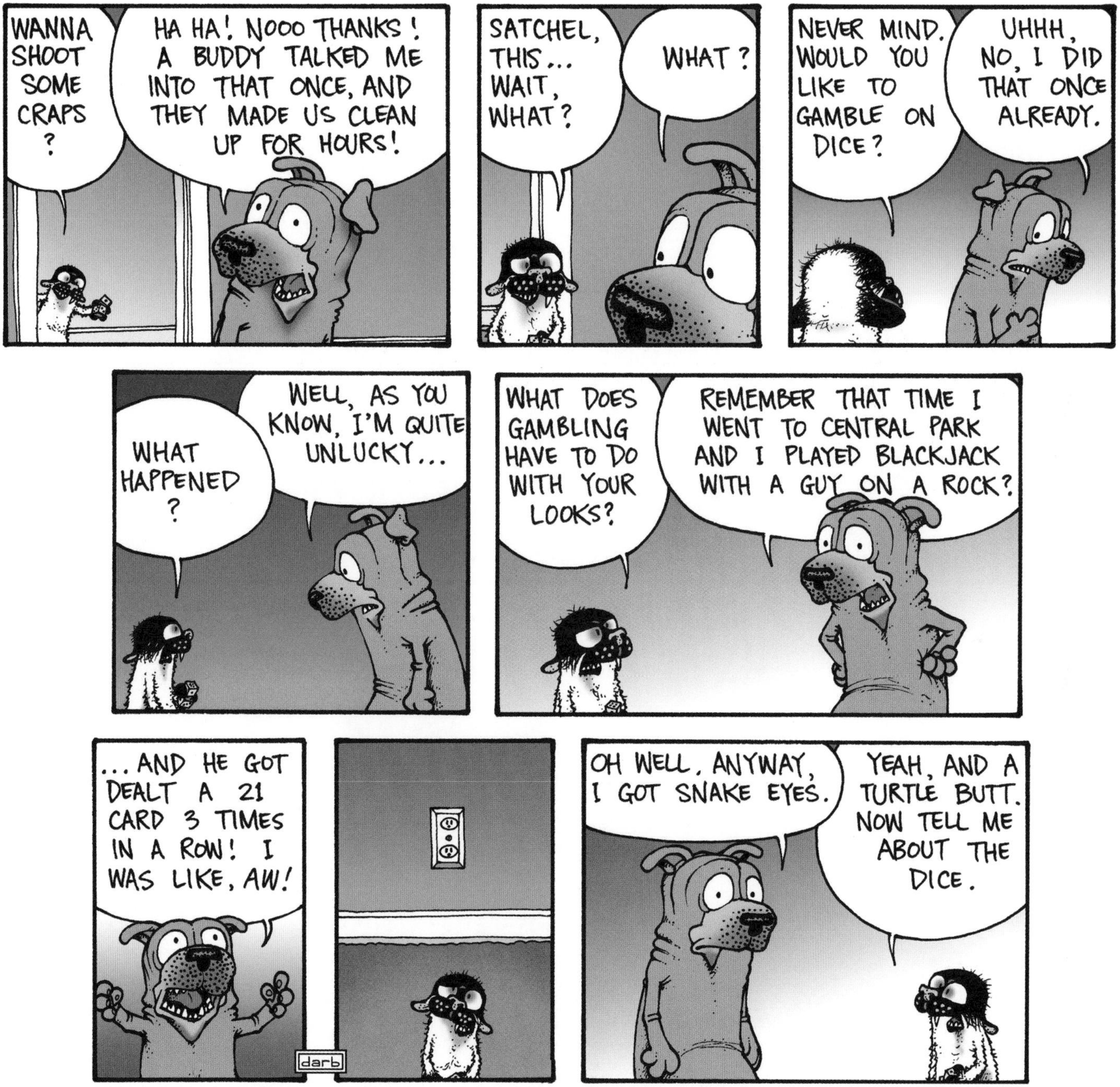
WANNA SHOOT SOME CRAPS ?
HA HA! NOOO THANKS! A BUDDY TALKED ME INTO THAT ONCE, AND THEY MADE US CLEAN UP FOR HOURS!
SATCHEL, THIS... WAIT, WHAT?
WHAT?
NEVER MIND. WOULD YOU LIKE TO GAMBLE ON DICE?
UHHH, NO, I DID THAT ONCE ALREADY.
WHAT HAPPENED ?
WELL, AS YOU KNOW, I'M QUITE UNLUCKY...
WHAT DOES GAMBLING HAVE TO DO WITH YOUR LOOKS?
REMEMBER THAT TIME I WENT TO CENTRAL PARK AND I PLAYED BLACKJACK WITH A GUY ON A ROCK?
...AND HE GOT DEALT A 21 CARD 3 TIMES IN A ROW! I WAS LIKE, AW!
darb
OH WELL, ANYWAY, I GOT SNAKE EYES.
YEAH, AND A TURTLE BUTT. NOW TELL ME ABOUT THE DICE.

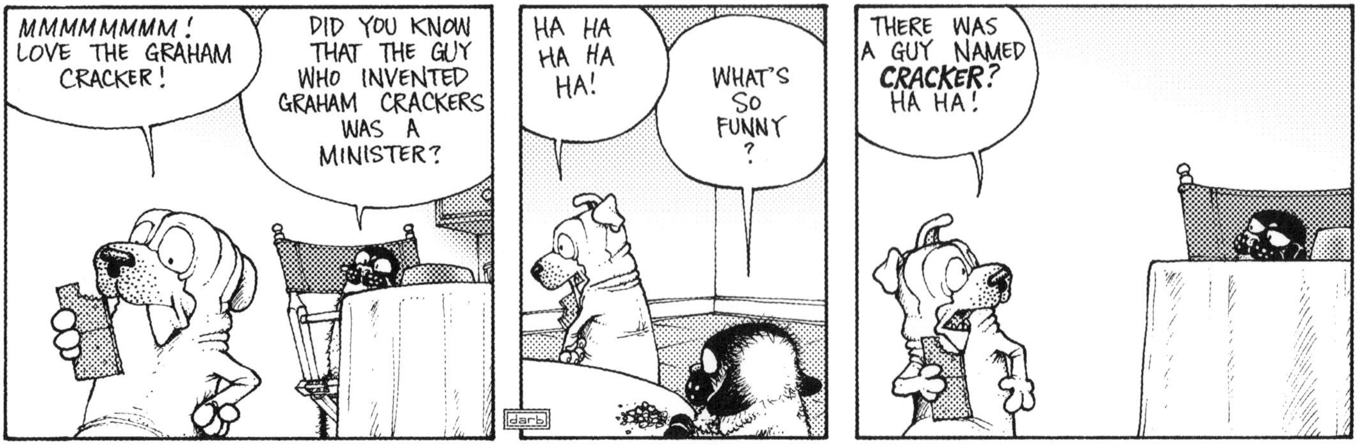
MMMMMMMM! LOVE THE GRAHAM CRACKER!
DID YOU KNOW THAT THE GUY WHO INVENTED GRAHAM CRACKERS WAS A MINISTER?
HA HA HA HA HA!
WHAT'S SO FUNNY?
THERE WAS A GUY NAMED **CRACKER?** HA HA!
darb

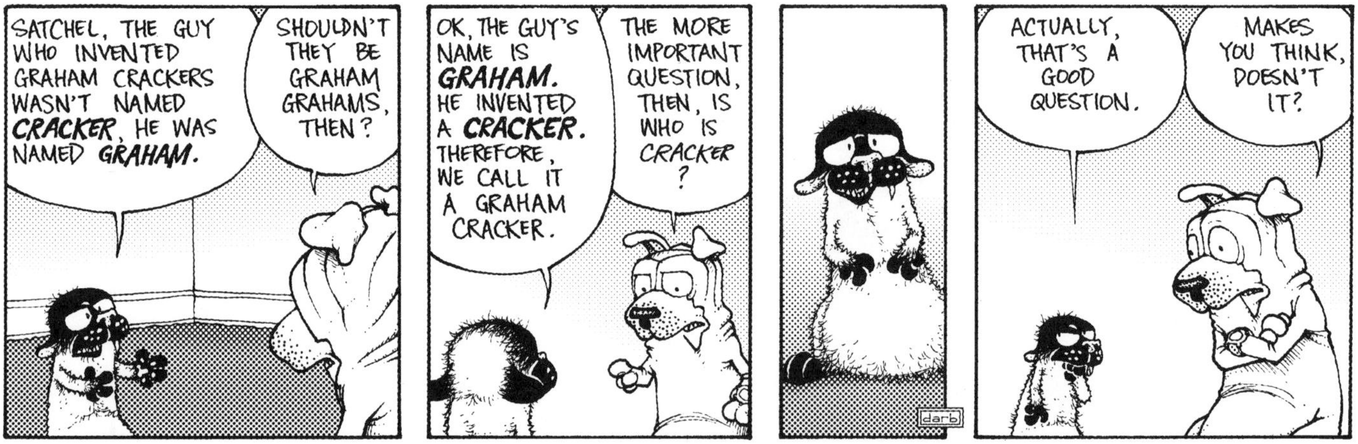
SATCHEL, THE GUY WHO INVENTED GRAHAM CRACKERS WASN'T NAMED ***CRACKER***, HE WAS NAMED ***GRAHAM.***
SHOULDN'T THEY BE GRAHAM GRAHAMS, THEN?
OK, THE GUY'S NAME IS ***GRAHAM.*** HE INVENTED A ***CRACKER.*** THEREFORE, WE CALL IT A GRAHAM CRACKER.
THE MORE IMPORTANT QUESTION, THEN, IS WHO IS *CRACKER*?
ACTUALLY, THAT'S A GOOD QUESTION.
MAKES YOU THINK, DOESN'T IT?
darb

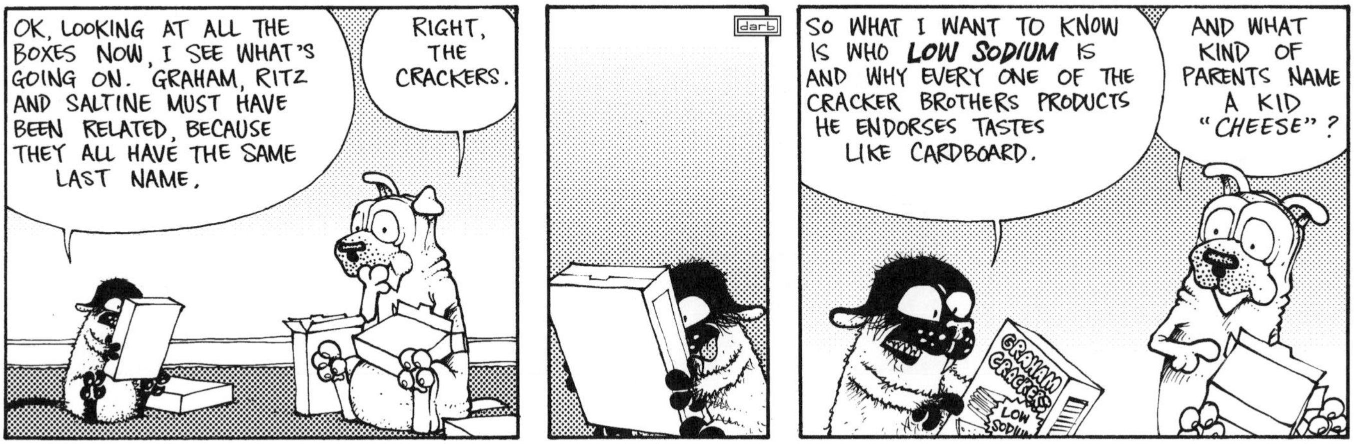
OK, LOOKING AT ALL THE BOXES NOW, I SEE WHAT'S GOING ON. GRAHAM, RITZ AND SALTINE MUST HAVE BEEN RELATED, BECAUSE THEY ALL HAVE THE SAME LAST NAME.
RIGHT, THE CRACKERS.
SO WHAT I WANT TO KNOW IS WHO ***LOW SODIUM*** IS AND WHY EVERY ONE OF THE CRACKER BROTHERS PRODUCTS HE ENDORSES TASTES LIKE CARDBOARD.
AND WHAT KIND OF PARENTS NAME A KID "*CHEESE*"?
GRAHAM CRACKERS
LOW SODIUM
darb

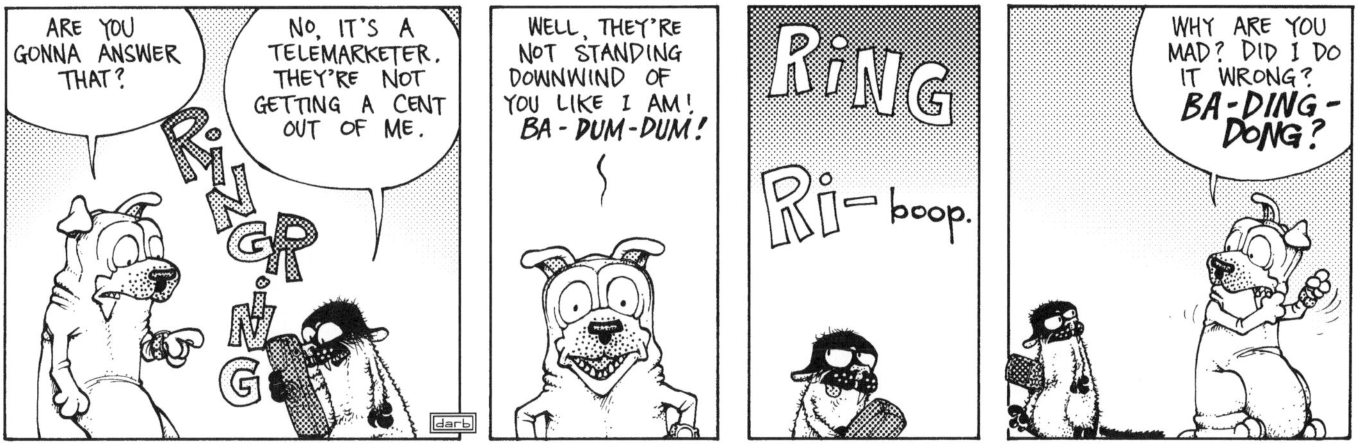
ARE YOU GONNA ANSWER THAT?
RING RING RING
NO, IT'S A TELEMARKETER. THEY'RE NOT GETTING A CENT OUT OF ME.
darb
WELL, THEY'RE NOT STANDING DOWNWIND OF YOU LIKE I AM! BA-DUM-DUM!
RING
RI- boop.
WHY ARE YOU MAD? DID I DO IT WRONG? BA-DING-DONG?

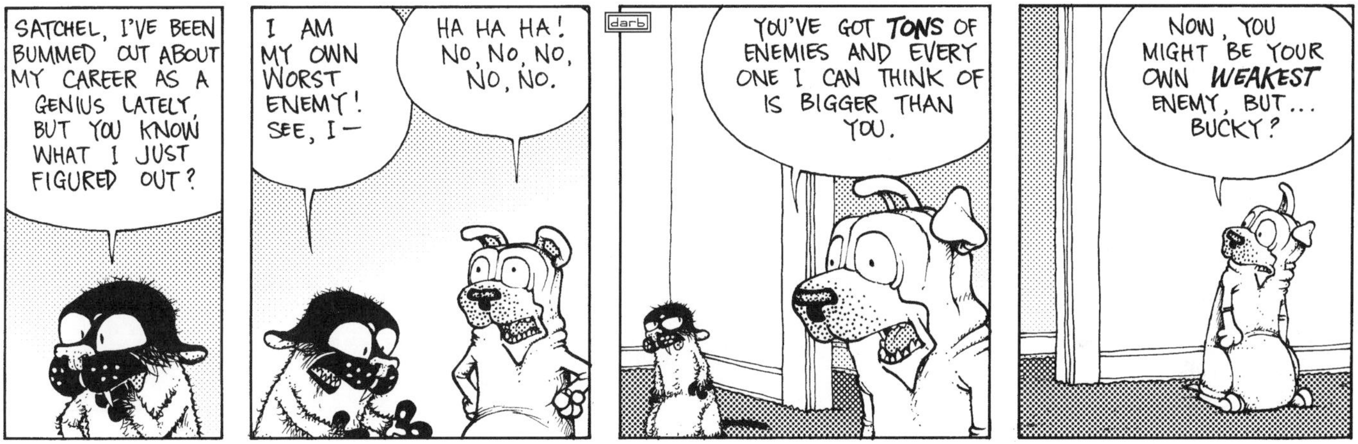
SATCHEL, I'VE BEEN BUMMED OUT ABOUT MY CAREER AS A GENIUS LATELY, BUT YOU KNOW WHAT I JUST FIGURED OUT?
I AM MY OWN WORST ENEMY! SEE, I—
HA HA HA! NO, NO, NO, NO, NO.
darb
YOU'VE GOT TONS OF ENEMIES AND EVERY ONE I CAN THINK OF IS BIGGER THAN YOU.
NOW, YOU MIGHT BE YOUR OWN WEAKEST ENEMY, BUT... BUCKY?

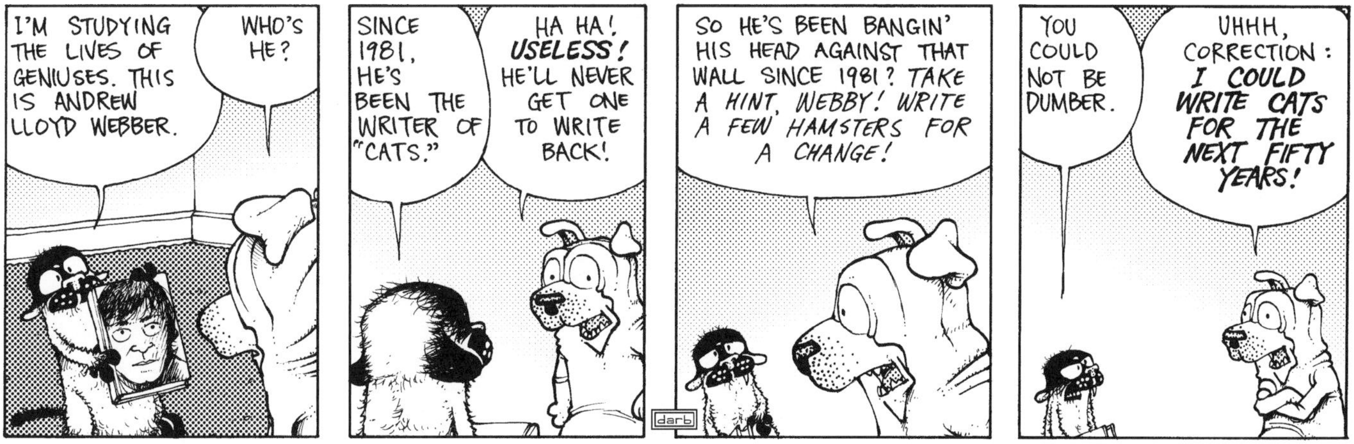
I'M STUDYING THE LIVES OF GENIUSES. THIS IS ANDREW LLOYD WEBBER.
WHO'S HE?
SINCE 1981, HE'S BEEN THE WRITER OF "CATS."
HA HA! USELESS! HE'LL NEVER GET ONE TO WRITE BACK!
darb
SO HE'S BEEN BANGIN' HIS HEAD AGAINST THAT WALL SINCE 1981? TAKE A HINT, WEBBY! WRITE A FEW HAMSTERS FOR A CHANGE!
YOU COULD NOT BE DUMBER.
UHHH, CORRECTION: I COULD WRITE CATS FOR THE NEXT FIFTY YEARS!

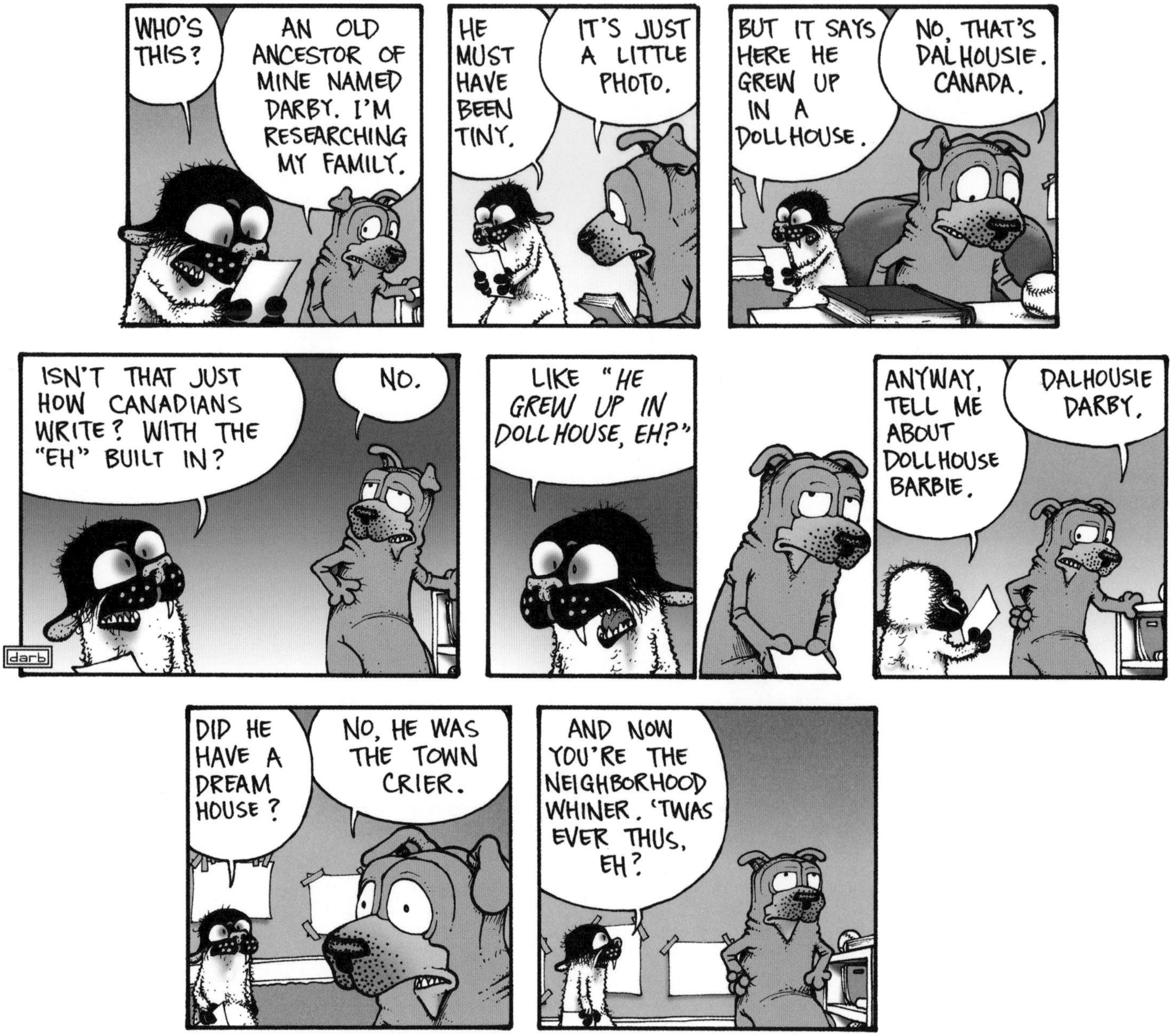
WHO'S THIS?
AN OLD ANCESTOR OF MINE NAMED DARBY. I'M RESEARCHING MY FAMILY.
HE MUST HAVE BEEN TINY.
IT'S JUST A LITTLE PHOTO.
BUT IT SAYS HERE HE GREW UP IN A DOLLHOUSE.
NO, THAT'S DALHOUSIE. CANADA.
ISN'T THAT JUST HOW CANADIANS WRITE? WITH THE "EH" BUILT IN?
NO.
darb
LIKE "HE GREW UP IN DOLLHOUSE, EH?"
ANYWAY, TELL ME ABOUT DOLLHOUSE BARBIE.
DALHOUSIE DARBY.
DID HE HAVE A DREAM HOUSE?
NO, HE WAS THE TOWN CRIER.
AND NOW YOU'RE THE NEIGHBORHOOD WHINER. 'TWAS EVER THUS, EH?

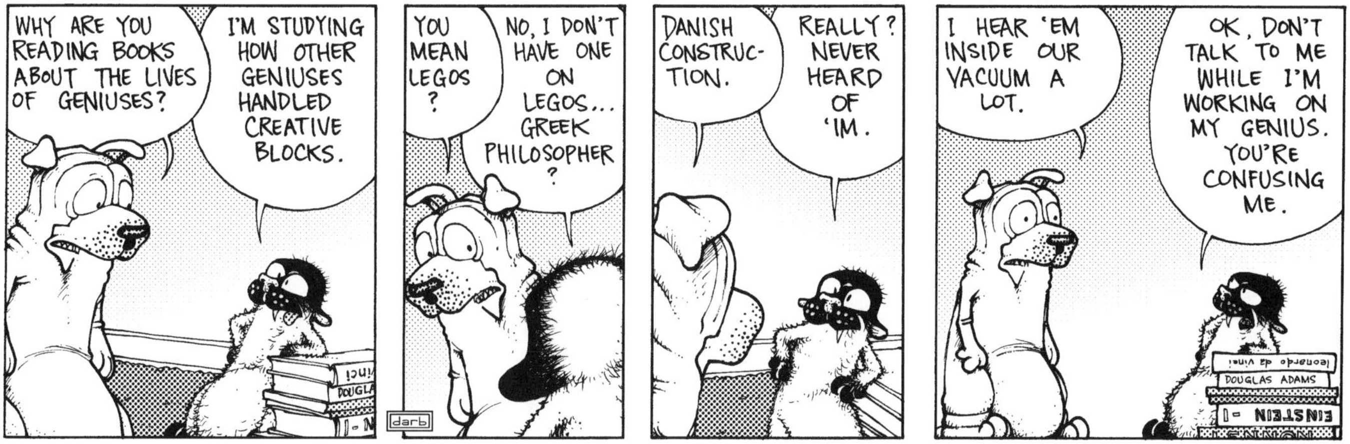
WHY ARE YOU READING BOOKS ABOUT THE LIVES OF GENIUSES?
I'M STUDYING HOW OTHER GENIUSES HANDLED CREATIVE BLOCKS.
YOU MEAN LEGOS?
NO, I DON'T HAVE ONE ON LEGOS... GREEK PHILOSOPHER?
DANISH CONSTRUCTION.
REALLY? NEVER HEARD OF 'IM.
I HEAR 'EM INSIDE OUR VACUUM A LOT.
OK, DON'T TALK TO ME WHILE I'M WORKING ON MY GENIUS. YOU'RE CONFUSING ME.
leonardo da vinci
DOUGLAS ADAMS
EINSTEIN

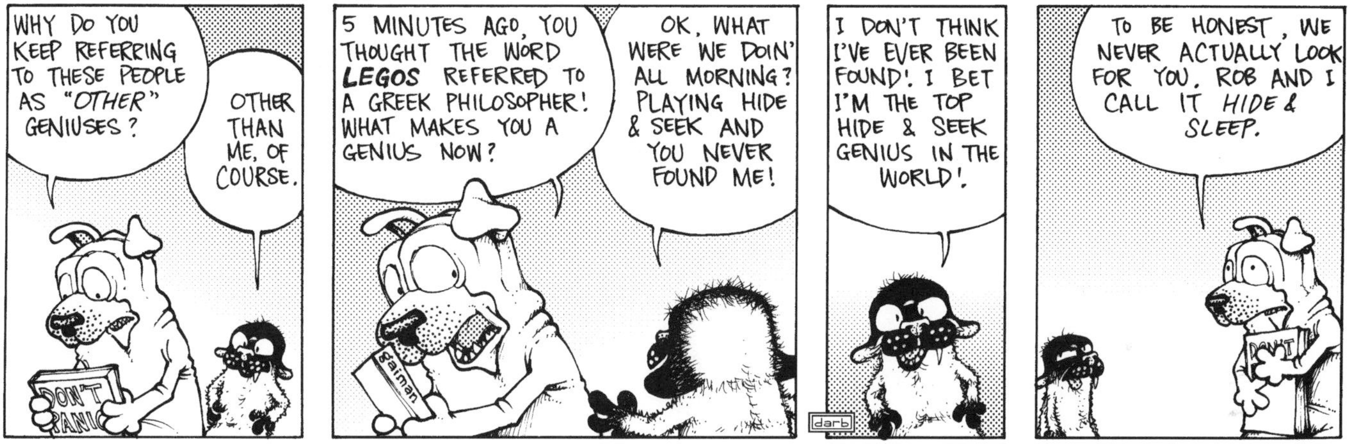
WHY DO YOU KEEP REFERRING TO THESE PEOPLE AS "OTHER" GENIUSES?
OTHER THAN ME, OF COURSE.
5 MINUTES AGO, YOU THOUGHT THE WORD **LEGOS** REFERRED TO A GREEK PHILOSOPHER! WHAT MAKES YOU A GENIUS NOW?
OK, WHAT WERE WE DOIN' ALL MORNING? PLAYING HIDE & SEEK AND YOU NEVER FOUND ME!
I DON'T THINK I'VE EVER BEEN FOUND! I BET I'M THE TOP HIDE & SEEK GENIUS IN THE WORLD!
TO BE HONEST, WE NEVER ACTUALLY LOOK FOR YOU. ROB AND I CALL IT *HIDE & SLEEP*.

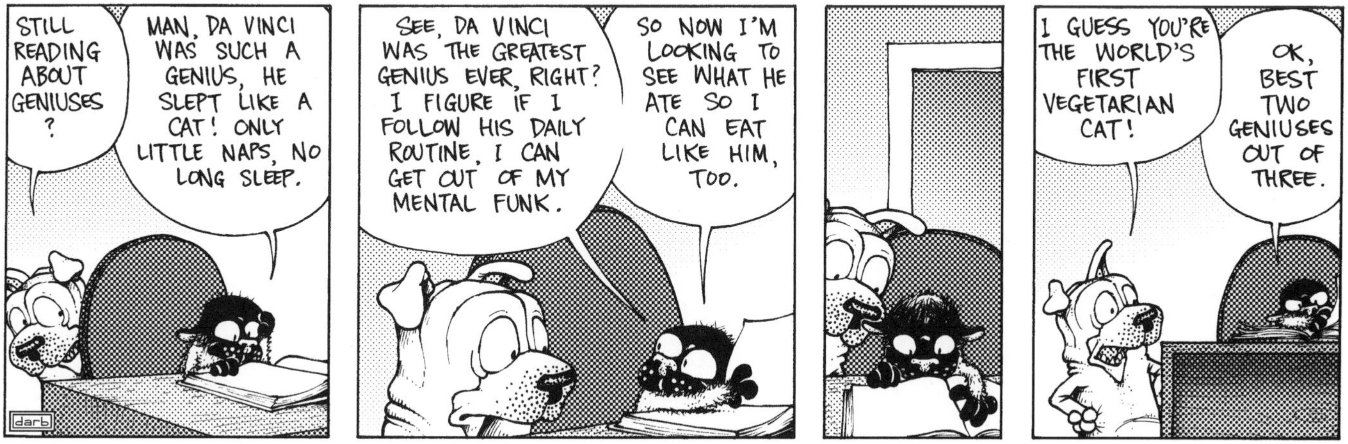
STILL READING ABOUT GENIUSES?
MAN, DA VINCI WAS SUCH A GENIUS, HE SLEPT LIKE A CAT! ONLY LITTLE NAPS, NO LONG SLEEP.
SEE, DA VINCI WAS THE GREATEST GENIUS EVER, RIGHT? I FIGURE IF I FOLLOW HIS DAILY ROUTINE, I CAN GET OUT OF MY MENTAL FUNK.
SO NOW I'M LOOKING TO SEE WHAT HE ATE SO I CAN EAT LIKE HIM, TOO.
I GUESS YOU'RE THE WORLD'S FIRST VEGETARIAN CAT!
OK, BEST TWO GENIUSES OUT OF THREE.

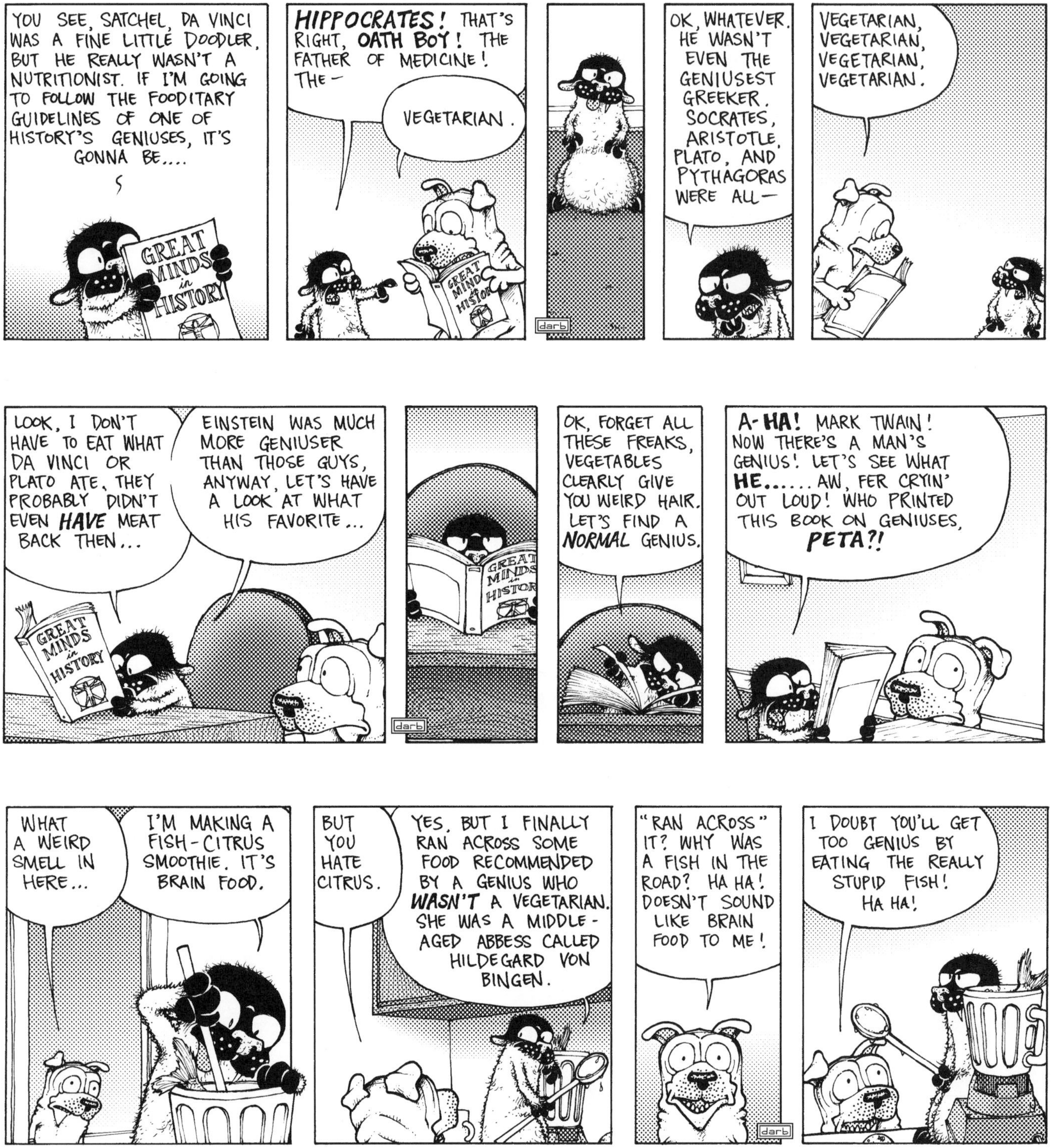
YOU SEE, SATCHEL, DA VINCI WAS A FINE LITTLE DOODLER, BUT HE REALLY WASN'T A NUTRITIONIST. IF I'M GOING TO FOLLOW THE FOODITARY GUIDELINES OF ONE OF HISTORY'S GENIUSES, IT'S GONNA BE....
GREAT MINDS in HISTORY
HIPPOCRATES! THAT'S RIGHT, OATH BOY! THE FATHER OF MEDICINE! THE—
VEGETARIAN.
darb
OK, WHATEVER. HE WASN'T EVEN THE GENIUSEST GREEKER. SOCRATES, ARISTOTLE, PLATO, AND PYTHAGORAS WERE ALL—
VEGETARIAN, VEGETARIAN, VEGETARIAN, VEGETARIAN.
LOOK, I DON'T HAVE TO EAT WHAT DA VINCI OR PLATO ATE. THEY PROBABLY DIDN'T EVEN HAVE MEAT BACK THEN...
EINSTEIN WAS MUCH MORE GENIUSER THAN THOSE GUYS, ANYWAY. LET'S HAVE A LOOK AT WHAT HIS FAVORITE...
darb
OK, FORGET ALL THESE FREAKS. VEGETABLES CLEARLY GIVE YOU WEIRD HAIR. LET'S FIND A NORMAL GENIUS.
A-HA! MARK TWAIN! NOW THERE'S A MAN'S GENIUS! LET'S SEE WHAT HE...... AW, FER CRYIN' OUT LOUD! WHO PRINTED THIS BOOK ON GENIUSES, PETA?!
WHAT A WEIRD SMELL IN HERE...
I'M MAKING A FISH-CITRUS SMOOTHIE. IT'S BRAIN FOOD.
BUT YOU HATE CITRUS.
YES, BUT I FINALLY RAN ACROSS SOME FOOD RECOMMENDED BY A GENIUS WHO WASN'T A VEGETARIAN. SHE WAS A MIDDLE-AGED ABBESS CALLED HILDEGARD VON BINGEN.
"RAN ACROSS" IT? WHY WAS A FISH IN THE ROAD? HA HA! DOESN'T SOUND LIKE BRAIN FOOD TO ME!
darb
I DOUBT YOU'LL GET TOO GENIUS BY EATING THE REALLY STUPID FISH! HA HA!

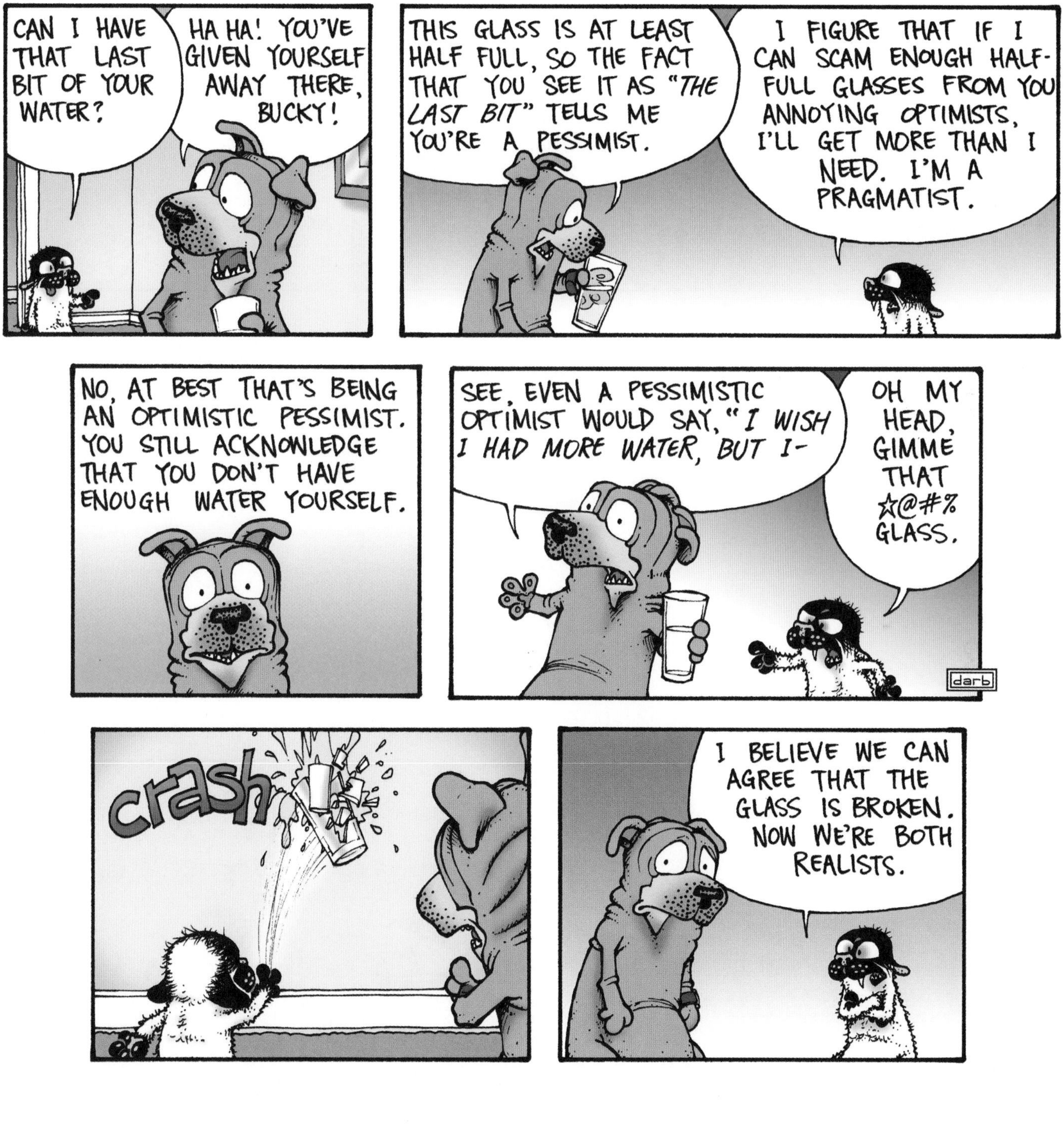
CAN I HAVE THAT LAST BIT OF YOUR WATER?
HA HA! YOU'VE GIVEN YOURSELF AWAY THERE, BUCKY!
THIS GLASS IS AT LEAST HALF FULL, SO THE FACT THAT YOU SEE IT AS "*THE LAST BIT*" TELLS ME YOU'RE A PESSIMIST.
I FIGURE THAT IF I CAN SCAM ENOUGH HALF-FULL GLASSES FROM YOU ANNOYING OPTIMISTS, I'LL GET MORE THAN I NEED. I'M A PRAGMATIST.
NO, AT BEST THAT'S BEING AN OPTIMISTIC PESSIMIST. YOU STILL ACKNOWLEDGE THAT YOU DON'T HAVE ENOUGH WATER YOURSELF.
SEE, EVEN A PESSIMISTIC OPTIMIST WOULD SAY, "*I WISH I HAD MORE WATER, BUT I-*
OH MY HEAD, GIMME THAT ☆@#% GLASS.
darb
crash
I BELIEVE WE CAN AGREE THAT THE GLASS IS BROKEN. NOW WE'RE BOTH REALISTS.

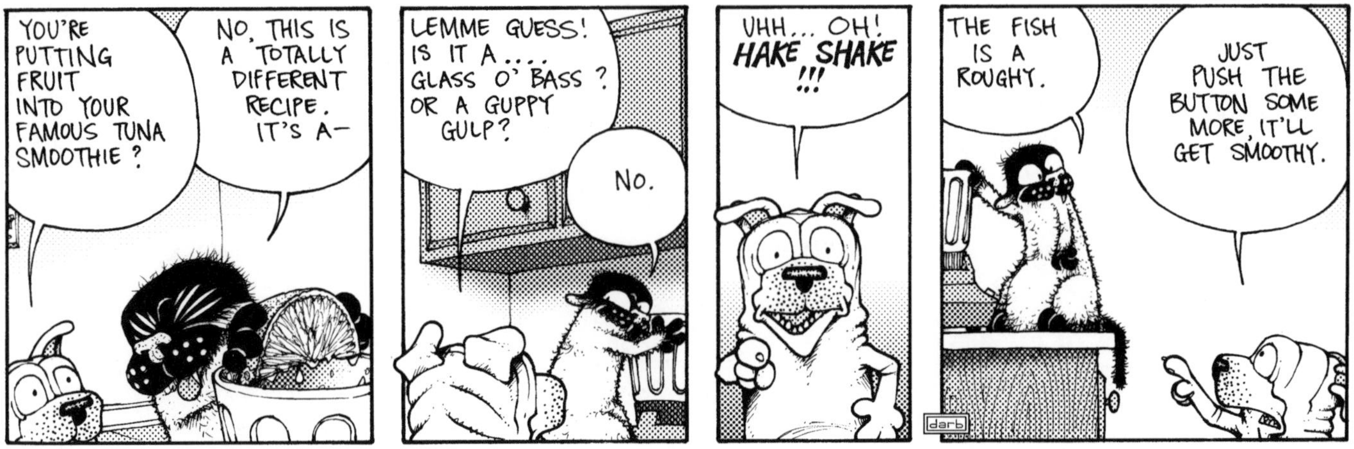
YOU'RE PUTTING FRUIT INTO YOUR FAMOUS TUNA SMOOTHIE?
NO, THIS IS A TOTALLY DIFFERENT RECIPE. IT'S A–
LEMME GUESS! IS IT A.... GLASS O' BASS? OR A GUPPY GULP?
NO.
UHH... OH! HAKE SHAKE!!!
THE FISH IS A ROUGHY.
JUST PUSH THE BUTTON SOME MORE, IT'LL GET SMOOTHY.
darb

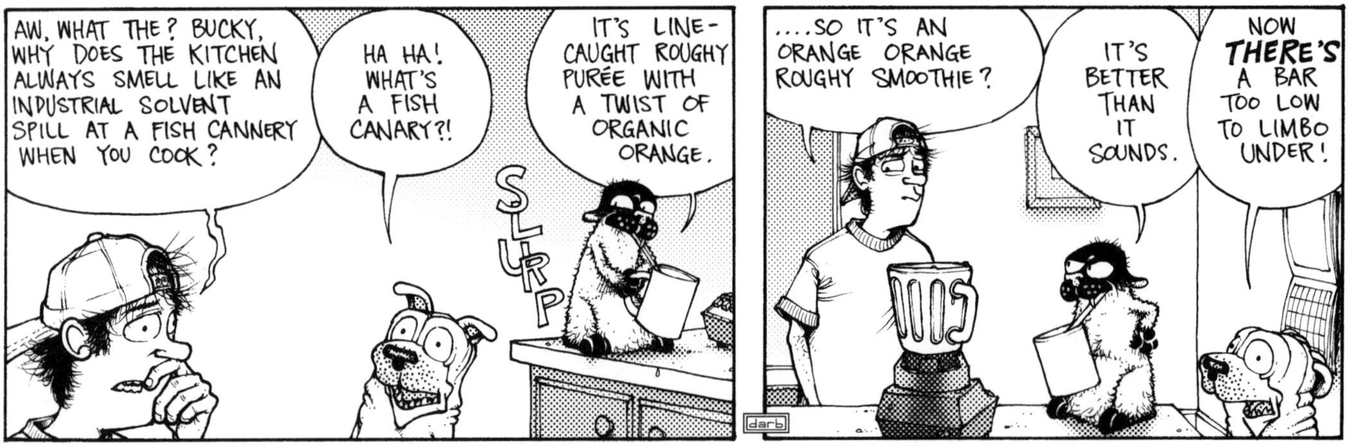
AW, WHAT THE? BUCKY, WHY DOES THE KITCHEN ALWAYS SMELL LIKE AN INDUSTRIAL SOLVENT SPILL AT A FISH CANNERY WHEN YOU COOK?
HA HA! WHAT'S A FISH CANARY?!
IT'S LINE-CAUGHT ROUGHY PURÉE WITH A TWIST OF ORGANIC ORANGE.
SLURP
....SO IT'S AN ORANGE ORANGE ROUGHY SMOOTHIE?
IT'S BETTER THAN IT SOUNDS.
NOW THERE'S A BAR TOO LOW TO LIMBO UNDER!
darb

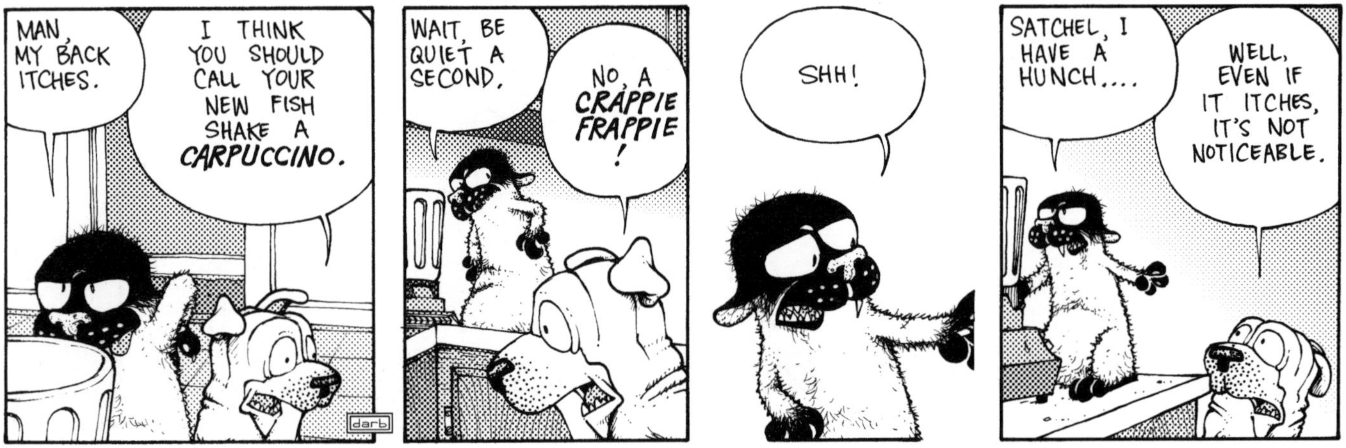
MAN, MY BACK ITCHES.
I THINK YOU SHOULD CALL YOUR NEW FISH SHAKE A CARPUCCINO.
darb
WAIT, BE QUIET A SECOND.
NO, A CRAPPIE FRAPPIE!
SHH!
SATCHEL, I HAVE A HUNCH....
WELL, EVEN IF IT ITCHES, IT'S NOT NOTICEABLE.

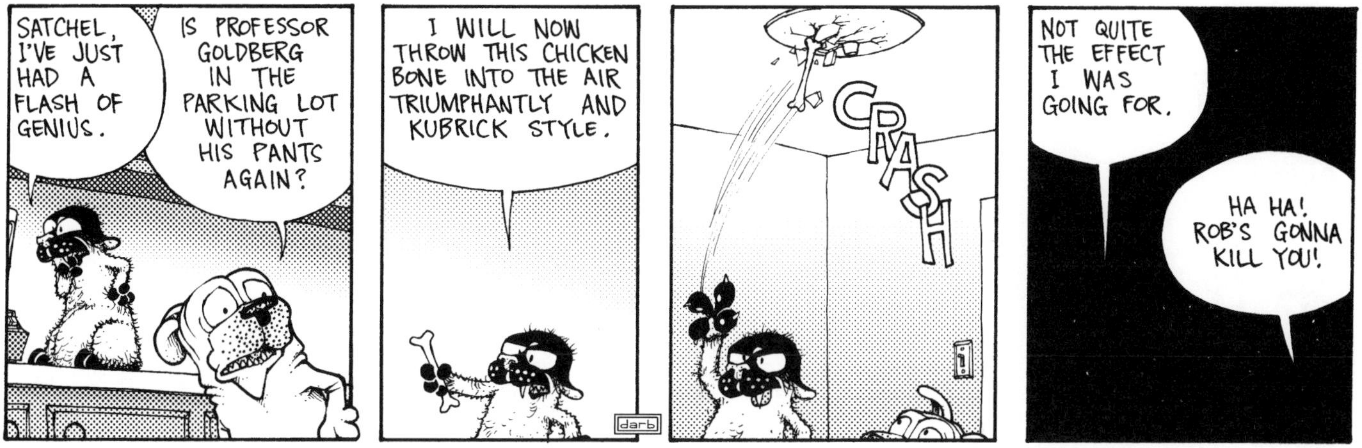
SATCHEL, I'VE JUST HAD A FLASH OF GENIUS.
IS PROFESSOR GOLDBERG IN THE PARKING LOT WITHOUT HIS PANTS AGAIN?
I WILL NOW THROW THIS CHICKEN BONE INTO THE AIR TRIUMPHANTLY AND KUBRICK STYLE.
CRASH
NOT QUITE THE EFFECT I WAS GOING FOR.
HA HA! ROB'S GONNA KILL YOU!
darb

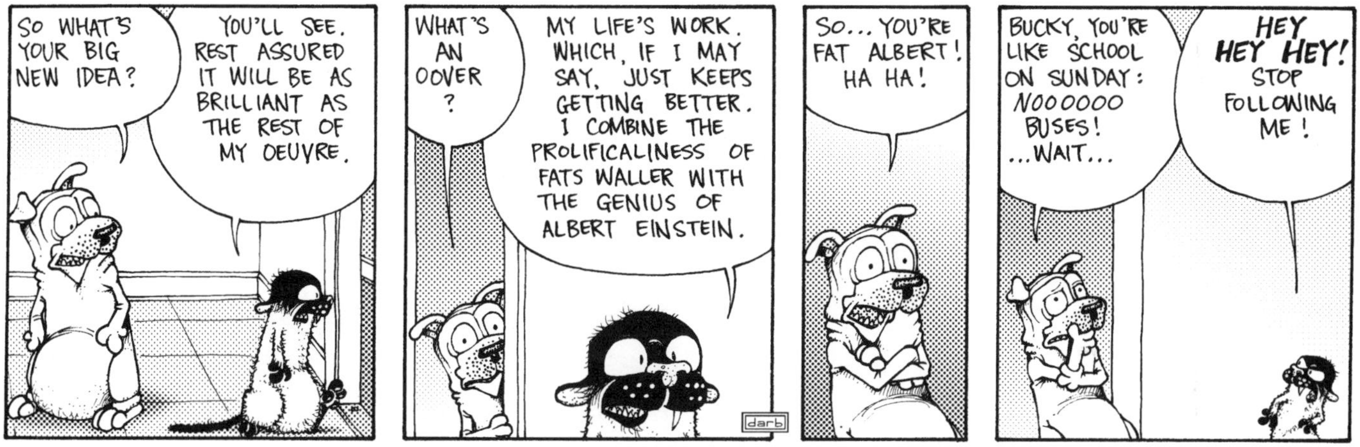
SO WHAT'S YOUR BIG NEW IDEA?
YOU'LL SEE. REST ASSURED IT WILL BE AS BRILLIANT AS THE REST OF MY OEUVRE.
WHAT'S AN OOVER?
MY LIFE'S WORK. WHICH, IF I MAY SAY, JUST KEEPS GETTING BETTER. I COMBINE THE PROLIFICALINESS OF FATS WALLER WITH THE GENIUS OF ALBERT EINSTEIN.
SO... YOU'RE FAT ALBERT! HA HA!
BUCKY, YOU'RE LIKE SCHOOL ON SUNDAY: NOOOOOO BUSES! ...WAIT...
HEY HEY HEY! STOP FOLLOWING ME!
darb

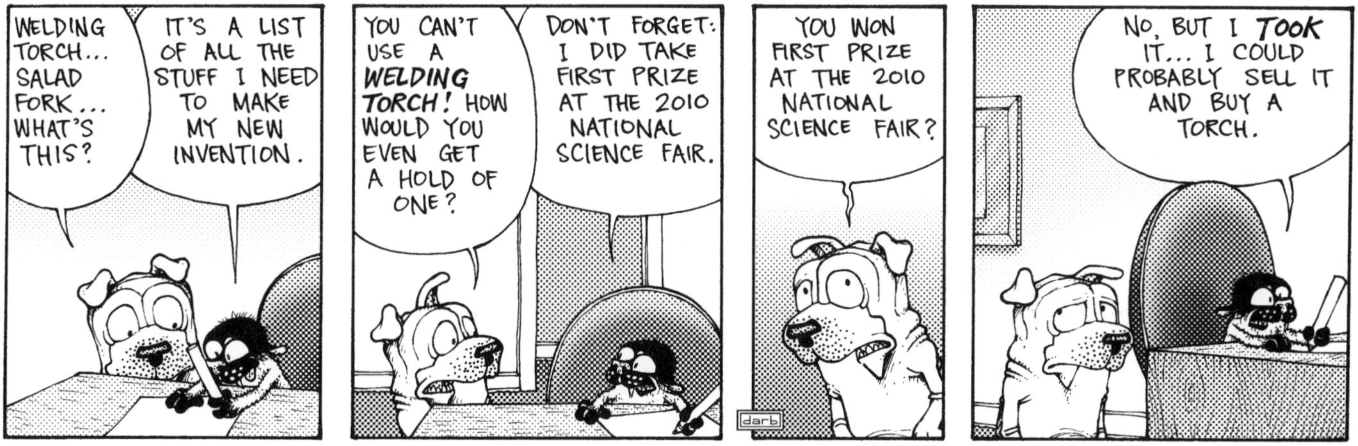
WELDING TORCH... SALAD FORK... WHAT'S THIS?
IT'S A LIST OF ALL THE STUFF I NEED TO MAKE MY NEW INVENTION.
YOU CAN'T USE A WELDING TORCH! HOW WOULD YOU EVEN GET A HOLD OF ONE?
DON'T FORGET: I DID TAKE FIRST PRIZE AT THE 2010 NATIONAL SCIENCE FAIR.
YOU WON FIRST PRIZE AT THE 2010 NATIONAL SCIENCE FAIR?
NO, BUT I TOOK IT... I COULD PROBABLY SELL IT AND BUY A TORCH.
darb

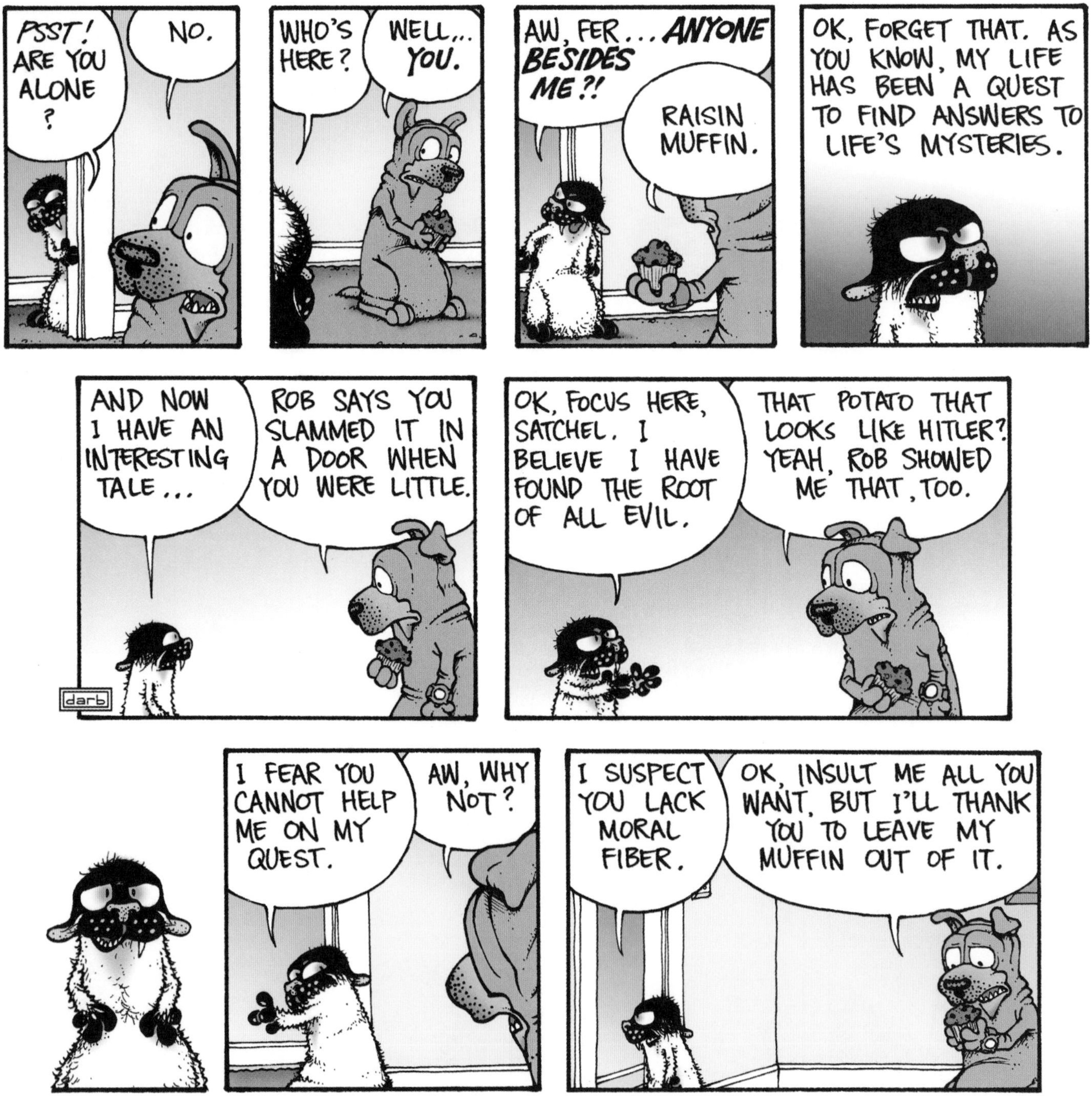
PSST! ARE YOU ALONE?
NO.
WHO'S HERE?
WELL... *YOU.*
AW, FER... ***ANYONE BESIDES ME?!***
RAISIN MUFFIN.
OK, FORGET THAT. AS YOU KNOW, MY LIFE HAS BEEN A QUEST TO FIND ANSWERS TO LIFE'S MYSTERIES.
AND NOW I HAVE AN INTERESTING TALE...
ROB SAYS YOU SLAMMED IT IN A DOOR WHEN YOU WERE LITTLE.
darb
OK, FOCUS HERE, SATCHEL. I BELIEVE I HAVE FOUND THE ROOT OF ALL EVIL.
THAT POTATO THAT LOOKS LIKE HITLER? YEAH, ROB SHOWED ME THAT, TOO.
I FEAR YOU CANNOT HELP ME ON MY QUEST.
AW, WHY NOT?
I SUSPECT YOU LACK MORAL FIBER.
OK, INSULT ME ALL YOU WANT, BUT I'LL THANK YOU TO LEAVE MY MUFFIN OUT OF IT.

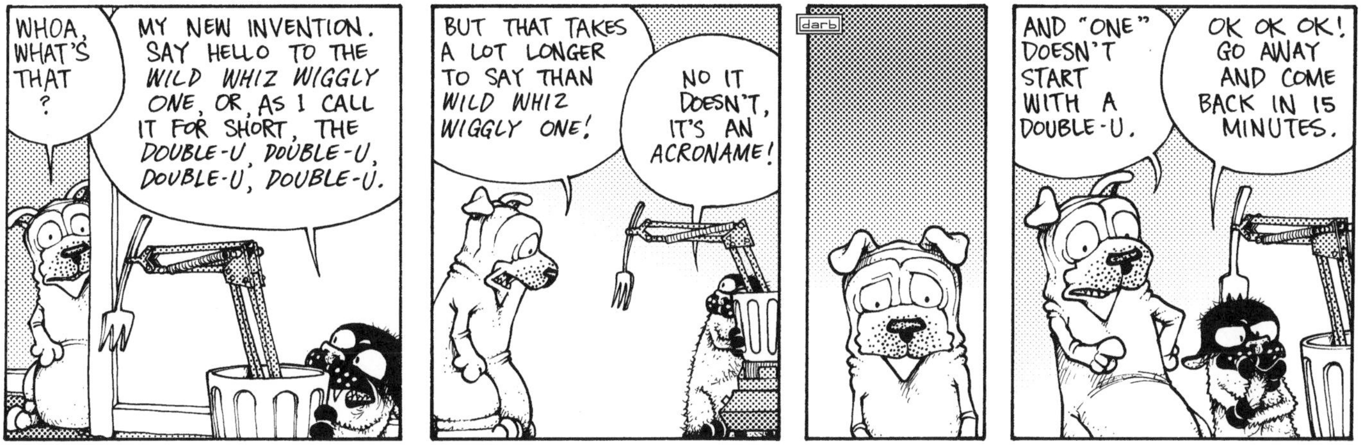
WHOA, WHAT'S THAT ?
MY NEW INVENTION. SAY HELLO TO THE WILD WHIZ WIGGLY ONE, OR, AS I CALL IT FOR SHORT, THE DOUBLE-U, DOUBLE-U, DOUBLE-U, DOUBLE-U.
BUT THAT TAKES A LOT LONGER TO SAY THAN WILD WHIZ WIGGLY ONE!
NO IT DOESN'T, IT'S AN ACRONAME!
darb
AND "ONE" DOESN'T START WITH A DOUBLE-U.
OK OK OK! GO AWAY AND COME BACK IN 15 MINUTES.

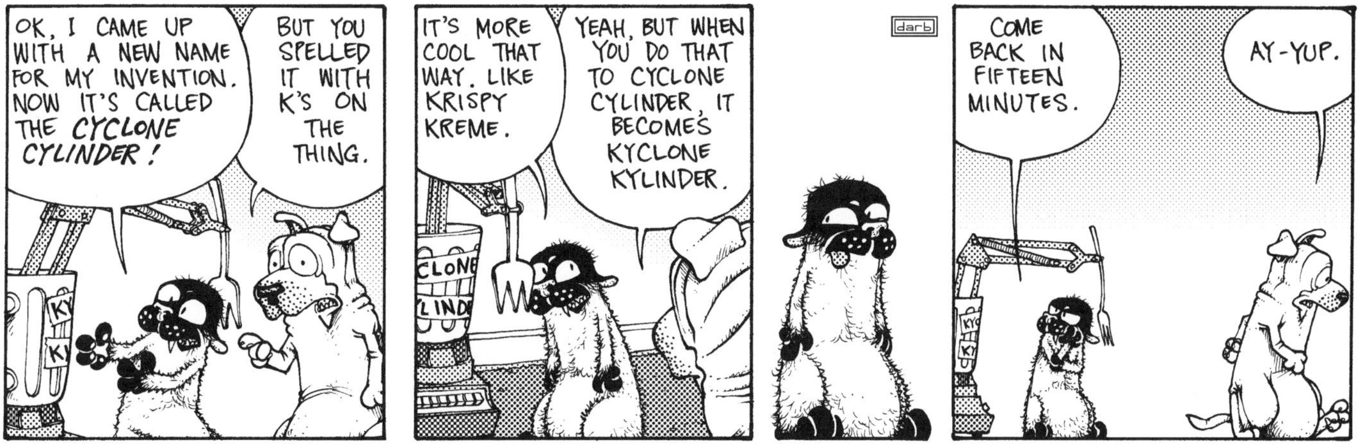
OK, I CAME UP WITH A NEW NAME FOR MY INVENTION. NOW IT'S CALLED THE CYCLONE CYLINDER!
BUT YOU SPELLED IT WITH K'S ON THE THING.
IT'S MORE COOL THAT WAY. LIKE KRISPY KREME.
YEAH, BUT WHEN YOU DO THAT TO CYCLONE CYLINDER, IT BECOMES KYCLONE KYLINDER.
darb
COME BACK IN FIFTEEN MINUTES.
AY-YUP.

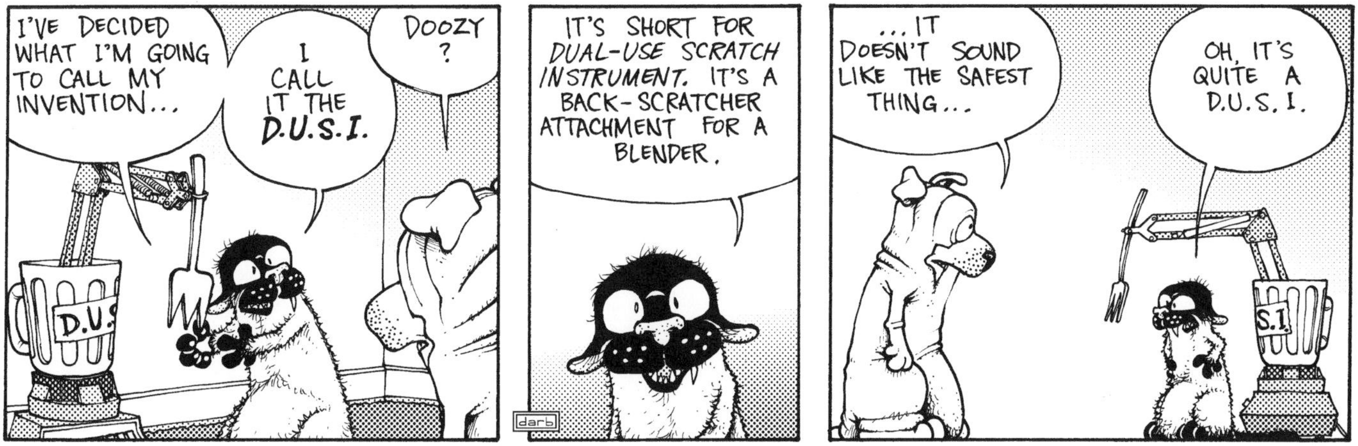
I'VE DECIDED WHAT I'M GOING TO CALL MY INVENTION...
I CALL IT THE D.U.S.I.
DOOZY ?
D.U.S
IT'S SHORT FOR DUAL-USE SCRATCH INSTRUMENT. IT'S A BACK-SCRATCHER ATTACHMENT FOR A BLENDER.
darb
...IT DOESN'T SOUND LIKE THE SAFEST THING...
OH, IT'S QUITE A D.U.S.I.
S.I

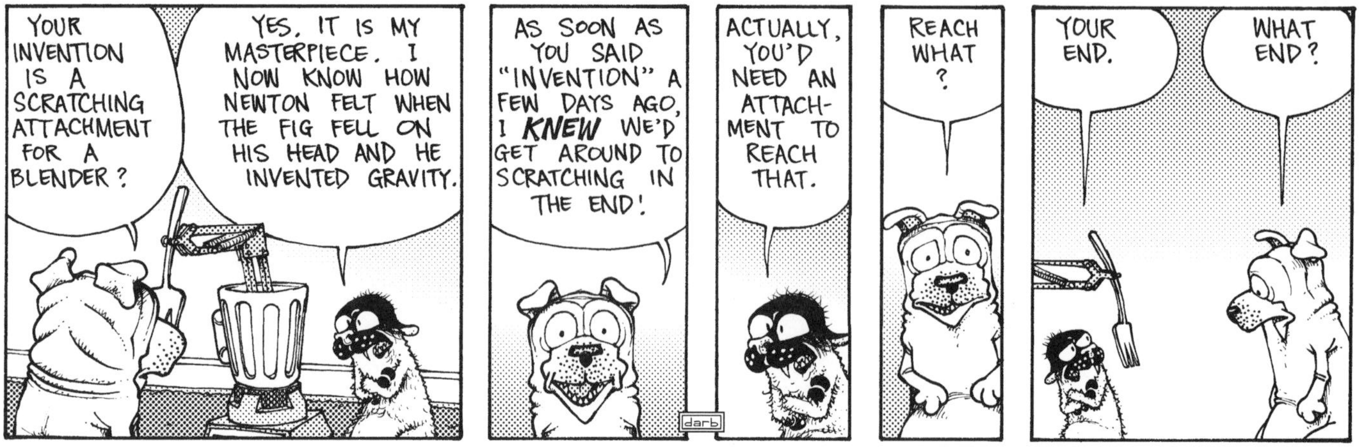
YOUR INVENTION IS A SCRATCHING ATTACHMENT FOR A BLENDER?
YES, IT IS MY MASTERPIECE. I NOW KNOW HOW NEWTON FELT WHEN THE FIG FELL ON HIS HEAD AND HE INVENTED GRAVITY.
AS SOON AS YOU SAID "INVENTION" A FEW DAYS AGO, I ***KNEW*** WE'D GET AROUND TO SCRATCHING IN THE END!
ACTUALLY, YOU'D NEED AN ATTACHMENT TO REACH THAT.
REACH WHAT?
YOUR END.
WHAT END?

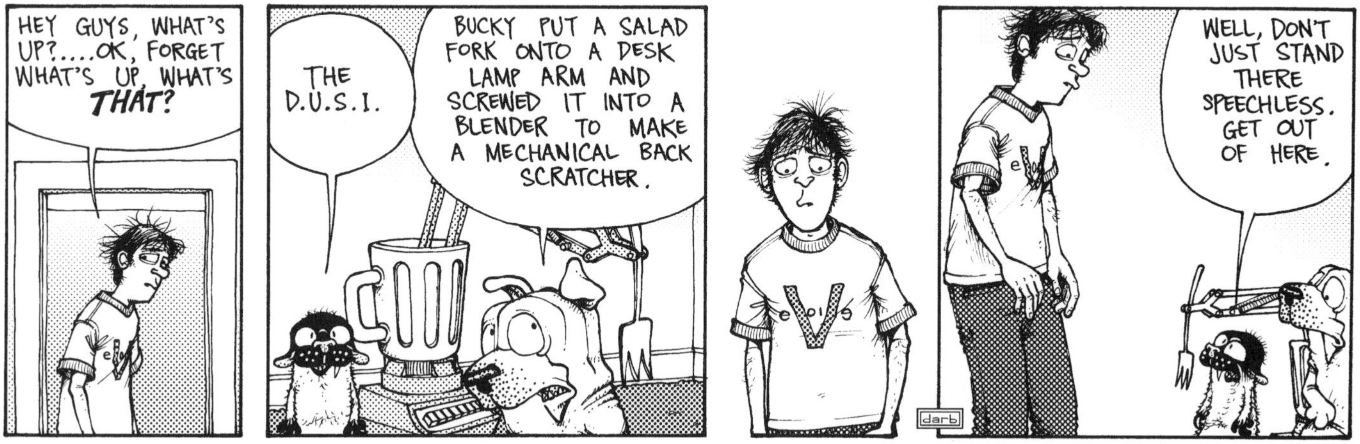
HEY GUYS, WHAT'S UP?....OK, FORGET WHAT'S UP, WHAT'S ***THAT?***
THE D.U.S.I.
BUCKY PUT A SALAD FORK ONTO A DESK LAMP ARM AND SCREWED IT INTO A BLENDER TO MAKE A MECHANICAL BACK SCRATCHER.
WELL, DON'T JUST STAND THERE SPEECHLESS. GET OUT OF HERE.

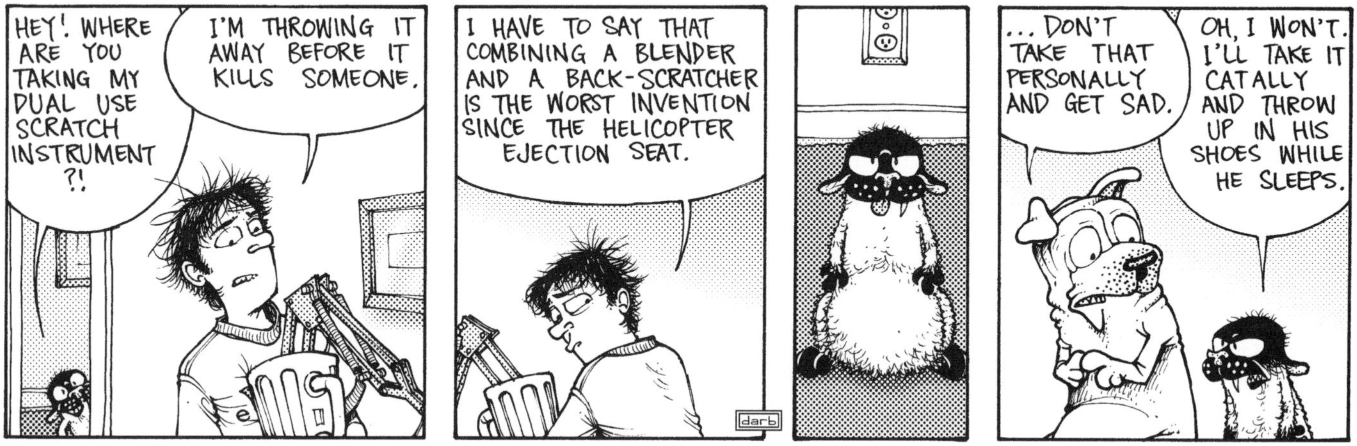
HEY! WHERE ARE YOU TAKING MY DUAL USE SCRATCH INSTRUMENT?!
I'M THROWING IT AWAY BEFORE IT KILLS SOMEONE.
I HAVE TO SAY THAT COMBINING A BLENDER AND A BACK-SCRATCHER IS THE WORST INVENTION SINCE THE HELICOPTER EJECTION SEAT.
...DON'T TAKE THAT PERSONALLY AND GET SAD.
OH, I WON'T. I'LL TAKE IT CATALLY AND THROW UP IN HIS SHOES WHILE HE SLEEPS.

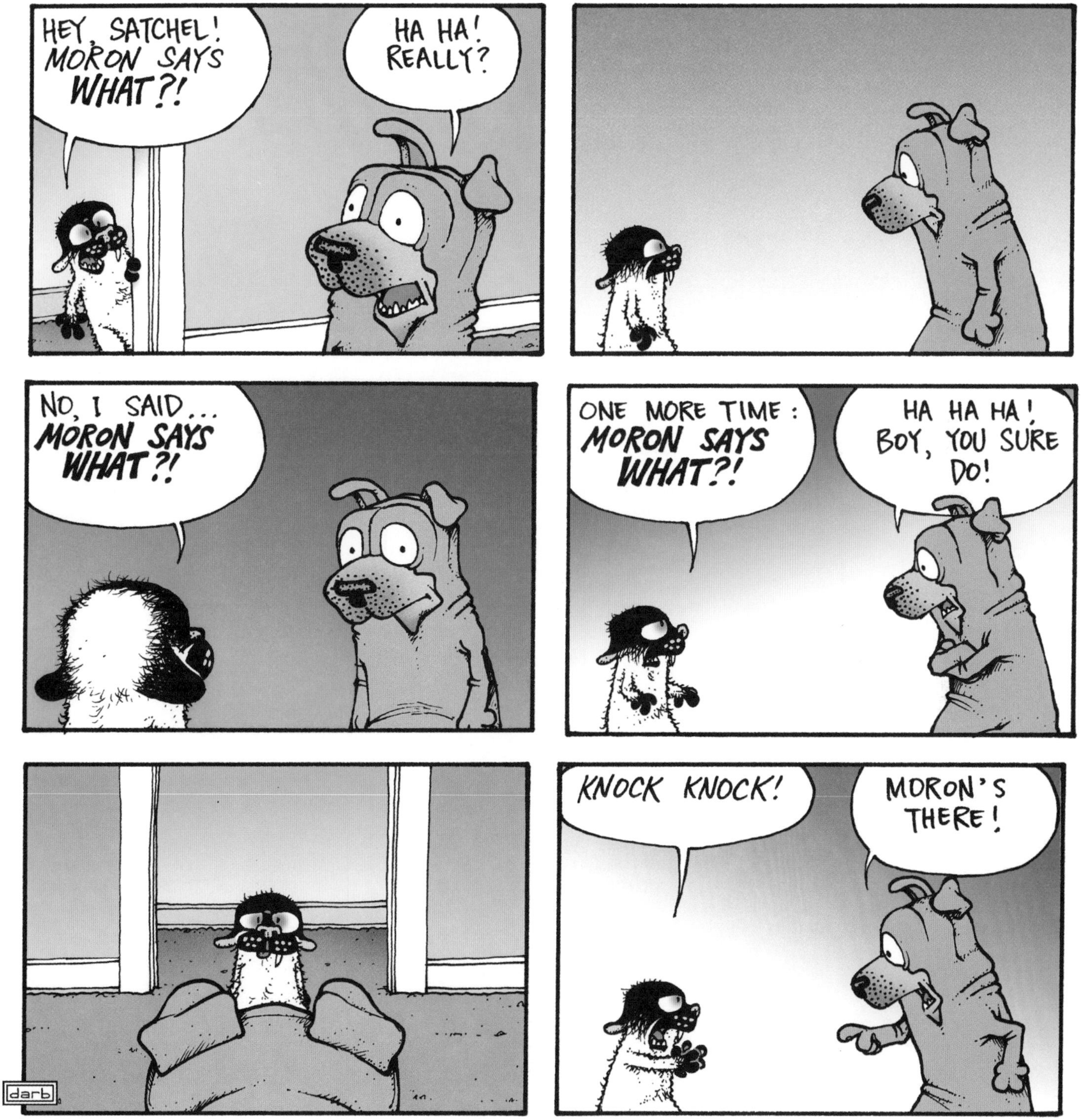
HEY, SATCHEL! MORON SAYS WHAT?!
HA HA! REALLY?
NO, I SAID... MORON SAYS WHAT?!
ONE MORE TIME: MORON SAYS WHAT?!
HA HA HA! BOY, YOU SURE DO!
KNOCK KNOCK!
MORON'S THERE!
darb

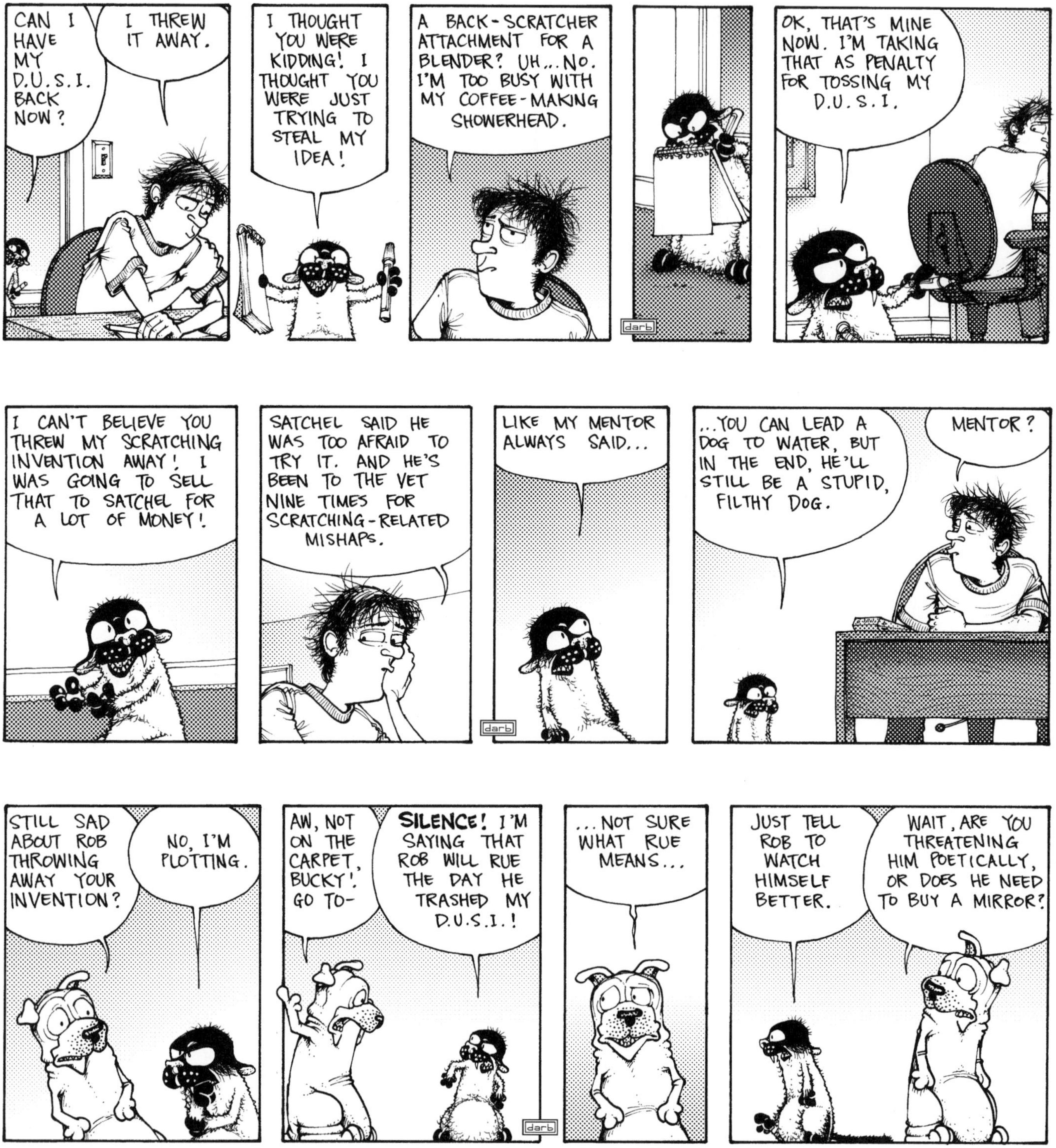
CAN I HAVE MY D.U.S.I. BACK NOW?
I THREW IT AWAY.
I THOUGHT YOU WERE KIDDING! I THOUGHT YOU WERE JUST TRYING TO STEAL MY IDEA!
A BACK-SCRATCHER ATTACHMENT FOR A BLENDER? UH...NO. I'M TOO BUSY WITH MY COFFEE-MAKING SHOWERHEAD.
darb
OK, THAT'S MINE NOW. I'M TAKING THAT AS PENALTY FOR TOSSING MY D.U.S.I.
I CAN'T BELIEVE YOU THREW MY SCRATCHING INVENTION AWAY! I WAS GOING TO SELL THAT TO SATCHEL FOR A LOT OF MONEY!
SATCHEL SAID HE WAS TOO AFRAID TO TRY IT. AND HE'S BEEN TO THE VET NINE TIMES FOR SCRATCHING-RELATED MISHAPS.
darb
LIKE MY MENTOR ALWAYS SAID...
...YOU CAN LEAD A DOG TO WATER, BUT IN THE END, HE'LL STILL BE A STUPID, FILTHY DOG.
MENTOR?
STILL SAD ABOUT ROB THROWING AWAY YOUR INVENTION?
NO, I'M PLOTTING.
AW, NOT ON THE CARPET, BUCKY! GO TO-
SILENCE! I'M SAYING THAT ROB WILL RUE THE DAY HE TRASHED MY D.U.S.I.!
darb
...NOT SURE WHAT RUE MEANS...
JUST TELL ROB TO WATCH HIMSELF BETTER.
WAIT, ARE YOU THREATENING HIM POETICALLY, OR DOES HE NEED TO BUY A MIRROR?

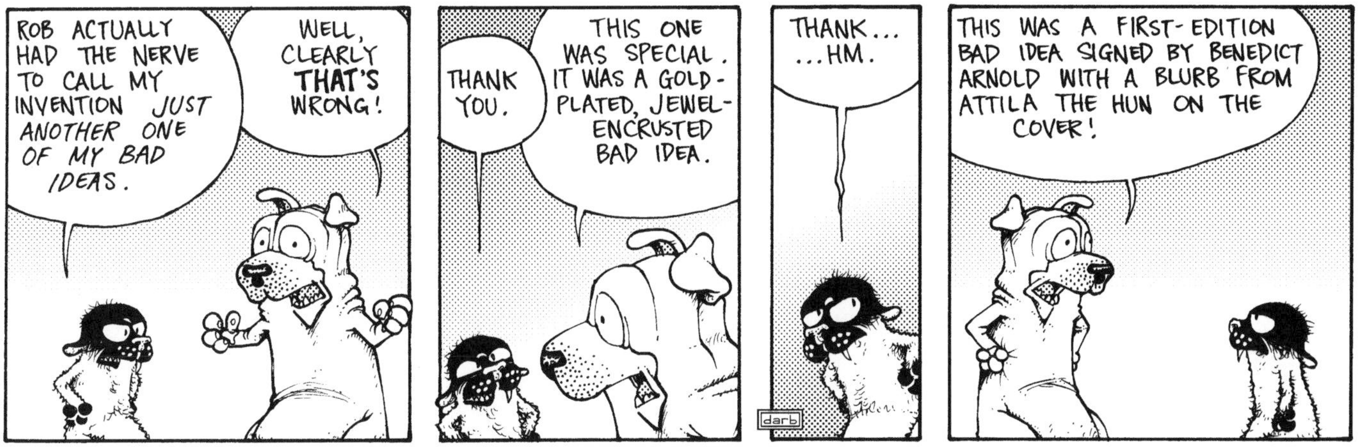
ROB ACTUALLY HAD THE NERVE TO CALL MY INVENTION *JUST ANOTHER ONE OF MY BAD IDEAS.*
WELL, CLEARLY **THAT'S** WRONG!
THANK YOU.
THIS ONE WAS SPECIAL. IT WAS A GOLD-PLATED, JEWEL-ENCRUSTED BAD IDEA.
THANK...
...HM.
THIS WAS A FIRST-EDITION BAD IDEA SIGNED BY BENEDICT ARNOLD WITH A BLURB FROM ATTILA THE HUN ON THE COVER!

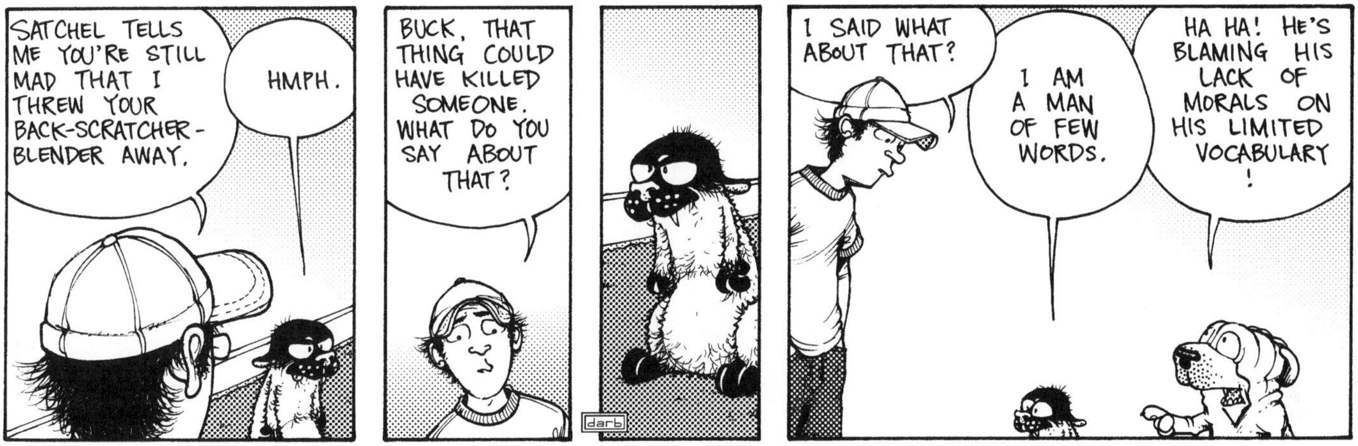
SATCHEL TELLS ME YOU'RE STILL MAD THAT I THREW YOUR BACK-SCRATCHER-BLENDER AWAY.
HMPH.
BUCK, THAT THING COULD HAVE KILLED SOMEONE. WHAT DO YOU SAY ABOUT THAT?
I SAID WHAT ABOUT THAT?
I AM A MAN OF FEW WORDS.
HA HA! HE'S BLAMING HIS LACK OF MORALS ON HIS LIMITED VOCABULARY!

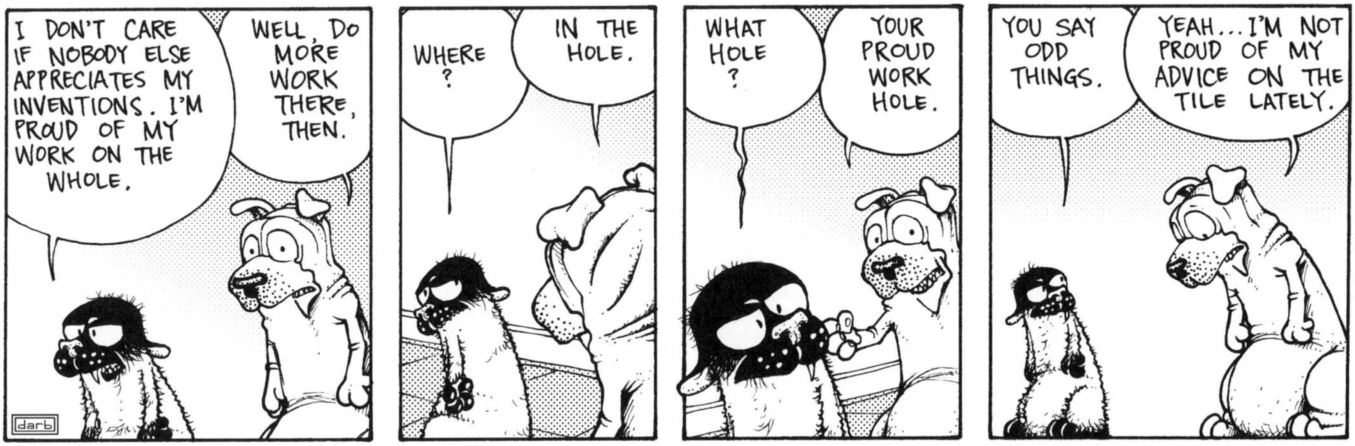
I DON'T CARE IF NOBODY ELSE APPRECIATES MY INVENTIONS. I'M PROUD OF MY WORK ON THE WHOLE.
WELL, DO MORE WORK THERE, THEN.
WHERE?
IN THE HOLE.
WHAT HOLE?
YOUR PROUD WORK HOLE.
YOU SAY ODD THINGS.
YEAH... I'M NOT PROUD OF MY ADVICE ON THE TILE LATELY.

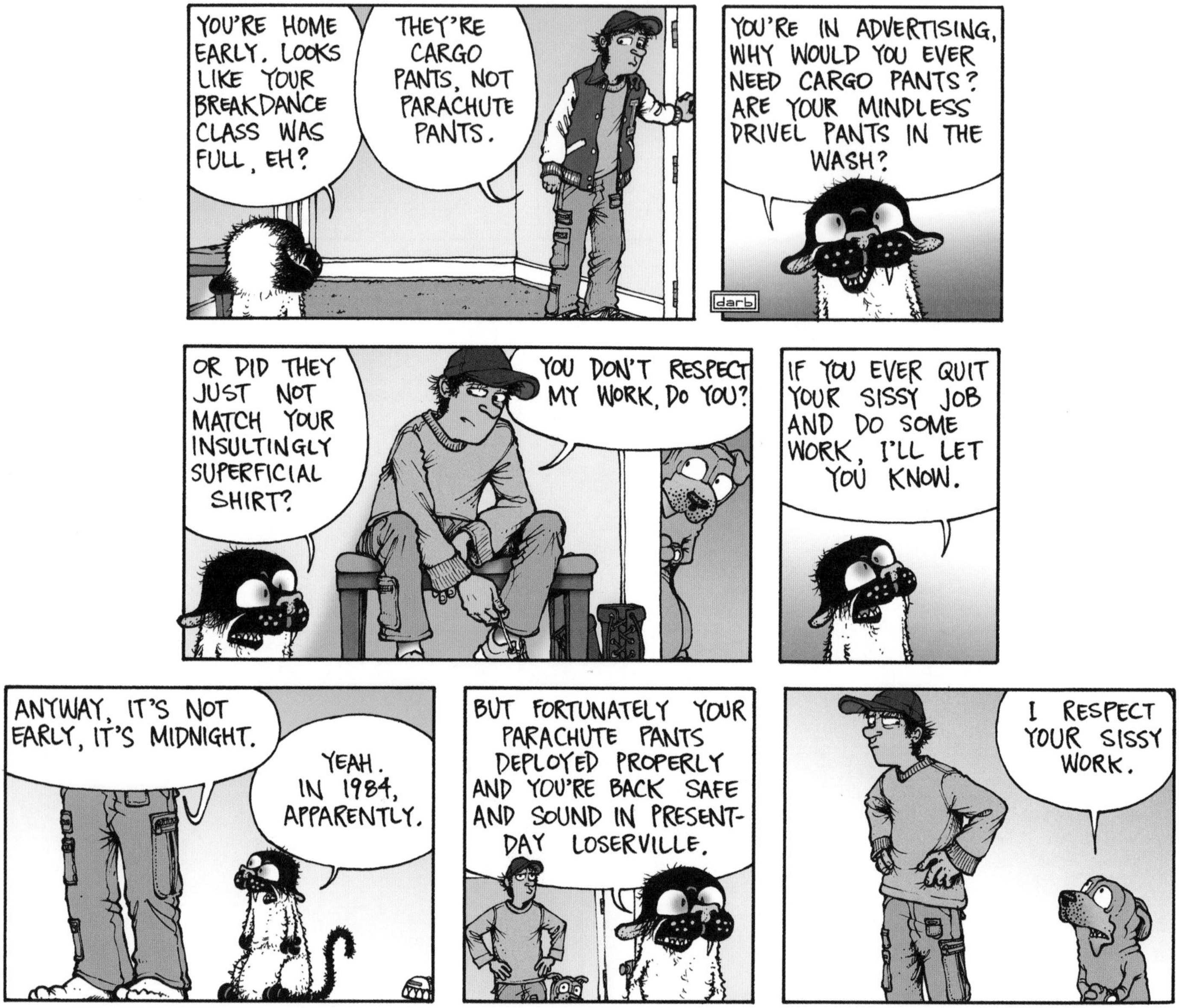

YOU'RE HOME EARLY. LOOKS LIKE YOUR BREAKDANCE CLASS WAS FULL, EH?
THEY'RE CARGO PANTS, NOT PARACHUTE PANTS.
YOU'RE IN ADVERTISING, WHY WOULD YOU EVER NEED CARGO PANTS? ARE YOUR MINDLESS DRIVEL PANTS IN THE WASH?
darb
OR DID THEY JUST NOT MATCH YOUR INSULTINGLY SUPERFICIAL SHIRT?
YOU DON'T RESPECT MY WORK, DO YOU?
IF YOU EVER QUIT YOUR SISSY JOB AND DO SOME WORK, I'LL LET YOU KNOW.
ANYWAY, IT'S NOT EARLY, IT'S MIDNIGHT.
YEAH. IN 1984, APPARENTLY.
BUT FORTUNATELY YOUR PARACHUTE PANTS DEPLOYED PROPERLY AND YOU'RE BACK SAFE AND SOUND IN PRESENT-DAY LOSERVILLE.
I RESPECT YOUR SISSY WORK.

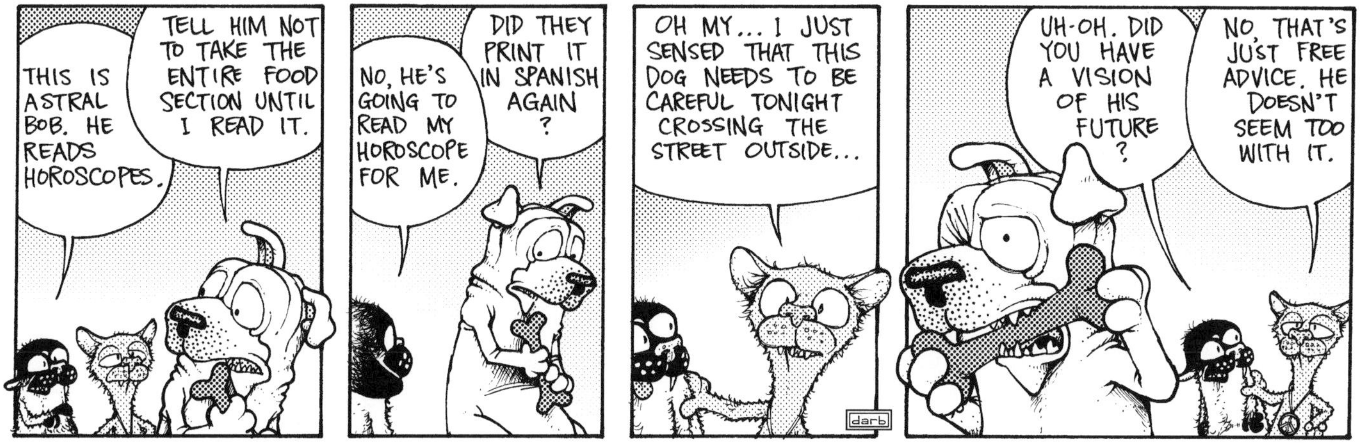
THIS IS ASTRAL BOB. HE READS HOROSCOPES.
TELL HIM NOT TO TAKE THE ENTIRE FOOD SECTION UNTIL I READ IT.
NO, HE'S GOING TO READ MY HOROSCOPE FOR ME.
DID THEY PRINT IT IN SPANISH AGAIN ?
OH MY... I JUST SENSED THAT THIS DOG NEEDS TO BE CAREFUL TONIGHT CROSSING THE STREET OUTSIDE...
UH-OH. DID YOU HAVE A VISION OF HIS FUTURE ?
NO, THAT'S JUST FREE ADVICE. HE DOESN'T SEEM TOO WITH IT.
darb

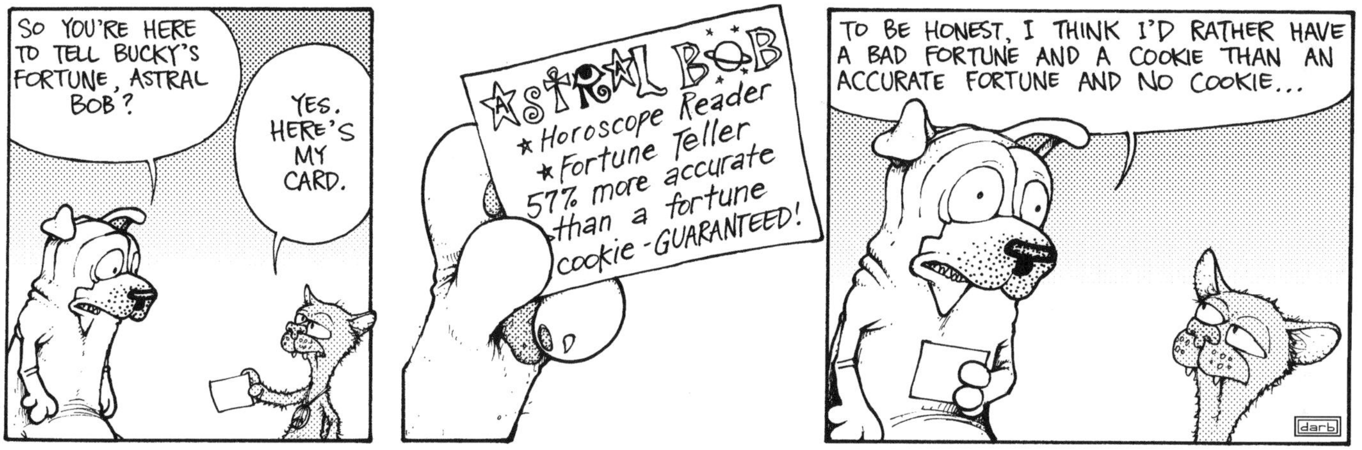
SO YOU'RE HERE TO TELL BUCKY'S FORTUNE, ASTRAL BOB?
YES. HERE'S MY CARD.
ASTRAL BOB
★Horoscope Reader
★Fortune Teller
57% more accurate than a fortune cookie - GUARANTEED!
TO BE HONEST, I THINK I'D RATHER HAVE A BAD FORTUNE AND A COOKIE THAN AN ACCURATE FORTUNE AND NO COOKIE...
darb

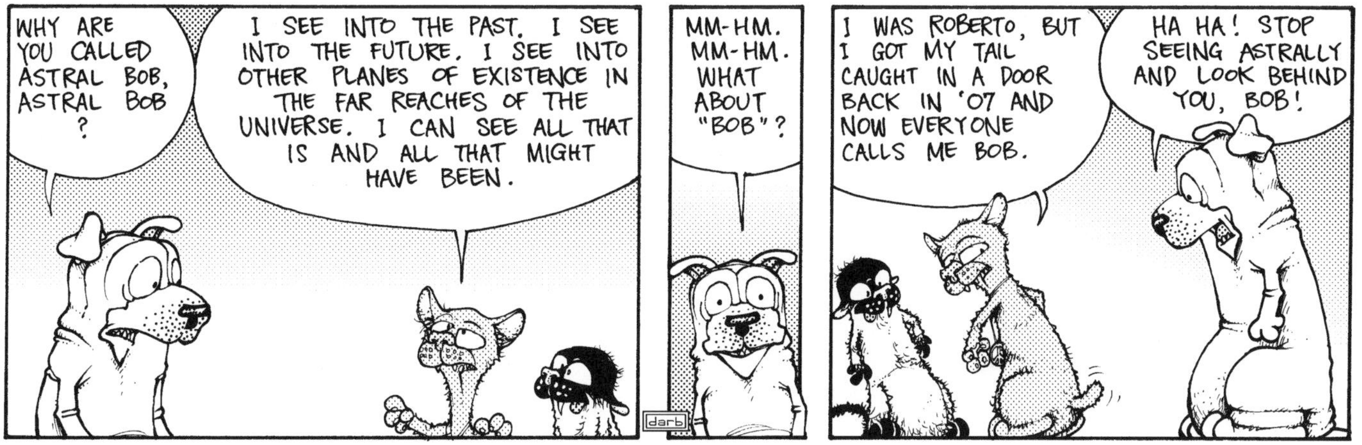
WHY ARE YOU CALLED ASTRAL BOB, ASTRAL BOB ?
I SEE INTO THE PAST. I SEE INTO THE FUTURE. I SEE INTO OTHER PLANES OF EXISTENCE IN THE FAR REACHES OF THE UNIVERSE. I CAN SEE ALL THAT IS AND ALL THAT MIGHT HAVE BEEN.
darb
MM-HM. MM-HM. WHAT ABOUT "BOB"?
I WAS ROBERTO, BUT I GOT MY TAIL CAUGHT IN A DOOR BACK IN '07 AND NOW EVERYONE CALLS ME BOB.
HA HA! STOP SEEING ASTRALLY AND LOOK BEHIND YOU, BOB!

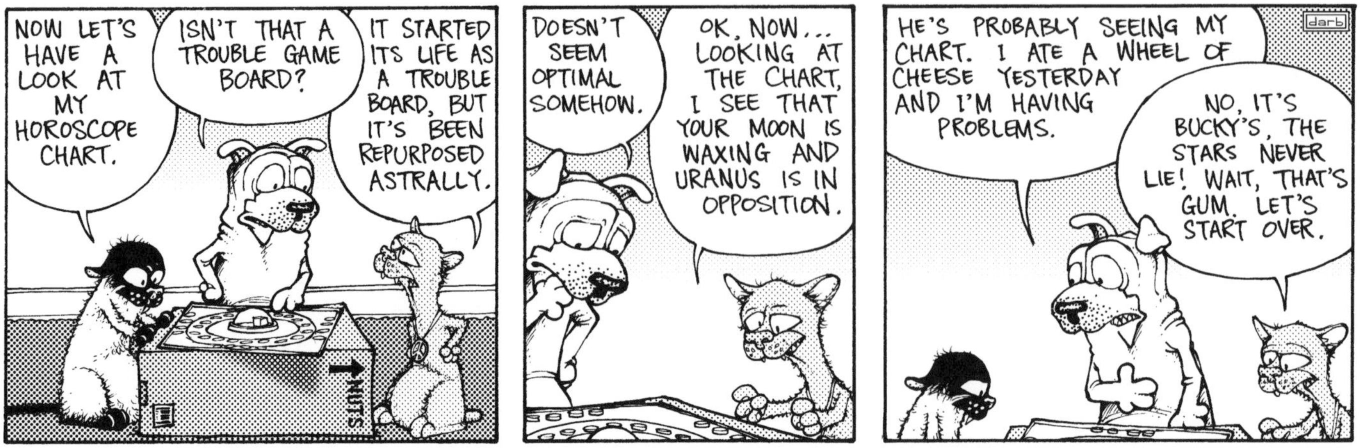
NOW LET'S HAVE A LOOK AT MY HOROSCOPE CHART.
ISN'T THAT A TROUBLE GAME BOARD?
IT STARTED ITS LIFE AS A TROUBLE BOARD, BUT IT'S BEEN REPURPOSED ASTRALLY.
DOESN'T SEEM OPTIMAL SOMEHOW.
OK, NOW... LOOKING AT THE CHART, I SEE THAT YOUR MOON IS WAXING AND URANUS IS IN OPPOSITION.
HE'S PROBABLY SEEING MY CHART. I ATE A WHEEL OF CHEESE YESTERDAY AND I'M HAVING PROBLEMS.
NO, IT'S BUCKY'S, THE STARS NEVER LIE! WAIT, THAT'S GUM. LET'S START OVER.

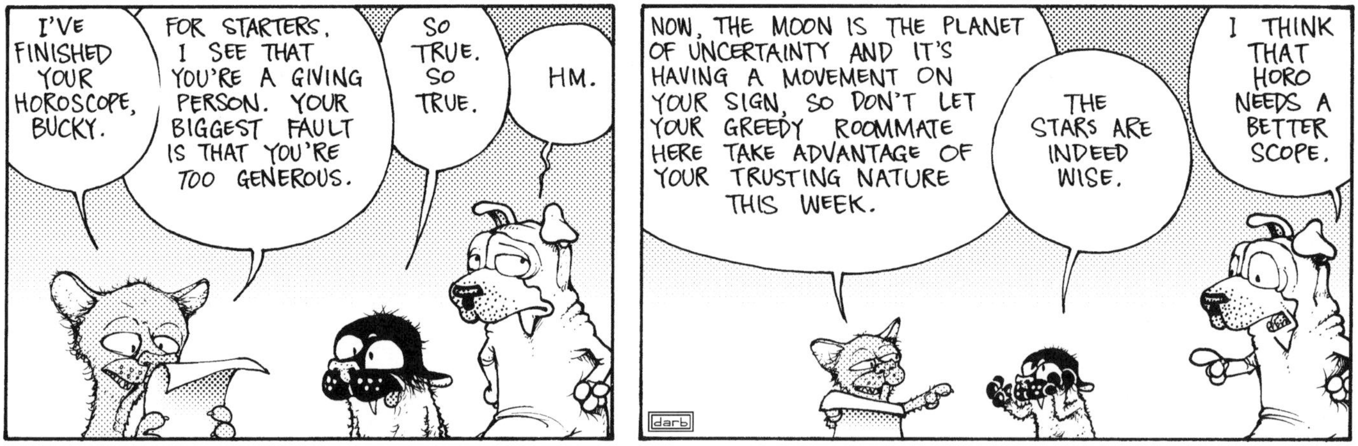
I'VE FINISHED YOUR HOROSCOPE, BUCKY.
FOR STARTERS, I SEE THAT YOU'RE A GIVING PERSON. YOUR BIGGEST FAULT IS THAT YOU'RE *TOO* GENEROUS.
SO TRUE. SO TRUE.
HM.
NOW, THE MOON IS THE PLANET OF UNCERTAINTY AND IT'S HAVING A MOVEMENT ON YOUR SIGN, SO DON'T LET YOUR GREEDY ROOMMATE HERE TAKE ADVANTAGE OF YOUR TRUSTING NATURE THIS WEEK.
THE STARS ARE INDEED WISE.
I THINK THAT HORO NEEDS A BETTER SCOPE.

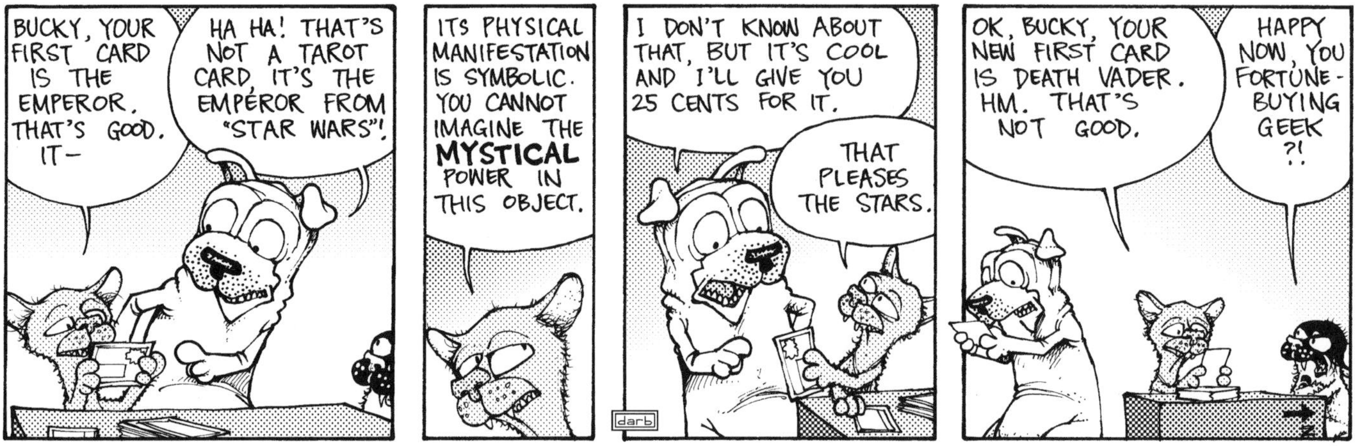
BUCKY, YOUR FIRST CARD IS THE EMPEROR. THAT'S GOOD. IT–
HA HA! THAT'S NOT A TAROT CARD, IT'S THE EMPEROR FROM "STAR WARS"!
ITS PHYSICAL MANIFESTATION IS SYMBOLIC. YOU CANNOT IMAGINE THE **MYSTICAL** POWER IN THIS OBJECT.
I DON'T KNOW ABOUT THAT, BUT IT'S COOL AND I'LL GIVE YOU 25 CENTS FOR IT.
THAT PLEASES THE STARS.
OK, BUCKY, YOUR NEW FIRST CARD IS DEATH VADER. HM. THAT'S NOT GOOD.
HAPPY NOW, YOU FORTUNE-BUYING GEEK?!

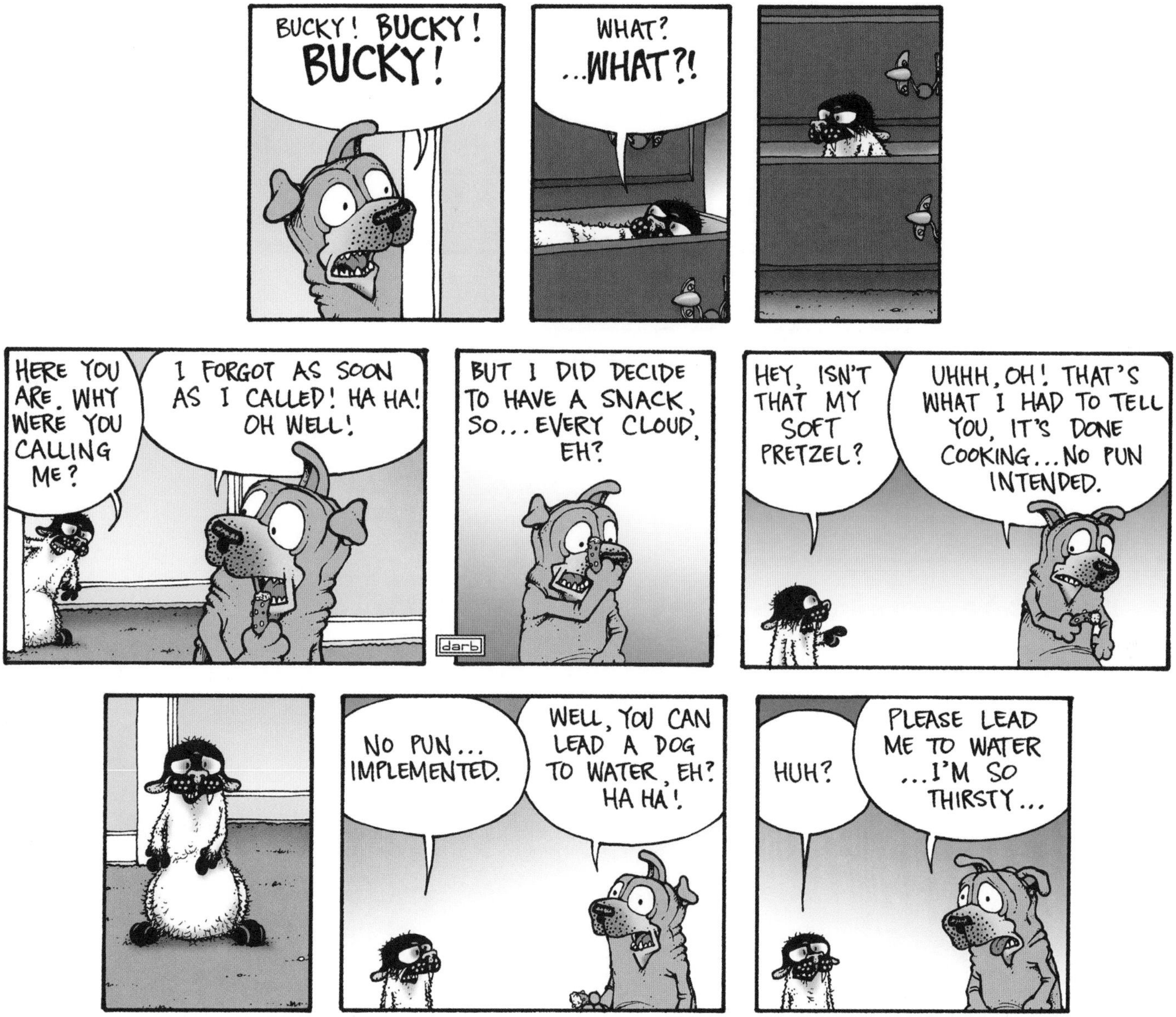

BUCKY! BUCKY! BUCKY!
WHAT? ...WHAT?!
HERE YOU ARE. WHY WERE YOU CALLING ME?
I FORGOT AS SOON AS I CALLED! HA HA! OH WELL!
BUT I DID DECIDE TO HAVE A SNACK, SO... EVERY CLOUD, EH?
darb
HEY, ISN'T THAT MY SOFT PRETZEL?
UHHH, OH! THAT'S WHAT I HAD TO TELL YOU, IT'S DONE COOKING... NO PUN INTENDED.
NO PUN... IMPLEMENTED.
WELL, YOU CAN LEAD A DOG TO WATER, EH? HA HA!
HUH?
PLEASE LEAD ME TO WATER ...I'M SO THIRSTY...

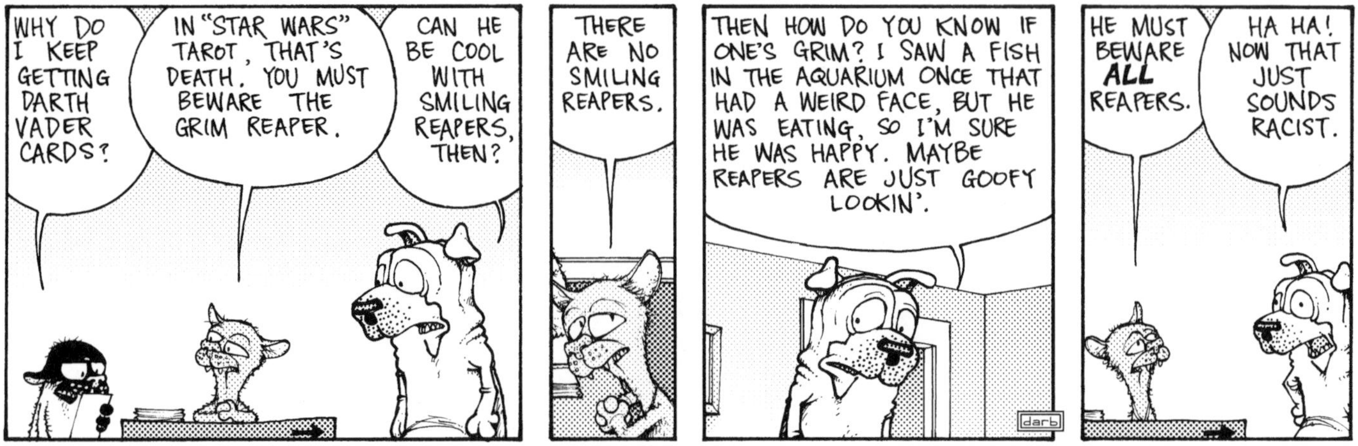
WHY DO I KEEP GETTING DARTH VADER CARDS?
IN "STAR WARS" TAROT, THAT'S DEATH. YOU MUST BEWARE THE GRIM REAPER.
CAN HE BE COOL WITH SMILING REAPERS, THEN?
THERE ARE NO SMILING REAPERS.
THEN HOW DO YOU KNOW IF ONE'S GRIM? I SAW A FISH IN THE AQUARIUM ONCE THAT HAD A WEIRD FACE, BUT HE WAS EATING, SO I'M SURE HE WAS HAPPY. MAYBE REAPERS ARE JUST GOOFY LOOKIN'.
darb
HE MUST BEWARE **ALL** REAPERS.
HA HA! NOW THAT JUST SOUNDS RACIST.

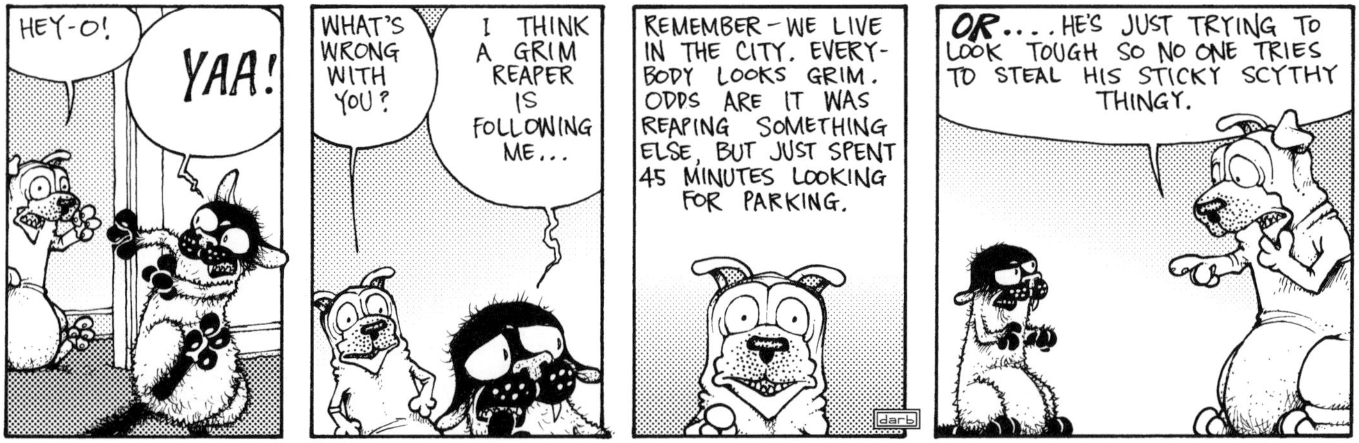
HEY-O!
YAA!
WHAT'S WRONG WITH YOU?
I THINK A GRIM REAPER IS FOLLOWING ME...
REMEMBER - WE LIVE IN THE CITY. EVERYBODY LOOKS GRIM. ODDS ARE IT WAS REAPING SOMETHING ELSE, BUT JUST SPENT 45 MINUTES LOOKING FOR PARKING.
darb
OR.... HE'S JUST TRYING TO LOOK TOUGH SO NO ONE TRIES TO STEAL HIS STICKY SCYTHY THINGY.

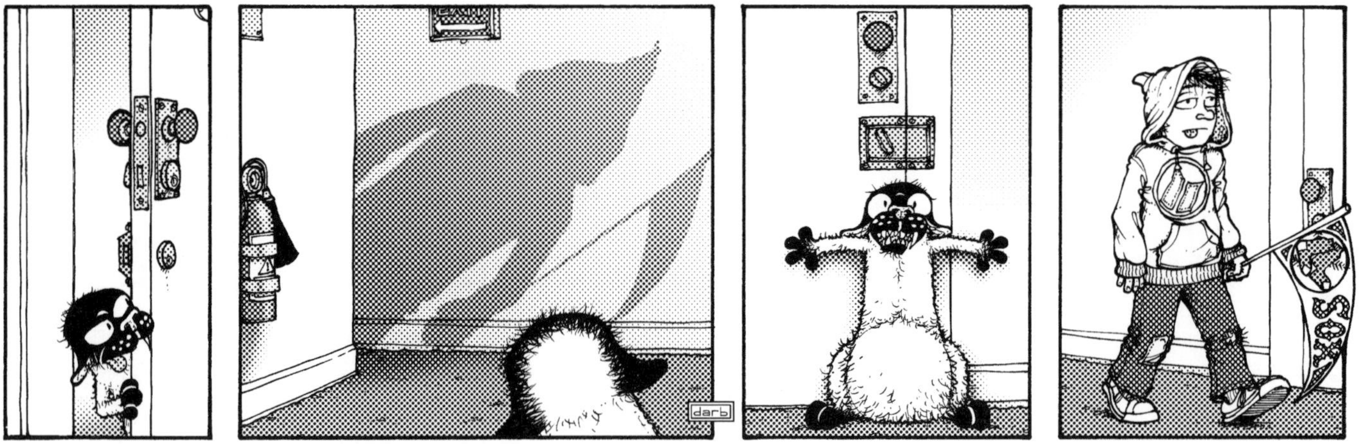
darb

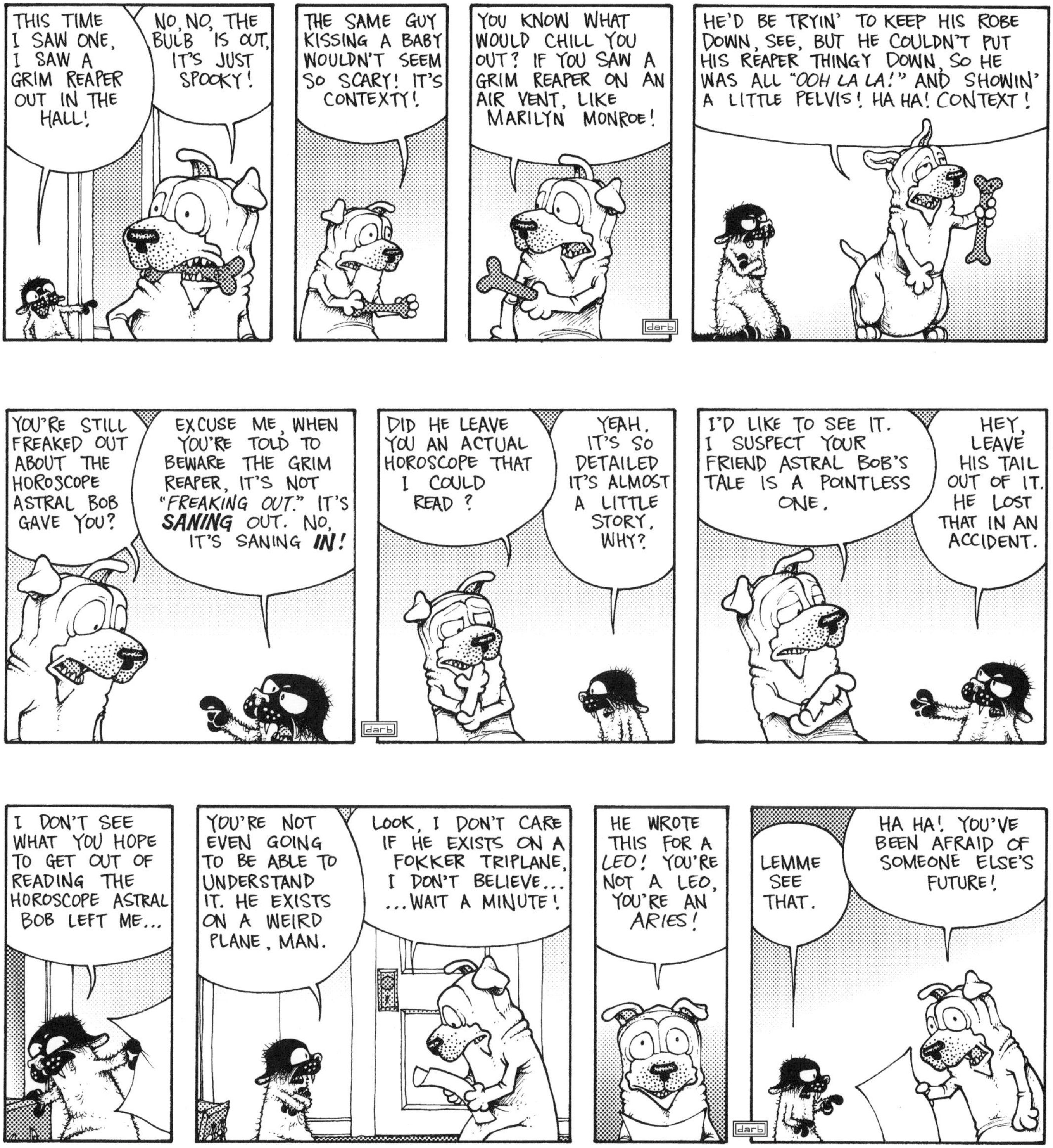
THIS TIME I SAW ONE, I SAW A GRIM REAPER OUT IN THE HALL!
NO, NO, THE BULB IS OUT, IT'S JUST SPOOKY!
THE SAME GUY KISSING A BABY WOULDN'T SEEM SO SCARY! IT'S CONTEXTY!
YOU KNOW WHAT WOULD CHILL YOU OUT? IF YOU SAW A GRIM REAPER ON AN AIR VENT, LIKE MARILYN MONROE!
darb
HE'D BE TRYIN' TO KEEP HIS ROBE DOWN, SEE, BUT HE COULDN'T PUT HIS REAPER THINGY DOWN, SO HE WAS ALL "*OOH LA LA!*" AND SHOWIN' A LITTLE PELVIS! HA HA! CONTEXT!
YOU'RE STILL FREAKED OUT ABOUT THE HOROSCOPE ASTRAL BOB GAVE YOU?
EXCUSE ME, WHEN YOU'RE TOLD TO BEWARE THE GRIM REAPER, IT'S NOT "*FREAKING OUT.*" IT'S ***SANING*** OUT. NO, IT'S SANING ***IN!***
darb
DID HE LEAVE YOU AN ACTUAL HOROSCOPE THAT I COULD READ?
YEAH. IT'S SO DETAILED IT'S ALMOST A LITTLE STORY. WHY?
I'D LIKE TO SEE IT. I SUSPECT YOUR FRIEND ASTRAL BOB'S TALE IS A POINTLESS ONE.
HEY, LEAVE HIS TAIL OUT OF IT. HE LOST THAT IN AN ACCIDENT.
I DON'T SEE WHAT YOU HOPE TO GET OUT OF READING THE HOROSCOPE ASTRAL BOB LEFT ME...
YOU'RE NOT EVEN GOING TO BE ABLE TO UNDERSTAND IT. HE EXISTS ON A WEIRD PLANE, MAN.
LOOK, I DON'T CARE IF HE EXISTS ON A FOKKER TRIPLANE, I DON'T BELIEVE... ...WAIT A MINUTE!
HE WROTE THIS FOR A *LEO!* YOU'RE NOT A LEO, YOU'RE AN *ARIES!*
darb
LEMME SEE THAT.
HA HA! YOU'VE BEEN AFRAID OF SOMEONE ELSE'S FUTURE!

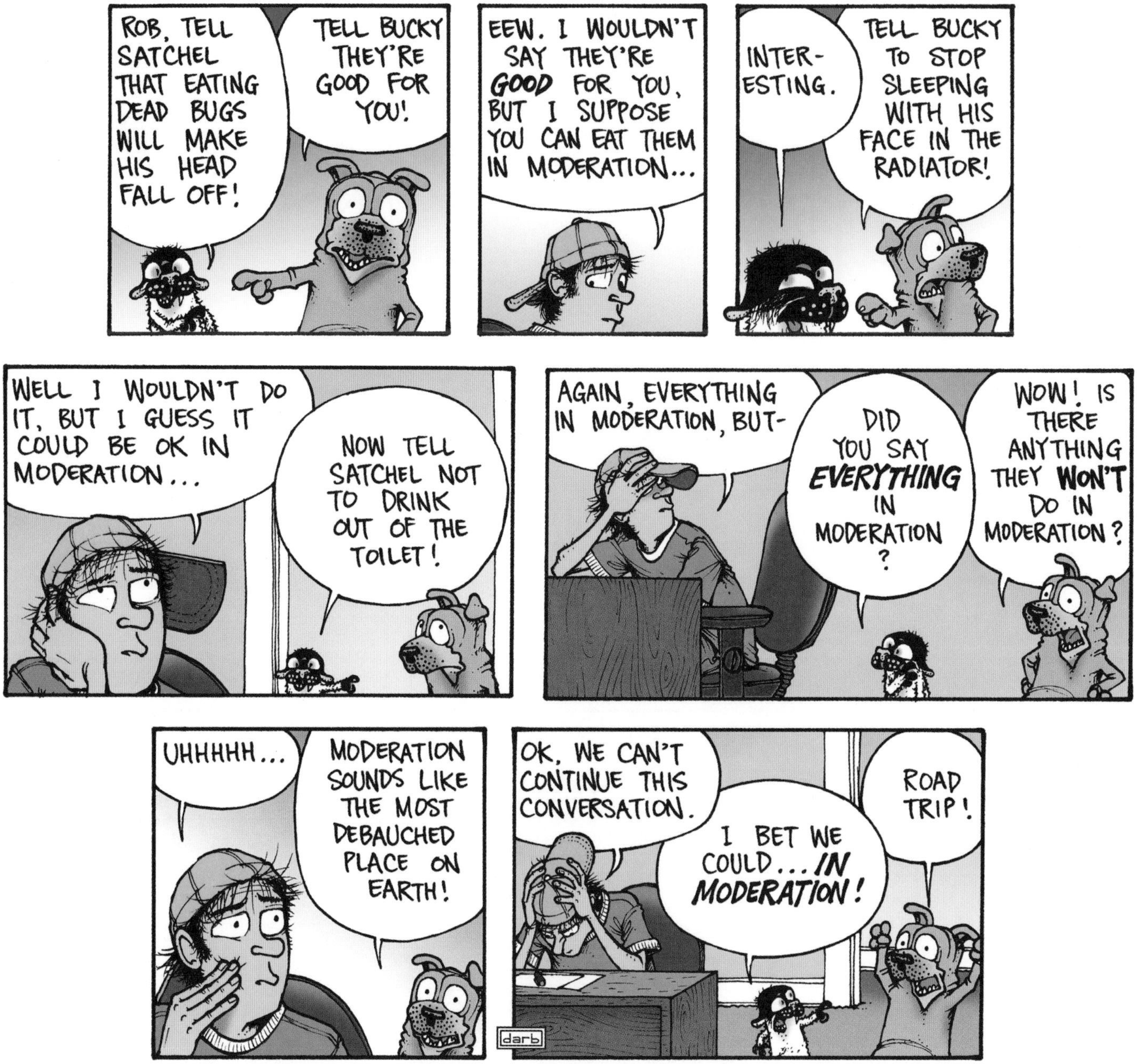
ROB, TELL SATCHEL THAT EATING DEAD BUGS WILL MAKE HIS HEAD FALL OFF!
TELL BUCKY THEY'RE GOOD FOR YOU!
EEW. I WOULDN'T SAY THEY'RE **GOOD** FOR YOU, BUT I SUPPOSE YOU CAN EAT THEM IN MODERATION...
INTER-ESTING.
TELL BUCKY TO STOP SLEEPING WITH HIS FACE IN THE RADIATOR!
WELL I WOULDN'T DO IT, BUT I GUESS IT COULD BE OK IN MODERATION...
NOW TELL SATCHEL NOT TO DRINK OUT OF THE TOILET!
AGAIN, EVERYTHING IN MODERATION, BUT-
DID YOU SAY **EVERYTHING** IN MODERATION?
WOW! IS THERE ANYTHING THEY **WON'T** DO IN MODERATION?
UHHHHH...
MODERATION SOUNDS LIKE THE MOST DEBAUCHED PLACE ON EARTH!
darb
OK, WE CAN'T CONTINUE THIS CONVERSATION.
I BET WE COULD... ***IN MODERATION!***
ROAD TRIP!

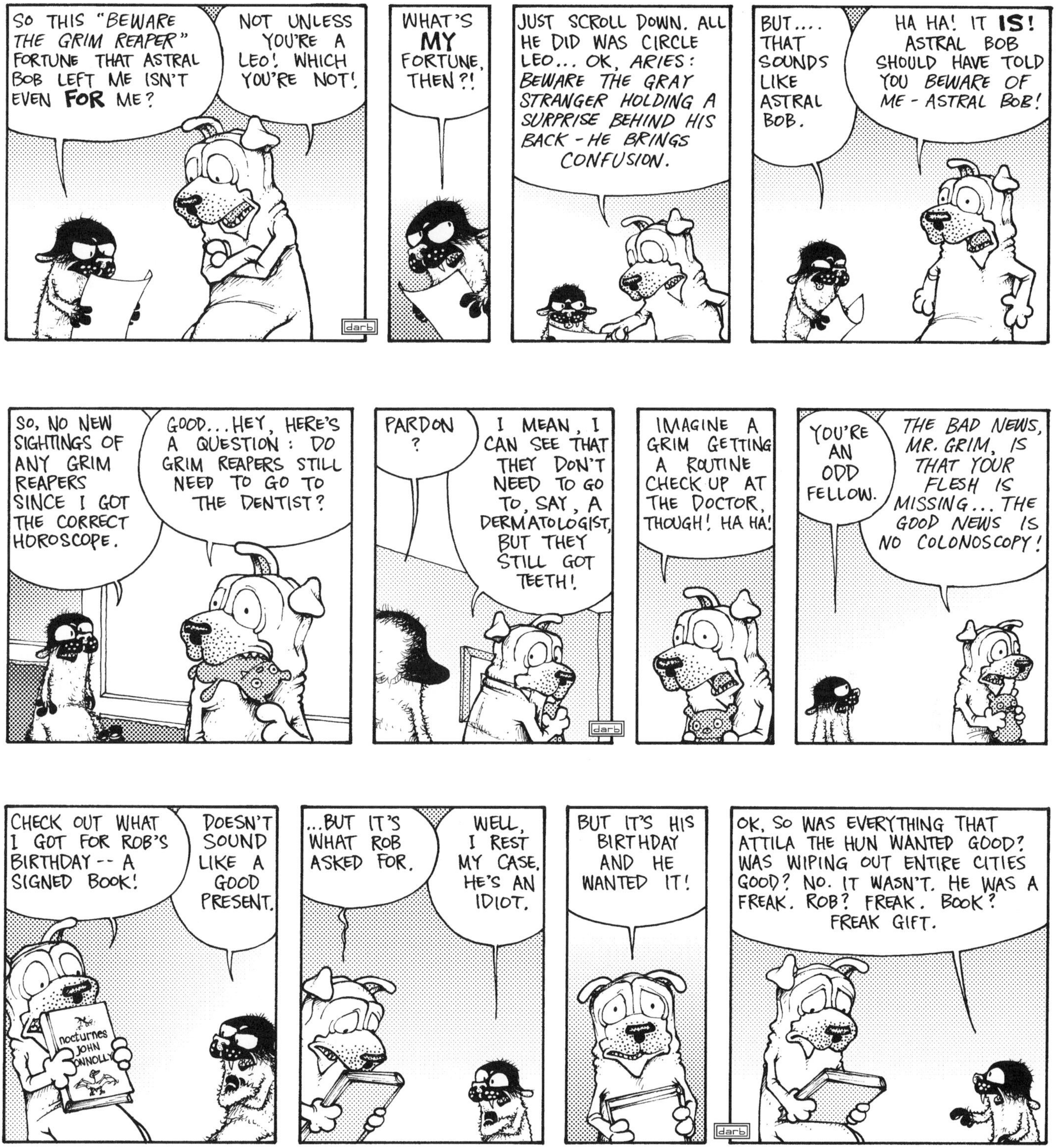
SO THIS "BEWARE THE GRIM REAPER" FORTUNE THAT ASTRAL BOB LEFT ME ISN'T EVEN FOR ME?
NOT UNLESS YOU'RE A LEO! WHICH YOU'RE NOT!
WHAT'S MY FORTUNE, THEN?!
JUST SCROLL DOWN. ALL HE DID WAS CIRCLE LEO... OK, ARIES: BEWARE THE GRAY STRANGER HOLDING A SURPRISE BEHIND HIS BACK - HE BRINGS CONFUSION.
BUT.... THAT SOUNDS LIKE ASTRAL BOB.
HA HA! IT IS! ASTRAL BOB SHOULD HAVE TOLD YOU BEWARE OF ME - ASTRAL BOB!
darb
SO, NO NEW SIGHTINGS OF ANY GRIM REAPERS SINCE I GOT THE CORRECT HOROSCOPE.
GOOD... HEY, HERE'S A QUESTION: DO GRIM REAPERS STILL NEED TO GO TO THE DENTIST?
PARDON?
I MEAN, I CAN SEE THAT THEY DON'T NEED TO GO TO, SAY, A DERMATOLOGIST, BUT THEY STILL GOT TEETH!
IMAGINE A GRIM GETTING A ROUTINE CHECK UP AT THE DOCTOR, THOUGH! HA HA!
YOU'RE AN ODD FELLOW.
THE BAD NEWS, MR. GRIM, IS THAT YOUR FLESH IS MISSING... THE GOOD NEWS IS NO COLONOSCOPY!
darb
CHECK OUT WHAT I GOT FOR ROB'S BIRTHDAY -- A SIGNED BOOK!
DOESN'T SOUND LIKE A GOOD PRESENT.
nocturnes JOHN CONNOLLY
...BUT IT'S WHAT ROB ASKED FOR.
WELL, I REST MY CASE. HE'S AN IDIOT.
BUT IT'S HIS BIRTHDAY AND HE WANTED IT!
OK, SO WAS EVERYTHING THAT ATTILA THE HUN WANTED GOOD? WAS WIPING OUT ENTIRE CITIES GOOD? NO. IT WASN'T. HE WAS A FREAK. ROB? FREAK. BOOK? FREAK GIFT.
darb

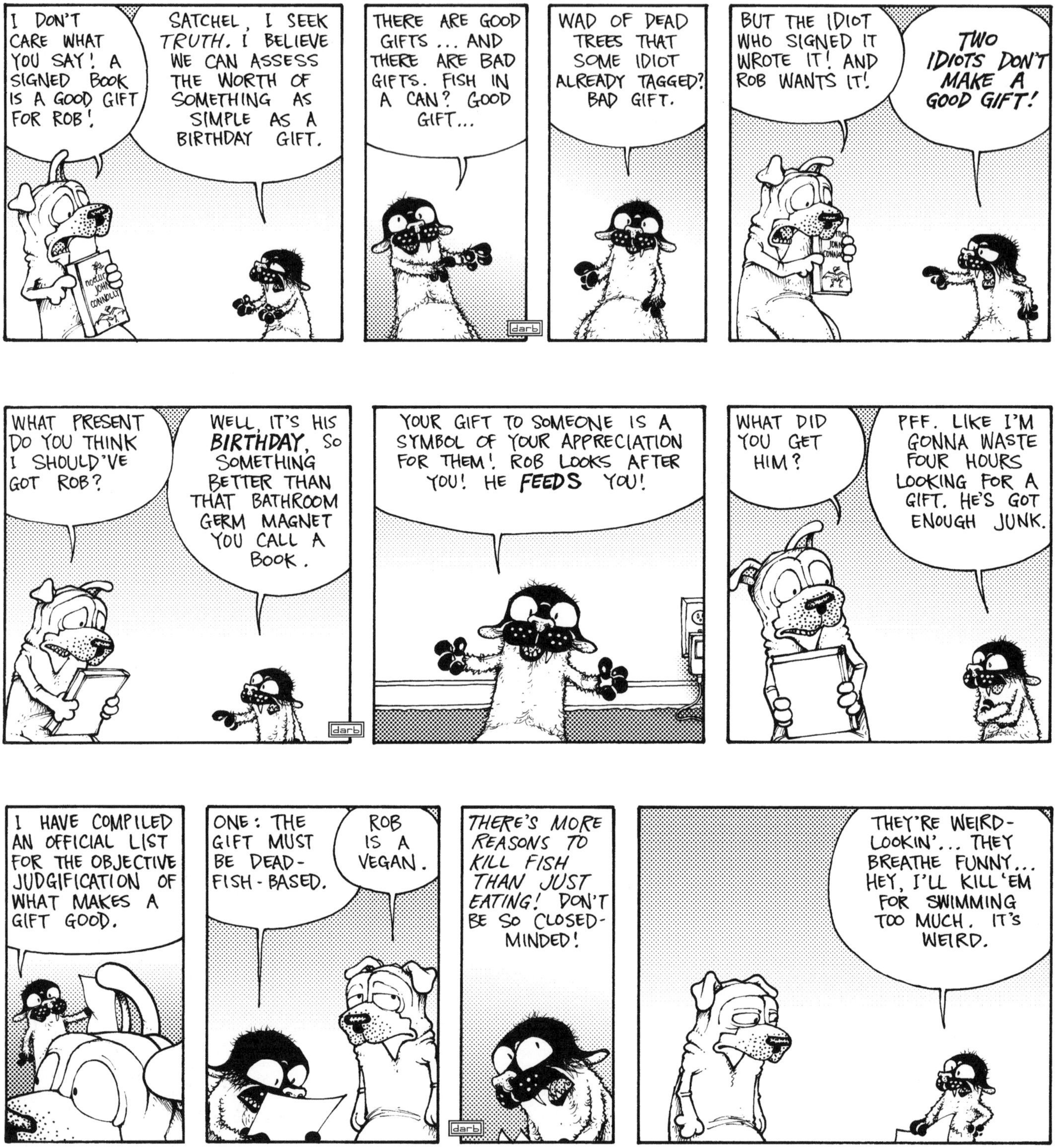
I DON'T CARE WHAT YOU SAY! A SIGNED BOOK IS A GOOD GIFT FOR ROB!
SATCHEL, I SEEK *TRUTH*. I BELIEVE WE CAN ASSESS THE WORTH OF SOMETHING AS SIMPLE AS A BIRTHDAY GIFT.
THERE ARE GOOD GIFTS... AND THERE ARE BAD GIFTS. FISH IN A CAN? GOOD GIFT...
WAD OF DEAD TREES THAT SOME IDIOT ALREADY TAGGED? BAD GIFT.
BUT THE IDIOT WHO SIGNED IT WROTE IT! AND ROB WANTS IT!
TWO IDIOTS DON'T MAKE A GOOD GIFT!
WHAT PRESENT DO YOU THINK I SHOULD'VE GOT ROB?
WELL, IT'S HIS **BIRTHDAY**, SO SOMETHING BETTER THAN THAT BATHROOM GERM MAGNET YOU CALL A BOOK.
YOUR GIFT TO SOMEONE IS A SYMBOL OF YOUR APPRECIATION FOR THEM! ROB LOOKS AFTER YOU! HE **FEEDS** YOU!
WHAT DID YOU GET HIM?
PFF. LIKE I'M GONNA WASTE FOUR HOURS LOOKING FOR A GIFT. HE'S GOT ENOUGH JUNK.
I HAVE COMPILED AN OFFICIAL LIST FOR THE OBJECTIVE JUDGIFICATION OF WHAT MAKES A GIFT GOOD.
ONE: THE GIFT MUST BE DEAD-FISH-BASED.
ROB IS A VEGAN.
THERE'S MORE REASONS TO KILL FISH THAN JUST EATING! DON'T BE SO CLOSED-MINDED!
THEY'RE WEIRD-LOOKIN'... THEY BREATHE FUNNY... HEY, I'LL KILL 'EM FOR SWIMMING TOO MUCH. IT'S WEIRD.

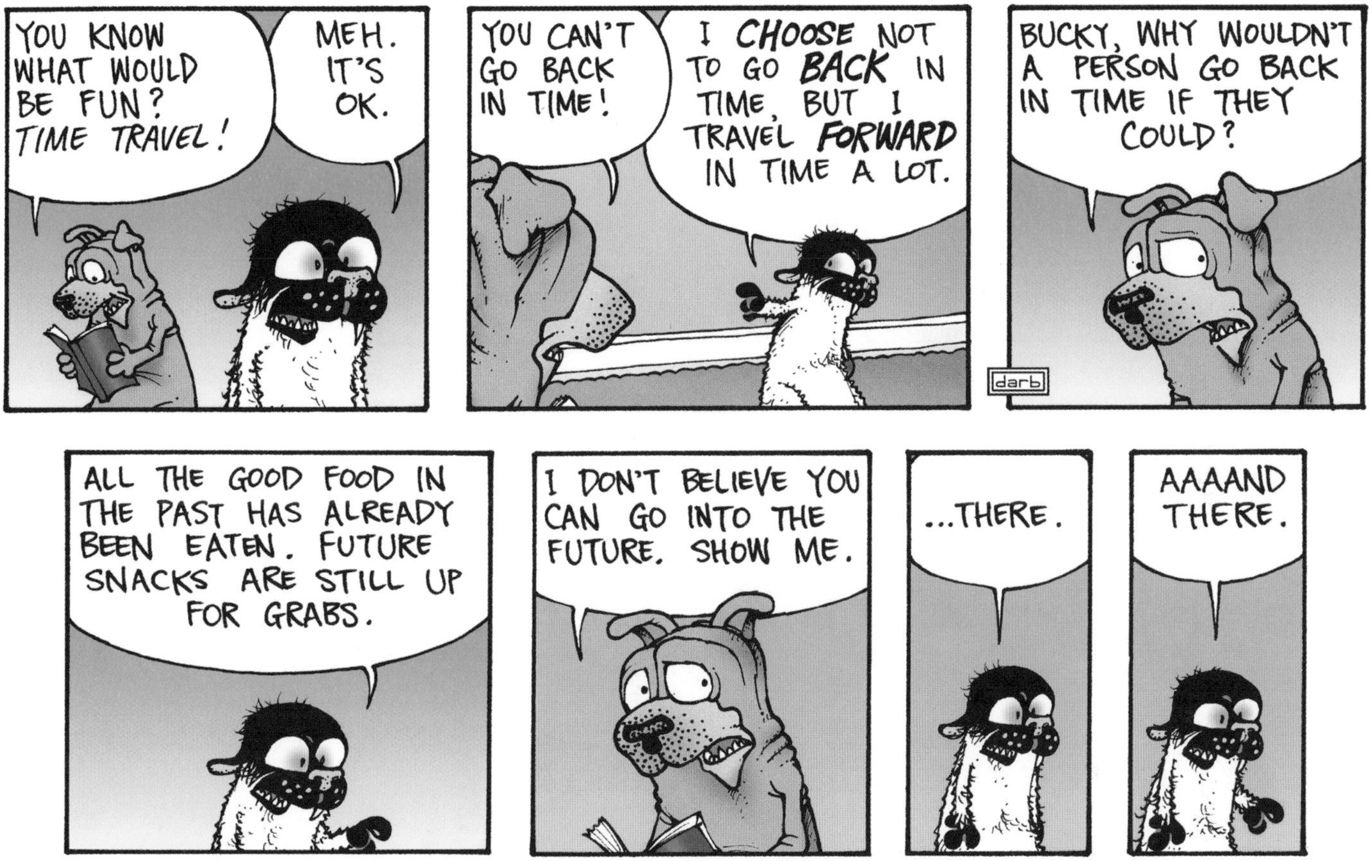
YOU KNOW WHAT WOULD BE FUN? TIME TRAVEL!
MEH. IT'S OK.
YOU CAN'T GO BACK IN TIME!
I CHOOSE NOT TO GO BACK IN TIME, BUT I TRAVEL FORWARD IN TIME A LOT.
BUCKY, WHY WOULDN'T A PERSON GO BACK IN TIME IF THEY COULD?
darb
ALL THE GOOD FOOD IN THE PAST HAS ALREADY BEEN EATEN. FUTURE SNACKS ARE STILL UP FOR GRABS.
I DON'T BELIEVE YOU CAN GO INTO THE FUTURE. SHOW ME.
...THERE.
AAAAND THERE.

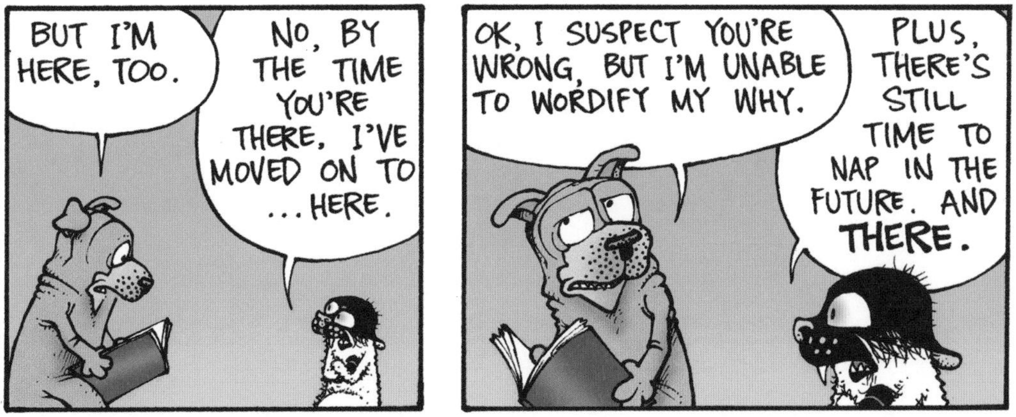
BUT I'M HERE, TOO.
NO, BY THE TIME YOU'RE THERE, I'VE MOVED ON TO ...HERE.
OK, I SUSPECT YOU'RE WRONG, BUT I'M UNABLE TO WORDIFY MY WHY.
PLUS, THERE'S STILL TIME TO NAP IN THE FUTURE. AND THERE.

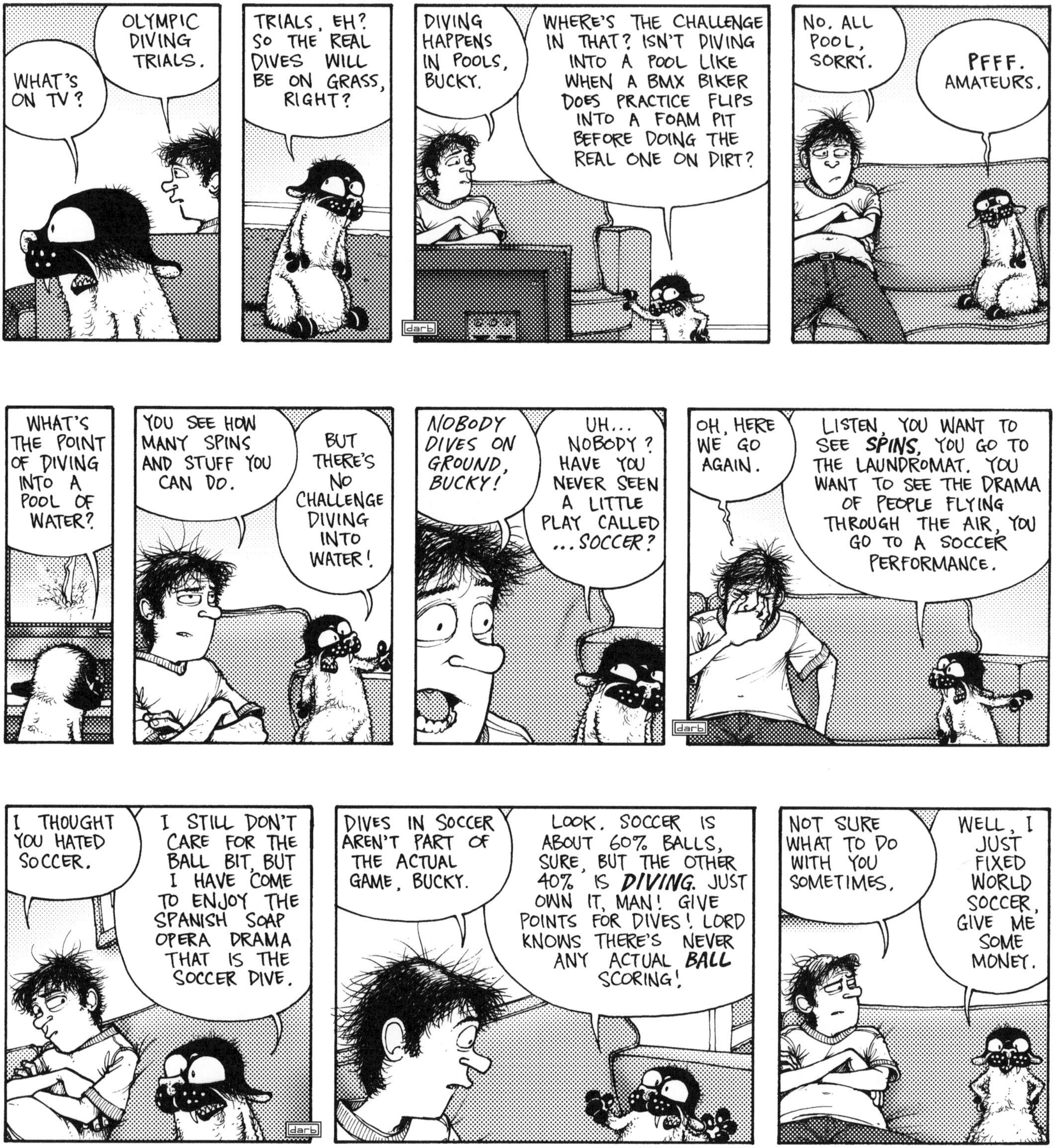
WHAT'S ON TV?
OLYMPIC DIVING TRIALS.
TRIALS, EH? SO THE REAL DIVES WILL BE ON GRASS, RIGHT?
DIVING HAPPENS IN POOLS, BUCKY.
WHERE'S THE CHALLENGE IN THAT? ISN'T DIVING INTO A POOL LIKE WHEN A BMX BIKER DOES PRACTICE FLIPS INTO A FOAM PIT BEFORE DOING THE REAL ONE ON DIRT?
NO. ALL POOL, SORRY.
PFFF. AMATEURS.
darb
WHAT'S THE POINT OF DIVING INTO A POOL OF WATER?
YOU SEE HOW MANY SPINS AND STUFF YOU CAN DO.
BUT THERE'S NO CHALLENGE DIVING INTO WATER!
NOBODY DIVES ON GROUND, BUCKY!
UH... NOBODY? HAVE YOU NEVER SEEN A LITTLE PLAY CALLED ...SOCCER?
OH, HERE WE GO AGAIN.
LISTEN, YOU WANT TO SEE SPINS, YOU GO TO THE LAUNDROMAT. YOU WANT TO SEE THE DRAMA OF PEOPLE FLYING THROUGH THE AIR, YOU GO TO A SOCCER PERFORMANCE.
darb
I THOUGHT YOU HATED SOCCER.
I STILL DON'T CARE FOR THE BALL BIT, BUT I HAVE COME TO ENJOY THE SPANISH SOAP OPERA DRAMA THAT IS THE SOCCER DIVE.
DIVES IN SOCCER AREN'T PART OF THE ACTUAL GAME, BUCKY.
LOOK. SOCCER IS ABOUT 60% BALLS, SURE, BUT THE OTHER 40% IS DIVING. JUST OWN IT, MAN! GIVE POINTS FOR DIVES! LORD KNOWS THERE'S NEVER ANY ACTUAL BALL SCORING!
NOT SURE WHAT TO DO WITH YOU SOMETIMES.
WELL, I JUST FIXED WORLD SOCCER, GIVE ME SOME MONEY.
darb

Panel 1:

WHY ARE YOU WATCHING AMERICAN DIVING, ANYWAY? WHY NOT WATCH ONE OF THE TOP COUNTRIES?

I'M NOT LISTENING TO YOU.

Panel 2:

APPROXIMATELY 90% OF THE WORLD'S BEST DIVERS PLAY SOCCER FOR EITHER PORTUGAL, ITALY, SPAIN OR BRAZIL.

YOU GET WITHIN 6 FEET OF AN ITALIAN IN A PENALTY BOX, YOU GET READY TO SEE THE BEST *BIRD-SHOT-IN-FLIGHT* IMPRESSION YOU'VE EVER SEEN.

Panel 3:

NOT LISTENING.

A SIX YEAR-OLD PORTUGAL KID DIVES AT AN AMERICAN COLLEGE LEVEL. FACT.

Panel 4:

BUCKY, NOT ALL PORTUGUESE AND ITALIAN SOCCER PLAYERS "DIVE."

ROBERT... WHY DO YOU THINK THEY CALL SLANTED LETTERS *ITALICS*?

Panel 5:

IT'S BECAUSE THEY LOOK LIKE ITALIAN SOCCER PLAYERS, FLYING THROUGH THE AIR LIKE THIS...

Panel 6:

AND EACH CULTURE'S TRADITIONS CELEBRATE A DIFFERENT ASPECT OF THE DIVING RITUAL.

Panel 7:

FOR SPANIARDS, IT'S ALL ABOUT THE SYMBOLIC REENACTMENT OF THE MOMENT OF PAIN... IT'S THE *PAIN*, OR, FOR SHORT, S'PAIN.

Panel 8:

NOW... THE PORTUGUESE TAKE SOCCER DIVING TO UNHEARD-OF NEW LEVELS.

Panel 9:

DON'T GET ME WRONG, THEY'LL DO A FACE-FIRST, DOUBLE-TUCK, OPEN-MOUTHED SHIN GRAB WITH THE BEST OF 'EM...

Panel 10:

BUT THEIR BRILLIANCE IS IN SHEER AIR TIME AND NOISE PRODUCED. IT'S SAID THEY MAKE ENOUGH NOISE FOR TWO GEESE...PARA...TWO...GEESE...PORTUGUESE.

Panel 11:

THE CONTENTS OF A PORTUGUESE TRAINER'S MEDICAL BAG CONSIST SOLELY OF SORE THROAT SPRAY AND HAIR GEL. FACT.

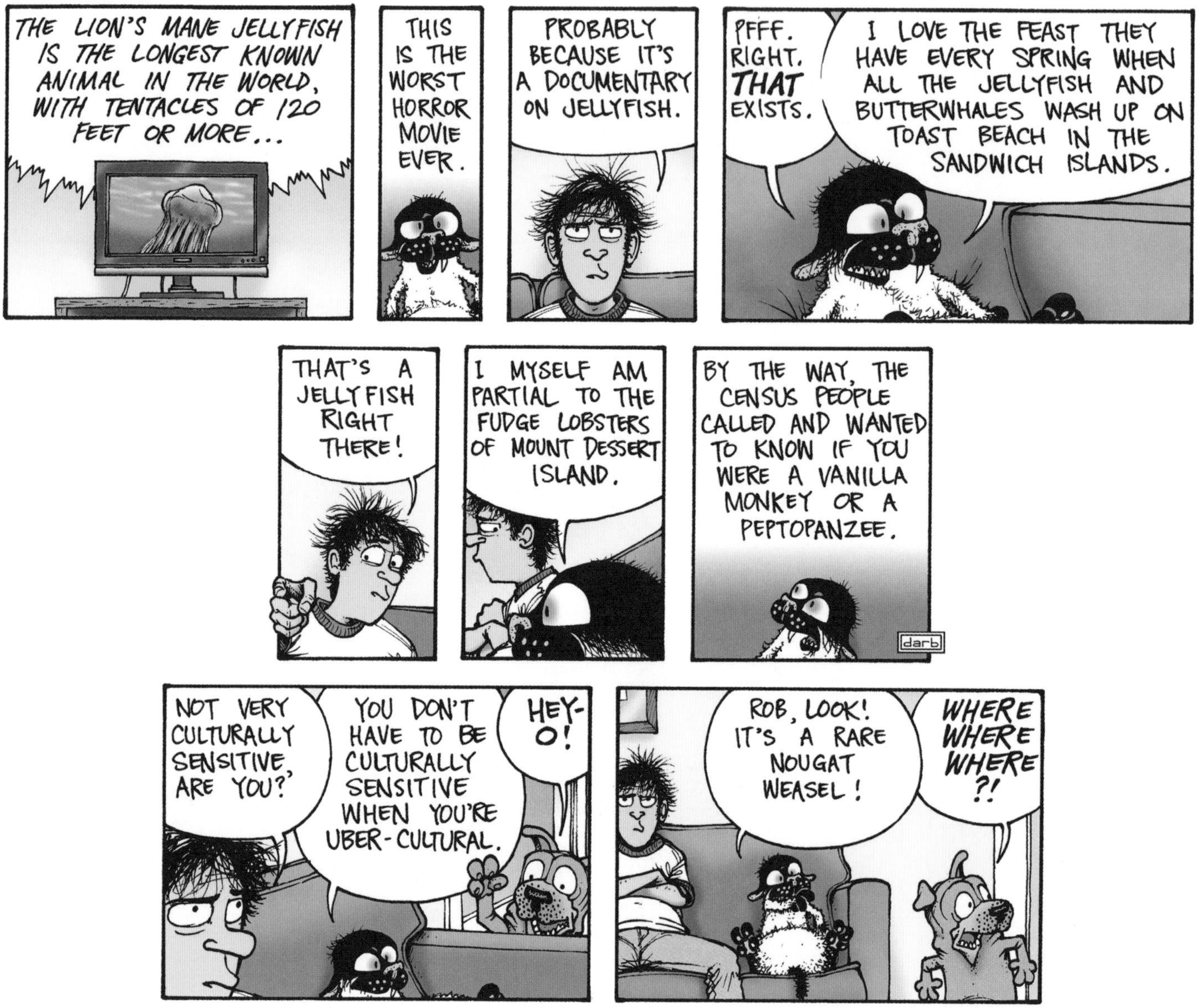
THE LION'S MANE JELLYFISH IS THE LONGEST KNOWN ANIMAL IN THE WORLD, WITH TENTACLES OF 120 FEET OR MORE...
THIS IS THE WORST HORROR MOVIE EVER.
PROBABLY BECAUSE IT'S A DOCUMENTARY ON JELLYFISH.
PFFF. RIGHT. THAT EXISTS.
I LOVE THE FEAST THEY HAVE EVERY SPRING WHEN ALL THE JELLYFISH AND BUTTERWHALES WASH UP ON TOAST BEACH IN THE SANDWICH ISLANDS.
THAT'S A JELLYFISH RIGHT THERE!
I MYSELF AM PARTIAL TO THE FUDGE LOBSTERS OF MOUNT DESSERT ISLAND.
BY THE WAY, THE CENSUS PEOPLE CALLED AND WANTED TO KNOW IF YOU WERE A VANILLA MONKEY OR A PEPTOPANZEE.
darb
NOT VERY CULTURALLY SENSITIVE, ARE YOU?
YOU DON'T HAVE TO BE CULTURALLY SENSITIVE WHEN YOU'RE UBER-CULTURAL.
HEY-O!
ROB, LOOK! IT'S A RARE NOUGAT WEASEL!
WHERE WHERE WHERE ?!

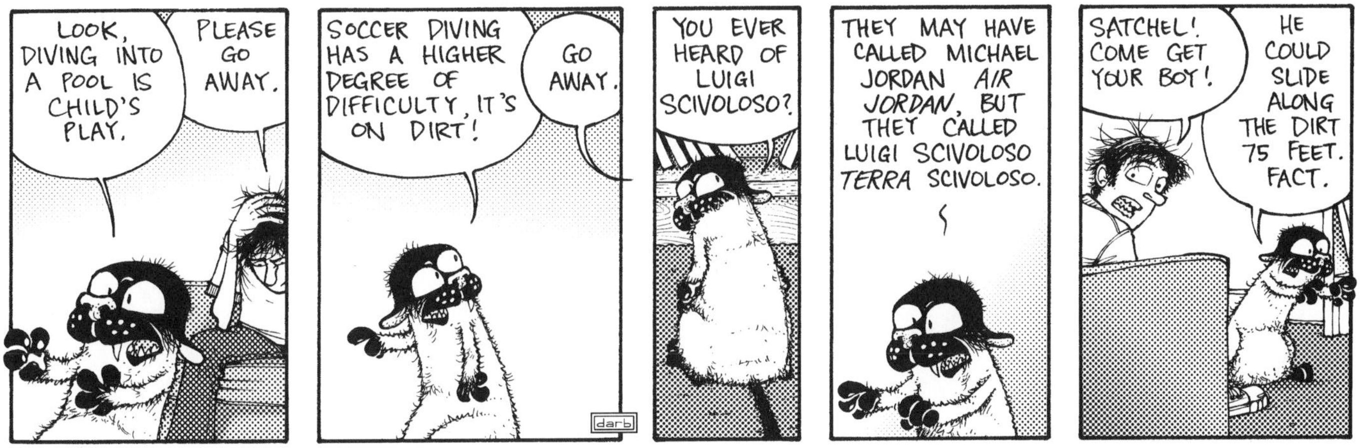
LOOK, DIVING INTO A POOL IS CHILD'S PLAY.
PLEASE GO AWAY.
SOCCER DIVING HAS A HIGHER DEGREE OF DIFFICULTY, IT'S ON DIRT!
GO AWAY.
YOU EVER HEARD OF LUIGI SCIVOLOSO?
THEY MAY HAVE CALLED MICHAEL JORDAN *AIR JORDAN*, BUT THEY CALLED LUIGI SCIVOLOSO *TERRA* SCIVOLOSO.
SATCHEL! COME GET YOUR BOY!
HE COULD SLIDE ALONG THE DIRT 75 FEET. FACT.
darb

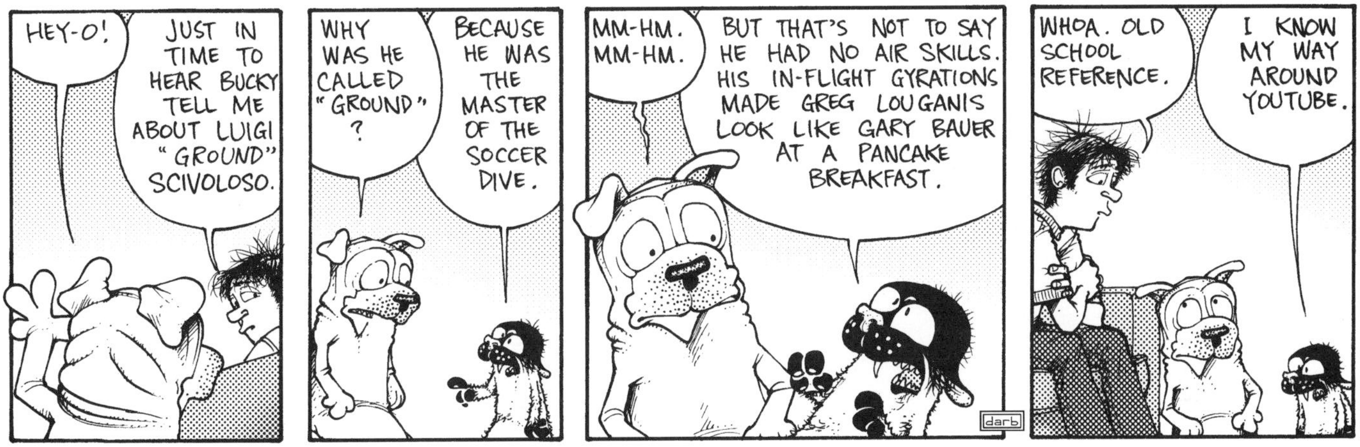
HEY-O!
JUST IN TIME TO HEAR BUCKY TELL ME ABOUT LUIGI "GROUND" SCIVOLOSO.
WHY WAS HE CALLED "GROUND"?
BECAUSE HE WAS THE MASTER OF THE SOCCER DIVE.
MM-HM. MM-HM.
BUT THAT'S NOT TO SAY HE HAD NO AIR SKILLS. HIS IN-FLIGHT GYRATIONS MADE GREG LOUGANIS LOOK LIKE GARY BAUER AT A PANCAKE BREAKFAST.
WHOA. OLD SCHOOL REFERENCE.
I KNOW MY WAY AROUND YOUTUBE.
darb

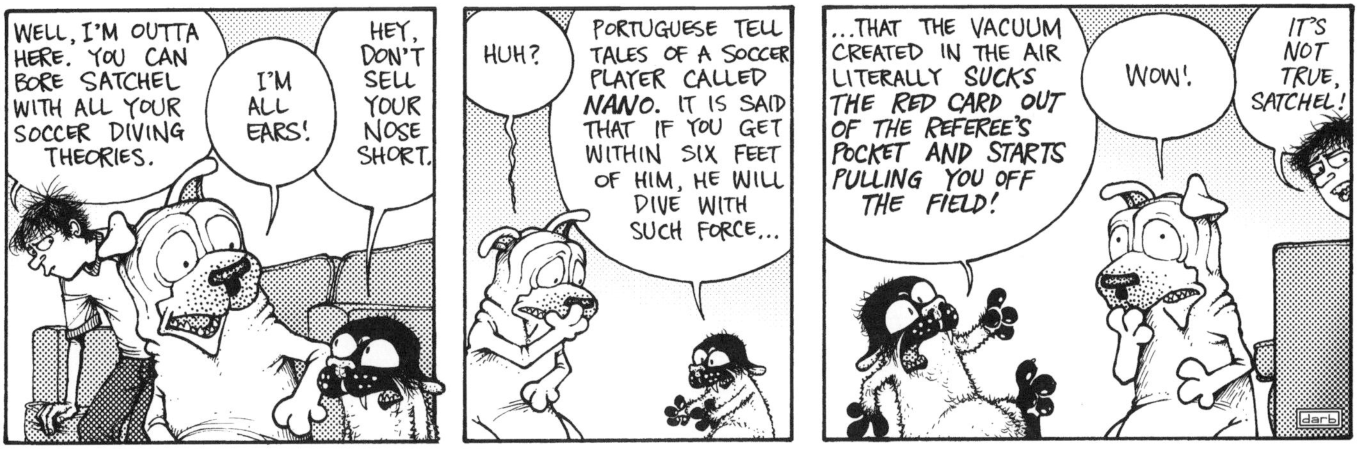
WELL, I'M OUTTA HERE. YOU CAN BORE SATCHEL WITH ALL YOUR SOCCER DIVING THEORIES.
I'M ALL EARS!
HEY, DON'T SELL YOUR NOSE SHORT.
HUH?
PORTUGUESE TELL TALES OF A SOCCER PLAYER CALLED *NANO*. IT IS SAID THAT IF YOU GET WITHIN SIX FEET OF HIM, HE WILL DIVE WITH SUCH FORCE...
...THAT THE VACUUM CREATED IN THE AIR LITERALLY *SUCKS THE RED CARD OUT OF THE REFEREE'S POCKET AND STARTS PULLING YOU OFF THE FIELD!*
WOW!
IT'S NOT TRUE, SATCHEL!
darb

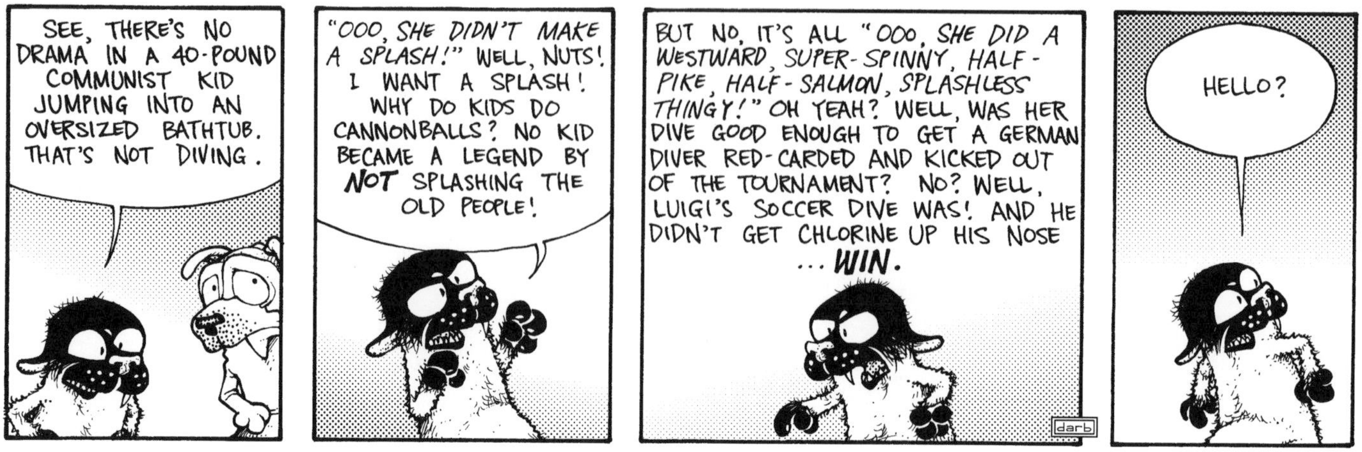
SEE, THERE'S NO DRAMA IN A 40-POUND COMMUNIST KID JUMPING INTO AN OVERSIZED BATHTUB. THAT'S NOT DIVING.
"OOO, SHE DIDN'T MAKE A SPLASH!" WELL, NUTS! I WANT A SPLASH! WHY DO KIDS DO CANNONBALLS? NO KID BECAME A LEGEND BY NOT SPLASHING THE OLD PEOPLE!
BUT NO, IT'S ALL "OOO, SHE DID A WESTWARD, SUPER-SPINNY, HALF-PIKE, HALF-SALMON, SPLASHLESS THINGY!" OH YEAH? WELL, WAS HER DIVE GOOD ENOUGH TO GET A GERMAN DIVER RED-CARDED AND KICKED OUT OF THE TOURNAMENT? NO? WELL, LUIGI'S SOCCER DIVE WAS! AND HE DIDN'T GET CHLORINE UP HIS NOSE ...WIN.
darb
HELLO?

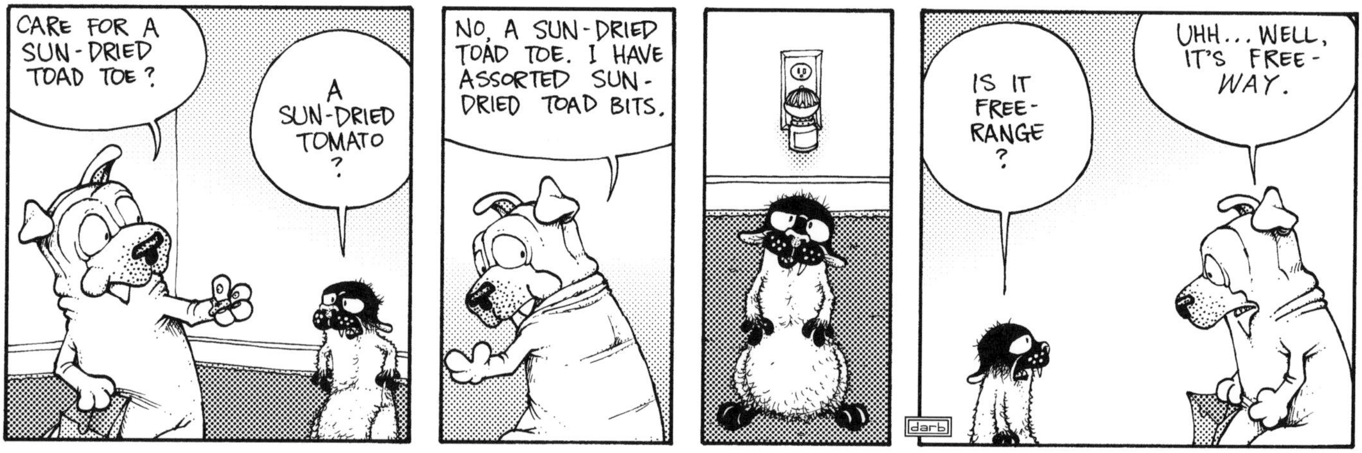
CARE FOR A SUN-DRIED TOAD TOE?
A SUN-DRIED TOMATO?
NO, A SUN-DRIED TOAD TOE. I HAVE ASSORTED SUN-DRIED TOAD BITS.
darb
IS IT FREE-RANGE?
UHH... WELL, IT'S FREE-WAY.

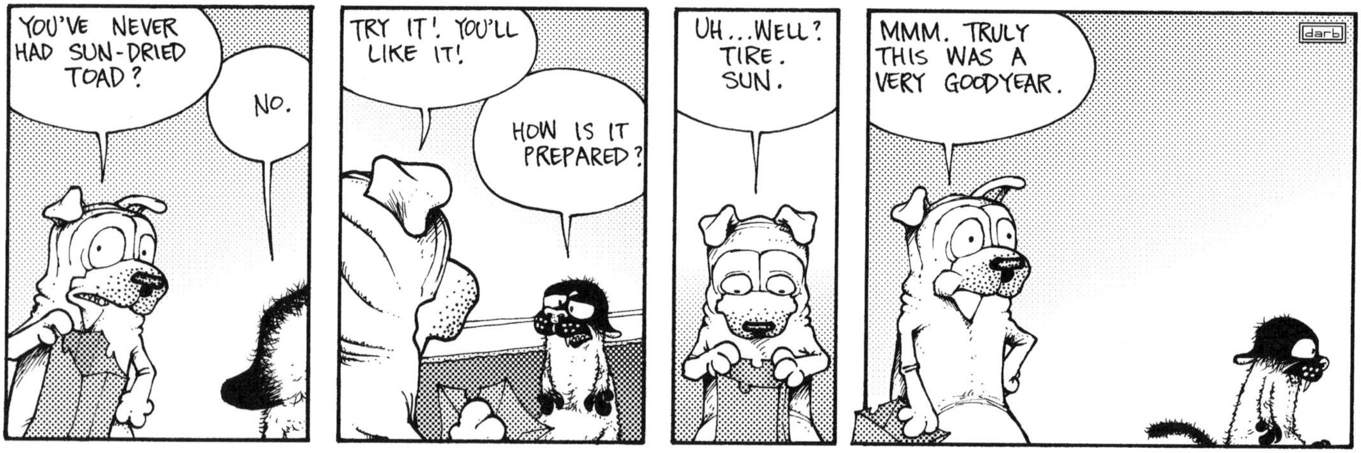
YOU'VE NEVER HAD SUN-DRIED TOAD?
NO.
TRY IT! YOU'LL LIKE IT!
HOW IS IT PREPARED?
UH... WELL? TIRE. SUN.
darb
MMM. TRULY THIS WAS A VERY GOODYEAR.

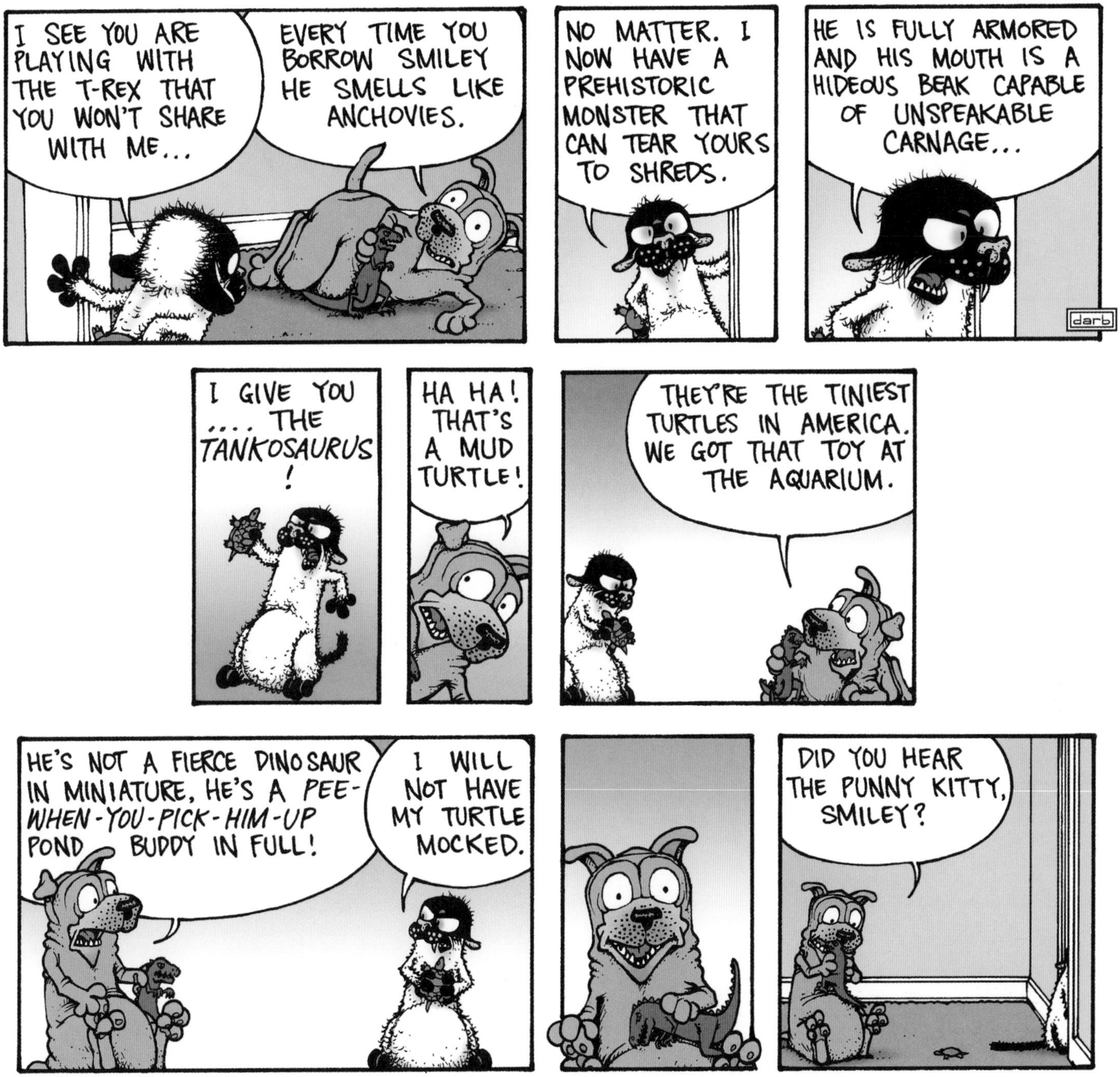
I SEE YOU ARE PLAYING WITH THE T-REX THAT YOU WON'T SHARE WITH ME...
EVERY TIME YOU BORROW SMILEY HE SMELLS LIKE ANCHOVIES.
NO MATTER. I NOW HAVE A PREHISTORIC MONSTER THAT CAN TEAR YOURS TO SHREDS.
HE IS FULLY ARMORED AND HIS MOUTH IS A HIDEOUS BEAK CAPABLE OF UNSPEAKABLE CARNAGE...
darb
I GIVE YOU .... THE TANKOSAURUS!
HA HA! THAT'S A MUD TURTLE!
THEY'RE THE TINIEST TURTLES IN AMERICA. WE GOT THAT TOY AT THE AQUARIUM.
HE'S NOT A FIERCE DINOSAUR IN MINIATURE, HE'S A PEE-WHEN-YOU-PICK-HIM-UP POND BUDDY IN FULL!
I WILL NOT HAVE MY TURTLE MOCKED.
DID YOU HEAR THE PUNNY KITTY, SMILEY?

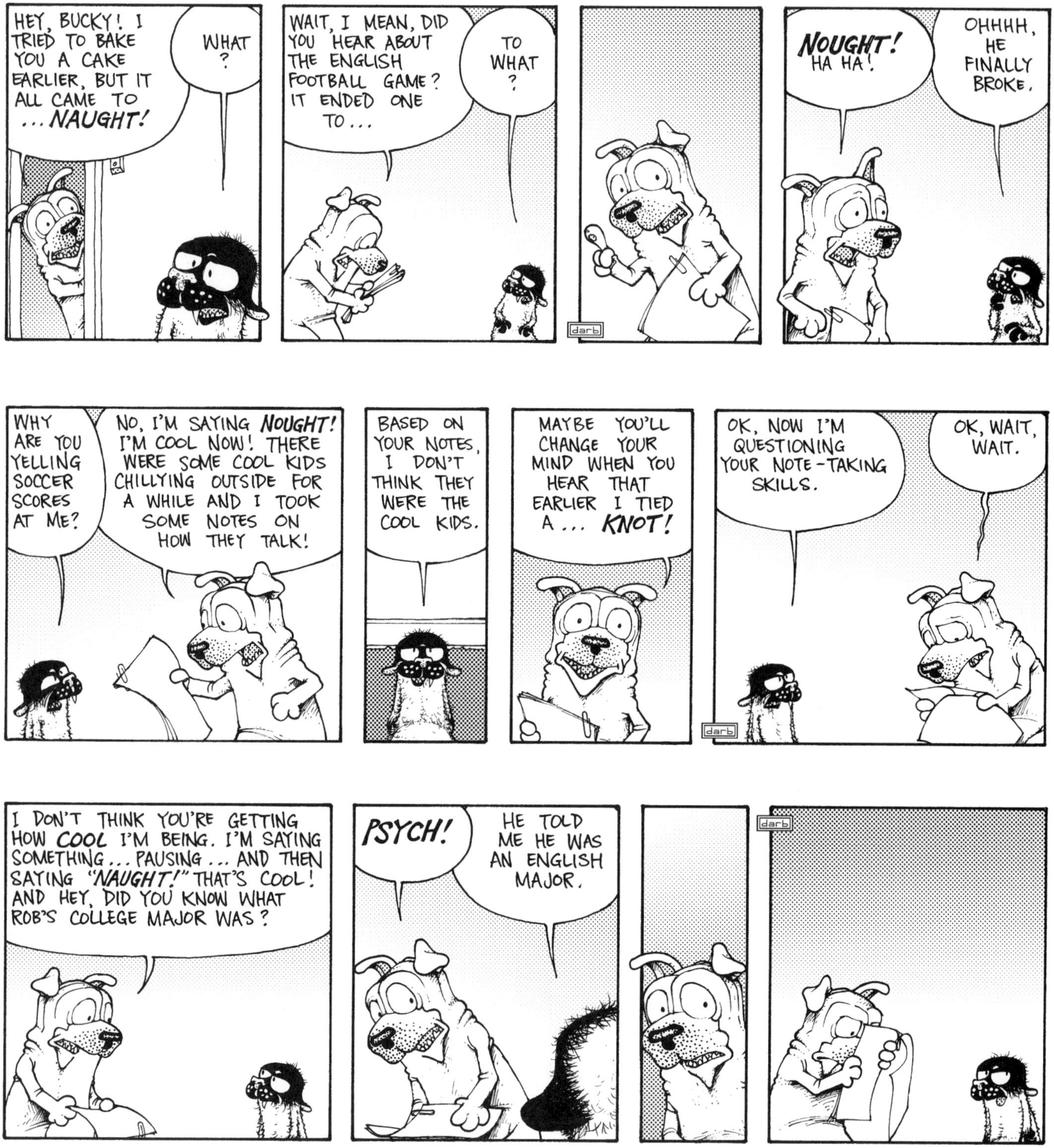
HEY, BUCKY! I TRIED TO BAKE YOU A CAKE EARLIER, BUT IT ALL CAME TO ...NAUGHT!
WHAT ?
WAIT, I MEAN, DID YOU HEAR ABOUT THE ENGLISH FOOTBALL GAME? IT ENDED ONE TO...
TO WHAT ?
darb
NOUGHT! HA HA!
OHHHH, HE FINALLY BROKE.
WHY ARE YOU YELLING SOCCER SCORES AT ME?
NO, I'M SAYING NOUGHT! I'M COOL NOW! THERE WERE SOME COOL KIDS CHILLYING OUTSIDE FOR A WHILE AND I TOOK SOME NOTES ON HOW THEY TALK!
BASED ON YOUR NOTES, I DON'T THINK THEY WERE THE COOL KIDS.
MAYBE YOU'LL CHANGE YOUR MIND WHEN YOU HEAR THAT EARLIER I TIED A... KNOT!
darb
OK, NOW I'M QUESTIONING YOUR NOTE-TAKING SKILLS.
OK, WAIT, WAIT.
I DON'T THINK YOU'RE GETTING HOW COOL I'M BEING. I'M SAYING SOMETHING... PAUSING... AND THEN SAYING "NAUGHT!" THAT'S COOL! AND HEY, DID YOU KNOW WHAT ROB'S COLLEGE MAJOR WAS?
PSYCH!
HE TOLD ME HE WAS AN ENGLISH MAJOR.
darb

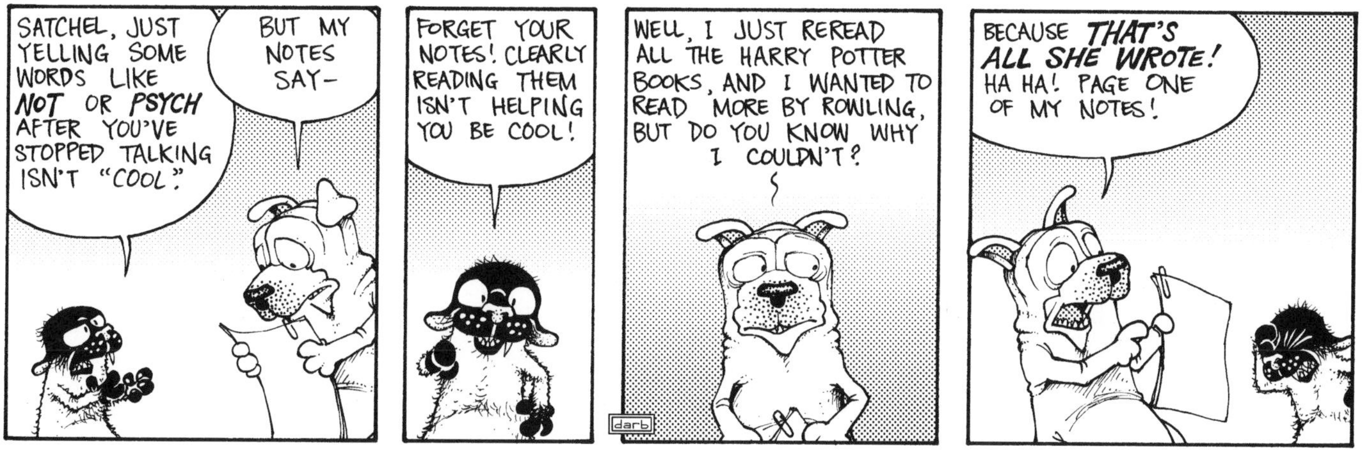
SATCHEL, JUST YELLING SOME WORDS LIKE NOT OR PSYCH AFTER YOU'VE STOPPED TALKING ISN'T "COOL."
BUT MY NOTES SAY–
FORGET YOUR NOTES! CLEARLY READING THEM ISN'T HELPING YOU BE COOL!
WELL, I JUST REREAD ALL THE HARRY POTTER BOOKS, AND I WANTED TO READ MORE BY ROWLING, BUT DO YOU KNOW WHY I COULDN'T?
BECAUSE THAT'S ALL SHE WROTE! HA HA! PAGE ONE OF MY NOTES!
darb

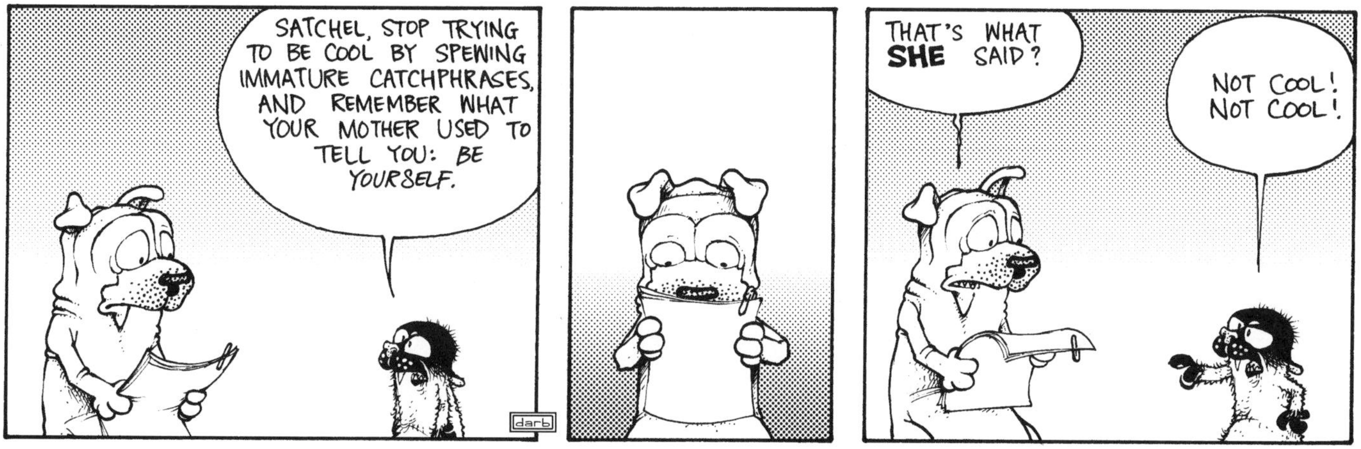
SATCHEL, STOP TRYING TO BE COOL BY SPEWING IMMATURE CATCHPHRASES, AND REMEMBER WHAT YOUR MOTHER USED TO TELL YOU: BE YOURSELF.
THAT'S WHAT SHE SAID?
NOT COOL! NOT COOL!
darb

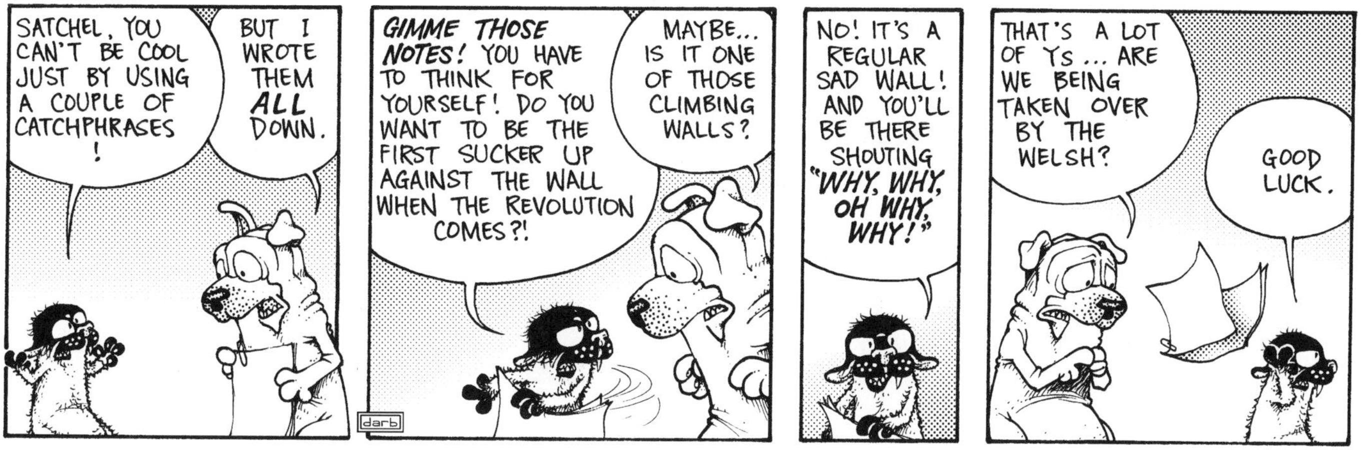
SATCHEL, YOU CAN'T BE COOL JUST BY USING A COUPLE OF CATCHPHRASES!
BUT I WROTE THEM ALL DOWN.
GIMME THOSE NOTES! YOU HAVE TO THINK FOR YOURSELF! DO YOU WANT TO BE THE FIRST SUCKER UP AGAINST THE WALL WHEN THE REVOLUTION COMES?!
MAYBE... IS IT ONE OF THOSE CLIMBING WALLS?
NO! IT'S A REGULAR SAD WALL! AND YOU'LL BE THERE SHOUTING "WHY, WHY, OH WHY, WHY!"
THAT'S A LOT OF Ys... ARE WE BEING TAKEN OVER BY THE WELSH?
GOOD LUCK.
darb

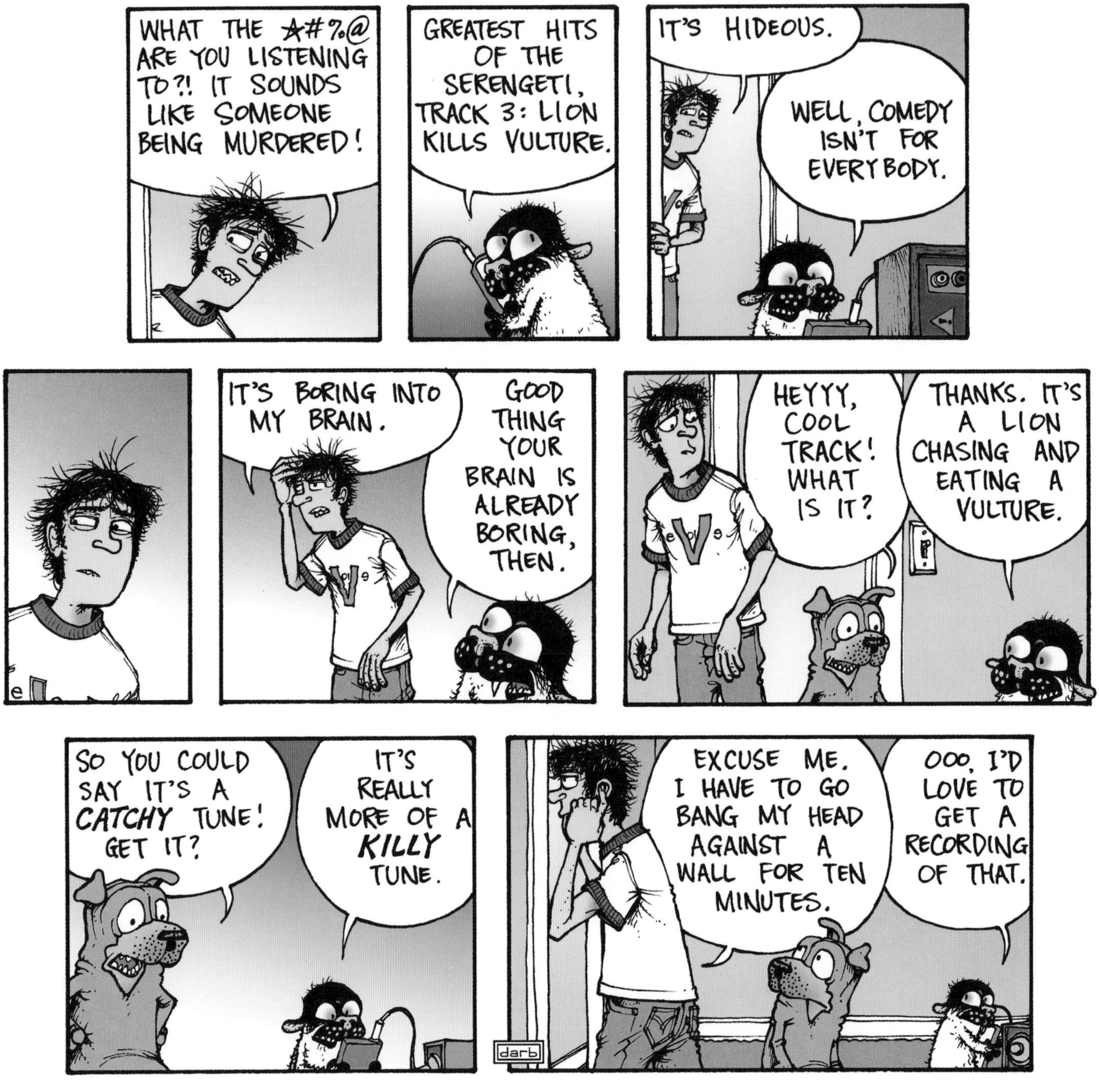
WHAT THE ☆#%@ ARE YOU LISTENING TO?! IT SOUNDS LIKE SOMEONE BEING MURDERED!
GREATEST HITS OF THE SERENGETI, TRACK 3: LION KILLS VULTURE.
IT'S HIDEOUS.
WELL, COMEDY ISN'T FOR EVERYBODY.
IT'S BORING INTO MY BRAIN.
GOOD THING YOUR BRAIN IS ALREADY BORING, THEN.
HEYYY, COOL TRACK! WHAT IS IT?
THANKS. IT'S A LION CHASING AND EATING A VULTURE.
SO YOU COULD SAY IT'S A *CATCHY* TUNE! GET IT?
IT'S REALLY MORE OF A *KILLY* TUNE.
EXCUSE ME. I HAVE TO GO BANG MY HEAD AGAINST A WALL FOR TEN MINUTES.
OOO, I'D LOVE TO GET A RECORDING OF THAT.
darb

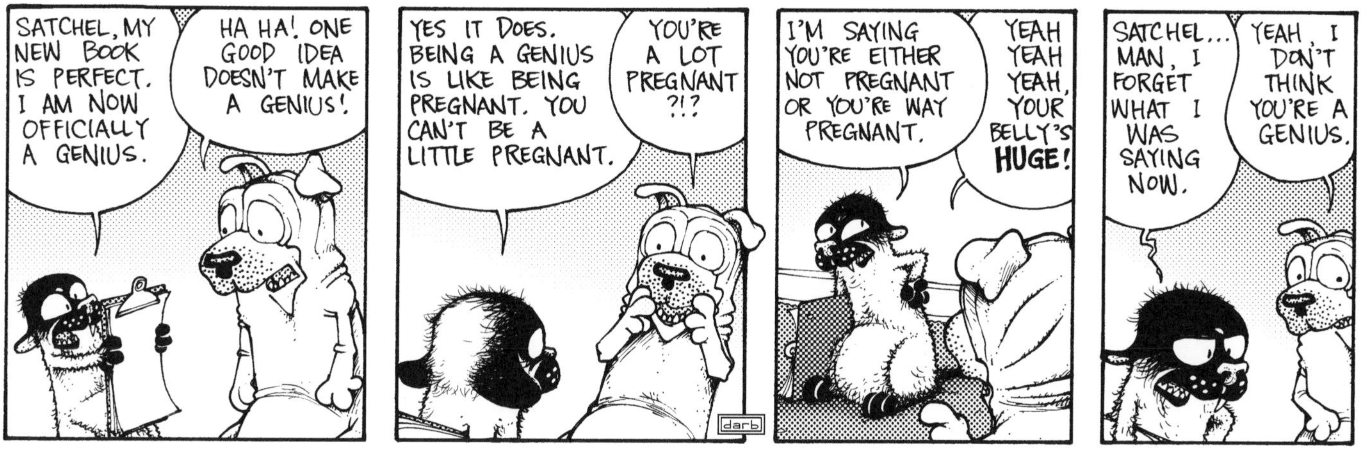
SATCHEL, MY NEW BOOK IS PERFECT. I AM NOW OFFICIALLY A GENIUS.
HA HA! ONE GOOD IDEA DOESN'T MAKE A GENIUS!
YES IT DOES. BEING A GENIUS IS LIKE BEING PREGNANT. YOU CAN'T BE A LITTLE PREGNANT.
YOU'RE A LOT PREGNANT ?!?
I'M SAYING YOU'RE EITHER NOT PREGNANT OR YOU'RE WAY PREGNANT.
YEAH YEAH YEAH, YOUR BELLY'S **HUGE**!
SATCHEL... MAN, I FORGET WHAT I WAS SAYING NOW.
YEAH, I DON'T THINK YOU'RE A GENIUS.

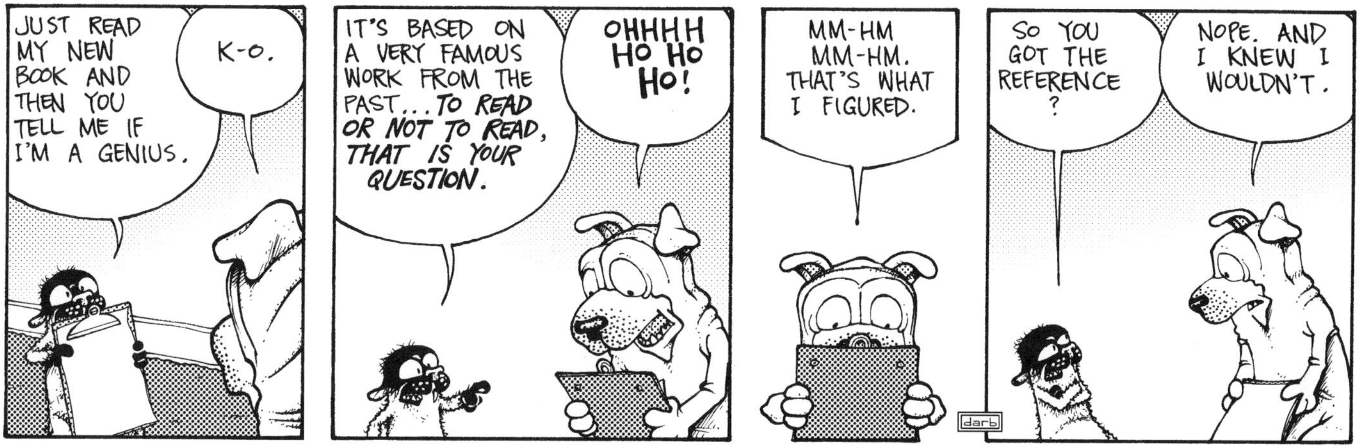
JUST READ MY NEW BOOK AND THEN YOU TELL ME IF I'M A GENIUS.
K-O.
IT'S BASED ON A VERY FAMOUS WORK FROM THE PAST... ***TO READ OR NOT TO READ, THAT IS YOUR QUESTION***.
OHHHH HO HO HO!
MM-HM MM-HM. THAT'S WHAT I FIGURED.
SO YOU GOT THE REFERENCE ?
NOPE. AND I KNEW I WOULDN'T.

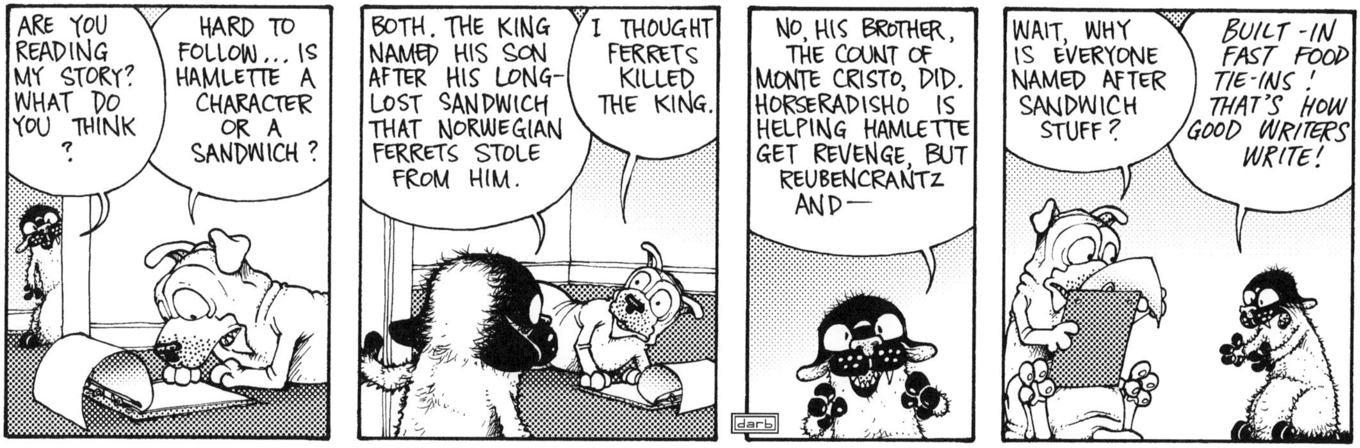
ARE YOU READING MY STORY? WHAT DO YOU THINK ?
HARD TO FOLLOW... IS HAMLETTE A CHARACTER OR A SANDWICH ?
BOTH. THE KING NAMED HIS SON AFTER HIS LONG-LOST SANDWICH THAT NORWEGIAN FERRETS STOLE FROM HIM.
I THOUGHT FERRETS KILLED THE KING.
NO, HIS BROTHER, THE COUNT OF MONTE CRISTO, DID. HORSERADISHO IS HELPING HAMLETTE GET REVENGE, BUT REUBENCRANTZ AND—
WAIT, WHY IS EVERYONE NAMED AFTER SANDWICH STUFF?
BUILT-IN FAST FOOD TIE-INS! THAT'S HOW GOOD WRITERS WRITE!

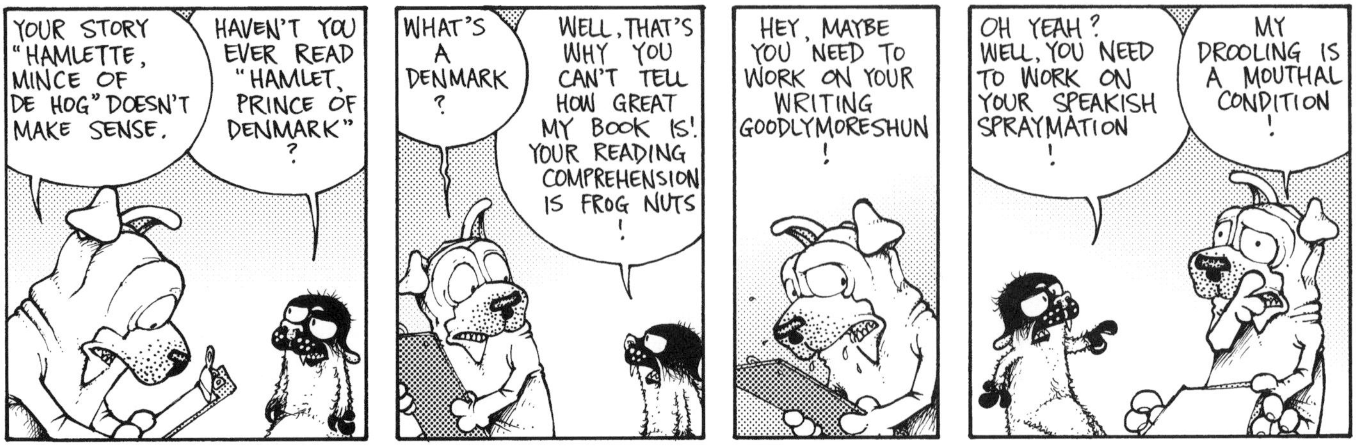
YOUR STORY "HAMLETTE, MINCE OF DE HOG" DOESN'T MAKE SENSE.
HAVEN'T YOU EVER READ "HAMLET, PRINCE OF DENMARK"?
WHAT'S A DENMARK?
WELL, THAT'S WHY YOU CAN'T TELL HOW GREAT MY BOOK IS! YOUR READING COMPREHENSION IS FROG NUTS!
HEY, MAYBE YOU NEED TO WORK ON YOUR WRITING GOODLYMORESHUN!
OH YEAH? WELL, YOU NEED TO WORK ON YOUR SPEAKISH SPRAYMATION!
MY DROOLING IS A MOUTHAL CONDITION!

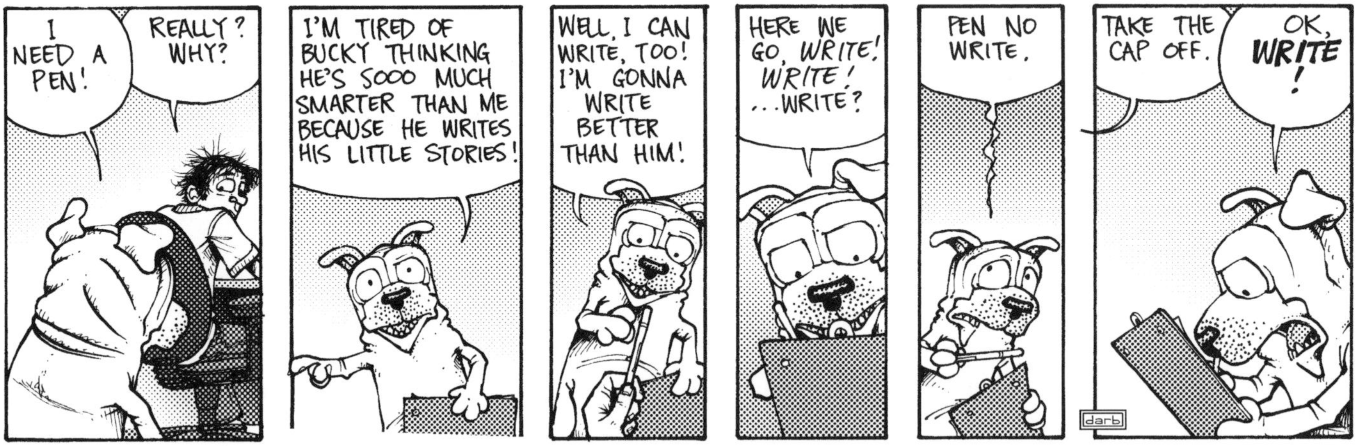
I NEED A PEN!
REALLY? WHY?
I'M TIRED OF BUCKY THINKING HE'S SOOO MUCH SMARTER THAN ME BECAUSE HE WRITES HIS LITTLE STORIES!
WELL, I CAN WRITE, TOO! I'M GONNA WRITE BETTER THAN HIM!
HERE WE GO, *WRITE*! *WRITE*! ...WRITE?
PEN NO WRITE.
TAKE THE CAP OFF.
OK, ***WRITE***!
darb

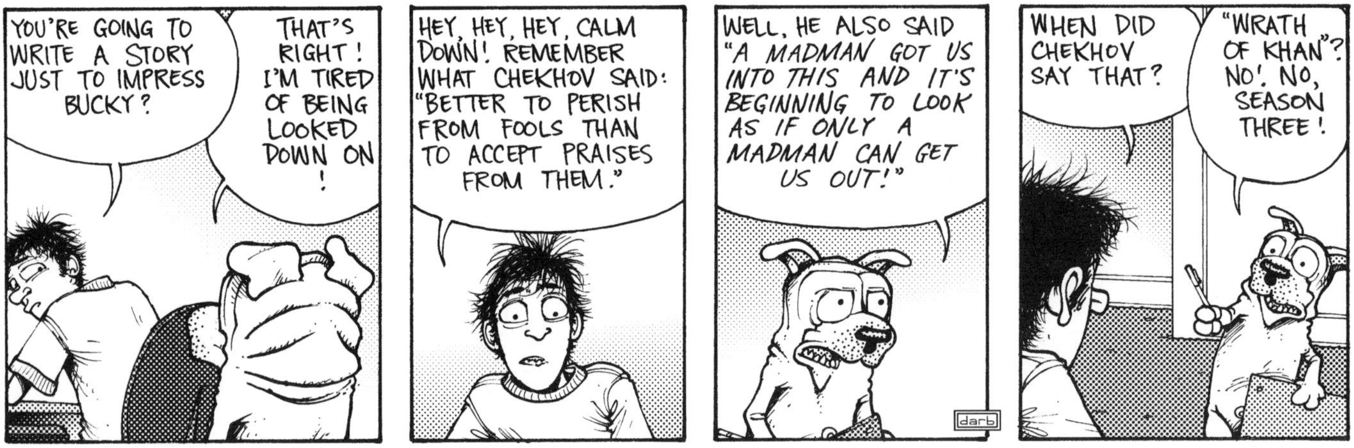
YOU'RE GOING TO WRITE A STORY JUST TO IMPRESS BUCKY?
THAT'S RIGHT! I'M TIRED OF BEING LOOKED DOWN ON!
HEY, HEY, HEY, CALM DOWN! REMEMBER WHAT CHEKHOV SAID: "BETTER TO PERISH FROM FOOLS THAN TO ACCEPT PRAISES FROM THEM."
WELL, HE ALSO SAID *"A MADMAN GOT US INTO THIS AND IT'S BEGINNING TO LOOK AS IF ONLY A MADMAN CAN GET US OUT!"*
darb
WHEN DID CHEKHOV SAY THAT?
"WRATH OF KHAN"? NO! NO, SEASON THREE!

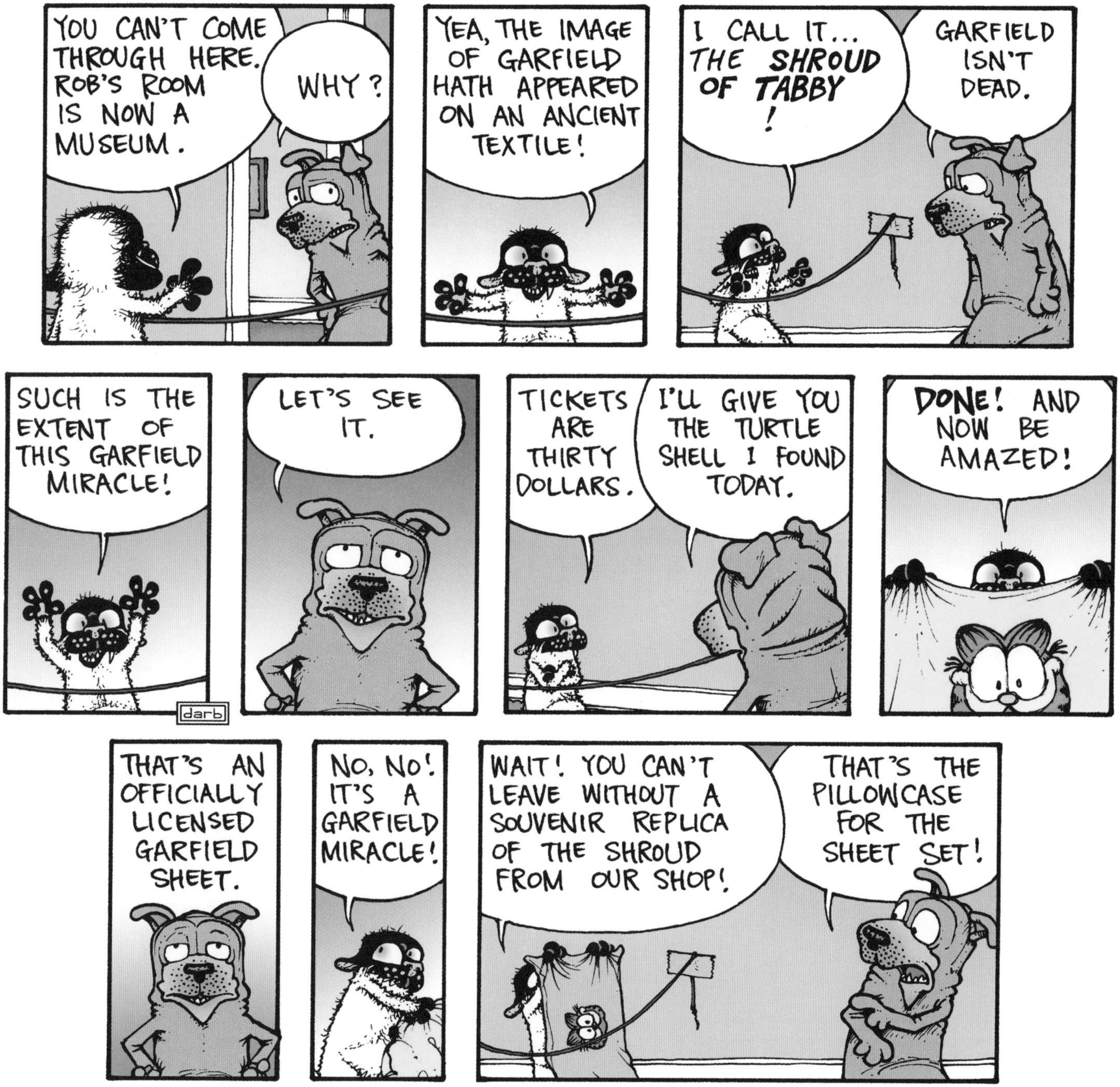
YOU CAN'T COME THROUGH HERE. ROB'S ROOM IS NOW A MUSEUM.
WHY?
YEA, THE IMAGE OF GARFIELD HATH APPEARED ON AN ANCIENT TEXTILE!
I CALL IT... THE SHROUD OF TABBY!
GARFIELD ISN'T DEAD.
SUCH IS THE EXTENT OF THIS GARFIELD MIRACLE!
darb
LET'S SEE IT.
TICKETS ARE THIRTY DOLLARS.
I'LL GIVE YOU THE TURTLE SHELL I FOUND TODAY.
DONE! AND NOW BE AMAZED!
THAT'S AN OFFICIALLY LICENSED GARFIELD SHEET.
NO, NO! IT'S A GARFIELD MIRACLE!
WAIT! YOU CAN'T LEAVE WITHOUT A SOUVENIR REPLICA OF THE SHROUD FROM OUR SHOP!
THAT'S THE PILLOWCASE FOR THE SHEET SET!

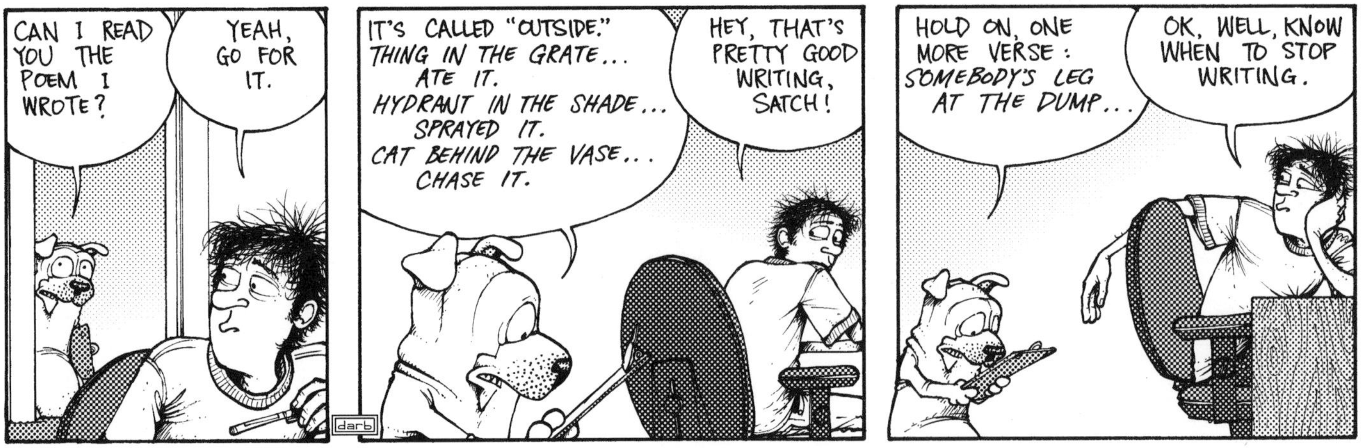
CAN I READ YOU THE POEM I WROTE?
YEAH, GO FOR IT.
IT'S CALLED "OUTSIDE." *THING IN THE GRATE... ATE IT. HYDRANT IN THE SHADE... SPRAYED IT. CAT BEHIND THE VASE... CHASE IT.*
HEY, THAT'S PRETTY GOOD WRITING, SATCH!
HOLD ON, ONE MORE VERSE: *SOMEBODY'S LEG AT THE DUMP...*
OK, WELL, KNOW WHEN TO STOP WRITING.
darb

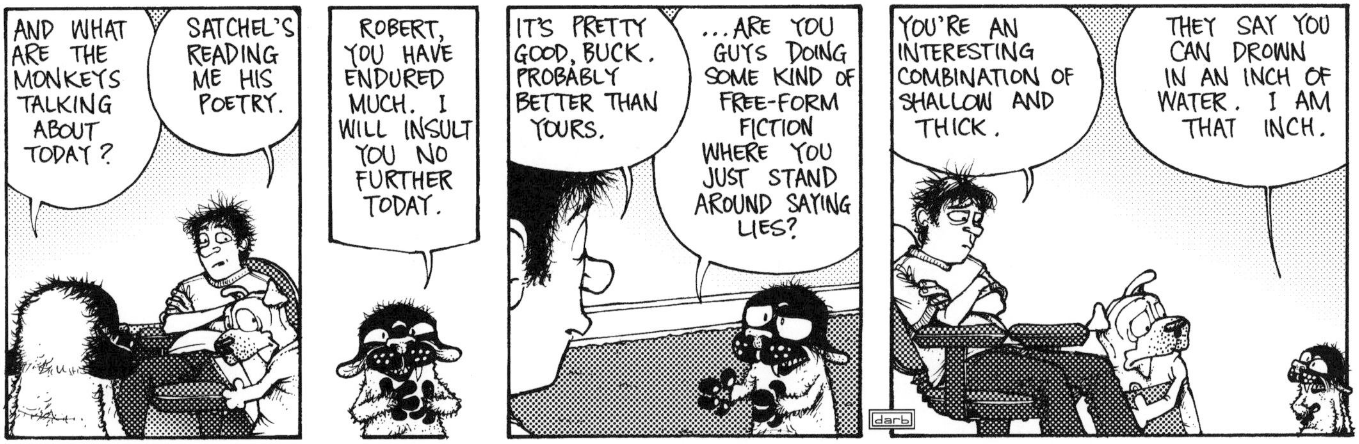
AND WHAT ARE THE MONKEYS TALKING ABOUT TODAY?
SATCHEL'S READING ME HIS POETRY.
ROBERT, YOU HAVE ENDURED MUCH. I WILL INSULT YOU NO FURTHER TODAY.
IT'S PRETTY GOOD, BUCK. PROBABLY BETTER THAN YOURS.
...ARE YOU GUYS DOING SOME KIND OF FREE-FORM FICTION WHERE YOU JUST STAND AROUND SAYING LIES?
darb
YOU'RE AN INTERESTING COMBINATION OF SHALLOW AND THICK.
THEY SAY YOU CAN DROWN IN AN INCH OF WATER. I AM THAT INCH.

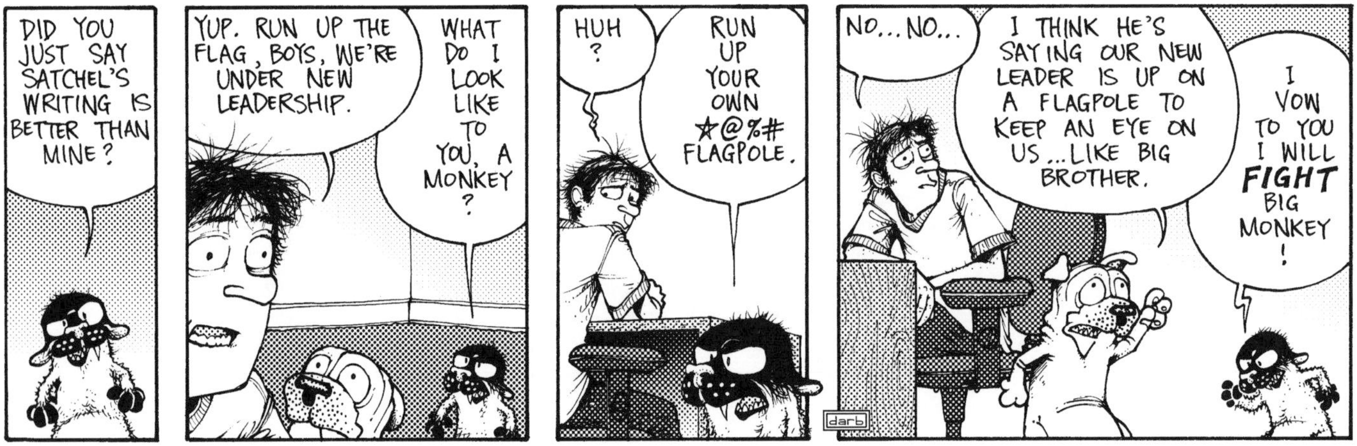
DID YOU JUST SAY SATCHEL'S WRITING IS BETTER THAN MINE?
YUP. RUN UP THE FLAG, BOYS, WE'RE UNDER NEW LEADERSHIP.
WHAT DO I LOOK LIKE TO YOU, A MONKEY?
HUH?
RUN UP YOUR OWN ☆@%# FLAGPOLE.
darb
NO... NO...
I THINK HE'S SAYING OUR NEW LEADER IS UP ON A FLAGPOLE TO KEEP AN EYE ON US... LIKE BIG BROTHER.
I VOW TO YOU I WILL **FIGHT** BIG MONKEY!

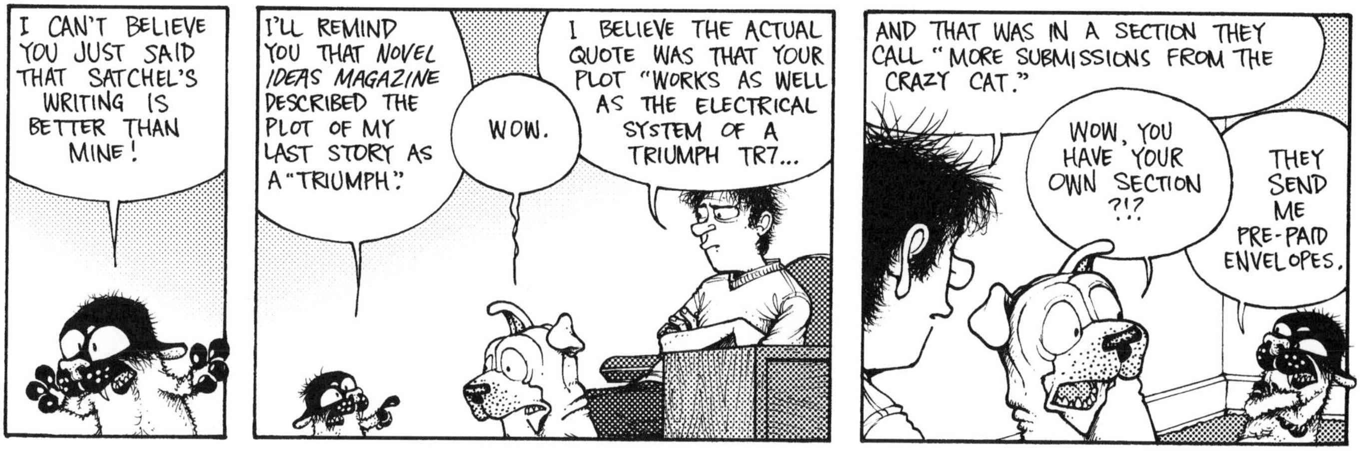
I CAN'T BELIEVE YOU JUST SAID THAT SATCHEL'S WRITING IS BETTER THAN MINE!
I'LL REMIND YOU THAT *NOVEL IDEAS MAGAZINE* DESCRIBED THE PLOT OF MY LAST STORY AS A "TRIUMPH."
WOW.
I BELIEVE THE ACTUAL QUOTE WAS THAT YOUR PLOT "WORKS AS WELL AS THE ELECTRICAL SYSTEM OF A TRIUMPH TR7...
AND THAT WAS IN A SECTION THEY CALL "MORE SUBMISSIONS FROM THE CRAZY CAT."
WOW, YOU HAVE YOUR OWN SECTION ?!?
THEY SEND ME PRE-PAID ENVELOPES.

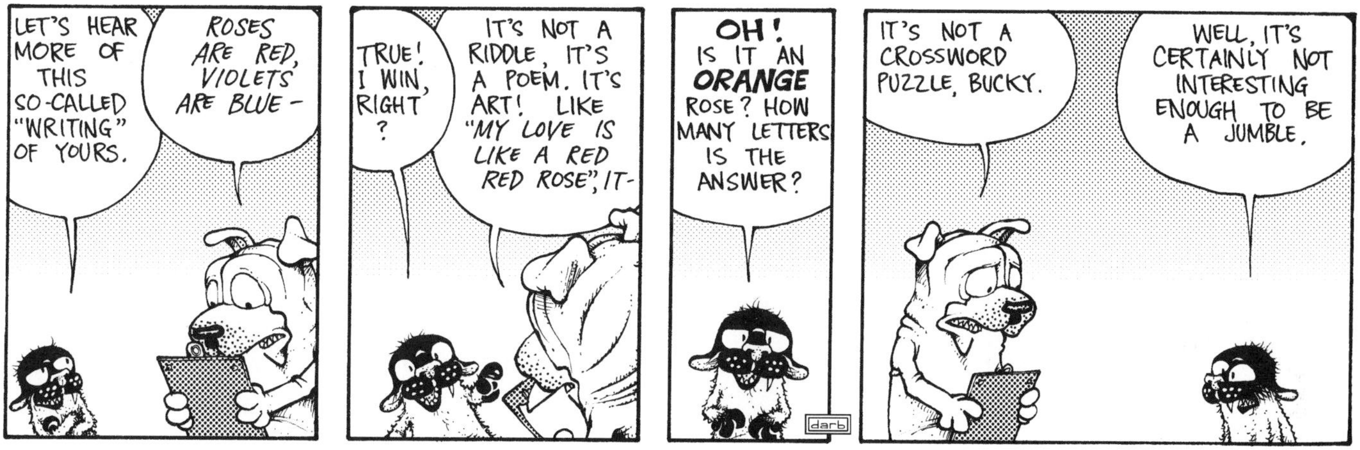
LET'S HEAR MORE OF THIS SO-CALLED "WRITING" OF YOURS.
ROSES ARE RED, VIOLETS ARE BLUE -
TRUE! I WIN, RIGHT?
IT'S NOT A RIDDLE, IT'S A POEM. IT'S ART! LIKE "*MY LOVE IS LIKE A RED RED ROSE*", IT-
OH! IS IT AN **ORANGE** ROSE? HOW MANY LETTERS IS THE ANSWER?
darb
IT'S NOT A CROSSWORD PUZZLE, BUCKY.
WELL, IT'S CERTAINLY NOT INTERESTING ENOUGH TO BE A JUMBLE.

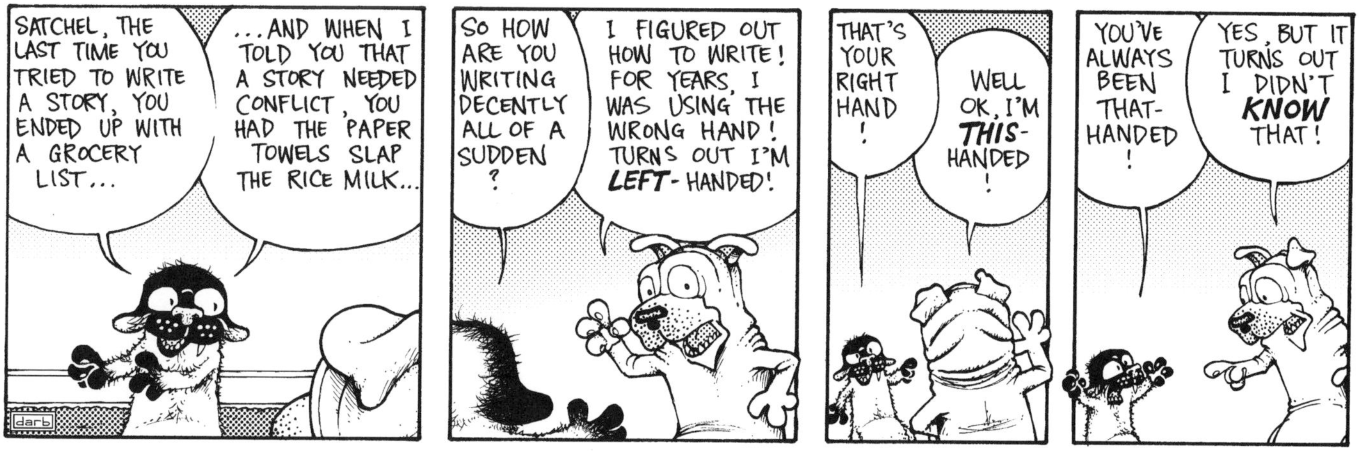
SATCHEL, THE LAST TIME YOU TRIED TO WRITE A STORY, YOU ENDED UP WITH A GROCERY LIST...
...AND WHEN I TOLD YOU THAT A STORY NEEDED CONFLICT, YOU HAD THE PAPER TOWELS SLAP THE RICE MILK...
darb
SO HOW ARE YOU WRITING DECENTLY ALL OF A SUDDEN?
I FIGURED OUT HOW TO WRITE! FOR YEARS, I WAS USING THE WRONG HAND! TURNS OUT I'M **LEFT**-HANDED!
THAT'S YOUR RIGHT HAND!
WELL OK, I'M **THIS**-HANDED!
YOU'VE ALWAYS BEEN THAT-HANDED!
YES, BUT IT TURNS OUT I DIDN'T **KNOW** THAT!

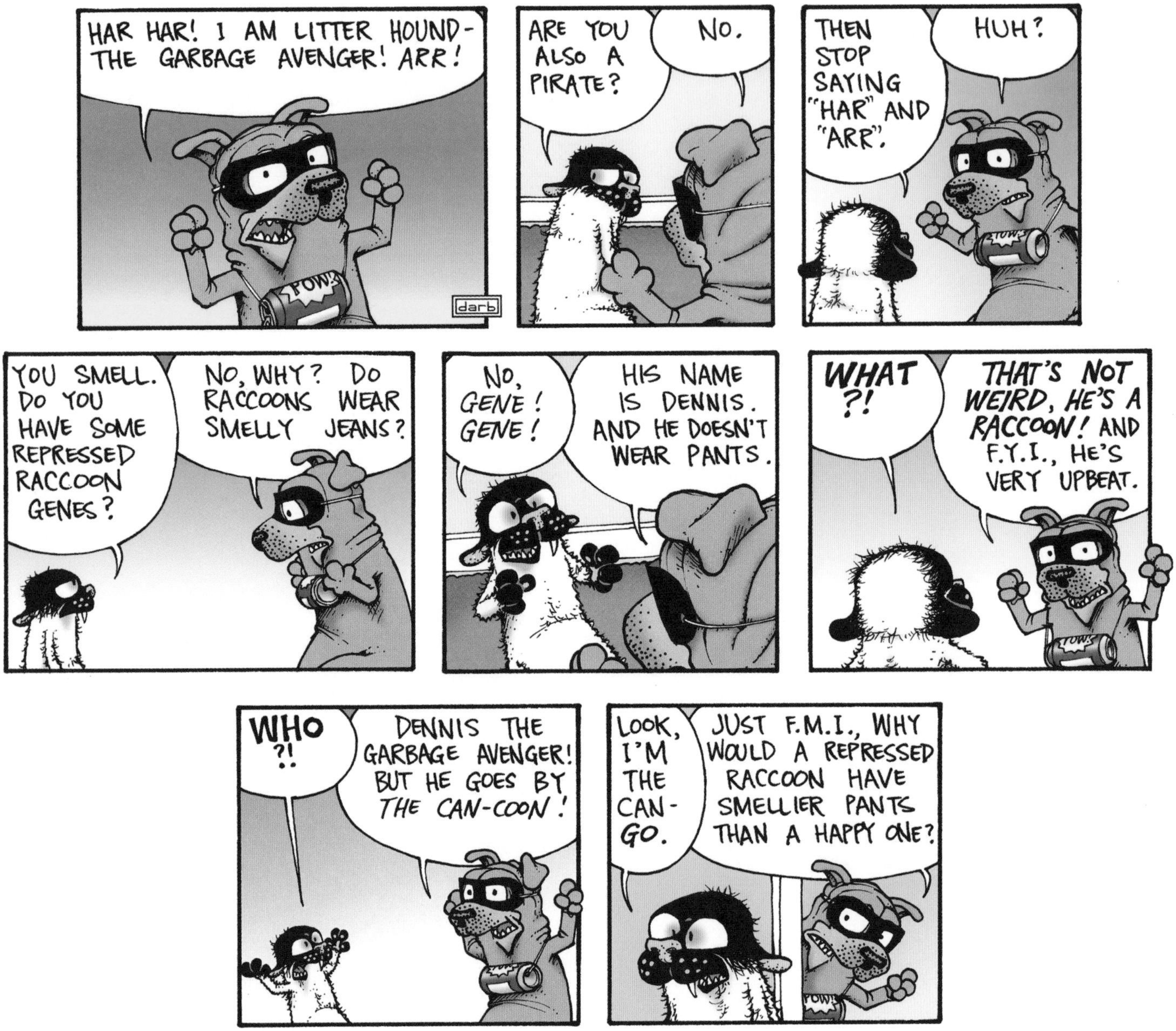
HAR HAR! I AM LITTER HOUND- THE GARBAGE AVENGER! ARR!
darb
ARE YOU ALSO A PIRATE?
NO.
THEN STOP SAYING "HAR" AND "ARR".
HUH?
POW!
YOU SMELL. DO YOU HAVE SOME REPRESSED RACCOON GENES?
NO, WHY? DO RACCOONS WEAR SMELLY JEANS?
NO, GENE! GENE!
HIS NAME IS DENNIS. AND HE DOESN'T WEAR PANTS.
WHAT ?!
THAT'S NOT WEIRD, HE'S A RACCOON! AND F.Y.I., HE'S VERY UPBEAT.
WHO ?!
DENNIS THE GARBAGE AVENGER! BUT HE GOES BY THE CAN-COON!
LOOK, I'M THE CAN-GO.
JUST F.M.I., WHY WOULD A REPRESSED RACCOON HAVE SMELLIER PANTS THAN A HAPPY ONE?

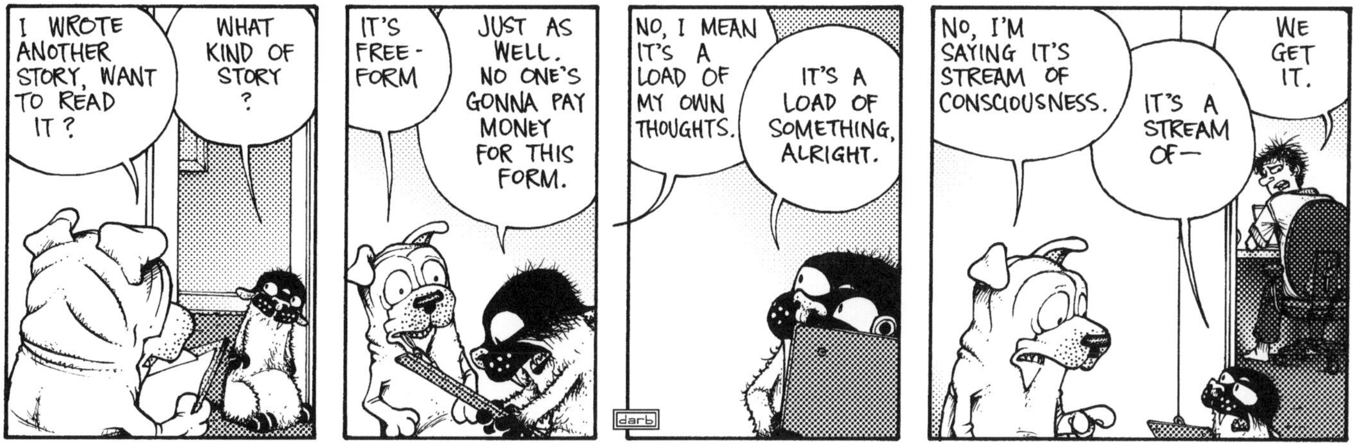
I WROTE ANOTHER STORY, WANT TO READ IT?
WHAT KIND OF STORY?
IT'S FREE-FORM
JUST AS WELL. NO ONE'S GONNA PAY MONEY FOR THIS FORM.
NO, I MEAN IT'S A LOAD OF MY OWN THOUGHTS.
IT'S A LOAD OF SOMETHING, ALRIGHT.
darb
NO, I'M SAYING IT'S STREAM OF CONSCIOUSNESS.
IT'S A STREAM OF—
WE GET IT.

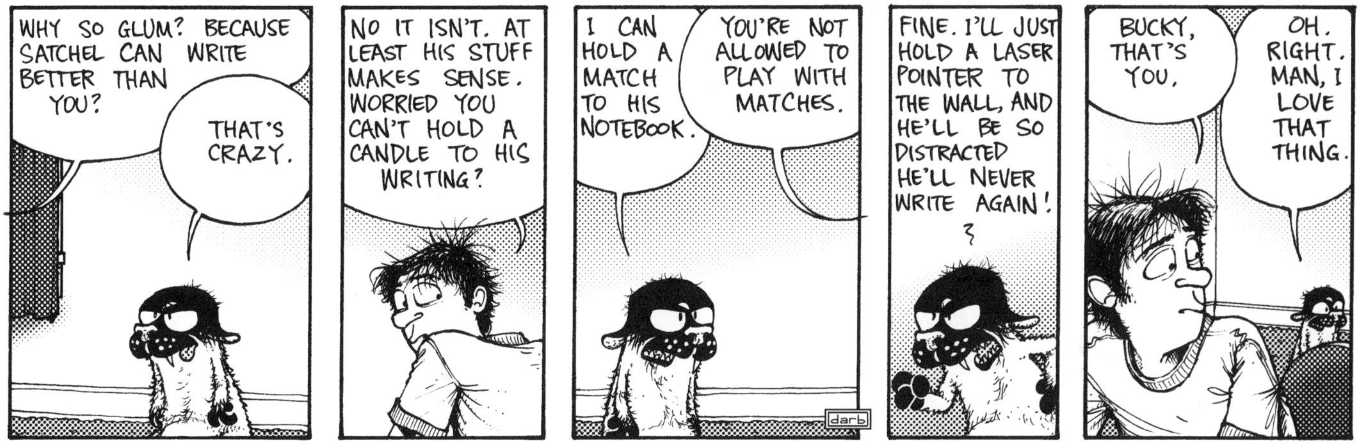
WHY SO GLUM? BECAUSE SATCHEL CAN WRITE BETTER THAN YOU?
THAT'S CRAZY.
NO IT ISN'T. AT LEAST HIS STUFF MAKES SENSE. WORRIED YOU CAN'T HOLD A CANDLE TO HIS WRITING?
I CAN HOLD A MATCH TO HIS NOTEBOOK.
YOU'RE NOT ALLOWED TO PLAY WITH MATCHES.
darb
FINE. I'LL JUST HOLD A LASER POINTER TO THE WALL, AND HE'LL BE SO DISTRACTED HE'LL NEVER WRITE AGAIN!
BUCKY, THAT'S YOU.
OH. RIGHT. MAN, I LOVE THAT THING.

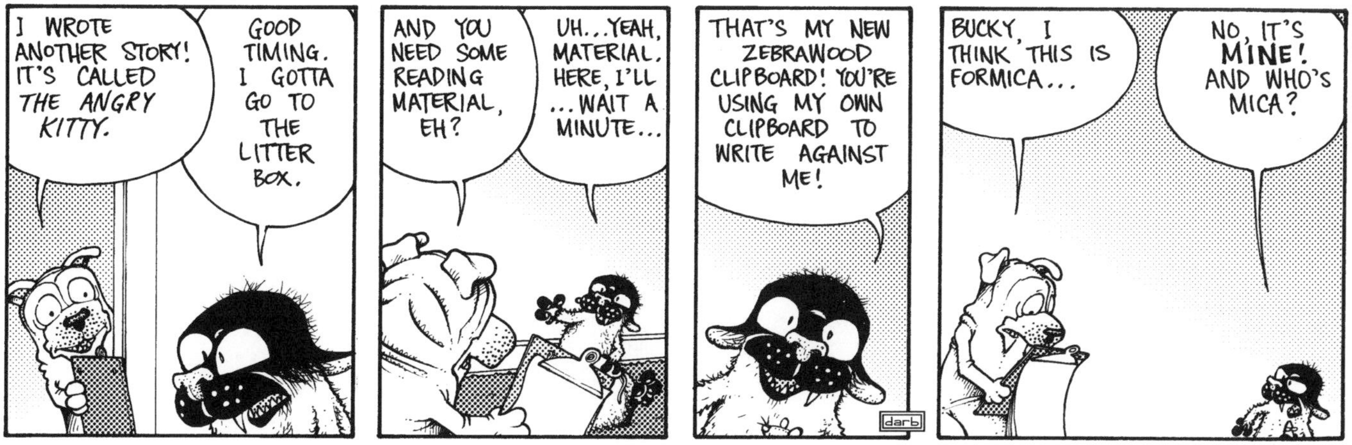
I WROTE ANOTHER STORY! IT'S CALLED *THE ANGRY KITTY.*
GOOD TIMING. I GOTTA GO TO THE LITTER BOX.
AND YOU NEED SOME READING MATERIAL, EH?
UH...YEAH, MATERIAL. HERE, I'LL ...WAIT A MINUTE...
THAT'S MY NEW ZEBRAWOOD CLIPBOARD! YOU'RE USING MY OWN CLIPBOARD TO WRITE AGAINST ME!
darb
BUCKY, I THINK THIS IS FORMICA...
NO, IT'S **MINE**! AND WHO'S MICA?

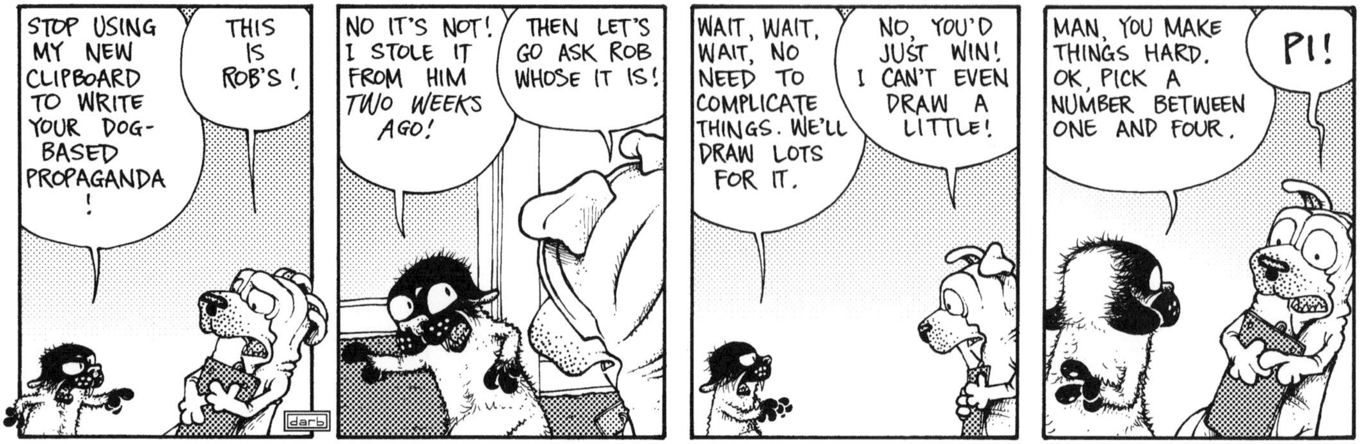
STOP USING MY NEW CLIPBOARD TO WRITE YOUR DOG-BASED PROPAGANDA!
THIS IS ROB'S!
darb
NO IT'S NOT! I STOLE IT FROM HIM TWO WEEKS AGO!
THEN LET'S GO ASK ROB WHOSE IT IS!
WAIT, WAIT, WAIT, NO NEED TO COMPLICATE THINGS. WE'LL DRAW LOTS FOR IT.
NO, YOU'D JUST WIN! I CAN'T EVEN DRAW A LITTLE!
MAN, YOU MAKE THINGS HARD. OK, PICK A NUMBER BETWEEN ONE AND FOUR.
PI!

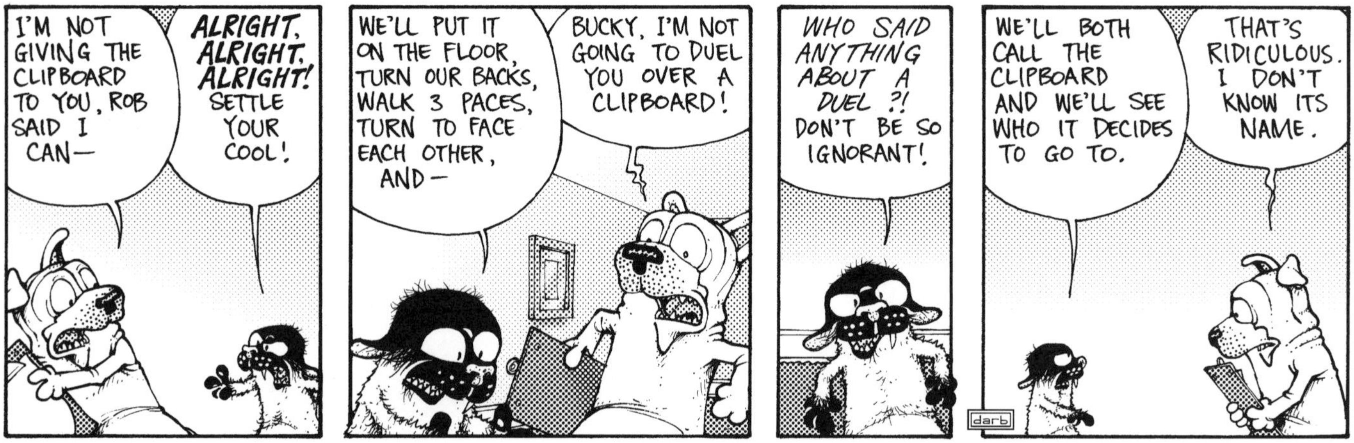
I'M NOT GIVING THE CLIPBOARD TO YOU, ROB SAID I CAN—
ALRIGHT, ALRIGHT, ALRIGHT! SETTLE YOUR COOL!
WE'LL PUT IT ON THE FLOOR, TURN OUR BACKS, WALK 3 PACES, TURN TO FACE EACH OTHER, AND—
BUCKY, I'M NOT GOING TO DUEL YOU OVER A CLIPBOARD!
WHO SAID ANYTHING ABOUT A DUEL ?! DON'T BE SO IGNORANT!
darb
WE'LL BOTH CALL THE CLIPBOARD AND WE'LL SEE WHO IT DECIDES TO GO TO.
THAT'S RIDICULOUS. I DON'T KNOW ITS NAME.

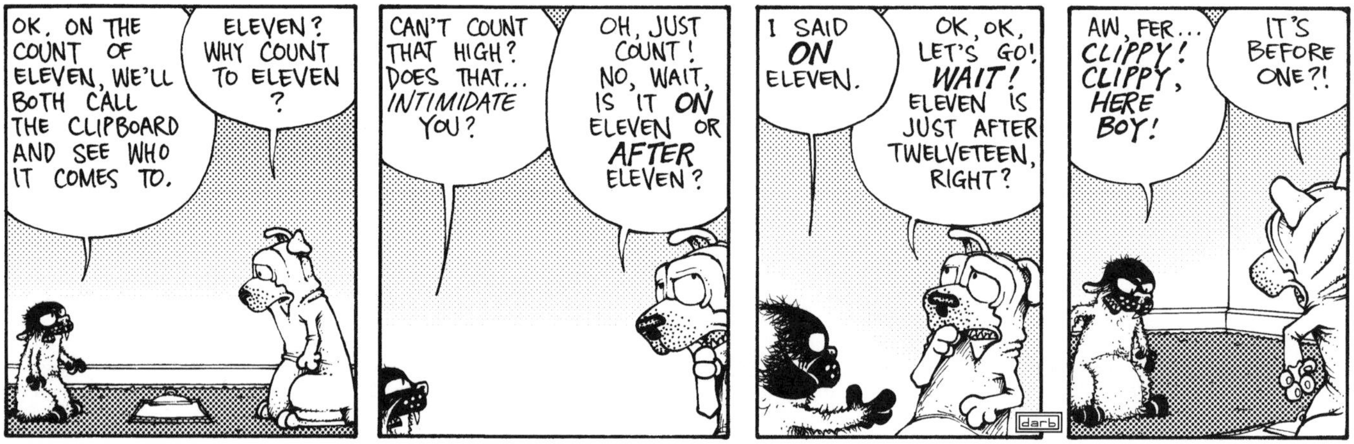
OK, ON THE COUNT OF ELEVEN, WE'LL BOTH CALL THE CLIPBOARD AND SEE WHO IT COMES TO.
ELEVEN? WHY COUNT TO ELEVEN?
CAN'T COUNT THAT HIGH? DOES THAT... INTIMIDATE YOU?
OH, JUST COUNT! NO, WAIT, IS IT ON ELEVEN OR AFTER ELEVEN?
I SAID ON ELEVEN.
OK, OK, LET'S GO! WAIT! ELEVEN IS JUST AFTER TWELVETEEN, RIGHT?
darb
AW, FER... CLIPPY! CLIPPY, HERE BOY!
IT'S BEFORE ONE?!

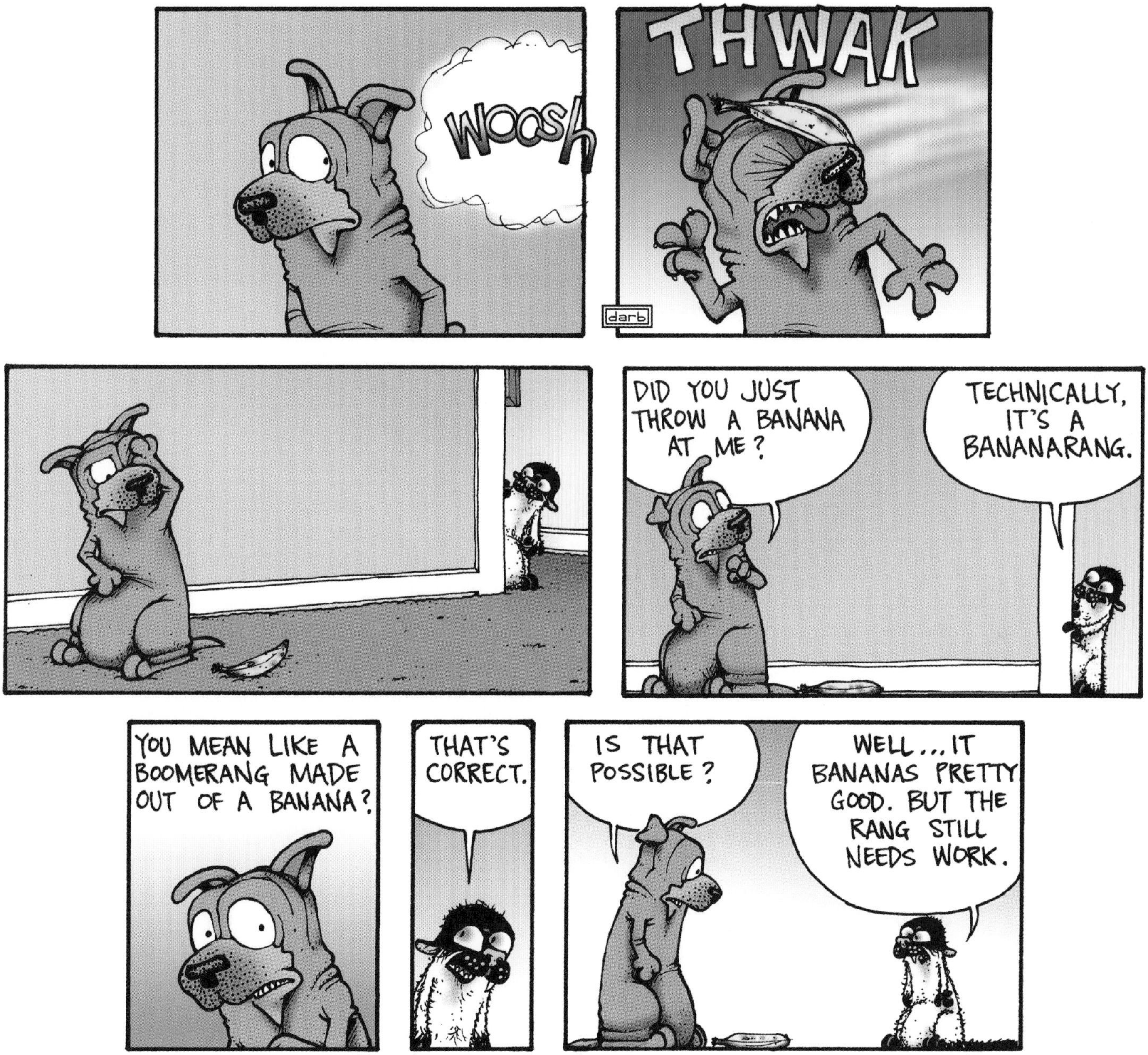
WOOSH
THWAK
darb
DID YOU JUST THROW A BANANA AT ME?
TECHNICALLY, IT'S A BANANARANG.
YOU MEAN LIKE A BOOMERANG MADE OUT OF A BANANA?
THAT'S CORRECT.
IS THAT POSSIBLE?
WELL... IT BANANAS PRETTY GOOD. BUT THE RANG STILL NEEDS WORK.

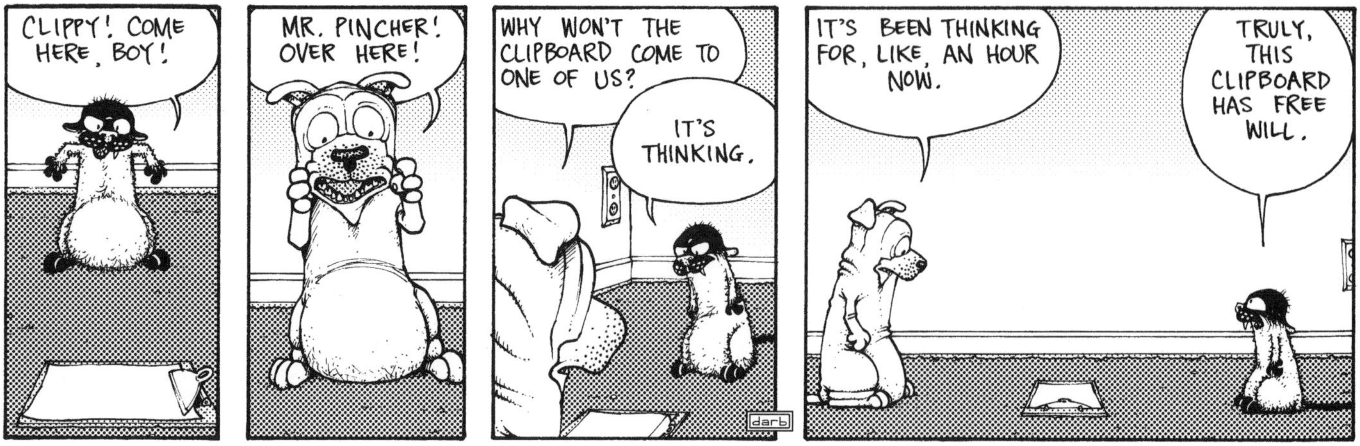
CLIPPY! COME HERE, BOY!
MR. PINCHER! OVER HERE!
WHY WON'T THE CLIPBOARD COME TO ONE OF US?
IT'S THINKING.
IT'S BEEN THINKING FOR, LIKE, AN HOUR NOW.
TRULY, THIS CLIPBOARD HAS FREE WILL.

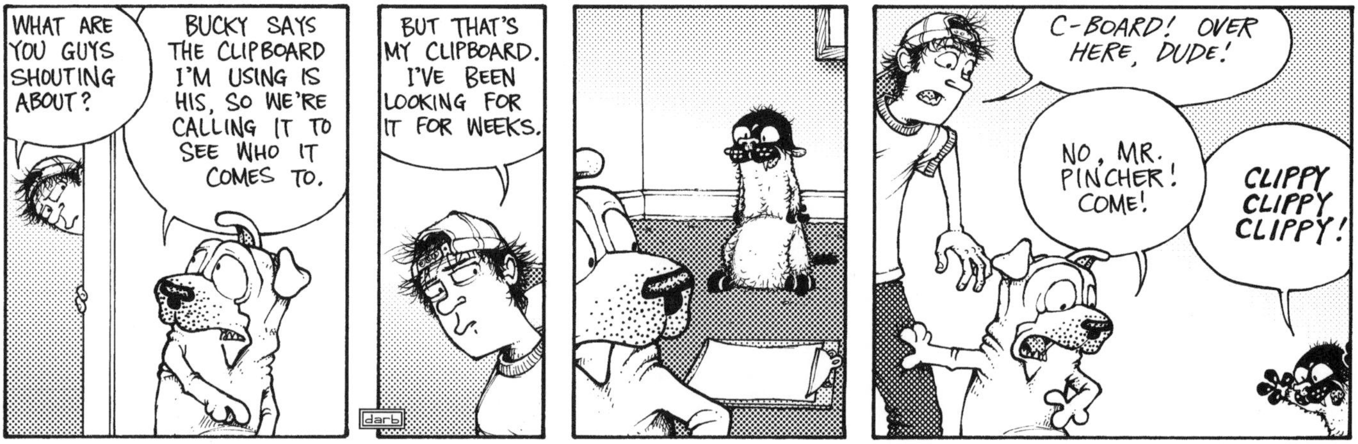
WHAT ARE YOU GUYS SHOUTING ABOUT?
BUCKY SAYS THE CLIPBOARD I'M USING IS HIS, SO WE'RE CALLING IT TO SEE WHO IT COMES TO.
BUT THAT'S MY CLIPBOARD. I'VE BEEN LOOKING FOR IT FOR WEEKS.
C-BOARD! OVER HERE, DUDE!
NO, MR. PINCHER! COME!
CLIPPY CLIPPY CLIPPY!

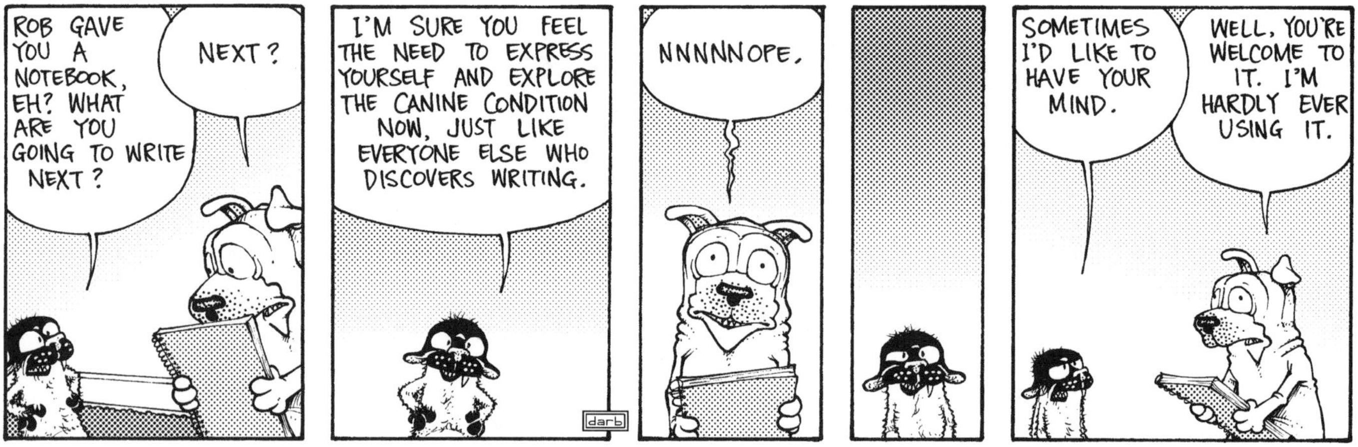
ROB GAVE YOU A NOTEBOOK, EH? WHAT ARE YOU GOING TO WRITE NEXT?
NEXT?
I'M SURE YOU FEEL THE NEED TO EXPRESS YOURSELF AND EXPLORE THE CANINE CONDITION NOW, JUST LIKE EVERYONE ELSE WHO DISCOVERS WRITING.
NNNNNOPE.
SOMETIMES I'D LIKE TO HAVE YOUR MIND.
WELL, YOU'RE WELCOME TO IT. I'M HARDLY EVER USING IT.

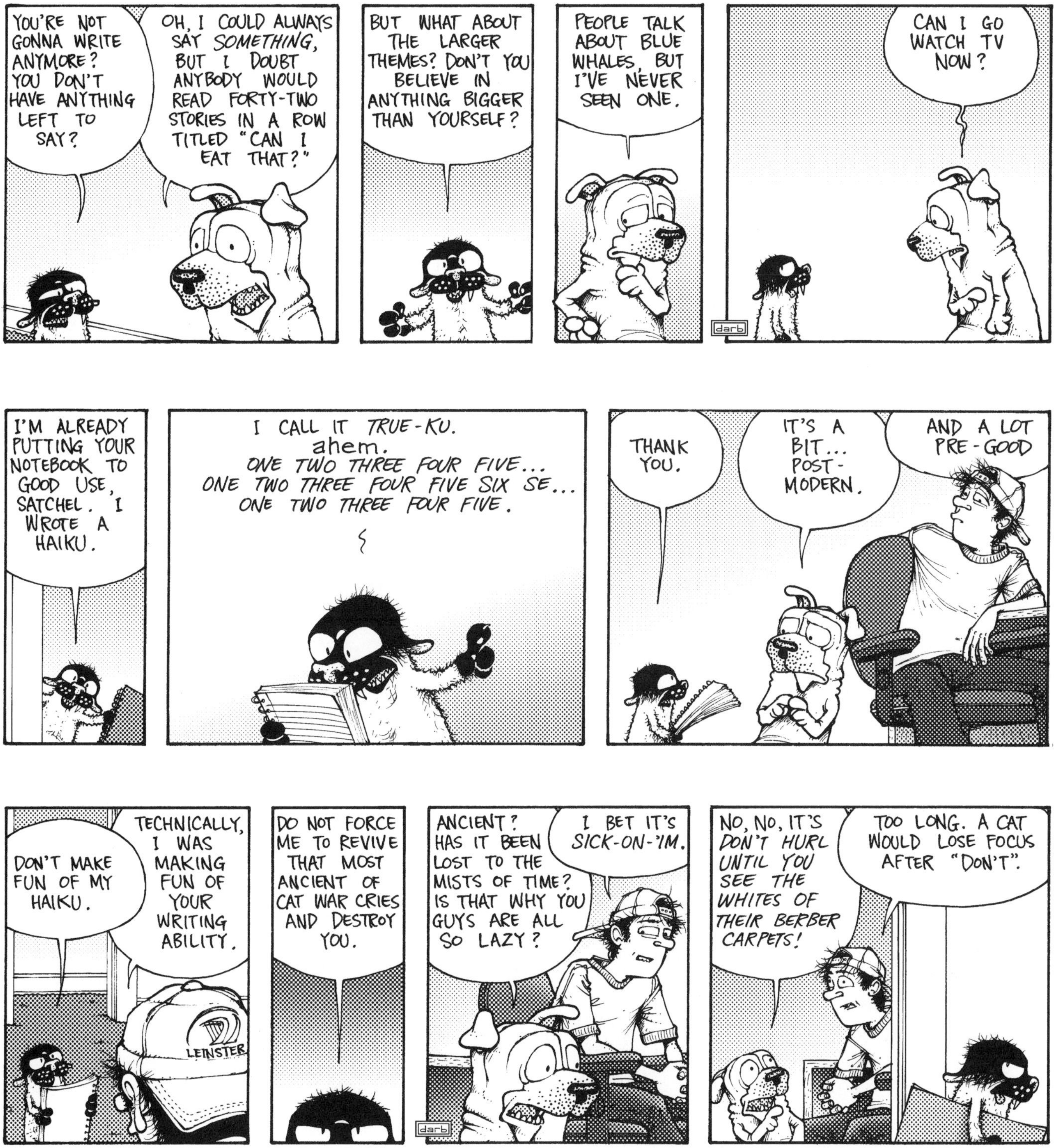
YOU'RE NOT GONNA WRITE ANYMORE? YOU DON'T HAVE ANYTHING LEFT TO SAY?
OH, I COULD ALWAYS SAY SOMETHING, BUT I DOUBT ANYBODY WOULD READ FORTY-TWO STORIES IN A ROW TITLED "CAN I EAT THAT?"
BUT WHAT ABOUT THE LARGER THEMES? DON'T YOU BELIEVE IN ANYTHING BIGGER THAN YOURSELF?
PEOPLE TALK ABOUT BLUE WHALES, BUT I'VE NEVER SEEN ONE.
darb
CAN I GO WATCH TV NOW?
I'M ALREADY PUTTING YOUR NOTEBOOK TO GOOD USE, SATCHEL. I WROTE A HAIKU.
I CALL IT TRUE-KU.
ahem.
ONE TWO THREE FOUR FIVE...
ONE TWO THREE FOUR FIVE SIX SE...
ONE TWO THREE FOUR FIVE.
THANK YOU.
IT'S A BIT... POST-MODERN.
AND A LOT PRE-GOOD
DON'T MAKE FUN OF MY HAIKU.
TECHNICALLY, I WAS MAKING FUN OF YOUR WRITING ABILITY.
LEINSTER
DO NOT FORCE ME TO REVIVE THAT MOST ANCIENT OF CAT WAR CRIES AND DESTROY YOU.
darb
ANCIENT? HAS IT BEEN LOST TO THE MISTS OF TIME? IS THAT WHY YOU GUYS ARE ALL SO LAZY?
I BET IT'S SICK-ON-'IM.
NO, NO, IT'S DON'T HURL UNTIL YOU SEE THE WHITES OF THEIR BERBER CARPETS!
TOO LONG. A CAT WOULD LOSE FOCUS AFTER "DON'T".

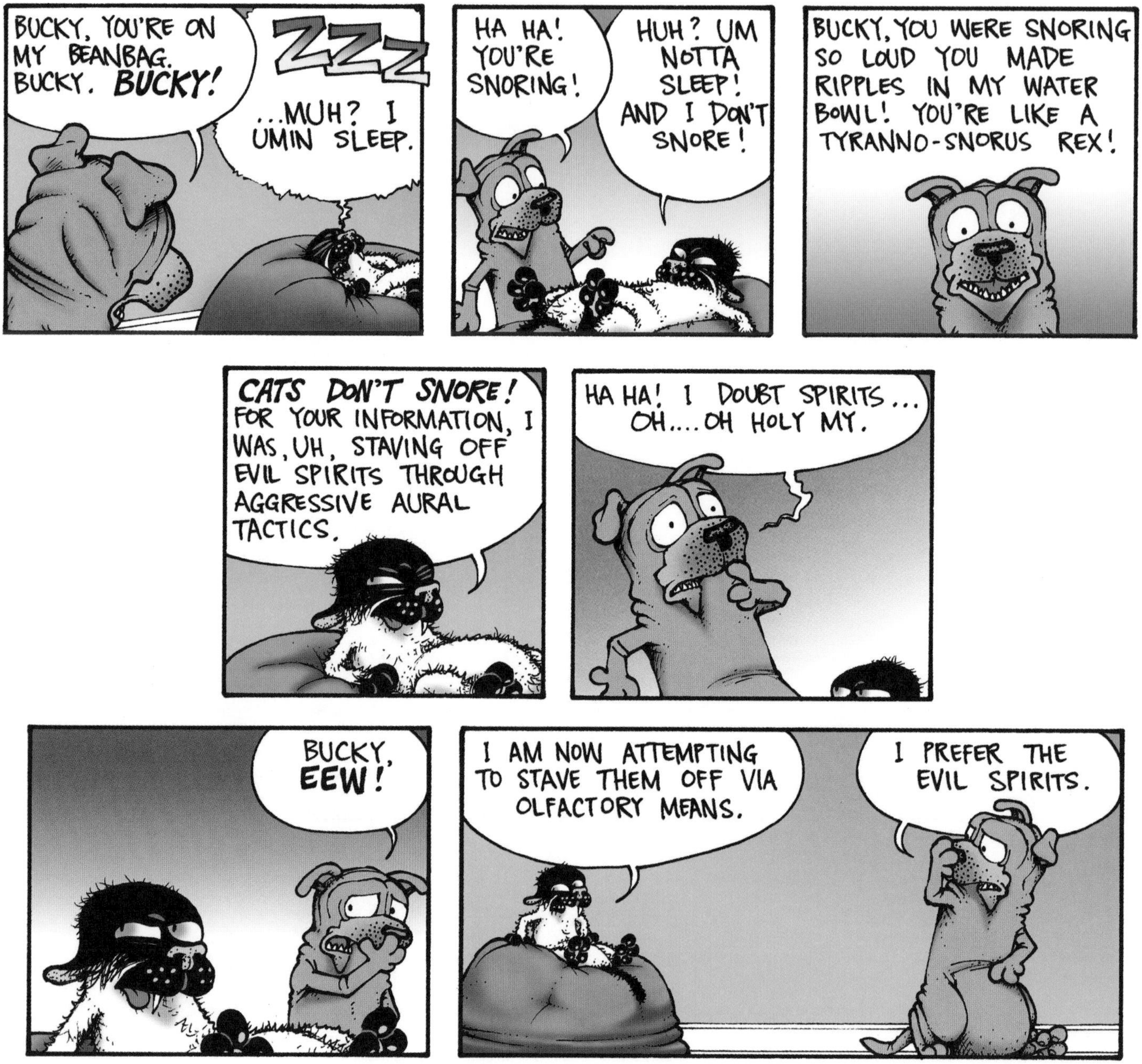
BUCKY, YOU'RE ON MY BEANBAG. BUCKY. BUCKY!
ZZZ
...MUH? I UMIN SLEEP.
HA HA! YOU'RE SNORING!
HUH? UM NOTTA SLEEP! AND I DON'T SNORE!
BUCKY, YOU WERE SNORING SO LOUD YOU MADE RIPPLES IN MY WATER BOWL! YOU'RE LIKE A TYRANNO-SNORUS REX!
CATS DON'T SNORE! FOR YOUR INFORMATION, I WAS, UH, STAVING OFF EVIL SPIRITS THROUGH AGGRESSIVE AURAL TACTICS.
HA HA! I DOUBT SPIRITS... OH.... OH HOLY MY.
BUCKY, EEW!
I AM NOW ATTEMPTING TO STAVE THEM OFF VIA OLFACTORY MEANS.
I PREFER THE EVIL SPIRITS.

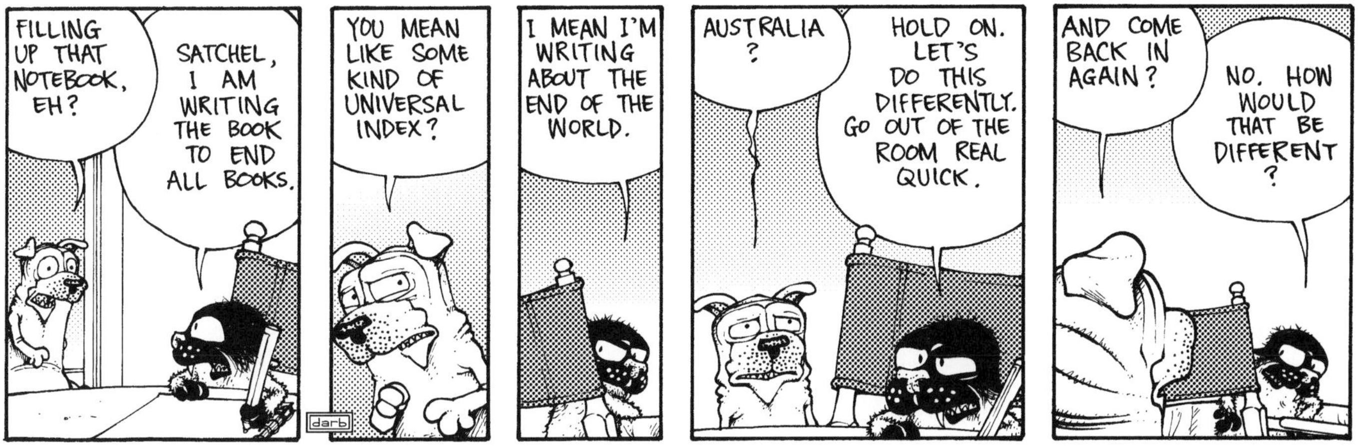

FILLING UP THAT NOTEBOOK, EH?
SATCHEL, I AM WRITING THE BOOK TO END ALL BOOKS.
darb
YOU MEAN LIKE SOME KIND OF UNIVERSAL INDEX?
I MEAN I'M WRITING ABOUT THE END OF THE WORLD.
AUSTRALIA?
HOLD ON. LET'S DO THIS DIFFERENTLY. GO OUT OF THE ROOM REAL QUICK.
AND COME BACK IN AGAIN?
NO. HOW WOULD THAT BE DIFFERENT?

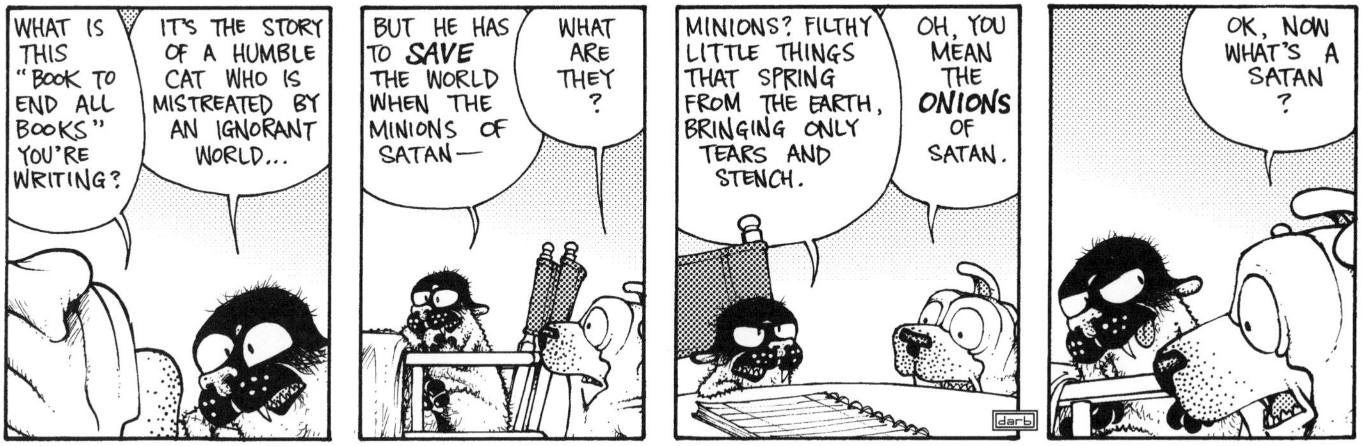

WHAT IS THIS "BOOK TO END ALL BOOKS" YOU'RE WRITING?
IT'S THE STORY OF A HUMBLE CAT WHO IS MISTREATED BY AN IGNORANT WORLD...
BUT HE HAS TO **SAVE** THE WORLD WHEN THE MINIONS OF SATAN—
WHAT ARE THEY?
MINIONS? FILTHY LITTLE THINGS THAT SPRING FROM THE EARTH, BRINGING ONLY TEARS AND STENCH.
OH, YOU MEAN THE **ONIONS** OF SATAN.
darb
OK, NOW WHAT'S A SATAN?

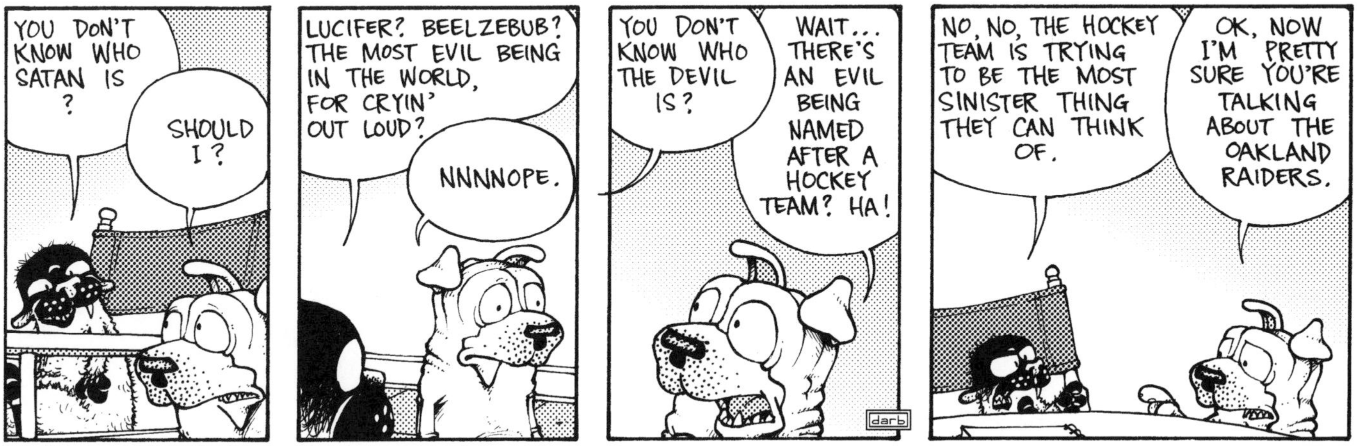

YOU DON'T KNOW WHO SATAN IS?
SHOULD I?
LUCIFER? BEELZEBUB? THE MOST EVIL BEING IN THE WORLD, FOR CRYIN' OUT LOUD?
NNNNOPE.
YOU DON'T KNOW WHO THE DEVIL IS?
WAIT... THERE'S AN EVIL BEING NAMED AFTER A HOCKEY TEAM? HA!
darb
NO, NO, THE HOCKEY TEAM IS TRYING TO BE THE MOST SINISTER THING THEY CAN THINK OF.
OK, NOW I'M PRETTY SURE YOU'RE TALKING ABOUT THE OAKLAND RAIDERS.

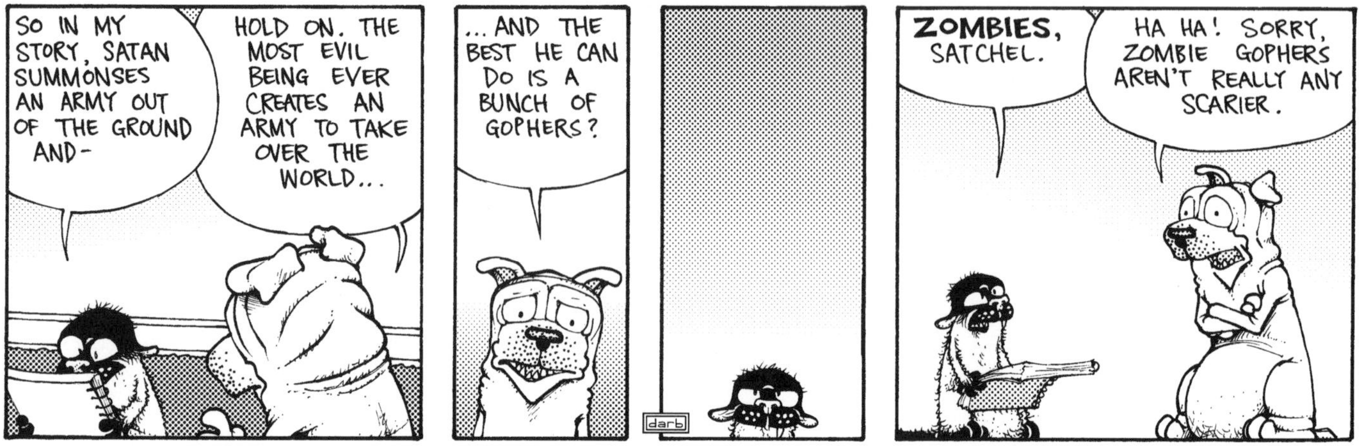
SO IN MY STORY, SATAN SUMMONSES AN ARMY OUT OF THE GROUND AND-
HOLD ON. THE MOST EVIL BEING EVER CREATES AN ARMY TO TAKE OVER THE WORLD...
...AND THE BEST HE CAN DO IS A BUNCH OF GOPHERS?
darb
ZOMBIES, SATCHEL.
HA HA! SORRY, ZOMBIE GOPHERS AREN'T REALLY ANY SCARIER.

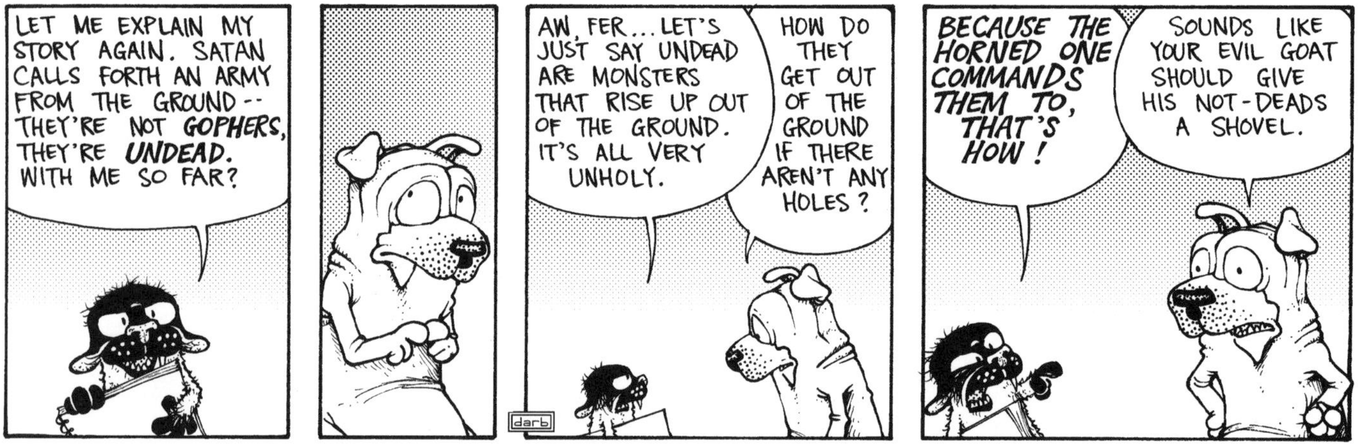
LET ME EXPLAIN MY STORY AGAIN. SATAN CALLS FORTH AN ARMY FROM THE GROUND-- THEY'RE NOT GOPHERS, THEY'RE UNDEAD. WITH ME SO FAR?
darb
AW, FER... LET'S JUST SAY UNDEAD ARE MONSTERS THAT RISE UP OUT OF THE GROUND. IT'S ALL VERY UNHOLY.
HOW DO THEY GET OUT OF THE GROUND IF THERE AREN'T ANY HOLES?
BECAUSE THE HORNED ONE COMMANDS THEM TO, THAT'S HOW!
SOUNDS LIKE YOUR EVIL GOAT SHOULD GIVE HIS NOT-DEADS A SHOVEL.

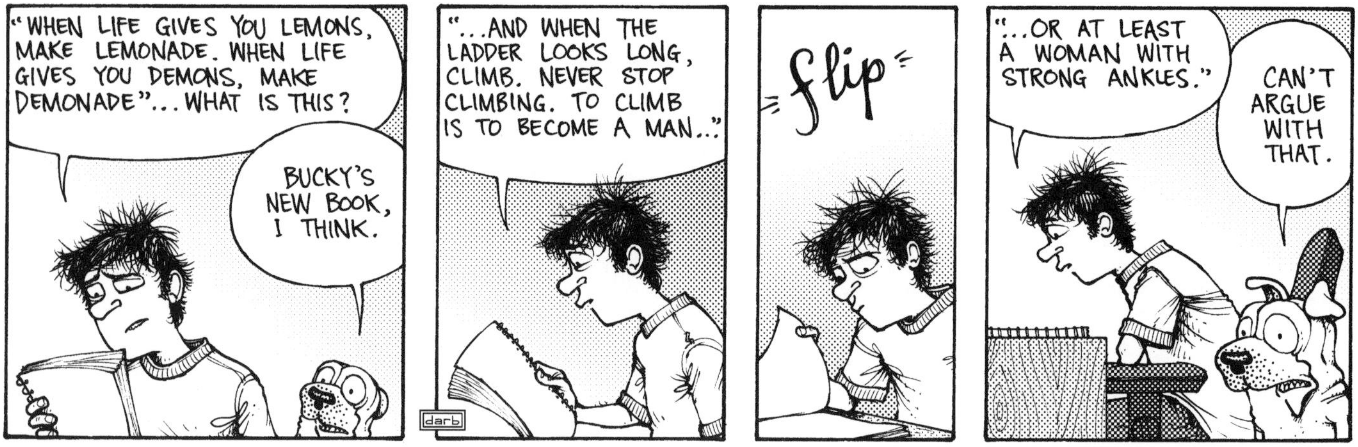
"WHEN LIFE GIVES YOU LEMONS, MAKE LEMONADE. WHEN LIFE GIVES YOU DEMONS, MAKE DEMONADE"... WHAT IS THIS?
BUCKY'S NEW BOOK, I THINK.
"...AND WHEN THE LADDER LOOKS LONG, CLIMB. NEVER STOP CLIMBING. TO CLIMB IS TO BECOME A MAN..."
darb
flip
"...OR AT LEAST A WOMAN WITH STRONG ANKLES."
CAN'T ARGUE WITH THAT.

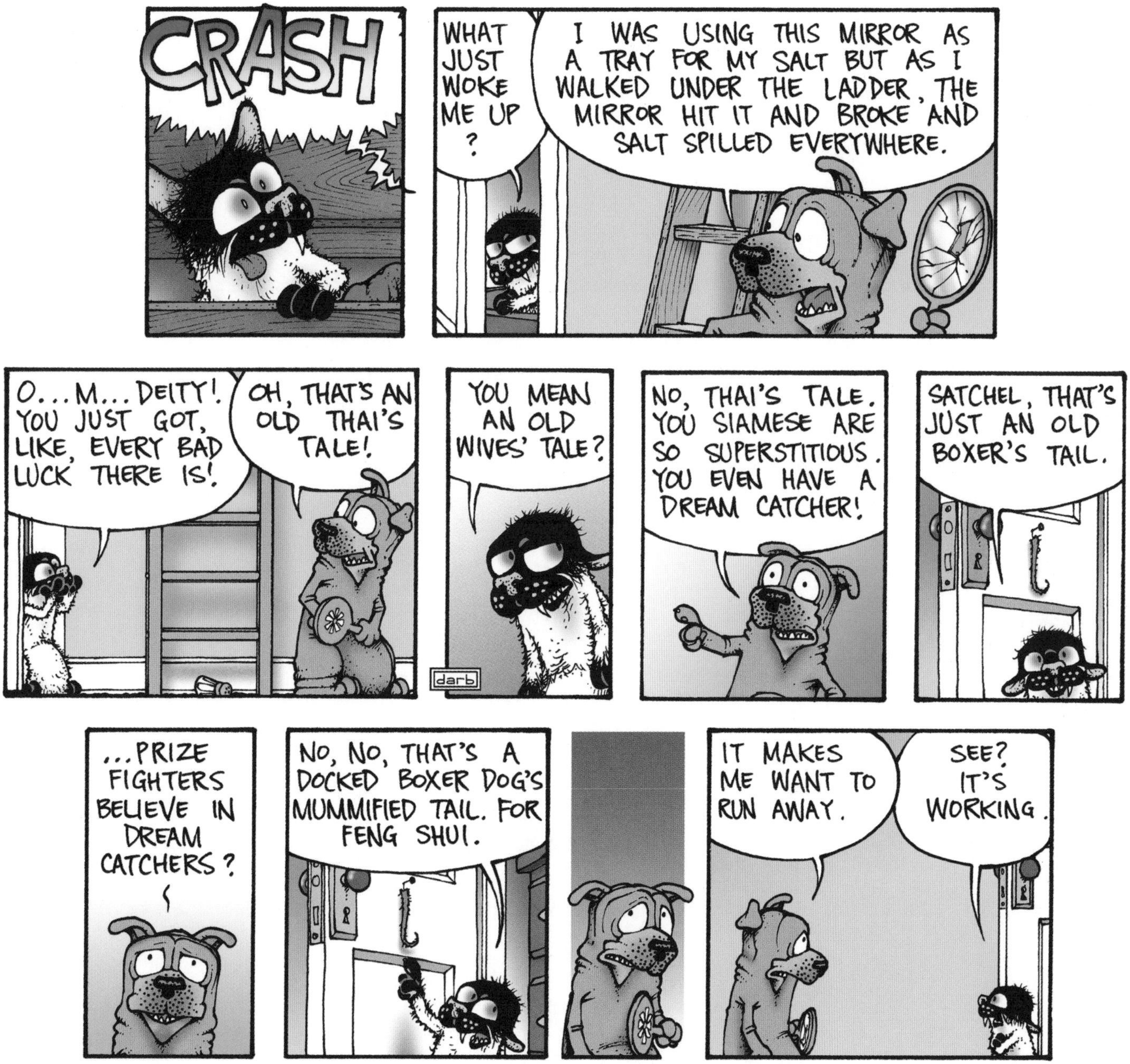
CRASH
WHAT JUST WOKE ME UP ?
I WAS USING THIS MIRROR AS A TRAY FOR MY SALT BUT AS I WALKED UNDER THE LADDER, THE MIRROR HIT IT AND BROKE AND SALT SPILLED EVERYWHERE.
O...M...DEITY! YOU JUST GOT, LIKE, EVERY BAD LUCK THERE IS!
OH, THAT'S AN OLD THAI'S TALE!
YOU MEAN AN OLD WIVES' TALE?
darb
NO, THAI'S TALE. YOU SIAMESE ARE SO SUPERSTITIOUS. YOU EVEN HAVE A DREAM CATCHER!
SATCHEL, THAT'S JUST AN OLD BOXER'S TAIL.
...PRIZE FIGHTERS BELIEVE IN DREAM CATCHERS?
NO, NO, THAT'S A DOCKED BOXER DOG'S MUMMIFIED TAIL. FOR FENG SHUI.
IT MAKES ME WANT TO RUN AWAY.
SEE? IT'S WORKING.

Panel 1: BUCKY! COME GET YOUR NOTEBOOK!

Panel 2: WHAT HO, PINKISH?

HERE. YOUR NEW STORY IS FREAKING SATCHEL OUT.

Panel 3: IT'S SUPPOSED TO. IT'S A HORROR STORY.

Panel 4: NO, I MEAN HE THINKS IT'S A SCRATCH-AND-SNIFF AND HE'S WEARING HIS CLAWS OUT ON IT.

Panel 5: AWWW! HE MADE A HOLE IN THE PROLOGUE!

RELAX, IT MATCHES ALL THE ONES YOU MADE IN THE PLOT.

Panel 6: WHAT DID YOU THINK OF MY NEW STORY?

WELL, IF YOU EVER THINK OF A PLOT, JOT IT DOWN. **ANY** PLOT. I'M NOT PICKY.

Panel 7: FRANKLY, I'M HAVING PROBLEMS WITH THE MIDDLE OF THIS BOOK.

YOU AND ME BOTH.

Panel 8: LIKE WHEN YOUR CAT GOES OFF TO FIGHT ZOMBIES BUT THEN YOU SPEND THE NEXT NINE PAGES TALKING ABOUT BIRDS ON A POWER LINE.

Panel 9: IT'S MEANT TO BE LIKE "ULYSSES."

IT CAME OUT LIKE USELESS-ES.

Panel 10: I READ YOUR NEW STORY EARLIER.

I KNOW. THANKS A LOT FOR SCRATCHING HOLES IN IT.

Panel 11: IN MY DEFENSE, YOUR TWO MAIN CHARACTERS WERE NAMED SCRATCH AND SNIFF AND THERE WAS TUNA ALL OVER THE PAPER.

Panel 12: WHATEVER. I'M REWRITING IT ALL NOW, ANYWAY. I NEED TO WRITE MORE ABOUT *MYSELF*.

Panel 13: I WILL WRITE OF MY OWN LIFE. FOR I HAVE EXPERIENCED MUCH, AND I HAVE ACQUIRED SOMETHING FROM EACH EXPERIENCE.

SO IT'S A MEDICAL TEXTBOOK?

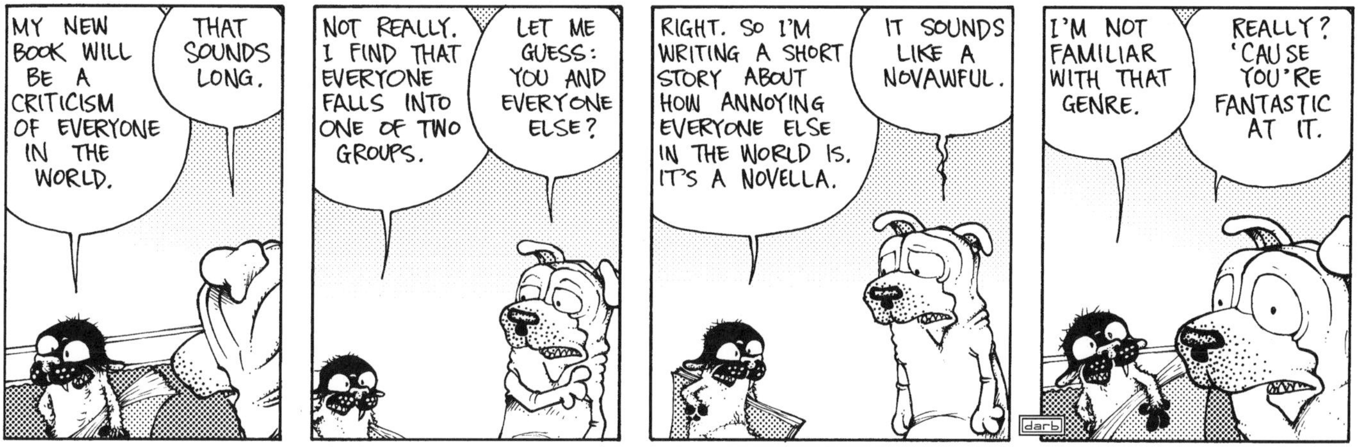
MY NEW BOOK WILL BE A CRITICISM OF EVERYONE IN THE WORLD.
THAT SOUNDS LONG.
NOT REALLY. I FIND THAT EVERYONE FALLS INTO ONE OF TWO GROUPS.
LET ME GUESS: YOU AND EVERYONE ELSE?
RIGHT. SO I'M WRITING A SHORT STORY ABOUT HOW ANNOYING EVERYONE ELSE IN THE WORLD IS. IT'S A NOVELLA.
IT SOUNDS LIKE A NOVAWFUL.
I'M NOT FAMILIAR WITH THAT GENRE.
REALLY? 'CAUSE YOU'RE FANTASTIC AT IT.
darb

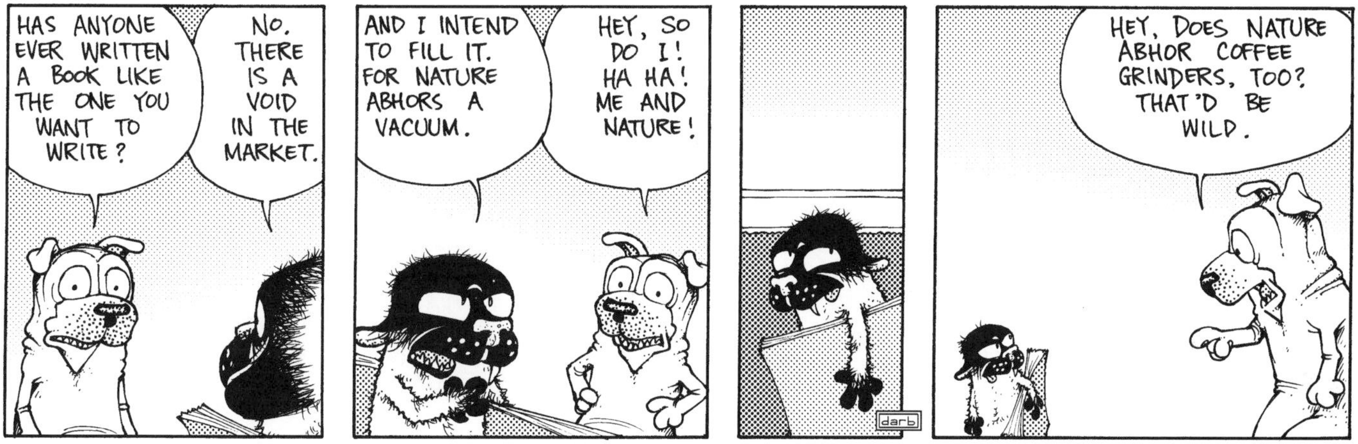
HAS ANYONE EVER WRITTEN A BOOK LIKE THE ONE YOU WANT TO WRITE?
NO. THERE IS A VOID IN THE MARKET.
AND I INTEND TO FILL IT. FOR NATURE ABHORS A VACUUM.
HEY, SO DO I! HA HA! ME AND NATURE!
darb
HEY, DOES NATURE ABHOR COFFEE GRINDERS, TOO? THAT'D BE WILD.

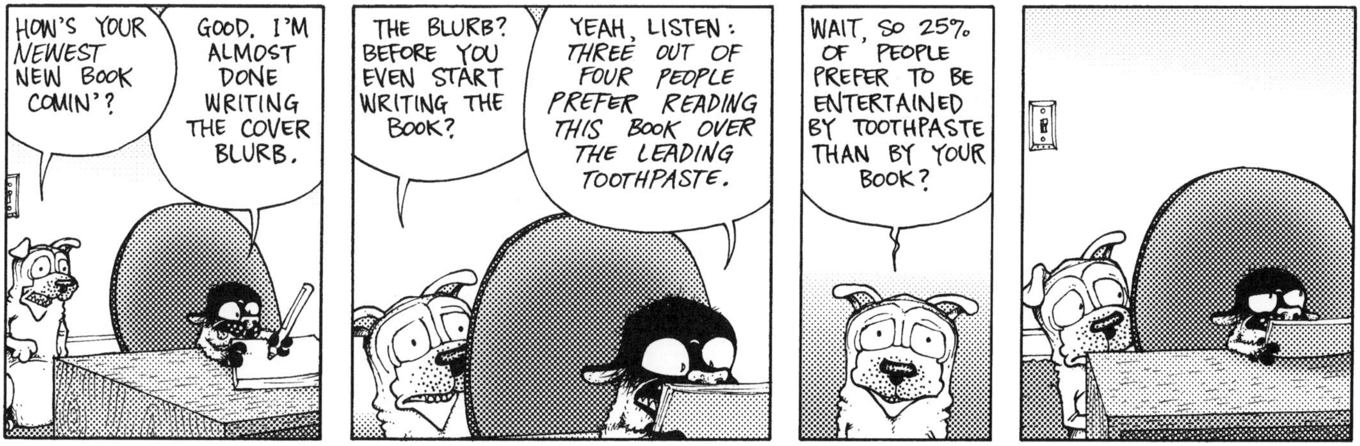
HOW'S YOUR NEWEST NEW BOOK COMIN'?
GOOD. I'M ALMOST DONE WRITING THE COVER BLURB.
THE BLURB? BEFORE YOU EVEN START WRITING THE BOOK?
YEAH, LISTEN: THREE OUT OF FOUR PEOPLE PREFER READING THIS BOOK OVER THE LEADING TOOTHPASTE.
WAIT, SO 25% OF PEOPLE PREFER TO BE ENTERTAINED BY TOOTHPASTE THAN BY YOUR BOOK?

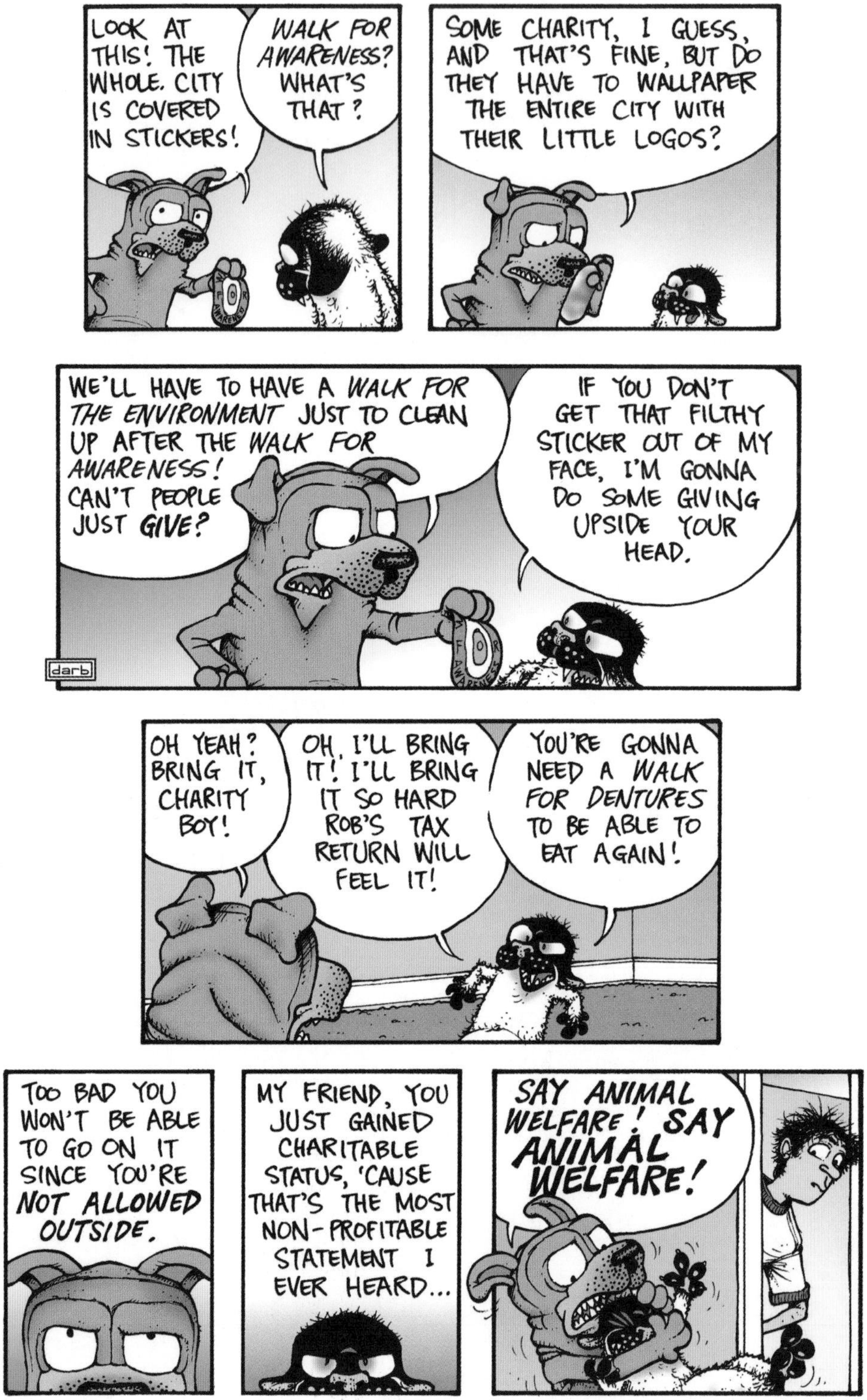
LOOK AT THIS! THE WHOLE CITY IS COVERED IN STICKERS!
WALK FOR AWARENESS? WHAT'S THAT?
SOME CHARITY, I GUESS, AND THAT'S FINE, BUT DO THEY HAVE TO WALLPAPER THE ENTIRE CITY WITH THEIR LITTLE LOGOS?
WE'LL HAVE TO HAVE A WALK FOR THE ENVIRONMENT JUST TO CLEAN UP AFTER THE WALK FOR AWARENESS! CAN'T PEOPLE JUST GIVE?
IF YOU DON'T GET THAT FILTHY STICKER OUT OF MY FACE, I'M GONNA DO SOME GIVING UPSIDE YOUR HEAD.
darb
OH YEAH? BRING IT, CHARITY BOY!
OH, I'LL BRING IT! I'LL BRING IT SO HARD ROB'S TAX RETURN WILL FEEL IT!
YOU'RE GONNA NEED A WALK FOR DENTURES TO BE ABLE TO EAT AGAIN!
TOO BAD YOU WON'T BE ABLE TO GO ON IT SINCE YOU'RE NOT ALLOWED OUTSIDE.
MY FRIEND, YOU JUST GAINED CHARITABLE STATUS, 'CAUSE THAT'S THE MOST NON-PROFITABLE STATEMENT I EVER HEARD...
SAY ANIMAL WELFARE! SAY ANIMAL WELFARE!

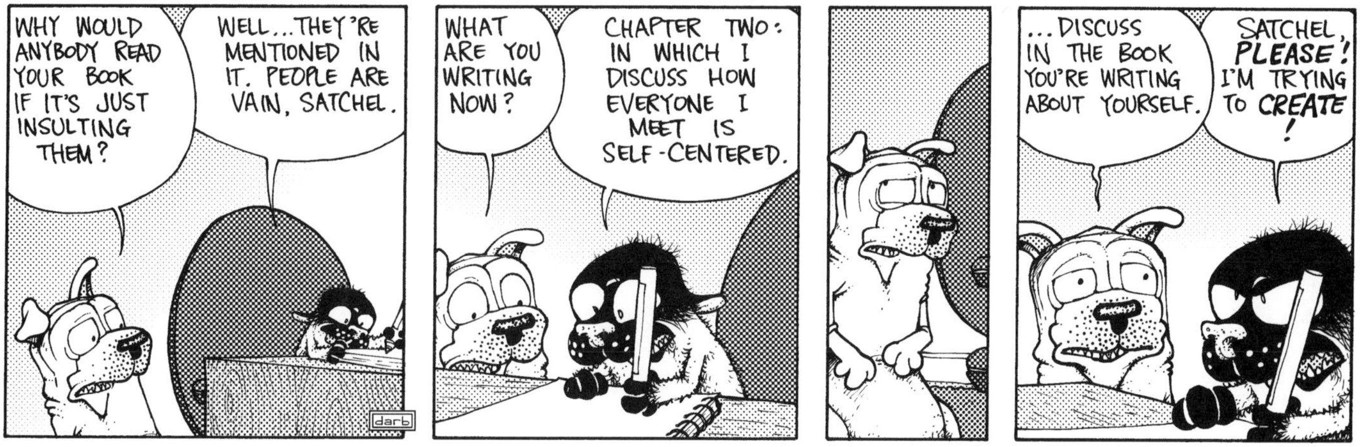
WHY WOULD ANYBODY READ YOUR BOOK IF IT'S JUST INSULTING THEM?
WELL... THEY'RE MENTIONED IN IT. PEOPLE ARE VAIN, SATCHEL.
darb
WHAT ARE YOU WRITING NOW?
CHAPTER TWO: IN WHICH I DISCUSS HOW EVERYONE I MEET IS SELF-CENTERED.
...DISCUSS IN THE BOOK YOU'RE WRITING ABOUT YOURSELF.
SATCHEL, **PLEASE!** I'M TRYING TO **CREATE!**

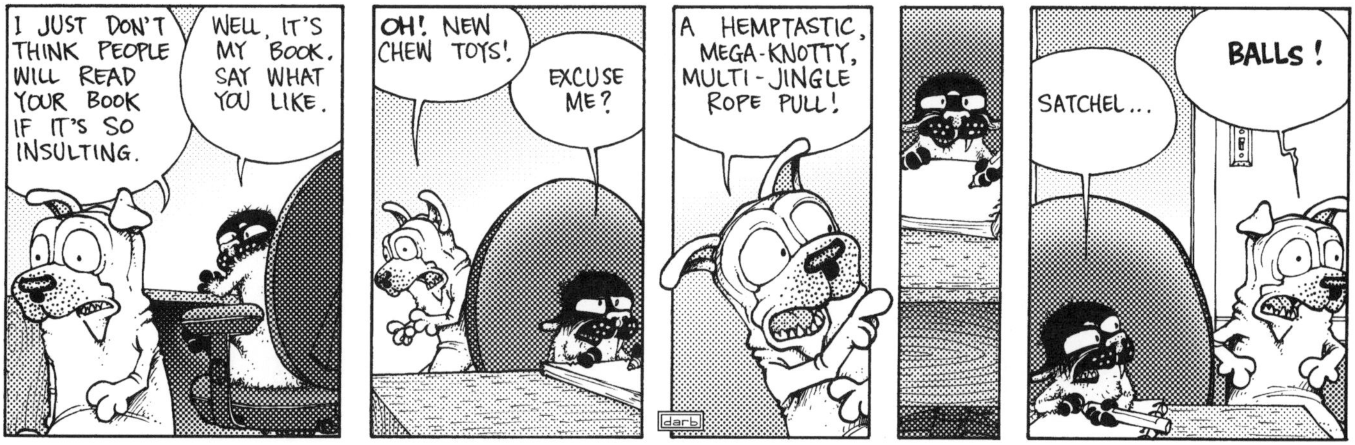
I JUST DON'T THINK PEOPLE WILL READ YOUR BOOK IF IT'S SO INSULTING.
WELL, IT'S MY BOOK. SAY WHAT YOU LIKE.
OH! NEW CHEW TOYS!
EXCUSE ME?
darb
A HEMPTASTIC, MEGA-KNOTTY, MULTI-JINGLE ROPE PULL!
SATCHEL...
BALLS!

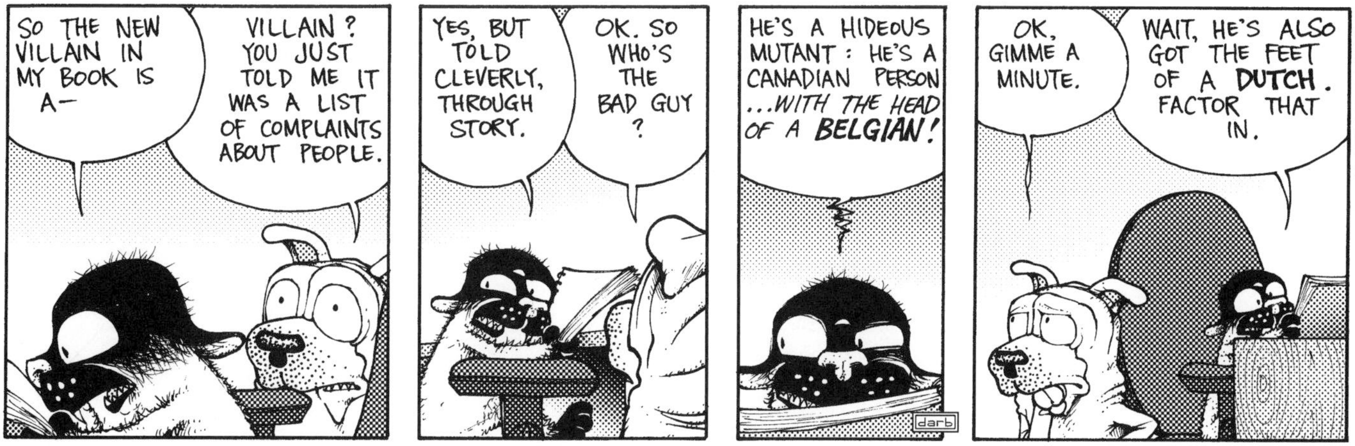
SO THE NEW VILLAIN IN MY BOOK IS A—
VILLAIN? YOU JUST TOLD ME IT WAS A LIST OF COMPLAINTS ABOUT PEOPLE.
YES, BUT TOLD CLEVERLY, THROUGH STORY.
OK. SO WHO'S THE BAD GUY?
HE'S A HIDEOUS MUTANT: HE'S A CANADIAN PERSON *...WITH THE HEAD OF A* ***BELGIAN!***
darb
OK, GIMME A MINUTE.
WAIT, HE'S ALSO GOT THE FEET OF A **DUTCH**. FACTOR THAT IN.

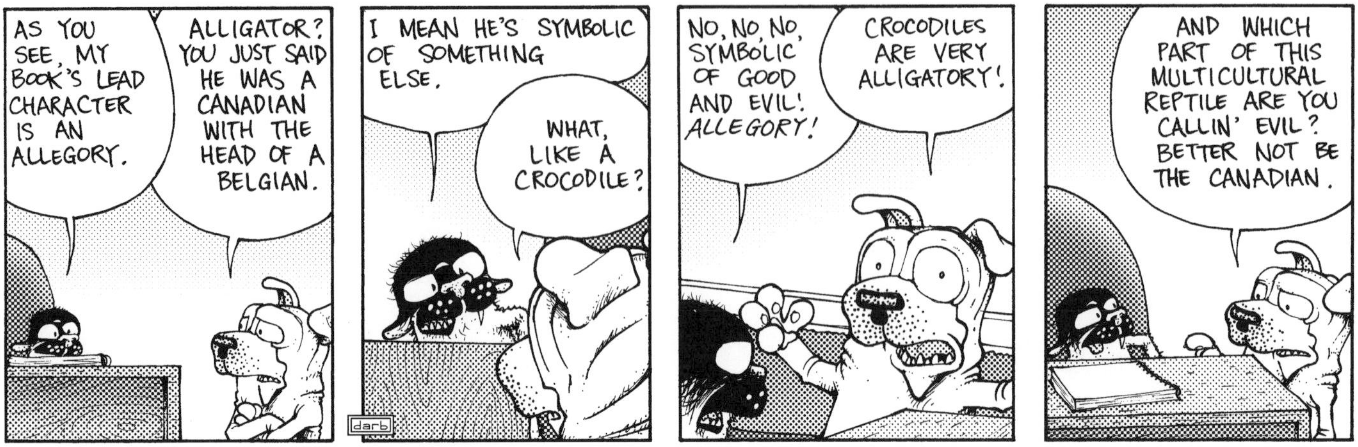
AS YOU SEE, MY BOOK'S LEAD CHARACTER IS AN ALLEGORY.
ALLIGATOR? YOU JUST SAID HE WAS A CANADIAN WITH THE HEAD OF A BELGIAN.
I MEAN HE'S SYMBOLIC OF SOMETHING ELSE.
WHAT, LIKE A CROCODILE?
darb
NO, NO, NO, SYMBOLIC OF GOOD AND EVIL! *ALLEGORY!*
CROCODILES ARE VERY ALLIGATORY!
AND WHICH PART OF THIS MULTICULTURAL REPTILE ARE YOU CALLIN' EVIL? BETTER NOT BE THE CANADIAN.

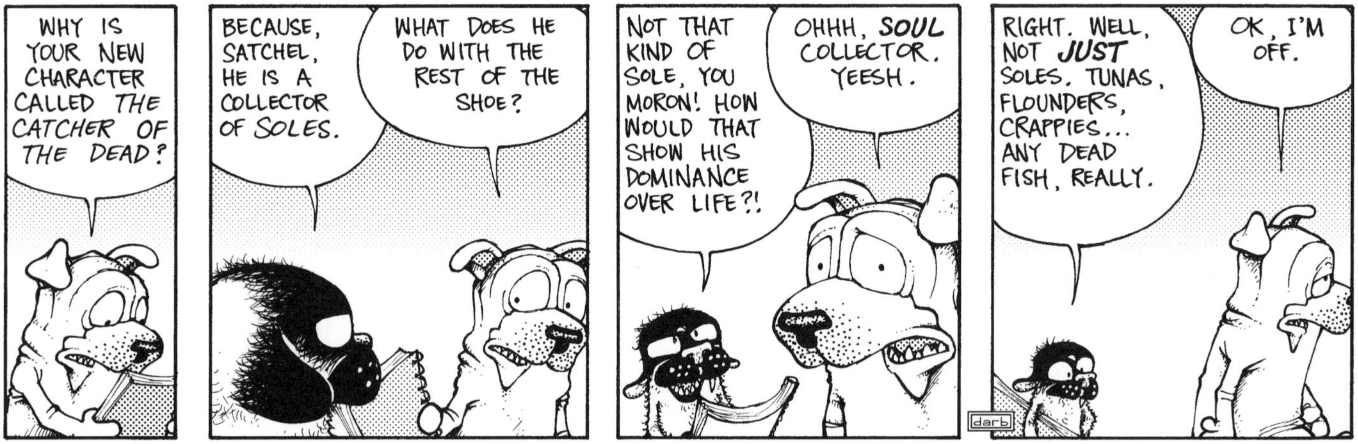
WHY IS YOUR NEW CHARACTER CALLED *THE CATCHER OF THE DEAD?*
BECAUSE, SATCHEL, HE IS A COLLECTOR OF *SOLES*.
WHAT DOES HE DO WITH THE REST OF THE SHOE?
NOT THAT KIND OF SOLE, YOU MORON! HOW WOULD THAT SHOW HIS DOMINANCE OVER LIFE?!
OHHH, **SOUL** COLLECTOR. YEESH.
darb
RIGHT. WELL, NOT ***JUST*** SOLES. TUNAS, FLOUNDERS, CRAPPIES... ANY DEAD FISH, REALLY.
OK, I'M OFF.

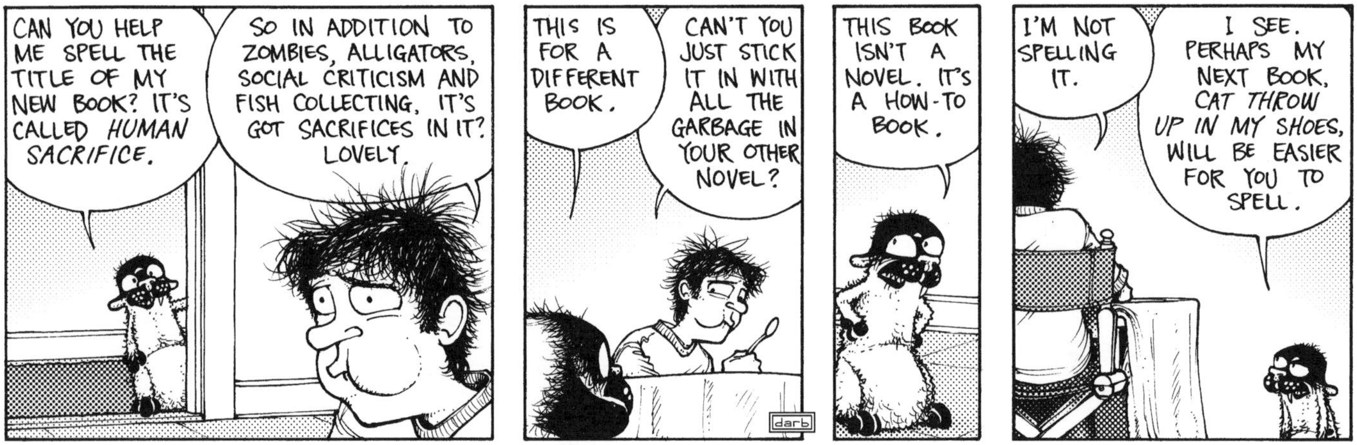
CAN YOU HELP ME SPELL THE TITLE OF MY NEW BOOK? IT'S CALLED *HUMAN SACRIFICE*.
SO IN ADDITION TO ZOMBIES, ALLIGATORS, SOCIAL CRITICISM AND FISH COLLECTING, IT'S GOT SACRIFICES IN IT? LOVELY.
THIS IS FOR A DIFFERENT BOOK.
CAN'T YOU JUST STICK IT IN WITH ALL THE GARBAGE IN YOUR OTHER NOVEL?
darb
THIS BOOK ISN'T A NOVEL. IT'S A HOW-TO BOOK.
I'M NOT SPELLING IT.
I SEE. PERHAPS MY NEXT BOOK, *CAT THROW UP IN MY SHOES*, WILL BE EASIER FOR YOU TO SPELL.

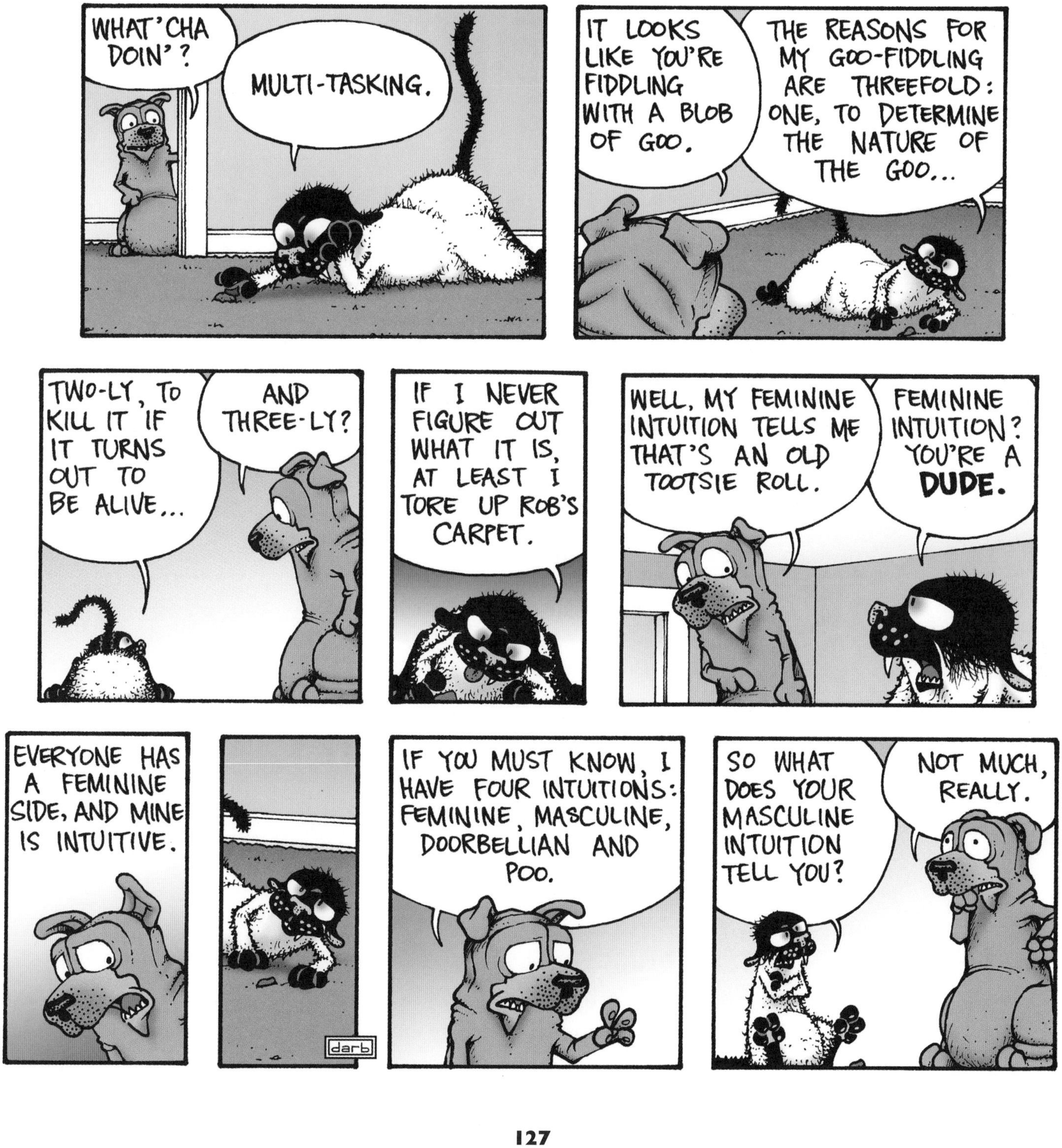
WHAT'CHA DOIN'?
MULTI-TASKING.
IT LOOKS LIKE YOU'RE FIDDLING WITH A BLOB OF GOO.
THE REASONS FOR MY GOO-FIDDLING ARE THREEFOLD: ONE, TO DETERMINE THE NATURE OF THE GOO...
TWO-LY, TO KILL IT IF IT TURNS OUT TO BE ALIVE...
AND THREE-LY?
IF I NEVER FIGURE OUT WHAT IT IS, AT LEAST I TORE UP ROB'S CARPET.
WELL, MY FEMININE INTUITION TELLS ME THAT'S AN OLD TOOTSIE ROLL.
FEMININE INTUITION? YOU'RE A **DUDE.**
EVERYONE HAS A FEMININE SIDE, AND MINE IS INTUITIVE.
darb
IF YOU MUST KNOW, I HAVE FOUR INTUITIONS: FEMININE, MASCULINE, DOORBELLIAN AND POO.
SO WHAT DOES YOUR MASCULINE INTUITION TELL YOU?
NOT MUCH, REALLY.

Get Fuzzy is distributed internationally by Universal Uclick.

Andrews McMeel Publishing, LLC
an Andrews McMeel Universal company
1130 Walnut Street
Kansas City, Missouri 64106
www.andrewsmcmeel.com

14 15 16 17 18 SDB 10 9 8 7 6 5 4 3 2 1

ISBN: 978-1-4494-5994-9

Library of Congress Control Number: 2014935613

Get Fuzzy can be viewed on the Internet at
www.gocomics.com/getfuzzy.